2.1
AUDITING

First edition May 1988
Second edition May 1989

ISBN 0 86277 240 0

A CIP catalogue record is available for this
book from the British Library

Published by

BPP Publishing Limited
BPP House, Aldine Place
142-144 Uxbridge Road
London W12 8AA

Printed in Great Britain by
Dotesios Printers Ltd, Trowbridge, Wiltshire

We are grateful to the Chartered Association of Certified
Accountants and the Institute of Chartered Accountants in England
and Wales for permission to reproduce past examination questions.
The suggested solutions have been prepared by BPP Publishing
Limited.

CONTENTS

CONTENTS

PREFACE

The syllabus originally introduced in 1982 was replaced in 1988 by a revised syllabus, which took effect from the December 1988 diet.

As the leading publisher of targeted ACCA texts, BPP welcomed the opportunity provided by the revised syllabus. In the first half of 1988 we brought out a completely new range of ACCA texts and kits. Even for subjects where the substantive syllabus changes were slight, we took the opportunity to reconsider existing material. The aim was to provide the freshest and most comprehensive study aids available for ACCA students.

This new edition of the 2.1 Auditing study text has been designed to cover the new syllabus reproduced on page (vi). Along with the new syllabus, the ACCA issued a study guide which is reproduced on pages (vii) to (x) below. All topics mentioned in the detailed study guide are included in this text.

BPP Publishing
May 1989

SYLLABUS AND STUDY GUIDE

Syllabus

Section 1: The nature and purpose of an audit

The role of the auditor
The audit concepts
The relationship with users of audited information
Responsibility for detection of fraud and other irregularities
The role of auditing standards and guidelines

Section 2: Professional and legal requirements

Procedures relating to the appointment, dismissal and
resignation of the external auditor
Professional requirements
Duties, powers and responsibilities under statute and case law

Section 3: Audit planning and control

Nature of client
Staffing the assignment
Setting objectives
Controlling the work
Recording the work done
Internal control evaluation and audit strategy
Audit programmes
Audit conclusions

Section 4: Audit procedures

System review and transaction testing
Final work and figure testing:
- analytical review
- the role of computer assisted audit techniques
- verification, valuation and disclosure of assets
- the ascertainment, verification and disclosure of
  liabilities and related profit and loss account headings
- post balance sheet events and contingencies
- letters of representation
- the role of sampling in transaction and figure testing

Section 5: The audit report

The nature and form of the audit report, unqualified
and qualified
Compliance with legal, professional and other requirements
The accountant's report

SYLLABUS AND STUDY GUIDE

Study guide

Objectives of the syllabus

The objective of the syllabus is to examine students' understanding of the nature and objectives of an audit and general auditing practice.

On completion of the course students should understand:

- the role of the auditor;
- the auditor's need for independence;
- the professional and regulatory requirements governing an audit and the audit report;
- the planning and execution of audit.

Format and standard of the examination paper

The examination paper has seven questions on it, with students being required to answer five. The paper is split into two sections. Section A is compulsory and students are required to answer both questions. In Section B students are required to answer three questions out of a choice of five. Section A will account for 40 marks, (although each question may not necessarily count for 20 marks) and Section B for 60 with each question worth 20 marks.

Paper 2.1 is the student's introduction to auditing and is intended to provide a firm foundation from which to study the Auditing and Investigations paper in level three. The standard of the paper is comparable to that required in the second year examinations of a three year UK honours degree.

Students will frequently be required to answer questions which draw on several syllabus topics. Thus it is important that the syllabus is studied as an integrated whole, rather than concentrating on selected topics. It should be noted that Section A will usually contain information about a particular set of circumstances and two related questions testing the students' ability to analyse and interpret that information in the audit context.

Please note:

1. Computers are becoming increasingly common in practice and students at level two are required to understand the basic problems facing the auditor as the result of their use within organisations subject to audit. Questions may be specifically directed towards the audit approach to computers but, frequently, questions will be set in a computer environment and students will be expected to reflect this in their answers.

2. There is some overlap in the syllabuses of Auditing 2.1 and Auditing and Investigations 3.4. In areas of overlap it should be noted that, generally, students at level two will be required to exhibit broad (B) knowledge of the areas specified in the syllabus, whereas students at level three will be generally required to exhibit full (F) knowledge. In a number of instances at level two, however, a fuller knowledge is felt to be necessary. By way of example, a full knowledge of verification, valuation and disclosure of certain assets and related profit and loss account headings is required to be demonstrated. This should not, however, be interpreted as requiring students to solve complex asset valuation problems.

Pre-requisite: paper 1.1, 1.2, 1.4 and 1.5

Content	Knowledge level

Section 1: The nature and purpose of an audit

The role of the auditor: B
- internal audit
- external audit
    - statutory
    - non-statutory

The audit concepts: B
- independence and other personal qualities of the auditor
- evidence
- truth and fairness, including materiality
- responsibility
- audit risk

The relationship with users of audited information   B
- the role of the engagement letter

Responsibility for detection of fraud and other irregularities   B

The role of auditing standards and guidelines   B

Section 2: Professional and legal requirements

Procedures relating to the appointment, dismissal and
resignation of the external auditor   F

Professional requirements, including those relating to
independence and professional ethics generally, and
accounting and auditing standards   B

Duties, powers and responsibilities under statute and
case law   B

Case law decisions affecting the auditor   B

Section 3: Audit planning and control

Planning the audit   B
Nature of client and audit strategy to be applied   B
Allocation of responsibility for the work   B
Setting objectives   B
Importance of staff briefing   B
Controlling the audit   B
Recording the work done including the use of standard
documentation such as internal control questionnaires
(ICQs) and internal control evaluation forms (ICEs)   F
Internal control evaluation and decision as to reliance
on client system   F
Audit programmes   F
Forming audit conclusions   B

Section 4: Audit procedures

System review and transaction testing
- recording systems, including narrative, internal
  control questionnaires and flowcharting   F
- compliance testing   F
- evaluation and setting scope of examination   F
- substantive testing   F
- sampling transactions for testing:
    role of sampling   B
    application of sampling   I
- special considerations in the audit of computer systems   B

Final work and figure testing
- analytical review   B
- the role of computer assisted audit techniques   B
- sampling items comprised in financial statement
  figures:
    role of sampling   B
    application of sampling   I
- verification, valuation and disclosure of assets and
  related profit and loss account headings   F
    - fixed assets, including depreciation
    - stock including stocktaking procedures and
      cut-off tests (in conjunction with sales and
      purchases)
    - debtors and sales, including debtors' circularisation
    - cash and bank

- the ascertainment, verification and disclosure of liabilities
  and related profit and loss account headings
    - the search for unrecorded liabilities   F
    - trade creditors and purchases   F
    - taxation   B
    - dividends   F
- post balance sheet events and contingencies   B
- letters of representation   B

Section 5: The audit report

The nature and form of the audit report, unqualified and qualified   F
Forms of qualification   B
- disagreement
- uncertainty
- meaning of fundamental and material but not fundamental in
  the context of the audit report
Examples of qualifications   B
Compliance with legal, professional and other requirements: B
- truth and fairness as the overriding requirement
- other legal requirements
- accounting standards
- auditing standards and guidelines
The accountant's report

SYLLABUS AND STUDY GUIDE

General notes

A knowledge is required of UK SSAPs and Auditing Standards and Guidelines, subject to the six month rule, and their effect on financial reporting and the duties of the auditor. Certain SSAPs and Auditing Guidelines will not be examined in detail at this level. These are:

SSAPs

SSAP   1, 4, 13, 14, 15, 20, 21, 22, 23, 24

Auditing guidelines

Industry guidelines

Students will also be required to have an appreciation of the accounting requirements of the Companies Act 1985, regarding general form of profit and loss account and balance sheet and disclosure of:

- Fixed assets and depreciation
- Stocks and work in progress
- Debtors (long and short-term) and related interest receivable
- Cash and bank balances and related interest payable
- Share capital and reserves
- Creditors (long and short-term) and related interest payable
- Taxation
- Dividends
- Remuneration of directors and higher paid employees
- Remuneration of the auditor.

Knowledge levels

Each topic in the syllabus is given a level of knowledge which defines the depth at which it needs to be studied. The three levels are:

I   *Introductory:* basic understanding of principles, concepts, theories and techniques

B   *Broad:* application of principles, concepts, theories and techniques in the solution of straightforward problems

F   *Full:* Identification and solution of more complex problems through the selection and application of principles, concepts, theories and techniques.

THE EXAMINATION PAPER

Paper format

Section A contains two compulsory questions worth 40 marks in total. (These questions will usually make use of common data.)

Section B contains five questions (each worth 20 marks) of which any three must be answered.

Details of changes in the format of the examination are published in the Students' Newsletter. You should check the Newsletter in the months leading up to the examination to determine whether there has been any change in the paper format or, indeed, the syllabus.

Recent legislation, auditing guidelines, SSAPs

The golden rule here is that you must read the 'Newsletter' to get the exact position.

On *legislation*, to quote from a recent Newsletter:

"The Association applies a six months' rule, in that questions requiring an understanding of new legislation will not be set until at least six calendar months after the last day of the month in which the legislation received Royal Assent....".

Auditing Standards and Guidelines are vital as you prepare for your examination. The ACCA rule is that Standards and Guidelines are relevant provided six months have passed from the last date of the month in which they were issued.

A full list of Standards and Guidelines dealt with in the text is set out in Chapter 4.

Auditing Guideline Exposure Drafts are strictly not examinable in paper 2.1. However, certain of the Exposure Drafts currently in issue are concerned with topics that are unquestionably within the syllabus, and, as they represent current best practice, they are dealt with in this text. A list of these Exposure Drafts is also provided in Chapter 4.

Additionally you should note, with reference to the full syllabus reproduced above, that a *detailed knowledge* of SSAPs 1, 4, 13, 14, 15, 20, 21, 22, 23 or 24 is not expected. This text deals with aspects of relevant SSAPs issued up to 30 April 1989.

Past examination papers

Compulsory (C)
Optional (O)

June 1986

1.	Identification of weaknesses in internal controls	C
2.	Audit of cash and bank balances; quality control	C
3.	Substantive audit of capital expenditure/fixed assets	O
4.	Planning and execution of stocktakes	O
5.	Substantive audit of creditors, accruals and provisions	O
6.	Audit report - small companies	O
7.	Explanation of various auditing terms	O

THE EXAMINATION PAPER

December 1986

1. Audit of fixed assets, including capitalisation of overheads
    and depreciation   C
2. Qualified audit reports   C
3. The auditor's independence   O
4. Computer auditing terms and techniques   O
5. Controls over a purchase system   O
6. Internal audit; risks of fraud in a retail environment and
    audit techniques to be adopted   O
7. Sampling techniques - comparison of random, stratified, statistical
    and judgmental approaches   O

June 1987

1. The auditor's independence; resignation and dismissal of auditors   C
2. Internal control - definition, examples, problems in a new company   C
3. Computer terminology; audit of trade debtors, including
    circularisation   O
4. The auditor's responsibility in signing the audit report   O
5. Definition of different types of audit test   O
6. Acquisition of a new computer; audit of the transactions and of
    the transfer of balances from the old to the new system   O
7. Post-balance sheet events   O

December 1987

1. Audit of stock   C
2. Audit working papers   C
3. Risk-based auditing; statistical sampling   O
4. Internal controls; fraud; design of tests of a purchase system   O
5. Computerised systems; terminology and internal control   O
6. Internal audit - its effect on the statutory audit   O
7. Letter of representation; audit of subjective areas; contingencies;
    auditor's responsibility with regard to SSAPs.   O

June 1988

1. Preparation of management letter   C
2. Preparation of audit report   C
3. Post balance sheet events; contingent gain   O
4. Audit implications of introducing microcomputer-based systems   O
5. Scope and purpose of standards and guidelines; techniques of
    audit testing; analytical review   O
6. Substantive testing of debtors and taxation   O
7. Independence of the auditor   O

THE EXAMINATION PAPER

December 1988

1.	Weaknesses in and audit of a given salaries and wages system	C
2.	Discuss audit implications of findings about wages and salaries system	C
3.	Audit of stock with standard cost system	O
4.	Meaning of standard wording of audit report; discussion of possible improvements	O
5.	Preparation of management letter on prior year adjustments and extraordinary and exceptional items	O
6.	Audit sampling techniques	O
7.	Reliance on internal audit; debtors' circularisation	O

A GUIDE TO THIS STUDY TEXT

The structure of this text

Although Paper 2.1 is the junior of the two auditing papers, the syllabus is rather daunting and questions cover a wide range of topics, some of which might be considered more appropriate to the level three examination. This text is therefore necessarily comprehensive, but it is organised so as to make the detailed syllabus coverage as palatable as possible.

It is important that the text is studied in the sequence in which it is presented. This can be summarised as follows:

- Chapters 1 and 2 set the scene by concentrating on the role of the auditor and the audit concepts.
- Chapters 3 to 5 set out the regulatory framework within which the auditor operates. Both statutory and professional regulations are covered in detail.
- Chapter 6 provides an overview of the audit in operation, identifying the key stages of the audit process from engagement through to the signing and dating of the audit report. The initial stages of the audit are discussed in chapter 7.
- Chapters 8-13 explore *in detail* the conduct of an audit through each of the stages identified in the chapter 6 overview. The majority of questions on the examination paper are likely to be derived from the subject matter of these chapters, in particular the two compulsory questions in Section A, totalling 40 marks.
- Chapter 14 is concerned with audit reporting. It discusses how the auditor, having completed his detailed work, drafts his report - the end product of the audit process.
- Chapter 15 concentrates on the special and topical problem of the audit of small businesses.
- Chapter 16 provides an appreciation of the audit implications of computerised accounting systems.

Each chapter incorporates the following features at the conclusion of the main text:

- a brief summary pinpointing the topics covered in the chapter of particular examination significance and indicating areas of lesser significance for study and revision purposes;
- a set of 'self-revision' questions which are tests of knowledge to be completed after the text has been studied. Answers should be checked against the paragraph references provided after each question.

Each *section* of the text ends with a bank of examination-style questions with suggested solutions.

This text is primarily concerned with the audit of limited companies. Although the examiner may occasionally require candidates to demonstrate, applying basic principles, how the audit of other enterprises might be conducted, questions requiring *detailed* knowledge of such specialised undertakings as building societies and charities are not set at level 2.

Looking things up in the text

A brief index of topics is provided at the end of the text. Legal cases affecting the work of the auditor are listed in the Table of Cases also at the end of the text.

Auditing Guidelines and Exposure Drafts are, as mentioned earlier, summarised in Chapter 4. Each is, of course, dealt with in more detail elsewhere in the text.

A GUIDE TO THIS STUDY TEXT

Confidence in the subject

Many ACCA students feel uneasy about auditing because of their lack of practical experience and familiarity with the subject. It is vital, however, that you should be able to write about auditing matters in your examination with confidence.

In order to give the student with little or no practical experience of auditing a flavour of the audit in operation, the text contains examples of documentation used by practising firms of accountants, large and small.

If you study this text conscientiously and are able to gain a good working understanding of its contents, then it will provide you with more than sufficient detail to establish a sound base of knowledge from which to answer examination questions with the necessary conviction.

Examination technique

Never forget that auditing is essentially a very practical subject where general knowledge and basic common sense need to be allied to a sound grasp of the basic principles involved. Remember also that this is a paper where the examiner is not merely seeking to test your knowledge of the underlying theory, but is also testing your ability to communicate clearly, in good English, to other people.

If an auditor in practice is to achieve the necessary quality control of the audit assignment then it is essential that he starts by carefully planning his work. If you wish to achieve quality control of your examination answers, it is essential for you to start by planning them carefully.

In practice, auditors are placing increasing reliance upon checklists to ensure that they do not omit any important aspects of their work. Given below is a checklist which you may like to use to assist in the planning of your auditing answers. Use of this checklist will ensure that you make best use of your knowledge.

When planning answers, ask yourself 'Should my answer be affected by all or any of the following?':
- Auditing standards and guidelines currently in issue.
- SSAPs currently in issue.
- Statutory provisions.
- Ethical considerations.
- Case law.

Finally, never forget to *read the question carefully* and in your answers to *state the obvious*.

SECTION 1

THE NATURE AND PURPOSE
OF AN AUDIT

Chapter 1

THE ROLE OF THE AUDITOR

Topics covered in this chapter:

- The definition of an audit
- The purpose of an audit
- The role of auditing standards and guidelines
- Statutory and non-statutory audits
- Internal and external audit
- The auditor's responsibility for detecting fraud

The definition of an audit

1. An audit has been defined as 'the independent examination of, and expression of opinion on, the financial statements of an enterprise by an appointed auditor in pursuance of that appointment and in compliance with any relevant statutory obligation'. The definition contains a number of important points which are discussed in the following paragraphs.

2. An auditor must be *independent*. A finance director who prepares a set of accounts may check his own work for accuracy or he may request a fellow director or subordinate to check it. This would not count as an audit of the accounts because the element of independence is absent. But if the finance director engaged an outside firm of accountants to check his work and express an opinion on the accounts, the external accountants would be performing an audit.

3. An auditor conducts an *examination* of the financial statements. He is *not* responsible for their preparation: this responsibility lies with the management of the enterprise. Some small enterprises have no staff with accounting expertise and may require the services of a firm of accountants to prepare their accounts. Frequently such enterprises engage the same firm of accountants to act as their auditors. But the preparation of the accounts and their subsequent audit are still two completely separate functions which ideally should be carried out by different members of the accountancy firm.

4. An auditor must *express an opinion* on the financial statements presented to him. He is *not* required to certify that the accounts are correct in every particular. Indeed, this would not be possible because many of the figures which appear in accounts are not objectively verifiable. In most cases the auditor will be required to say whether, in his opinion, the accounts show a true and fair view. (The meaning of the phrase 'true and fair view' will be explained in the next chapter.)

5.   An auditor acts *in pursuance of an appointment*. In the case of a limited company, the members will appoint an auditor, whose duty it will be to report to them on the results of their work. In simple cases the auditor will be able to report that he has carried out his work in accordance with approved auditing standards and that, in his opinion, the accounts show a true and fair view and comply with the Companies Act 1985.

6.   Finally, the appointment of an auditor is often a matter of *statutory obligation*. This is particularly the case with limited companies who are obliged by the Companies Act 1985 to publish audited accounts annually. But other organisations, too, are obliged by law to appoint auditors; we shall return to this point later in the chapter.

The purpose of an audit

7.   Various reasons might be identified for performing an audit, but most commentators would agree that the main purpose is bound up with the way in which business enterprises have developed over the centuries.

8.   At one time, a business enterprise might consist of a single venture with a limited life. For example, a merchant might charter a ship to purchase goods from abroad for sale in his own country. In such cases it was easy to measure the success of the enterprise: it was represented by the amount of cash in hand after the goods had been sold.

9.   Modern businesses of course are much more complicated. For the most part they are long-standing enterprises which will continue to trade for the foreseeable future. They seldom have a single owner (in fact some very large enterprises, such as British Telecom, may be owned by literally millions of shareholders). Frequently the owners are not involved in the day-to-day running of the business but appoint managers to act on their behalf.

10. For all these reasons it is desirable that businesses should produce accounts which will indicate how successfully they are performing. But the owners of a business require something more than the mere preparation of accounts because the managers responsible for preparing them may, either unintentionally or by deliberate manipulation, produce accounts which are misleading. An independent examination of the accounts is needed so that the owners of the business can assess how well management have discharged their stewardship.

11. It may be claimed that in the *small company* - or 'proprietary' company - both shareholders' funds and day-to-day management are provided by the same people and consequently that there are no other interested parties. The requirement for an independent auditor to review and report on the record of the financial implications of transactions is therefore superfluous and is moreover an unnecessary expense. Further, the small size of such enterprises normally means a limited and simple organisation structure compensated by close managerial supervision of staff and detailed involvement in the day-to-day routine of transacting and recording business. It is also maintained that the owners of such enterprises are better equipped to evaluate the progress and financial position of their company both past and future because of the above factors than the independent auditor whose work is concerned with reporting on historical performance and financial strength frequently for accounting periods some months in the past.

12. Such arguments, however, fail to recognise a number of important considerations. First, the provision of funds by proprietors is not the only requirement for the business entity to exist. The environment both social and economic in which an enterprise operates (for example, the provision and maintenance of roads, law and order etc) must be paid for, and the revenue for such services is raised by the fiscal system instituted by central and local government. A large proportion of this revenue is raised by direct taxation of the profits of the business unit. The accuracy and honesty of the financial statements used as the basis for tax assessments is relied upon very heavily by the Inland Revenue and Customs and Excise authorities, and hence the viability and credibility of such statements is supported by the opinion of the independent auditor.

13. Secondly, there are interested parties other than the ultimate proprietors who place great reliance on financial information. Trade and loan creditors, bankers and potential investors, for example, will all at some stage be approached by both the large and small company to provide considerable credit or finance. Such users place great store upon the accuracy of financial statements, and presently have that assurance through the independent opinion of auditors. The importance of these other interested parties, or *users*, to the modern auditor cannot be overstressed. As we shall see later, the auditor may in certain circumstances owe a duty of care to these users.

14. It may be useful to list the categories of people who might be interested in the audited accounts of a business enterprise. Seven such categories were identified in a 1975 discussion paper published by the UK accountancy bodies and entitled *The corporate report*. They were:

    (a) the equity investor group, ie existing shareholders and potential investors;
    (b) the loan creditor group, eg debenture holders;
    (c) the employee group, including both employees and their trade union or staff association representatives;
    (d) the analyst-adviser group, eg merchant banks, stockbrokers;
    (e) the business contact group, eg customers and trade creditors;
    (f) the government, eg the Inland Revenue and Customs and Excise;
    (g) the public.

The role of auditing standards and guidelines

15. The work of an auditor is governed by two principal sets of regulations:

    (a) those contained in statutes. Later in this chapter we will be looking briefly at the statutory framework of auditing;

    (b) those contained in the auditing standards and guidelines. These are pronouncements issued by the Auditing Practices Committee (APC). (It was from the Explanatory Foreword to these Auditing Standards and Guidelines that the definition of an audit in paragraph 1 above was taken.) The APC is a sub-committee of the Consultative Committee of Accountancy Bodies (CCAB), which includes as its members all the six major accountancy bodies of the UK.

16. The Auditing Standards lay down the basic principles and practices which auditors are expected to follow in the conduct of an audit. Apparent failures by an auditor to observe the Standards may be investigated by the appropriate committee of the auditor's professional body and disciplinary action may result. It is also worth noting that a court of law may, when

considering the adequacy of the work of an auditor, take into account any pronouncements or publications that describe current best practice. The Standards and Guidelines would fall into this category.

17. The APC emphasise that it would be impracticable to establish a code of rules sufficiently detailed to cover all situations and circumstances that an auditor might encounter. Furthermore, any attempt at laying down a set of all embracing standards would tend to hinder the future development of auditing techniques. It is essential, therefore, that in following the Standards, the auditor exercises his judgment in determining the auditing procedures necessary in the circumstances.

18. The Auditing Guidelines are designed to help the auditor apply the standards. In particular, they give guidance on:

(a) procedures by which the Standards may be applied;
(b) the application of the Standards to specific items appearing in financial statements;
(c) techniques currently being used in auditing; and
(d) audit problems relating to particular commercial or legal circumstances or to specific industries.

19. A summary of the standards, guidelines and other pronouncements currently in issue, together with those topics that are under consideration by the APC - and will hence form the subject matter of future pronouncements - is provided in chapter 4.

Statutory and non-statutory audits

20. Audits are compulsory under statute in the case of a large number of undertakings including the following:

Undertaking	Principal Act
Limited companies	Companies Act 1985
Building societies	Building Societies Act 1986
Trade unions and employers' associations	Trade Union and Labour Relations Act 1974
Housing Associations	Various acts depending on the legal constitution of the housing association, but including: Industrial Provident Societies Act 1964; Friendly and Industrial and Provident Societies Act 1968; Housing Act 1980; Companies Act 1985.
Certain charities	Various acts depending on the status of the charity, but including: Industrial and Provident Societies Act 1965; Friendly and Industrial and Provident Societies Act 1968; Companies Act 1985; Special Act of Parliament.

21. Non-statutory audits are performed by independent auditors because the owners, proprietors, members, trustees, professional and governing bodies or other interested parties desire them, not because the law requires them. In consequence, auditing may and will extend to every type of undertaking which produces accounts, and will include therefore:

    (a) clubs;
    (b) charities (assuming an audit is not in any event statutory);
    (c) sole traders; and
    (d) partnerships.

22. It may also extend to forms of financial statement other than the annual reported figures where those responsible for the statement, or those to whom the statement is made, wish an independent opinion to be expressed as to whether it gives a *true and fair view*. Examples would include:

    (a) summaries of sales in support of a statement of royalties payable where goods are sold under licence;

    (b) statements of expenditure in support of applications for regional development or other government grants; and

    (c) the circulation figures of a newspaper or magazine, used when soliciting advertising.

23. In all such audits the auditor must have regard to any regulations concerning financial statements which are contained in the internal rules or constitution of the undertaking. Examples of the regulations which would be essential reference material for the auditor in such assignments would include:

    (a) the Rules of clubs, societies and charities (in the latter case the Charities Commissioner is empowered in certain instances to require an independent audit into certain aspects of any registered charity - thus specific terms of reference from the Commissioner together with the rules, regulations and objects of the charity would be the governing features determining the scope and reporting responsibility of the auditor);

    (b) partnership agreements. The audit of a partnership is not normally required by statute and so the auditor must agree with the client what his rights and duties are going to be. The auditor must obtain written confirmation of his terms of engagement and must take care to distinguish clearly between audit and accountancy work and ensure that the client appreciates the distinction.

24. In addition to the advantages common to all forms of audit, namely, the verification of accounts and the possible detection of errors and fraud, the audit of the accounts of a partnership may also be seen to have the following advantages.

    (a) It will provide a convenient means of settling accounts between the partners, thus avoiding the possibility of future disputes.

    (b) The auditor may be able to make useful comments on the firm's accounting and control systems, where necessary making recommendations as to how areas of weakness could be eliminated.

    (c) The settlement or adjustment of accounts between partners on the occasion of any change in the partnership structure will be facilitated where audited accounts are available.

(d) Where audited accounts are available this will perhaps make them more readily acceptable to the Inland Revenue when it comes to agreeing an individual partner's liability to tax. The partners may well wish to take advantage of the auditor's services in the additional role of tax adviser.

(e) The sale of the business or the negotiation of loan or overdraft facilities may well be facilitated if the firm is able to produce properly prepared and audited accounts.

(f) An audit on behalf of a 'sleeping partner' is highly advisable since generally such a person will have little other means of checking the accounts of the business, or confirming the share of profits due to him.

25. Apart from the advantages discussed above, which would be peculiar to a partnership, similar advantages may be found in the audit of the accounts of a sole trader, club or charity. Whatever the nature of the business, the auditor will find himself concerned with compliance with Auditing Standards.

Internal and external audit

26. So far we have discussed auditing in the context of the APC definition quoted at the start of this chapter. The definition relates to the work of an *external* auditor, ie an independent person brought in from outside an organisation to review the accounts prepared by management. It is worthwhile at this stage to mention the rather different work performed by an *internal* auditor.

27. The management of an organisation will wish to establish systems to ensure that business activities are carried out efficiently. They will institute clerical, administrative and financial controls. Even in very small businesses with informal accounting systems it will be found that some limited checks and controls are present.

28. Larger organisations may appoint full-time staff whose function is to monitor and report on the running of the company's operations. Such *internal audit* staff would constitute an elaborate example of the kind of control mentioned in the previous paragraph. Although some of the work carried out by internal auditors is similar to that performed by external auditors, there is an important distinction between the nature of the two functions: whereas the external auditor is independent of the organisation, the internal auditor is an employee.

29. This distinction has several consequences:

(a) Internal auditors are responsible to the management of the organisation. The responsibility of external auditors is normally fixed by statute; in the case of a limited company, the external auditor is responsible not to management (the directors) but to the members.

(b) The work performed by the external auditor is that which is required for him to fulfil the terms of his engagement, usually to express an opinion on the true and fair view shown by the accounts. The work performed by an internal auditor may range over any aspect of the organisation's activities, and is determined by what management consider to be the best interests of the company.

30. In a later chapter we will look in more detail at the relationship of the external auditor with the internal audit function.

Fraud and other irregularities

31. In discussing the reasons why audits are considered necessary we stated that a principal purpose is to ensure, for the benefit of an organisation's owners, that management are exercising their stewardship function in a proper manner. This is very different from a popularly held view of auditors, which is that they are appointed by management to discover any frauds or other irregularities that may have been committed. We will conclude this chapter by examining the development of this viewpoint over the history of auditing. In a later chapter we will look in detail at a draft auditing guideline which attempts to set out the modern view of an auditor's responsibilities in this area.

32. The judgement in *Nicol's case* in 1859 stated that it was part of the appointed auditor's duties to discover fraudulent misrepresentations. For many years after this, detection of fraud and error was held by many to be the major objective of the company audits. Gradually, however, the view was taken that the auditor should not be held responsible for detecting every fraud and error perpetrated within a company, and that the management of a concern must take a greater responsibility in this area.

33. Lindlay L J in *re The London and General Bank Limited* (1895) said:

   "He (the auditor) is not an insurer; he does not guarantee that the books do correctly show the true position of the company's affairs......... His obligation is not so onerous as this. Such I take to be the duty of an auditor: he must be honest - that is, he must not certify what he does not believe to be true, and he must take reasonable care and skill before he believes what he certifies is true."

34. In 1896, Lopes J, in the *Kingston Cotton Mill* case, said the following in relation to the auditor's failure to detect a fraud on the part of the management of that company:

   "It is the duty of an auditor to bring to bear on the work he has to perform that skill, care and caution which a reasonably competent, careful and cautious auditor would use. What is reasonable skill, care and caution must depend on the particular circumstances of each case. An auditor is not bound to be a detective, or, as was said, to approach his work with suspicion, or with a foregone conclusion that there is something wrong. He is a *watchdog*, but not a *bloodhound*. He is justified in believing tried servants of the company in whom confidence is placed by the company. He is entitled to assume that they are honest and to rely upon their representation, provided he takes reasonable care. If there is anything calculated to excite suspicion, he should probe it to the bottom; but in the absence of anything of that kind he is only bound to be *reasonably cautious* and *careful....*"

35. However, it was also held, in *Irish Woollen Co Limited v Tyson & Others* (1900), that the auditor was liable for any damage sustained by the company due to his failure, because of a lack of reasonable care and skill on his part, to detect fraud. What all these decisions perhaps show is that, as the approach to auditing became more professional, so there was a corresponding expectation of improvement in the standards of auditing by the courts.

36. The modern view, in simple terms, is that an auditor should not normally make the discovery of fraud an objective in itself. But he should plan his work so as to give himself a reasonable chance of discovering any fraud sufficiently major to affect the true and fair view shown by the accounts.

Summary of the chapter

37. (a) This chapter began with a definition of an audit which should be learnt by heart.

   (b) The purpose of an audit is bound up with the modern concept of organisational management as a stewardship function.

   (c) The users of audited information may be grouped into seven main categories identified by the discussion paper *The corporate report*.

   (d) The two main sources of regulations affecting the external auditor are:

   (i)   statute;
   (ii) auditing standards and guidelines.

   (e) Some organisations may employ internal audit staff. The distinction between internal and external auditors is principally that external auditors are independent of the organisation, whereas internal auditors are not.

   (f) An auditor has only a limited responsibility for the detection of fraud and other irregularities.

TEST YOUR KNOWLEDGE
Numbers in brackets refer to paragraphs in this chapter

1. Define an audit. (1)

2. What is the main reason why audits are considered to be necessary? (10)

3. List the seven categories of people identified in *The corporate report* as users of audited information. (14)

4. Who is responsible for issuing auditing standards and guidelines? (15)

5. List four types of undertaking for which audits are a statutory obligation. (20)

6. Summarise the judgement in the *Kingston Cotton Mill* case. (34)

Chapter 2

THE AUDIT CONCEPTS

Points covered in this chapter:

- Independence of the auditor
- Audit evidence
- 'True and fair'
- Materiality
- Responsibility of the auditor
- Audit risk

Independence of the auditor

1. Why should the auditor be independent? It is helpful to be reminded of the arguments.

    (a) The accounting information contained in the annual financial statements presented to company shareholders lacks sufficient credibility, on the whole, to be used by them with confidence in an unaudited state.

    (b) The auditor acts as a bridging point which helps to make management accountable to the shareholders through its annually required financial statements. It is vital to the strength of this bridging point that the auditor is not only independent in mind, but is also seen to be independent.

    (c) The shareholders and other users have a pressing need, in the majority of cases, for an objective and honest assessment and evaluation of the accounting information presented to them by management. If such an assessment is made, then they will be better prepared to use the information with confidence.

    (d) Consequently, user confidence in the information is closely related to the position of independence which the auditor adopts. The more independent he is, the greater is the probability of the shareholders and others having confidence in his work and opinion.

2. The main purpose of independence is that the report made by the auditor to the shareholders on the company's accounts should be independent of those responsible for preparing the accounts, ie the directors. In practice, this means that the audit report must not be influenced in any way by the relationship the auditors have with the directors. Furthermore, if the audit report is to give credibility to the accounts it is not enough that such independence exists, it must be clearly seen to exist.

3. The major problem in determining independence is that, between the situation where the auditor is the puppet of the directors and a situation of absolute independence (if there ever is such a thing), lies a whole spectrum of degrees of dependency, and to some extent the auditor must always depend on representations of the directors in forming his opinion on the accounts. The current debate on independence is concerned to determine what position in the spectrum should be viewed as representing an acceptable degree of independence.

4. Many statutory regulations relating to auditors are designed to ensure their independence. These regulations will be discussed in detail in the next chapter, but in the meantime you should note that:

   (a) management can only recommend the appointment or removal of the auditor. The final decision rests with the members in general meeting;

   (b) on resignation or removal, the auditor has the right to bring to the attention of the members any matters of which in his opinion they should be aware;

   (c) officers, servants, and their partners and employees are disqualified from acting as auditor;

   (d) the auditor is given the necessary freedom with which to exercise his independence of mind when collecting and assessing audit evidence.

5. There are also two other important regulations which are designed to protect the auditor's position.

   (a) Any attempt by the directors or members of the company to restrict the duties and rights of the auditor is void. This is even true if such a provision is included in the company's articles of association.

   (b) Any officer or servant of the company who knowingly or recklessly makes a statement to the auditors which is misleading or false in a material particular shall be guilty of a criminal offence (s393 CA85).

6. The subject of auditor independence is covered by statement 1 contained in the 'Rules of professional conduct' issued by the Association. The Rules will be discussed more fully in the next chapter but it is convenient at this stage to set out their requirements on the subject of independence.

7. The three paragraphs which summarise statement 1 are now given in full:

   " Professional independence is a concept fundamental to the accountancy profession. It is essentially an attitude of mind characterised by integrity and an objective approach to professional work.

   A member in public practice should be, and be seen to be, free in each professional assignment he undertakes of any interest which might detract from objectivity. The fact that this is self-evident in the exercise of the reporting function must not obscure its relevance in respect of other professional work.

Although a member not in public practice may be unable to be, or be seen to be, free of any interest which might conflict with a proper approach to his professional work, this does not diminish his duty of objectivity in relation to that work."

8. The explanatory notes to the statement which give specific guidance on the question of independence are reproduced in full below. It is important to appreciate that these notes are intended to apply to the practising accountant in general, not merely the auditor. Nevertheless, many of the guidelines apply specifically to the audit role.

---

1. *General*
    It is the duty of an accountant to present or report on information objectively. That duty is the essence of professionalism and is appropriate to all accountants in public practice, in commerce, in industry and in the public service.

2. In the guidance that follows, paragraphs 3 to 27 concern largely, but not exclusively, members in practice. Paragraphs 28-40 deal exclusively with the position of members who are not in practice.

3. *Responsibility of members in public practice*
    It is the responsibility of practising members to use their best endeavours to ensure that the guidance given in paragraphs 4 to 27 below is followed in their practices. The specific responsibility of practising members does not in any way detract from the general responsibilities of all members towards their professional body.

4. *Fees*
    It is undesirable that a practice should derive too great a part of its professional income from one client or group of connected clients. A practice, therefore, should endeavour to ensure that the recurring fees paid by one client or group of connected clients do not exceed 15 per cent of the gross fees of the practice or, in the case of a member practising part-time, 15% of his gross earned income. It is recognised that a new practice seeking to establish itself or an old practice running itself down may well not, in the short term, be able to comply with this criterion.

5. In circumstances where a member is dependent for his income on the profits of any one office within a practice and the gross income of that office is regularly dependent on one client or a group of connected clients for more than 15 per cent of its gross fees, a partner from another office of the practice should take final responsibility for any report made by the practice on the affairs of that client.

6. *Personal relationships*
    Personal relationships can affect objectivity. There is a particular need, therefore, for a practice to ensure that its objective approach to any assignment is not endangered as a consequence of any personal relationship. By way of example, problems may arise where the same partner or senior staff member works for a number of years on the same audit or where anyone in the practice has a mutual business interest with an officer or employees of a client or has an interest in a joint venture with a client. Such problems can also exist in cases of close friendship or relationship by blood or marriage or where work is being done for a company dominated by one individual.

---

7. *Financial involvement with or in the affairs of clients - General*
Financial involvement with a client may affect objectivity. Such involvement can arise in a number of ways of which a shareholding in a company upon which the practice is retained to report is a typical example.

8. *Beneficial shareholdings - audit clients*
A practice should ensure that it does not have as an audit client a company in which a partner in the practice, the spouse or minor child of such a partner, is the beneficial holder of shares in that company, nor should it employ on the audit any member of staff who is a beneficial holder of such shares.

9. (a) Shares in an audit client may be involuntarily acquired as where, for example, a partner inherits such shares or marries a shareholder or in a take-over situation. In such cases the shares should be disposed of at the earliest practicable date, being a date which the transaction would not amount to insider dealing. Similar action should be taken where shares are held in a company becoming an audit client.

    (b) Where a provision in an Act of Parliament requires the auditor of a company to be a shareholder therein the auditor should hold no more than the minimum number of shares necessary to comply with that provision.

    (c) Where a provision in the articles of association of a client company requires an auditor to be a shareholder therein the auditor should hold no more than the minimum number of shares necessary to comply with that provision in the articles as it stood on 31 December 1977.

    (d) Shares held under this paragraph should be disclosed in the accounts or in the directors' report or, if not so disclosed, in the audit report, except that any insignificant shareholding to which sub paragraph (a) applies need not be disclosed.

10. *Beneficial shareholdings - clients upon which a practice reports other than as auditor*
Where a practice is asked to report on a company other than as auditor, every effort should be made to ensure that no partner or member of staff engaged on the assignment or the spouse or minor child of such a partner, has any beneficial interest in the company. If it is discovered that such is the case immediate steps should be taken to remove from the assignment as soon as possible the partner or staff member concerned.

11. *Beneficial shareholdings - general exceptions*
The guidance given in paragraphs 8,9 and 10 is not intended to preclude a beneficial holding in an authorised unit trust, listed investment trust or Lloyds syndicate which holds shares in a client company, except where the unit or investment trust or syndicate is itself a client on which the practice reports. Nor is it intended to preclude personal savings in a client building society or industrial or provident society, except where such savings are of an amount significant in relation to the assets of the saver.

12. *Trustee shareholdings - public companies*
A practice should not have as an audit client a public company if a partner in the practice, or the spouse of a partner, is a trustee of a trust holding shares in that company and the holding is in excess of 10 per cent of the issued share capital of the company or of the total assets comprised in the trust. In other cases, unless the trust is an approved charity, a partner who is a trustee or is the spouse of the trustee should not personally take part in the audit and the shareholding should be disclosed in the accounts or in the directors' report or if not so disclosed in the audit report. Where more than one trust is involved it is sufficient that the number of trusts and aggregate holding is disclosed. Where a practice is asked to report on a company other than as auditor, the principles set out in paragraph 10 apply.

13. *Trustee shareholdings - private companies*
Where a practice is retained to report as auditor or otherwise on a private company, shares of which are held by a trust of which a partner or the spouse of a partner in the practice is a trustee, the shareholding should be disclosed in the accounts or in the directors' report or, if not so disclosed, in the report made by the practice. Where possible a review of the files in such a case should be undertaken by another partner.

14. *Corporate trustees*
Similar considerations to those set out in paragraphs 12 and 13 apply when a partner or spouse of a partner is a director or employee of a trust company which acts as a trustee, other than a mere custodian trustee, of a trust holding shares in a company on which the practice reports.

15. *Voting on audit appointments*
Where any shares are held in an audit company they should not be voted at any general meeting of the company in relation to the appointment or remuneration of auditors.

16. *Beneficiaries' interests in trusts*
A partner should not personally take part in the audit of a client company if he, his spouse or minor child, is a beneficiary drawing income or entitled to accumulated income from a trust which, to his knowledge, holds shares in the company. Similar principles apply where a practice is asked to report on a company other than as auditor.

17. *Nominee shareholdings*
Similar considerations to those set out in paragraph 12 apply to nominee shareholdings in public companies on which the practice reports.

18. *Loans to and from clients - practice loans*
(a) A practice should not make a loan to a client, nor guarantee a client's borrowings, nor for the future accept a loan from a client or have borrowings guaranteed by a client. This guidance does not preclude a practice from having a current account in credit or a deposit account with a client clearing bank or similar banking institution.

Loans to and from clients - individual loans

(b) Neither a partner in a practice, nor the spouse or minor child of a partner, should make a loan to a client, or guarantee a client's borrowings, or for the future accept a loan from a client or have borrowings guaranteed by a client. This guidance is not intended to preclude loans between close relations such as may be regarded as a normal consequence of family life. In the context of this sub-paragraph the word 'loan' does not include a current or deposit account with a clearing bank or similar banking institution, nor does it include a loan or overdraft from a clearing bank.

(c) A loan from or overdraft with a clearing bank does not preclude a member from being appointed by that bank to be a receiver.

19. *Goods and services*

Acceptance of goods or services from a client may be a threat to independence. These should not be accepted by a partner, his spouse or minor child or by the staff of the practice save on terms no more favourable than those available to the generality of the employees of the client. Acceptance of undue hospitality poses a similar threat.

20. *Commission*

Where advice given to a client is such that, if acted upon, it will result in commission being earned by the practice or anyone in it, special care should be taken that the advice is in fact in the best interests of the client. The client should be informed, in writing, both of the fact that commission will be received and, as soon as practicable, of the amount and terms of such commission.

21. *Conflicts of interest*

(a) *General*

In cases where conflicts of interest arise there should be a full and frank explanation to those involved, coupled with any action necessary to disengage from one or both positions, the conflicting interests which have occasioned the difficulty. Conflicts should, so far as possible, be avoided by not accepting any appointment or assignment in which conflict seems likely to occur.

(b) *Competing clients*

As an example, a practice which advises a company upon the figures on which it bases a tender for a contract should avoid the conflict of interest which would arise if it knowingly became involved in advising a rival company tendering for the same contract.

(c) *Clients in dispute*

Another example is where a practice which is financial adviser to a company also deals with the personal affairs of its directors and there is a dispute between the company and one of those directors. In such a case a practice should select which of its clients it is to advise. It should not advise both and it may well be preferable that it advises neither although it may, if asked by both clients, put forward proposals for settling the dispute. Similar considerations apply in the case of a partnership dispute.

22. *Provision of other services to audit clients*

Whilst it is right that members should provide, for audit clients, other services beyond performing the audit, nevertheless care must be taken not to perform executive functions or to make executive decisions. These are the duties of management. This theme runs through the examples below. In particular, members should beware lest, in providing such services they drift into a situation in which they step across the border-line of what is proper.

23. *Preparation of accounting records*

(a) A practice should not participate in the preparation of the accounting records of a public company audit client save in exceptional circumstances.

(b) In the case of private company audit clients, it is frequently necessary to provide a much fuller service than would be appropriate in the case of a public company audit client and this may include participation in the preparation of accounting records.

(c) In all cases in which a practice is concerned in the preparation of accounting records of an audit client particular care must be taken to ensure that the client accepts full responsibility for such records and that objectivity in carrying out the audit is not impaired.

24. *Current appointment in a company reported on*

A practice, wherever it may be situated, should not report on a company, even if the law of the country in which the company is registered would so permit, if a partner or employee of the practice is an officer or employee of the company. Nor should a practice report on a company if a company associated with the practice fills the appointment of secretary to the client. It should be particularly noted that this guidance is applicable to members whether they are within or without the United Kingdom and whether they are in practice or not.

25. *Previous appointments in a company reported on*

No-one should personally take part in the exercise of the reporting function on a company if he has, during the period upon which the report is to be made, or at any time in the two years prior to the first day thereof, been an officer (other than auditor) or employee of that company.

26. *Audit following receivership*

Where a partner in or an employee of a practice has been receiver of any of the assets of a company, neither the practice nor any partner in or employee of the practice should accept appointment as auditor of the company, or of any company which was under control of the receiver, for any accounting period during which the receiver acted or exercised control.

27. *New clients*

Whenever a practice is asked to accept an appointment, consideration will need to be given to whether acceptance might give rise to a situation in which independence may be compromised whether by a prospective conflict of interest or otherwise. All reasonable steps should be taken to establish that acceptance is unlikely to threaten independence.

28. *Integrity*. A member, including one working outside the areas normally associated with accountancy, must maintain a high standard of conduct. In conforming with this standard, a member should not knowingly mislead or misrepresent facts to others and should use due care to avoid doing so unintentionally. At all times, a member should be conscious that integrity must be an overriding principle.

29. *Objectivity*. A member has a duty to be objective in carrying out professional work, and should maintain an independent approach to that work. Thus a member performing professional work in commerce, industry or the public sector, should recognise the problems created by personal relationships or financial involvements which by reason of their nature or degree may threaten his objectivity.

30. *Confidentiality - disclosure of information*. Confidentiality should be preserved both within and outside a member's organisation.

31. However, in the course of his work, a member may find himself faced with conflicts between his loyalty to his employers or colleagues on the one hand, and his duties as a member of a profession or as a citizen on the other hand. When faced with such conflict a member should make disclosure only with proper authority or where there is a professional obligation, a right, a legal requirement or a public duty to disclose.

32. Where a member is in doubt as to whether he has a right or duty to disclose he should, if appropriate, initially discuss the matter fully within the organisation in which he works. If that is not appropriate, or if it fails to resolve his problem, he should take legal advice and/or consult his professional body.

Confidentiality: misuse of information
33. Information acquired by a member in the course of his duties and to which he would not otherwise have access should not be used for personal advantage nor for the advantage of a third party. When a member changes his employment he must distinguish between experience he has gained in his previous employment and confidential information acquired there.

Published information
34. When a member has sole responsibility for the preparation and approval of information, including management information, which is to be made public or is to become available, on however restricted a basis, outside the organisation to which it refers, he should ensure that such information complies with professional pronouncements or, if it does not so comply, that the reasons for non-compliance are stated truthfully, unambiguously and fairly.

35. When his is not the sole responsibility, he should use his best endeavours to achieve compliance or, if the information does not comply with professional pronouncements, that the reasons for non-compliance are stated truthfully, unambiguously and fairly.

36. Professional pronouncements include, for example, statements of standard accounting practice, the City Code on Take-overs and Mergers and the Rules and Regulations of the Stock Exchange.

Conflict of interest: disclosure

37. A member should always make full and proper disclosures of any conflict of interest unless to do so would be inconsistent with the advice given under the heading Confidentiality - Disclosure of information.

Trade Union membership

38. It is recognised that a member has a statutory right to belong to a trade union. He should not, however, take part in industrial action which is a contravention of the law or puts him in conflict with the provisions of the rules of professional conduct.

39. *Share dealings.* Subject to:
    (a) relevant legislation;
    (b) Stock Exchange and other non-statutory requirements;
    (c) his own terms of service and;
    (d) awareness of the risks attendant on financial involvement referred to in paragraph 29 hereof;
    a member may own and deal in shares in any organisation in which he is employed or holds office.

40. *Gifts.* A member should be aware of the difficulties which may arise from the offer or the acceptance of any gift, favour or hospitality which may be interpreted as intended to influence the recipient.

Future developments in auditor independence

9. Many proposals have been put forward for safeguarding the independence of auditors. In the following paragraphs we will discuss:

   (a) rotation of audit appointments;
   (b) setting up an audit court;
   (c) appointment of auditors by government or government agency;
   (d) setting up a state auditing board;
   (e) peer reviews.

10. In addition, the EEC's Eighth Company Directive, which is enacted in the Companies Bill 1989 to be in force from 1990 onwards, will have further impact on auditor independence.

11. *Rotation of auditor appointments.* It has been argued that the long-term nature of the company audit engagement tends to create a loss of auditor independence, due to an increasing familiarity with the company's management and staff, which works against the shareholders' and the public's interest. For this reason, it has been argued that there should be a rotation of the audit appointment every few years, allowing several firms of professional accountants periodically to conduct the engagement, and thereby preventing any unnecessary loss of physical independence which the present situation is thought to cause. Research findings have proved that this type of procedure does not appear to be very popular in practice, owing mainly to the attendant disadvantages of upsetting the client company with continual changes of audit staff, the high costs of recurring first audits, and the present ability of auditors to retain a fresh approach to the audit by rotating members of the audit staff internally so that no member is permanently assigned to it, including the reporting partner.

12. *The audit court*. It has been suggested that auditor independence has been eroded beyond repair in many cases, mainly because of the lack of apparent independence in his position when he is permitted to own shares in a client company, conduct management services on its behalf and be effectively employed by the company directors. Because of these factors, it is argued that the task of independent audit judgment should be removed from the auditor and given to a judicial court where eminent professional accountants would be appointed to judge the suitability of the accounting practices utilised by the company in producing its annual financial statements. The auditor in this situation would act as an evidence gatherer, responsible only for presenting the accounting facts to the court for its judgment and opinion.

13. *Appointment by government or a government agency*. It has been suggested that the auditor's appointment by the shareholders implies a certain lack of independence, firstly because it tends to ignore the interests of other important users of company financial statements; and secondly, because it tends to cause company directors to be the employers of the auditor, with the shareholders merely endorsing prior recommendations. It therefore has been proposed that the auditor should be appointed by a government agency such as the Department of Trade and Industry. The audit fees would be paid by this body out of levies on the companies based on their past fee record. The main argument for this suggestion is that it would give the auditor security of employment and leave him free to give a totally objective opinion on the accounting information in the company's financial statements. The main arguments against it are that it would be difficult to administer, could cause the costs of audits to rise substantially, and might well be the first step towards nationalising the accountancy profession.

14. *A state auditing board*. Commentators argue that the approach of the Sandilands Committee a few years back has proved that a government sponsored body has a useful role in shaping accountancy thinking and far from leading to increased party political interference has created an important contribution to the wider understanding of accountancy reports.

It has therefore been argued that a state auditing board will become inevitable. Its role would be to:

(a) influence new company legislation;
(b) formulate national accounting and auditing policy;
(c) co-operate with the Union Europeenne des Experts Comptables Economiques et Financiers (UEC);
(d) enforce Accounting Standards (SSAPs) and International Accounting Standards (IASs);
(e) oversee the appointment of auditors as envisaged in paragraph 13 above.

Any form of nationalisation is likely to be opposed by the accountancy profession.

15. *Audit committees*. One American innovation which is gathering momentum slowly in this country is the audit committee. In the US already 80% of large companies have such committees and the Security and Exchange Commission have made it compulsory for all listed companies. One of the main reasons for audit committees arises from the difficulty auditors have in combating instances where the executive directors of a company are determined to mislead them. As a result it is felt that an audit committee preferably drawn from 'non-executive' directors of a client company would provide an invaluable independent liaison between the board and the auditors, thus strengthening the auditors' position and improving communication. Other advantages that are claimed to arise from the existence of an audit committee include:

(a) it will lead to increased confidence in the credibility and objectivity of financial reports;

(b) by specialising in the problems of financial reporting and thus, to some extent, fulfilling the directors' responsibility in this area, it will allow the executive directors to devote their attention to management; and

(c) in cases where the interests of the company, the executive directors and the employees conflict, the audit committee might provide an impartial body for the auditors to consult.

16. Opponents of audit committees argue that:

(a) there may be difficulty selecting sufficient non-executive directors with the necessary competence in auditing matters for the committee to be really effective; and

(b) the establishment of such a formalised reporting procedure may dissuade the auditors from raising matters of judgement and limit them to reporting only on matters of fact.

17. *Peer reviews*. Some people have suggested that a system of 'auditing the auditors' should be established and indeed there have already been examples of such reviews being carried out on a mandatory basis in the USA. It would involve either:

(a) the profession as a whole establishing panels of experts to review and report on the practices and procedures of a firm of auditors; or simply,

(b) another independent firm of auditors carrying out the review.

The main object of such an exercise is to improve the quality and performance of audit work generally, but undoubtedly an important part of the 'brief' of the reviewer would be to consider whether the firm under review was sufficiently independent of its clients.

Independence and the EEC Eighth Directive

18. The EEC Eighth Directive was formally adopted in Brussels in 1984. Its provisions are included in the Companies Bill which at the time of writing is still before Parliament.

19. One controversial area of the Directive concerns a proposed new regulatory framework for audit firms. Only approved persons shall be permitted to carry out statutory audits, and the responsibility for approving such persons cannot be carried out by a private sector institution such as the Association. The UK profession favours implementation of this proposal by vesting ultimate control in the Secretary of State for Trade and Industry. A joint monitoring board for the regulation of auditors would then be set up by the accountancy bodies whose members are entitled by statute to act as auditors. The main area of interest to us in this section of the text is the question of auditor independence.

20. In a consultative document published by the Department of Trade and Industry a number of proposals were advanced for implementing the Directive's rules on independence. One suggestion was that audit appointments should be rotated every five years (see paragraph 11 above). Another suggestion was that audit firms should be prohibited from offering other services (eg consultancy services). Neither suggestion was welcomed by the accountancy bodies and the Government has now decided not to proceed with either of these proposals.

21. Another issue raised by the Eighth Directive is the possibility of audit firms becoming corporate bodies. In general the profession has welcomed the Directive's proposal that audit firms should be allowed to incorporate, although some commentators have argued that the auditor's unlimited liability is the best guarantee that standards will be maintained. Discussion has focused mainly on the extent to which shares in an incorporated audit firm may be held by persons outside the firm. The Directive allows up to 49% of the shares to be owned by outsiders, but most UK commentators have felt that the auditor's independence may be prejudiced if more than 25% of the shares are held externally.

Independence: conclusion

22. It is clear that the question of auditor independence is one that is of continuing concern to the profession. Although the current Rules of professional conduct provide an invaluable framework, there are still problems to be resolved. It is to be hoped that their solution can be found from within the profession rather than from outside. It should be borne in mind, however, that the fact of independence, rather than its mere appearance, is something which depends more on mental attitudes than on physical attributes. As such the only sure way of obtaining auditor independence is by generating a sufficiently high standard of professional ethics in those who are qualified to carry out audits.

Audit evidence

23. The APC auditing standards state that 'the auditor should obtain *relevant* and *reliable* audit evidence, *sufficient* to enable him to draw reasonable conclusions therefrom'. The three key words, 'relevant', 'reliable' and 'sufficient' are interpreted in the auditing guideline *Audit evidence*.

    (a) *Sufficiency*
    The auditor can rarely be certain of the validity of the financial statements. However, he needs to obtain sufficient relevant and reliable evidence to form a reasonable basis for his opinion thereon. The auditor's judgement as to what constitutes sufficient relevant and reliable audit evidence is influenced by such factors as:

    (i)   his knowledge of the business of the enterprise and the industry in which it operates;

    (ii) the degree of risk of misstatement through errors or irregularities; this risk may be affected by such factors as:
    - the nature and materiality of the items in the financial statements;
    - the auditor's experience as to the reliability of the management and staff of the enterprise and of its records;
    - the financial position of its records;
    - possible management bias;

    (iii) the persuasiveness of the evidence.

    (b) *Relevance*
    The relevance of the audit evidence should be considered in relation to the overall audit objective of forming an opinion and reporting on the financial statements. To achieve this objective the auditor needs to obtain evidence to enable him to draw reasonable conclusions in answer to the following questions.

Balance sheet items

(i)   Have all of the assets and liabilities been recorded?

(ii)   Do the recorded assets and liabilities exist?

(iii)   Are the assets owned by the enterprise and are the liabilities properly those of the enterprise?

(iv)   Have the amounts attributed to the assets and liabilities been arrived at in accordance with the stated accounting policies, on an acceptable and consistent basis?

(v)   Have the assets, liabilities and capital and reserves been properly disclosed?

Profit and loss account items

(vi)   Have all income and expenses been recorded?

(vii) Did the recorded income and expense transactions in fact occur?

(viii) Have the income and expenses been measured in accordance with the stated accounting policies, on an acceptable and consistent basis?

(ix)   Have income and expenses been properly disclosed where appropriate?

The audit objectives (i) to (ix) above can be summarised conveniently for each accounting area as:
- completeness
- existence
- ownership
- valuation
- disclosure

(c) *Reliability*

Although the reliability of audit evidence is dependent upon the particular circumstances, the following general presumptions may be found helpful:

(i)   documentary evidence is more reliable than oral evidence;

(ii)   evidence obtained from independent sources outside the enterprise is more reliable than that secured solely from within the enterprise;

(iii)   evidence originated by the auditor by such means as analysis and physical inspection is more reliable than evidence obtained from others.

The auditor should consider whether the conclusions drawn from differing types of evidence are consistent with one another. When audit evidence obtained from one source appears inconsistent with that obtained from another, the reliability of each remains in doubt until further work has been done to resolve the inconsistency. However, when the individual items of evidence relating to a particular matter are all consistent, then the auditor may obtain a cumulative degree of assurance higher than that which he obtains from the individual items.

24.   The reliability presumptions (i), (ii) and (iii) above have profoundly influenced the techniques that the auditor has developed to obtain sufficient audit evidence - particularly in respect of balance sheet items. It is useful to reinforce the reliability concept from the guideline with the legal viewpoint. Legally types of evidence may be divided into:

(a) *primary evidence:* this is simply the best evidence of a fact or of the contents of a document that exists. For example, the best evidence of the contents of a document is the original itself not a carbon copy, photocopy or microfilm of it. Similarly, the best evidence of the existence of a physical object is the inspection of it. With few exceptions, the courts always insist on primary evidence;

(b) *secondary evidence:* this is any other form of direct evidence that is not the best available. Examples include a copy of an original document or oral evidence as to its contents and a photograph of a physical object or a document stating that it exists;

(c) *circumstantial evidence:* this is of an indirect nature. It is evidence of one fact from which the fact at issue may be inferred. For example, the fact that a company has taken out fire insurance on a property is indirect evidence of its existence. One of the most important ways in which an auditor uses circumstantial evidence is when he relies on evidence showing that the controls over the accounting records are strong to infer that the records are accurate;

(d) *hearsay:* although the courts will accept oral evidence from a person of what he has seen, they will rarely accept evidence of what he has heard from another person who has not been called as a witness. This is known as hearsay. Although the courts will only accept hearsay in exceptional circumstances, the auditor may adopt a more flexible approach depending on his judgement of the situation.

'True and fair'

25. The accounts of a limited company are required by s228 (2) of the Companies Act 1985 to show a true and fair view of the company's financial position as at the balance sheet date and of its profit or loss for the year ending on that date. The auditor is required to state in his report whether, in his opinion, the accounts satisfy that requirement.

26. Although the Companies Act 1985 contains many detailed requirements as to the form and content of company accounts, it does not attempt to define what is meant by the term 'true and fair view'. This is surprising because the requirement to present a true and fair view is stated in the Act to override any other requirement with which it might conflict. The expression was first used in the Companies Act 1947 and has therefore been a part of company law for over 40 years. Its meaning can best be understood by considering a written opinion from counsel prepared for the Accounting Standards Committee (ASC). The ASC's particular interest was in the question of compliance with accounting standards, but counsel's opinion ranges more widely than that.

27. The following paragraphs are a paraphrase of the rather lengthy opinion.

"The ASC has recently undertaken a review of the standard setting process and decided that future standards will 'deal only with those matters which are of major and fundamental importance and affect the generality of companies' but that, as in the past, the standards will apply 'to all accounts which are intended to show a true and fair view of financial position and profit or loss'. A SSAP is therefore a declaration by the ASC, on behalf of its constituent professional bodies, that save in exceptional circumstances accounts which do not comply with the standard will not give a true and fair view."

28. 'True and fair view' is also a legal concept and the question of whether company accounts comply with section 228 (2) Companies Act 1985 can be authoritatively decided only by a court. The nature of the 'true and fair view' as used in the Companies Act:

"Is an abstraction or philosophical concept expressed in simple English. The law uses many similar concepts, of which 'reasonable care' is perhaps the most familiar example. It is a common feature of such concepts that there is seldom any difficulty in understanding what they mean but frequent controversy over their application to particular facts. One reason for this phenomenon is that because such concepts represent a very high level of abstraction which has to be applied to an infinite variety of concrete facts, there can never be a sharply defined line between, for example, what is reasonable care and what is not. There will always be a penumbral area in which views may reasonably differ.

It is however important to observe that the application of the concept involves judgement in questions of degree. The information contained in accounts must be accurate and comprehensive (to mention two of the most obvious elements which contribute to a true and fair view) to within acceptable limits. What is acceptable and how is this to be achieved? Reasonable businessmen and accountants may differ over the degree of accuracy or comprehensiveness which in particular cases the accounts should attain. Equally, there may sometimes be room for differences over the method to adopt in order to give a true and fair view, cases in which there may be more than one 'true and fair view' of the same financial position. Again, because 'true and fair view' involves questions of degree, we think that cost-effectiveness must play a part in deciding the amount of information which is sufficient to make accounts true and fair.

In the end, as we have said, the question of whether accounts give a true and fair view in compliance with the Companies Acts must be decided by a judge. But the courts look for guidance on this question to the ordinary practices of professional accountants. This is not merely because accounts are expressed in a language which judges find difficult to understand. This may sometimes be true but it is a minor reason for the importance which the courts attach to evidence of accountancy practice. The important reason is inherent in the nature of the 'true and fair' concept. Accounts will not be true and fair unless the information they contain is sufficient in quantity and quality to satisfy the reasonable expectations of the readers to whom they are addressed. On this question, accountants can express an informed professional opinion on what, in current circumstances, it is thought that accounts should reasonably contain. But they can do more than that. The readership of accounts will consist of businessmen, investors, bankers and so forth, as well as professional accountants. But the expectations of the readers will have been moulded by the practices of accountants because by and large they will expect to get what they ordinarily get and that in turn will depend upon the normal practices of accountants.

For these reasons, the courts will treat compliance with accepted accounting principles as prima facie evidence that the accounts are true and fair. Equally, the deviation from accepted principles will be prima facie evidence that they are not."

29. *Relationship between generally accepted accounting principles and the legal concept of 'true and fair'*

(a) "The function of the ASC is to formulate what it considers should be generally accepted accounting principles. Thus the value of a SSAP to a court which has to decide whether accounts are true and fair is two-fold. First, it represents an important statement of professional opinion about the standards which readers may reasonably expect in accounts which are intended to be true and fair. The SSAP is intended to crystallise professional opinion and reduce penumbral areas in which divergent practices exist and can each have a claim to being 'true and fair'. Secondly, because accountants are professionally obliged to comply with a SSAP, it creates in the readers an expectation that the accounts will be in conformity with the prescribed standards. This is in itself a reason why accounts which depart from the standard without adequate justification or explanation may be held not to be true and fair. The importance of expectations was emphasised by the Court of Appeal in what may be regarded as a converse case, *re Press Caps* (1949). An ordinary historic cost balance sheet was said to be 'true and fair' notwithstanding that it gave no information about the current value of freehold properties because, it was said, no one familiar with accounting conventions would expect it to include such information.

(b) A SSAP therefore has no direct legal effect. It is simply a rule of professional conduct for accountants. But in our opinion it is likely to have an indirect effect on the content which the courts will give to the 'true and fair' concept."

Materiality

30. The concept of 'true and fair' is linked with the concept of materiality, which is fundamental to the whole process of accounting. The auditor's task is to decide whether accounts show a true and fair view, not to establish that they are correct in every particular. It can take a great deal of time and trouble to check the correctness of even a very small transaction and the resulting benefit may not justify the effort.

31. To take account of this practical difficulty, neither company law nor accounting standards require that accounts should be correct in every particular. But preparers of accounts, as well as auditors, need to think carefully about the degree of latitude that is permitted to them; in other words, they need to decide which items are material and which are not. Although there is no statutory definition of the term, it is usual to regard an item as material if its non-disclosure, misstatement or omission would be likely to distort the view given by the accounts.

32. Materiality can only be considered in relative terms. In a small business £100 may be material whereas £1 million may not be material in the context of a very large undertaking. It is often useful to use a percentage difference as a guide to materiality. While percentage comparisons can, properly used, constitute useful broad guides, it must be kept in mind that they are no more than rough rules of thumb, and should not be applied indiscriminately without regard to the particular. For example, if it was estimated during the course of an audit that stocks with a total value of £750,000 had been over-valued by £20,000 (or about 2.7%), this might at first be considered to be immaterial. If, however, the profit for the period was given as £50,000, then the over-valuation becomes highly significant.

33. From the example in the last paragraph, it can be seen that an item can be material either in a general or a particular sense. Where an item is not material in the general context, the degree of latitude acceptable in the particular context may depend on its nature. It is important to distinguish between cases where the amount at issue can only be estimated or is based on the exercise of judgement (eg depreciation) and those where it can be determined precisely (eg share capital). For the former a margin of error which is high in relation to the item itself may be acceptable when viewed in the context of the accounts as a whole. On the other hand items such as directors' remuneration and investment income may have a particular interest to the shareholders so that an error that is trivial in the general context, and indeed not large in relation to the item, may nevertheless be considered material. In some cases the relevant statutory provisions do not allow any latitude at all.

34. Occasionally it is found that an item of small amount is nevertheless material in the context of the company's particular circumstances, for example, where the context leads the user to expect the item to be of substantial amount.

35. It frequently happens that two items, which are material taken separately, will be of opposite effect. Care should be taken before offsetting such items. For example, a company with profits before tax of £500,000 has made a profit on the disposal of an investment of £220,000 and a loss on the closure of a factory of £225,000. Both of these results should be disclosed as extraordinary items despite the fact that the net effect is a loss of only £5,000. It may also be necessary, where there are a large number of small items, for them to be aggregated to ascertain if they are material in total.

36. In a later chapter we will be looking in more detail at the concept of materiality and its practical effects on the work of the auditor.

Responsibility of the auditor

37. The responsibility borne by the auditor is a topic on which views have changed over the years. In the early days of auditing (and even now in the layman's conception of the profession) an auditor was thought to be responsible for ensuring the accuracy of accounts and for discovering fraud. But we have already seen that complete accuracy in accounts is unattainable and that the auditor's responsibilities in relation to fraud are very limited.

38. Even in the previous century, the limitations on the auditor's responsibility had begun to be recognised. Lindlay L J (already quoted in chapter 1) in re *The London and General Bank* 1895 said that:

> "He (the auditor) is not an insurer; he does not guarantee that the books do correctly show the position of the company's affairs ... His obligation is not so onerous as this. Such I take to be the duty of an auditor: he must be honest - that is, he must not certify what he does not believe to be true, and he must take reasonable care and skill before he believes what he certifies is true."

39. In modern times the responsibility of the auditor is determined by statute and by the rules of his profession. These aspects are examined in the next two chapters.

Audit risk

40. A draft audit brief issued by the APC in April 1987 says that:
    "Audit risk (or ultimate risk) is the term given to the risk that the auditor will draw an invalid conclusion from his audit procedures."

41. Common sense suggests that audit risk is in fact a combination of:

    (a) the risk that there is something wrong in the organisation which results in a material misstatement of some account figure; and
    (b) the risk that the audit does not discover a material misstatement, either through error, or because the auditor's sample just did not happen to pick up the relevant transactions.

42. The audit brief defines these commonsense ideas more precisely:

> "*Inherent risk*. Inherent risk derives from the characteristics of the entity and of its environment prior to the establishment of internal controls. It derives in large part from the type of industry in which the entity operates (eg there may be more risk of material misstatement occurring in the financial statements of a high technology company than there is in a stable industry). Inherent risk will vary between particular account headings (eg stock is usually subject to the possibility of more material errors than cash at bank because its valuation is more subjective). The occurrence of errors in previous years may be indicative of a higher inherent risk either in the business as a whole or in particular account areas.
>
> *Control risk* is the risk that internal controls will not prevent or detect material errors.
>
> *Detection risk* is the risk that the auditor's substantive procedures and his review of the financial statements will not detect material errors."

43. These definitions are fairly clear, even though you may not at this stage know exactly what 'internal controls' and 'substantive procedures' are. The important points to remember are the *definition* of audit risk, and the fact that audit risk is actually the combination of three other types of risk.

44. We will return to the subject of audit risk later in the text.

Summary of the chapter

45. In this chapter, we have looked at the audit concepts identified by your syllabus. You will find that there is a certain amount of overlap with the next section of the text on professional and legal requirements (because the regulatory framework is an attempt to put audit concepts into a workable practical structure).

TEST YOUR KNOWLEDGE
Numbers in brackets refer to paragraphs in this chapter

1. Why is it important that auditors should be independent? (1)

2. Describe the rules relating to beneficial shareholdings in audit clients. (8 (8))

3. What is an 'audit court'? What is an 'audit committee'? (12,15)

4. What are the three essential characteristics of the evidence required by an auditor? (23)

5. What is meant by the term 'material' in relation to an accounting item? (31)

6. Summarise the judgement in *re The London and General Bank* 1895. (38)

7. Describe the elements comprised in audit risk. (41)

SECTION 1: ILLUSTRATIVE QUESTIONS

1. In some cases, the application of the concept of prudence in financial statements may be inconsistent with a true and fair view being shown.

   You are required to discuss the proposition and reach a conclusion.

2. You are required to discuss the advantages and disadvantages of accounting and auditing standards and guidelines to the auditor and the consequences of such standards and guidelines being enforceable by statute.

SECTION 1: SUGGESTED SOLUTIONS

1. Statement of Standard Accounting Practice 2 (SSAP 2) defines the prudence concept in the following terms:

    "Revenue and profits are not anticipated, but are recognised by inclusion in the profit and loss account only when realised in the form either of cash or of other assets, the ultimate cash realisation of which can be assessed with reasonable certainty: provision is made for all known liabilities (expenses and losses) whether the amount of these is known with certainty or is a best estimate in the light of the information available."

    This definition is supported by the 4th Schedule, Companies Act 1985, which adds that liabilities and losses between the balance sheet date and the date of the directors signing of the financial statements should also be taken into account.

    The concept of prudence is basically an asymmetric concept, in that:
    - profits are recognised only when they are realised; but
    - losses are provided for immediately they are foreseen.

    It can be reasonably assumed that those who drafted SSAP 2 and the Companies Act 1985 would not agree that the application of the prudence concept could be inconsistent with a true and fair view being shown.

    Examples of how 'prudence' can contribute towards a true and fair view might be:
    - that prudence not only avoids overstating profits but prevents excessive distribution of profits, which would lead to a shortage of cash;
    - that prudence produces positive, more quantifiable results, as opposed to 'best estimates'.

    However, the principal cause of the type of conflict envisaged by the proposition in the question is where the prudence concept and the accruals concept appear to dictate different treatments for certain items in financial statements. Where this conflict arises, SSAP 2 requires that prudence should be applied, thus prevailing over the accruals concept.

    If a set of financial statements is to give a true and fair view it is necessary for a fair balance to be struck between the application of the prudence concept and the accruals concept. This is particularly important where the aim is to produce a profit figure which can be compared over periods of time.

    Examples of circumstances where a balance needs to be struck between the application of the prudence and the accruals concepts are:

    (a) *SSAP 9 - Accounting for stocks and long-term contracts*
        If the application of the prudence concept were taken to extremes then no profit would be recognised until a long-term contract was completed. This would make comparison of profits over a number of years difficult. This policy would also conflict with the accruals concept in that profit in any year would not reflect work performed in that year.

        In this case, SSAP 9 requires profit to be taken in the year in which the work is performed provided that the outcome of the contract can be foreseen with reasonable certainty. In this way, provided that such attributable profit is taken on a prudent basis, the two concepts are broadly compatible.

    (b) *SSAP 13 - Accounting for research and development*
        Again, if the application of the prudence concept were taken to extremes, all research and development expenditure would be charged to the profit and loss account in the year in which it was incurred.

SSAP 13, however, allows certain development expenditure to be carried forward and matched against future revenues which will be earned as a result of the development expenditure. The standard lays down criteria which must be met in order for this carry forward of development expenditure to be permitted. The aim of these criteria is to ensure a balance between the accruals and prudence concepts.

(c) *SSAP 16 - Current cost accounting* (now withdrawn)
In drawing up accounts on a CCA basis the resulting adjustments to the profit and loss account will tend to make the profit lower than on an historical cost basis. However, the corresponding net credits to the current cost reserve are regarded as realised gains by SSAP 16, so that after adding these amounts to the current cost profit attributable to shareholders, the resulting distributable profit will tend to be higher than the CCA profit.

Other examples could be found of similar potential conflicts between the prudence concept on the one hand and commercial reality on the other. The requirement to show a true and fair view encompasses not only the accuracy of the figures themselves in financial statements (often ascribed to 'truth') but also the way in which those figures are presented (which may be termed 'fairness'). A true and fair view cannot be given without the use of common sense and commercial realism. Taken to extremes, the prudence concept could in many cases conflict with those ideas; but it is not normally necessary to take such concepts to extremes and it could be said that the concept of truth and fairness is itself the antithesis of extremes. It should in the great majority of cases be possible to achieve a compromise and to prepare financial statements on a prudent yet realistic basis.

2. The major advantages of accounting standards and auditing standards and guidelines can be summarised as follows:

Accounting standards
- Reduce the areas of uncertainty and subjectivity in accounts.
- Narrow the areas where different accounting policies can be adopted.
- Increase the comparability of financial statements.
- Codify what is considered in most circumstances to be best accounting practice.
- Give an indication of the interpretation of the concept 'true and fair' in many circumstances.

Auditing standards and guidelines
- Give a framework for all audits around which a particular audit can be developed.
- Help to standardise the approach of all auditors to the common objective of forming an opinion.
- Assist the court in interpretation of the concept of 'due professional care' and may assist auditors when defending their work.
- Increase public awareness of what an audit comprises and the work behind the production of an audit report.
- Provide support for an auditor in a dispute with a client regarding the audit work necessary.

The disadvantages might include:

Accounting standards
- They are considered to be too rigid in some areas and too general in others making their application difficult in some circumstances.
- They can be onerous for small companies to adopt.

- Their proliferation could be said to increase proportionately the number of qualified audit reports thereby reducing the impact of such qualifications.
- They can create divisions within the profession of those who agree and those who disagree with a particular standard. This has been clearly demonstrated with the SSAP 16 debates, and has brought bad publicity to the Association and the profession.
- They would be difficult to change once they become statutory as alterations to company law can take years rather than months to enact.

Auditing standards and guidelines
- It may appear that they impinge on, rather than assist, professional judgement.
- They are considered by some to stifle initiative and developments of new auditing methods.
- They may create additional and unnecessary work and thus raise fees, particularly on the audit of small companies.

If either type of standard were to be enforceable by statute it would mean that there would be government intervention in areas currently controlled solely by the profession itself. This might ultimately lead to a diminished role in self-regulation.

To be enforceable by statute the standards and guidelines would have to be applicable to all circumstances and thus need to be very general and broad in their instructions. This might reduce their usefulness to the auditor.

Auditors might spend unnecessary time ensuring that they have complied with the law rather than considering the quality of their service to their clients.

Finally, it should be considered whether statutory backing for standards and guidelines would force auditors into narrow views and approaches which might gradually impair the quality of accounting and auditing practices.

SECTION 2

PROFESSIONAL AND LEGAL REQUIREMENTS

Chapter 3

THE LEGAL FRAMEWORK

Topics covered in this chapter:

- The qualifications required of an auditor
- The appointment, dismissal and resignation of an auditor
- The statutory duties and powers of auditors

The Companies Act 1985

1. Following the consolidation of the Companies Acts 1948 - 1981 into the Companies Act 1985, the majority of enactments concerned with the office of auditor are now conveniently, and sensibly, contained within one chapter of the 1985 Act - part xi chapter 5 - embracing sections 384-394; the exceptions are auditor's duties and powers which are to be found in part viii chapter 1 - sections 236 and 237.

The qualifications required of an auditor

2. Prior to the 1976 Companies Act, the relevant law was embodied in S161 CA 48 and S13 CA67. Together these sections (now S389 CA 1985) stipulated in general terms that members of recognised accountancy bodies and certain others who obtained Department of Trade (now the Department of Trade and Industry (DTI)) approval were eligible to act as auditors of limited companies.

3. In practice these accountancy bodies recognised by the DTI are restricted to:

   (a) the Institute of Chartered Accountants in England and Wales;
   (b) the Institute of Chartered Accountants of Scotland;
   (c) the Chartered Association of Certified Accountants;
   (d) the Institute of Chartered Accountants in Ireland.

4. S13 CA76 for the first time specifically named the above accountancy bodies, as the only ones whose members would be given universal recognition by the DTI. The Secretary of State is, however, empowered to amend the list of approved bodies by adding or deleting any body. To date no such amendments have been made although a couple of bodies have attempted unsuccessfully to obtain approval over the last few years.

5. Certain disqualification provisions are contained in the CA85.

    (a) None of the following persons is qualified for appointment as auditor of a company (S389 (b)):
         (i)   an officer or servant of the company;
         (ii)   a person who is a partner of or in the employment of an officer or servant of the company;
         (iii) a body corporate.

    (b) A person is also not qualified for appointment as auditor of a company if he is disqualified, under (a) above, for appointment as auditor of any other company within the same group of companies as that company (S389 (7)).

    (c) No person may act as auditor when he knows that he is disqualified from holding such office; and if an auditor knowingly becomes disqualified during his term of office he must vacate his office and give written notice to the company that he has so vacated his office by reason of such disqualification. Any person acting as auditor, or failing to vacate his office, knowing that he is not qualified to do so, "is guilty of an offence and liable to a fine and, for continued contravention, to a daily default fine" (S389 (9) and (10)).

6. It should be appreciated that although the above provisions ensure a degree of independence, the *legislation* does not disqualify the following from being an auditor of a limited company:

    (a) a shareholder of the company;
    (b) a debtor or creditor of the company;
    (c) a close relative (eg a husband, wife, son, daughter, etc of an officer or servant of the company).

    However, the self-imposed regulations of the accountancy bodies are stricter than statute in this respect.

7. It is, in part, because of the shortcomings in the legislation that the S389 accountancy bodies have established guidelines containing additional measures and recommendations intended to enhance auditor independence. These were examined in the previous chapter.

The appointment of an auditor

8. The Act, in its provisions governing the appointment of auditors, provides further recognition of the need for auditor independence. It requires, essentially, that the auditor be appointed *by the shareholders* (and he is therefore answerable to the shareholders).

9. The basic rule as regards appointment is that every company shall at each annual general meeting (AGM) appoint an auditor to hold office from the conclusion of that meeting until the conclusion of the next AGM (S384 (1)). The retiring auditor may be reappointed at the general meeting but by positive resolution only - it is not automatic.

10. Exceptions to the basic rule stated above are as follows.

    (a) The directors may appoint the auditor:
       (i)   at any time before the first AGM, such auditor to hold office until the conclusion of the first AGM (S384 (2));
       (ii) to fill any casual vacancy in the office of auditor (S384 (4)).

    (b) Where at any general meeting of a company, at which accounts are laid before the members, no auditors are appointed or re-appointed, the Secretary of State may appoint a person to fill the vacancy (S385(5)). The company must inform the Secretary of State within one week of his power under this subsection becoming exercisable.

11. In certain cases relating to appointment of an auditor special notice (28 days) is required for the appropriate resolutions at a general meeting (S388 (1)). Such resolutions are those:

    (a) appointing as auditor a person other than the retiring auditor;
    (b) filling a casual vacancy in the office of auditor;
    (c) re-appointing as auditor a retiring auditor who was appointed by the directors to fill a casual vacancy.

12. On receipt of notice of one of these resolutions the company must immediately send a copy thereof (S388 (2)) to:

    (a) the person proposed to be appointed;
    (b) the retiring auditor in 11 (a) above;
    (c) the auditor who resigned, where a casual vacancy was caused by a resignation.

13. The remuneration of the auditor, which will include any sums paid by the company in respect of the auditor's expenses, will be fixed (S385) either by:

    (a) whoever made his appointment, viz either
       (i)   the members; or
       (ii)   the directors; or
       (iii) the Secretary of State; or
    (b) in such manner as the company in general meeting may determine.

14. In practice the most common method is (b), with the members authorising the directors to fix the remuneration. Regardless of the manner in which the auditor's remuneration is fixed it must be disclosed in the annual accounts of the company (Paragraph 53(7) schedule 4).

The resignation of an auditor

15. Certain provisions introduced by the Companies Act 1976 (and now embodied in CA 1985) are designed to ensure that auditors do not just resign without any explanation of their action. If an auditor wishes to resign part-way through his term of office he must:

    (a) deposit written notice of such resignation at the registered office of the company, resignation being effective on the day the notice is received, unless the auditor has specified some later date;

(b) accompany such notice with a statement (S390 (2)) that either:
  (i) there were no circumstances connected with this resignation which he considers should be brought to the notice of the members or *creditors* of the company; or
  (ii) a statement detailing any such 'surrounding circumstances'.

16. It should be carefully noted that unless there is a statement as required by S390 (2) then the auditor's resignation will not be effective. (It is also interesting to see that some responsibility on the part of the auditor towards creditors of a client company is recognised.)

17. On receipt of such notice of the auditor's resignation the company must send a copy of it to the Registrar of Companies within 14 days. If the statement of circumstances dictates so, then further copies must be sent to all members and all debenture holders of the company. However, if aggrieved, the company or any other person may apply to the court within 14 days for it to rescind this requirement. If the court is satisfied that the auditor is using the notice to obtain needless publicity for defamatory matters, it will remove this obligation and direct that the applicant's costs be wholly or partly paid by the auditor. In this case the company will merely need to circulate a copy of the court's order. In the event of the court ruling in favour of the auditor the company must send out the notice within 14 days of the date of this ruling.

18. In addition to depositing the explanatory statement at the company's registered office the auditor may, if he feels the circumstances warrant it, attach a signed requisition for the directors to convene an extraordinary general meeting, the purpose simply being for the company to have such circumstances brought to its attention. Section 391 (4) requires that this meeting takes place within 28 days of the notice convening the meeting. Before the general meeting is convened, the auditor may request the company to circulate to its members a written statement of circumstances. This prerogative persists whether the auditor himself requested the meeting or a meeting is to be held anyway. The company must circulate this statement to all members to whom notice of the meeting is being sent. If for any reason this fails to happen the statement can be read out at the meeting. Section 391 (6) provides the same safeguard as mentioned in paragraph 17 above against abuse of the auditor's right to do this.

19. In any case an auditor who has resigned may exercise his right to attend and receive relevant communications about any forthcoming meeting at which either his vacant office is to be filled or a meeting at which his term of office would have finished. (S391 (7)). He may also be heard at any such meeting which he attends on any part of the business which concerns him as former auditor of the company.

20. An anomaly in these rules is that auditors can apparently avoid giving the required reasons for relinquishing their office merely by not seeking re-appointment at the next AGM rather than formally resigning. A leading firm of accountants a few years back gave up an audit by not seeking re-appointment after issuing a four page audit report with nineteen qualifications. In this way they avoided having to make a statement giving reasons for their action, claiming that the audit report was comprehensive enough.

The dismissal of an auditor

21. It has been stressed that an auditor must be able to preserve an independent viewpoint and must be prepared to stand his ground without fear or favour. He should not, therefore, be subjected to pressure from directors or members and should not be liable to 'summary dismissal'. The

detailed provisions relating to the removal of the auditor, set out in S386 - 388, place the authority for removal with the members in general meeting. The objects of these provisions are again:

(a) to preserve the right of the members to appoint the auditor of their choice; and
(b) to preserve the auditor's independence of the directors by not permitting directors, who may be in disagreement with the auditor, to dismiss him.

22. Removal of the auditor before the expiration of his term of office requires the passing of an *ordinary* resolution of which special notice (28 days) has been given, the auditor being entitled to receive a copy of this resolution. If the resolution is passed then the company must notify the Registrar within 14 days of the date of the meeting (S386(2)).

23. Where an attempt is being made to remove an auditor during his term of office or where notice of a resolution to appoint another person in his place has been received by the company, the auditor may make representations as to why he thinks he ought to stay in office. Provided they are not received too late and are of reasonable length, he may require the company (S388(3)) to:

(a) state in any notice of the resolution given to the members that representations have been made; and
(b) send a copy of the representations to the members.

24. If the representations are not sent out either because they were received too late or because of the company's default, the auditor may require that they are read out at the meeting. This will not prejudice his normal right to speak at the meeting (S388(4)).

25. As with statements made on resignation, the representations need neither be sent out nor read at the meeting if, on the application either of the company or any other person who claims to be aggrieved, the court is satisfied that the auditor's right is being abused to obtain needless publicity for defamatory matter (S388 (5)).

26. The removed auditor is given two further rights by the Act (S387(2)). They are:

(a) he is entitled to receive all notices relating to:
   (i) the general meeting at which his term of office would have expired;
   (ii) any general meeting at which it is proposed to fill the casual vacancy caused by his removal;
(b) he is entitled to attend such meetings and to speak at them on any part of the business which concerns him as former auditor.

27. It should be appreciated therefore that the directors, as such, cannot remove the auditor from office. If the directors are also members it is only in that capacity that they can move a resolution to remove him (subject to their having the minimum specified voting rights).

Statutory duties of an auditor

28. The statutory duties of an auditor in respect of the audit of a limited company are enshrined in S236 and 237 CA85. The requirements are intended to enable the auditor to report on every balance sheet and profit and loss account laid before the company in general meeting. The detailed contents of that report are left to chapter 14, but the statutory duties of the auditor can be summarised as follows. He must consider whether:

(a) the accounts have been prepared in accordance with the Act (S236(2)(a));

(b) the balance sheet shows a true and fair view of the state of the company's affairs at the end of the period, and the profit and loss account shows a true and fair view of the results for the period (S236(2)(b));

(c) proper accounting records have been kept (and proper returns adequate for the audit received from branches not visited by the auditor) (S237(1)(a));

(d) the accounts are in agreement with the accounting records (S237 (1)(b));

(e) the directors' report is consistent with the accounts (S237 (6)).

The auditor may provide other services for the company, but he does not carry these out as auditor acting under statute.

Statutory rights of an auditor

29. To enable him to carry out his statutory duties the Act has given the auditor the following rights:

(a) a right of access at all times to the books, accounts and vouchers of the company (S237 (3));

(b) a right to all such information and explanations as he thinks necessary for the performance of his duties (ie what he requires, not what the directors think he should have) (S237(3));

(c) a right to attend any general meeting and to receive all notices and communications relating to such meetings which any member of the company is entitled to receive (S387 (1));

(d) a right to speak at general meetings on any part of the business that concerns him as auditor (S387 (1)).

With regard to (c) and (d) remember that the resigning and removed auditor respectively have the additional rights conferred by the Act discussed above.

3: THE LEGAL FRAMEWORK

Summary of the chapter

30. (a) The Companies Act 1985 restricts the office of auditor to members of defined accountancy bodies, of which the Chartered Association of Certified Accountants is one.

    (b) A company's auditors are normally appointed by the shareholders, but in certain cases the appointment may be made by the directors.

    (c) Auditors are not allowed to resign their office without giving formal notice of their reasons.

    (d) The Companies Act 1985 confers a number of rights on auditors who are dismissed from office.

TEST YOUR KNOWLEDGE
Numbers in brackets refer to paragraphs in this chapter

1. What bodies are recognised by the DTI as the only ones whose members may act as auditors of limited companies? (3)

2. What persons are disqualified from appointment as auditors of limited companies? (5)

3. For what period does an auditor hold office? (9)

4. In what circumstances is 'special notice' required in the context of auditors' appointment? (11)

5. How may an auditor resign part way through his term of office? (15)

6. What rights regarding meetings does an auditor have who has resigned? (26)

7. Where an attempt is made to remove an auditor during his term of office, what rights does the auditor have? (23-26)

8. What are the statutory duties of an auditor? (28)

9. What are the statutory rights of an auditor? (29)

Chapter 4

PROFESSIONAL REQUIREMENTS

Topics covered in this chapter:

- Rules of professional conduct
- Auditing standards and guidelines

Introduction

1. The members of any profession owe duties to the public, including those who retain or employ them, to the profession itself and to their fellow members. These duties may at times be contrary to a member's personal self-interest. The Association's 'Rules of professional conduct', on which these notes are based, are an aid to members in the identification of occasions upon which they might unwittingly fail to recognise or to fulfil any of those duties.

2. All of the major accounting bodies, and in particular the Chartered Association of Certified Accountants, require the observance of strict rules of conduct as a condition of membership. The Association's bye-laws specifically require members to refrain from what is described as misconduct; for this purpose, misconduct includes any act or default likely to bring discredit to themselves, the Association or the accountancy profession.

3. The Association recognises that it is not possible to specify all those combinations of circumstances in which a member may be held to have committed professional misconduct as defined above, but nonetheless, considers it desirable to be more explicit in specific areas.

Rules of professional conduct

4. The rules are contained in section 2 of the Certified Accountants Members' Handbook. They consist of a series of statements on the Association's ethical requirements in relation to those professional situations which most commonly arise. At the time of writing the list of statements is as follows:

Statement	Title
2.1	Professional independence
2.2	The professional duty of confidence
2.3	Advertising, publicity and obtaining professional work
2.4	Descriptions
2.5	Changes in professional appointments
2.6	Ownership of books and papers
2.7	Retention of working papers
2.8	Activities through corporate or non-corporate organisations
2.9	Remuneration
2.10	The obligations of consultants
2.11	Professional liability of accountants and auditors
2.12	Membership of trade unions
2.13	Incapacity or death of a sole practitioner
2.14	Clients' moneys
2.15	Formation of companies
2.16	Estates of deceased persons
2.17	The Prevention of Fraud (Investments) Act 1958
2.18	Insider dealing
2.19	Disciplinary action in respect of convictions before the Courts
2.20	Insolvency practice

5.   For examination purposes, the most important of these are the first three. We have already looked in detail at the statement on professional independence in an earlier chapter, and later in this chapter we will examine statements 2.2 and 2.3. Statement 2.11 on the professional liability of accountants and auditors is discussed in detail in chapter 5. The remaining statements, to the extent that they have any examination importance, are summarised very briefly in the paragraphs which follow.

6.   *Statement 2.4: Descriptions.* This statement regulates the use by members of the initials ACCA and FCCA, and the use of the title 'Certified Accountant(s)' both by individuals and by firms. You should note that the title may not be used by a firm unless *all* its partners are Certified Accountants.

7.   *Statement 2.5: Changes in professional appointments.* This statement sets out the procedures to be followed when a member takes over an appointment previously conducted by another accountant. This topic is covered in chapter 7.

8.   *Statement 2.6: Ownership of books and papers.* Except where he is acting as an agent, the working papers of a professional person belong to him, and an accountant, when preparing accounts, conducting an audit or advising on professional matters is not an agent. However, when an accountant is negotiating with the Inland Revenue about a client's tax liability, he is acting as an agent and correspondence with the Revenue therefore belongs to the client.

9. Statement 2.6 also discusses the question of an accountant's lien on books and papers.

   'A lien is a right of a person to retain possession of the owner's property until the owner pays what he owes to the person in possession. A general lien entitles a person in possession of property to retain that property until all his claims or accounts against the owner are satisfied. Such liens can rarely be established. A particular lien is a right over property which can be retained only until payment of a particular debt due in respect of it is paid.'

10. In the course of doing their ordinary professional work of producing and auditing accounts, advising on financial problems and carrying on relations with the Inland Revenue, accountants have at least a particular lien over any books of account, files and papers which their clients have delivered to them and also over any documents which have come into their possession in the course of their ordinary professional work.

11. A right of lien will only exist where all of the following conditions are present:

   (a) the documents must have come into the possession of the member by proper means;
   (b) the documents retained by the member must be the property of the client who owes the money and not of a third party, no matter how closely connected with the client;
   (c) the member must have carried out work upon the documents;
   (d) the fees for which the lien is exercised must be outstanding in respect of such work and not in respect of other related work.

12. *Statement 2.7: Retention of working papers.* This statement discusses the length of time for which accountants are required by statute or other authority, to retain working papers. In summary the required minimum retention periods are as follows:

Audit working papers	7 years
Files on clients' chargeable assets and gifts	11 years (then return them to the client or obtain authority from the client for their destruction)
Files of member as trustee	For the period of trusteeship and 7 years thereafter
Liquidator's working papers in a voluntary liquidation	5 years or a lesser period if approved by the creditors or members

13. *Statement 2.8: Activities through corporate or non-corporate organisations.* This provides guidance for members wishing to participate in limited companies offering accountancy services or in non-accountancy organisations (whether incorporated or not).

14. *Statement 2.9: Remuneration.* Work of a recurring nature should normally be charged out on the basis of the time spent on the work calculated at appropriate hourly rates. A member in practice is not permitted to charge or accept a fee for professional work which is calculated on a percentage basis, except where sanctioned by statute or custom; nor, except in certain defined circumstances, should he charge fees on a contingency basis.

Statement 2.2: The professional duty of confidence

15. It is the duty of a member to make it clear to a client that he may only act for him if the client agrees to disclose in full to the member all information relevant to the engagement.

16. Where a member agrees to serve a client in a professional capacity both the member and the client should be aware that it is an implied term of that agreement that the member will not disclose the client's affairs to any other person save with the client's consent or within the terms of certain recognised exceptions.

17. The recognised exceptions are as follows:

    (a) *Obligatory disclosure.* If a member knows or suspects his client to have committed the offence of treason he is obliged to disclose all the information at his disposal to a competent authority.

    (b) *Voluntary disclosure.* In certain cases voluntary disclosure may be made by the member:

        (i)   where disclosure is reasonably necessary to protect the member's interests, eg to enable him to sue for fees or defend an action for, say, negligence;

        (ii) where disclosure is compelled by process of law, eg where in an action a member is required to give evidence or discovery of documents;

        (iii) where there is a public duty to disclose, eg where an offence has been committed which is contrary to the public interest.

18. If a member is requested to assist the police, the Inland Revenue or other authority by providing information about a client's affairs in connection with enquiries being made, he should first enquire under what statutory authority the information is demanded. Unless he is satisfied that such statutory authority exists he should decline to give any information until he has obtained his client's authority. If the client's authority is not forthcoming and the demand for information is pressed the member should not accede unless so advised by his solicitor. The position is the same whether the enquiries relate to a civil or criminal matter.

19. If a member knows or suspects that a client has committed a wrongful act he must give careful thought to his own position. He is under no obligation, even in a criminal matter (save only treason), to convey his information to a competent authority, but he must ensure that he has not prejudiced himself by, for example, relying on information given by the client which subsequently proves to be incorrect.

    However, it would be a criminal offence for a member to act positively, without lawful authority or reasonable excuse, in such a manner as to impede with intent the arrest or prosecution of a client whom he knows or believes to have committed an 'arrestable offence'.

Statement 2.3: Advertising, publicity and obtaining professional work

20. The key requirements on advertising and publicity are contained in the statement's first four paragraphs, reproduced below:

1. A member may obtain or seek professional work by direct approaches to existing or prospective clients by mail or any other means unless prohibited by the law of the land in which the member practises and subject to the requirements in paragraphs 2 and 3 below.

2. A member may inform the public of the services he is capable of providing by means of advertising or other forms of promotion subject to the general requirement that the medium should not, in the opinion of Council, reflect adversely on the member, the Association or the accountancy profession, nor should the advertisement or promotional material, in the opinion of Council:

   (a) as to content or presentation, bring the Association into disrepute or bring discredit to the member, firm or the accountancy profession;
   (b) discredit the services offered by others whether by claiming superiority for the member's or firm's own services or otherwise;
   (c) contain comparisons with other members or firms;
   (d) be misleading, either directly or by implication;
   (e) fall short of the requirements of the Advertising Standards Authority as to legality, decency, honesty and truthfulness.

3. Advertisements and other promotional material may refer to the basis on which fees are calculated, or to hourly or other charging rates, provided that the information given is not misleading.

4. Subject to paragraphs 2(a) and 3 above, a member may advertise:

   (a) for staff, a partnership, salaried employment or for sub-contract work;
   (b) on behalf of a client;
   (c) in a fiduciary or other capacity;
   (d) the commencement of a practice, the opening of a new office, members' appointments, changes in the membership of a firm and changes in the name, address or telephone number of a practice or firm.

21. The statement also includes detailed guidance on the extent to which members may publicise their services by less direct means, eg by sponsorship agreements, exhibitions and seminars.

22. Other requirements of the statement which should be learnt relate to obtaining professional work and advertising of fees:

   (a) 'A practising member may not give any commission, fee or reward to a third party, not being either his employee or another public accountant, in return for the introduction of a client.'

   (b) 'Members may advertise services at a fixed fee, provided the advertisement makes clear the extent and limits of the services covered in that fee. In the event of business arising as a result of the advertisement, the member should, for the avoidance of misunderstanding, send to the client an engagement letter specifying the precise range of services covered by the fee.'

Auditing standards and guidelines

23. It is generally accepted that the statutory audit in the UK, as we know it today, effectively came into being with the Companies Act 1948. From that date the UK profession, led, arguably, by the large international chartered firms, has been steadily developing sophisticated, cost-effective audit techniques. It is fair to say that the inspiration for many of these UK techniques was US methodology - their codification of auditing standards was achieved much earlier than ours.

24. Before 1980, it was left to the initiative of each individual practising firm to develop and apply its own techniques. However, in 1980 the APC issued authoritative Auditing Standards - supported by an initial tranche of guidelines - having first sounded out the profession by publishing them in draft form for comment. For the most part these standards represent no more than the formalisation of existing good practice.

Scope of auditing standards and guidelines

25. To establish the authority of Standards and Guidelines one can do no better than quote from the Explanatory Foreword (paras 3-7) to the Auditing Standards and Guidelines:

> 3 Auditing Standards prescribe the basic principles and practices which members are expected to follow in the conduct of an audit. Unless otherwise indicated in the text, Auditing Standards apply whenever an audit is carried out. Each Auditing Standard will consist of a text to which there may be added an explanatory note. Explanatory notes have the same status and purpose as Auditing Guidelines.
>
> 4 It would be impracticable to establish a code of rules sufficiently elaborate to cater for all situations and circumstances which an auditor might encounter. Such a code could not provide for innovations in business and financial practice and might hinder necessary development and experiment in auditing practice. In the observance of Auditing Standards, therefore, the auditor must exercise his judgement in determining both the auditing procedures necessary in the circumstances to afford a reasonable basis for his opinion and the wording of his report.
>
> 5 Auditing Guidelines give, or will give, guidance on:
>   (a) procedures by which the Auditing Standards may be applied;
>   (b) the application of the Auditing Standards to specific items appearing in the financial statements of enterprises;
>   (c) techniques currently being used in auditing;
>   (d) audit problems relating to particular commercial or legal circumstances or to specific industries;
>   but do not prescribe basic principles and practices.
>
> 6 Existing pronouncements on auditing matters approved by the respective Councils of the accountancy bodies should be considered by their members as having the same status as Auditing Guidelines. They will remain in force until withdrawn.
>
> 7 Members are advised that a court of law may, when considering the adequacy of the work of an auditor, take into account any pronouncements or publications which it thinks may be indicative of good practice. Auditing Standards and Guidelines are likely to be so regarded.

26. In summary, note the following.

   (a) Each Auditing Standard (there are in fact only two at present as we shall see) consists of a definitive text to which there may be added *both* an 'Explanatory note' and 'Auditing guidelines', which, although not definitive, give guidance on procedures by which the Standards may be applied (paras 3 and 5).

   (b) Auditing Standards and Guidelines are likely to be taken by a court of law as indicative of good practice (para 7).

   (c) The Guidelines will gradually replace any other existing ACCA statements, but such statements remain in force until withdrawn and have the same status as Auditing Guidelines (para 6).

27. In January 1989 a revised Explanatory Foreword to Auditing Standards and Guidelines was issued. The two most important changes from the original 1980 Foreword are:

   (a) a reminder that the principles of Auditing Standards apply to other forms of work carried out by accountants or auditors which are not usually regarded as audits, such as special reports or value for money reviews;

   (b) a statement that auditors should normally follow Auditing Guidelines in conducting their work and should be prepared to justify any departure from the Guidelines. The original Explanatory Foreword did not define the status of Guidelines at all.

28. The two Auditing Standards currently in issue are as follows:

		Issued
1.	The auditor's operational standard	April 1980
2.	The audit report.	March 1989

29. As its title implies, standard (1) above is concerned with the practical conduct of the audit, while standard (2) deals with the discipline to be applied to the audit report, addressed to the shareholders in the case of a limited company. The audit report is, to a large extent, the 'end product' of the auditor's work. Because of this we shall postpone further discussion of the reporting standard until we have thoroughly covered the audit in operation.

The auditor's operational standard

30. Throughout the next chapters, constant reference will be made to the Operational Standard. Here is the full text:

"The auditor's operational standard (Issued April 1980)
This Auditing Standard should be read in conjunction with the Explanatory Foreword to Auditing Standards and Guidelines. General guidance on procedures by which this auditing standard may be complied with are given in auditing guidelines:

> Planning, controlling and recording
> Accounting systems
> Audit evidence
> Internal controls
> Review of financial statements

1. This auditing standard applies whenever an audit is carried out.

Planning, controlling and recording
2. The auditor should adequately plan, control and record his work.

Accounting systems
3. The auditor should ascertain the enterprise's system of recording and processing transactions and assess its adequacy as a basis for the preparation of financial statements.

Audit evidence
4. The auditor should obtain relevant and reliable audit evidence sufficient to enable him to draw reasonable conclusions therefrom.

Internal controls
5. If the auditor wishes to place reliance on any internal controls, he should ascertain and evaluate those controls and perform compliance tests on their operation.

Review of financial statements
6. The auditor should carry out such a review of the financial statements as is sufficient, in conjunction with the conclusions drawn from the other audit evidence obtained, to give him a reasonable basis for his opinion on the financial statements.

Effective date
7. This auditing standard is effective for the audit of financial statements relating to accounting periods starting on or after 1 April 1980.

31. Although the standard comprises 7 paragraphs, it is clearly paragraphs 2 - 6 that are the heart of the matter in an operational sense. Each of these key paragraphs has an associated guideline, as indicated in the introduction to the standard. We will look at each of these guidelines in detail in the following chapters.

The development of auditing guidelines

32. The Explanatory Foreword to the Auditing Standards and Guidelines states that guidelines give, or will give, guidance on:

    (a) procedures by which the auditing standards may be applied;
    (b) the application of the auditing standards to specific items appearing in the financial statements of enterprises;
    (c) techniques currently being used in auditing;
    (d) audit problems relating to particular commercial or legal circumstances or to specific industries;

    but do not prescribe basic principles and practices.

33. Since 1980 we have seen the publication of a series of guidelines within categories (b) (c) and (d) above joining the original six category (a) guidelines issued with, and supporting, the three standards. In the jargon of the APC, category (b) and (c) guidelines are termed 'detailed operational guidelines' and category (d) 'industry guidelines'.

34. Each of the guidelines issued to date within the syllabus is discussed at the appropriate point in the text. However, as the situation with these guidelines is so fluid, and because of their sheer numbers, it is useful to provide a summary of the 'state of the art' with respect to the guidelines, indicating their title, date of issue and reference to the chapter in the text where principal coverage is provided. This appears on the following page.

AUDITING GUIDELINES

Category		Reference in text chapter
Operational guidelines:		
Planning, controlling and recording	April 1980	7
Accounting systems	"	8
Audit evidence	"	9/10
Internal controls	"	8
Review of financial statements	"	12
Detailed operational guidelines:		
Bank reports for audit purposes	June 1982	10
Events after the balance sheet date	November 1982	13
Amounts derived from the preceding financial statements	November 1982	7
Representations by management	July 1983	13
Detailed operational guidelines:		
Attendance at stocktaking	October 1983	10
Engagement letters	May 1984	7
Auditing in a computer environment	June 1984	16
Reliance on internal audit	November 1984	8
Quality control	January 1985	13
The auditor's considerations in respect of going concern	August 1985	13
Financial information issued with audited financial statements	September 1985	12
Prospectuses and the reporting accountant	February 1986	*
Reliance on other specialists	May 1986	10
Reports to management	December 1986	8
Group financial statements - reliance on the work of other auditors	December 1986	*
Applicability to the public sector of Auditing Standards and Guidelines	July 1987	-
Analytical review	April 1988	7
Reporting guidelines:		
Auditors' reports and SSAP 16 *Current cost accounting*	October 1980	*
Industry guidelines:		
Charities	October 1981	*
Building societies	January 1982	*
Trade unions and employers' associations	August 1984	*
Housing associations	November 1984	*
Impact of regulations on public sector audits	March 1988	*
Pension schemes in the United Kingdom	December 1988	-

* - not examinable at 2.1

EXPOSURE DRAFTS IN ISSUE		
Audit sampling	April 1987	9
Audit reports under company legislation in the United Kingdom	June 1987	14
Audit reports and information on the effects of changing prices	August 1987	-
The auditor's responsibility for detecting and reporting fraud and other illegal acts	January 1988	5
The implications for auditors of the Financial Services Act 1986	February 1988	-
Guidance for internal auditors	November 1988	8

Summary of the chapter

35. (a) The work of auditors is governed partly by professional statements issued by the Association. The most important for examination purposes are those covering the topics of independence, confidentiality and advertising and publicity.

    (b) Auditing standards and guidelines issued by the APC provide detailed operational guidance on auditing principles and procedures.

TEST YOUR KNOWLEDGE
Numbers in brackets refer to paragraphs in this chapter

1. Summarise the content of the statements on:
    (a) descriptions; (6)
    (b) retention of working papers. (12)

2. What are the two exceptional cases in which a member may disclose information about a client to a third party? (17)

3. How should a member act if he suspects that a client has committed a wrongful act? (19)

4. What is the requirement of Statement 2.3 on the subject of obtaining professional work? (22 (a))

5. What is the legal status of the Auditing Standards and Guidelines? (25 (7))

Chapter 5

LIABILITY OF THE AUDITOR

Topics covered in this chapter:

- Civil liability
- Criminal liability
- Liability to clients under contract law
- Liability to third parties
- Liability to detect fraud

Background

1. In the USA litigation against accountants (and especially auditors) has long been familiar. The trend is now spreading to the UK. Newspaper reports of legal actions, involving huge sums claimed in compensation for negligence, have become commonplace.

2. The traumatic aspect of legal action against accountants lies, of course, in their unlimited liability status - partners of firms which are sued have all their assets on the line, including their homes. The accountancy profession may claim, with some justification, that its member firms are being victimised unfairly. They argue that the combination of unlimited liability and substantial insurance cover makes accountants an easy target.

3. The principal topic that concerns us in this chapter is liability of the statutory auditor for professional negligence but we can also consider more generally the relationship between an accountant and his client and between an accountant and third parties.

4. By no means all the major actions against auditors arise because of alleged failure to detect fraud. Nevertheless, the auditor's responsibility to detect fraud is an important debating point. This issue is discussed in detail in connection with the draft auditing guideline 'The auditor's responsibility for detecting and reporting fraud and other illegal acts'.

5. Auditor's liability can be determined under the following distinct headings:

    (a) Liability under statute - civil and criminal;

    (b) Negligence under the common law:
        (i)   to clients under contract law (and possibly law of tort);
        (ii) to third parties under law of tort.

6. Each of these specific headings will be considered separately in the following sections, but first a few comments concerning the nature of negligence and the auditor/accountant's duty of care summarised from an ethical guidance statement entitled 'Professional liability of accountants and auditors' issued in November 1983. We shall return to this statement from time to time in this chapter.

7. Negligence means some act or omission which occurs because the person concerned has failed to exercise that degree of professional care and skill, appropriate to the circumstances of the case, which is expected of accountants and auditors. It would be a defence to an action for negligence to show (i) that there has been no negligence, or (ii) that no duty of care was owed to the plaintiff in the circumstances, or (iii) in the case of actions in tort that no financial loss has been suffered by the plaintiff. The third defence would not be available to a claim in contract, but only nominal damages would be recoverable and in those circumstances it is unlikely that such an action would be brought.

8. In recent years there have been a number of cases where substantial sums have been claimed as damages for negligence against accountants and auditors. In a number of cases it appears that the claims may have arisen as a result of some misunderstanding as to the degree of responsibility which the accountant was expected to assume in giving advice or expressing an opinion. It is therefore important to distinguish between (i) disputes arising from misunderstandings regarding the duties assumed and (ii) negligence in carrying out agreed terms.

Civil liability

9. S218 Insolvency Act 1986 provides that *officers* of the company may be liable for financial damages in respect of the civil offences of 'misfeasance' and 'breach of trust'. The decisions in both the *Kingston Cotton Mill* and *London and General Bank* cases imply that, for the purposes of this section, the auditor may be regarded as an officer of the company. This section, which relates only to a winding up, refers to the situation where officers have mis-used their positions of authority for personal gain.

10. There is, however, a relieving provision such that in any proceedings for negligence, default, breach of duty or breach of trust against an officer or an auditor of a company, the court may relieve him wholly or in part from his liability on such terms as it thinks fit, if it appears to the court that:

   (a) he is or may be liable; but
   (b) he acted honestly and reasonably; and
   (c) having regard to all the circumstances of the case, including those connected with his appointment, he ought fairly to be excused for the negligence, default etc.

   This section applies to both civil and criminal actions.

Criminal liability

11. The principal statutory provisions under which it is possible for an auditor to be held criminally liable are:
   (a) Sections 206-211 Insolvency Act 1986;
   (b) Sections 17, 18 and 19 Theft Act 1968:
   (c) Section 47(1) Financial Services Act 1986.

12. Sections 206-211 Insolvency Act 1986 relate to criminal offences involving officers in a winding-up. These provisions are hence not of general application, but it should be noted that, as in Section 218 discussed above, the term officer may again include the auditor for the purpose of these sections (even though for eligibility purposes an auditor of a company *cannot* be an officer of that company-S389(6) CA 1985).

13. Section 17 Theft Act 1968 states that a person commits an offence who dishonestly, with a view to gain for himself or another or with intent to cause loss to another:

    (a) destroys, defaces, conceals or falsifies any account or any record or document made or required for any accounting purpose; or

    (b) in furnishing information for any purpose produces or makes use of any account, or any such record or document as aforesaid, which to his knowledge is or may be misleading, false or deceptive in a material particular.

14. Section 18 states that where an offence is committed by a body corporate under Section 17 with the consent or connivance of any officer of the body corporate then he as well as the body corporate shall be guilty of that offence.

15. Under Section 19 an officer of a company will be guilty of an offence if he publishes or concurs in the publication of a written statement or account which to his knowledge is or may be misleading, false or deceptive in a material particular with intent to deceive members or creditors of the company about its affairs. A written statement may be considered false within the meaning of this section not only by what it actually states, but also by virtue of any significant matter which it may have concealed, omitted or implied. An officer found guilty may be imprisoned for up to 7 years.

16. The term 'officer' may include an auditor for the purposes of Section 17, 18 and 19. It can be assumed that any auditor found guilty under this Act would also be expelled from membership of his professional body under the application of the disciplinary code.

17. Under S47(1) Financial Services Act 1986 any person who:

    (a) makes a statement, promise or forecast which he knows to be misleading, false or deceptive or dishonestly conceals any material facts; or

    (b) recklessly makes (dishonestly or otherwise) a statement, promise or forecast which is misleading, false or deceptive,

    is guilty of an offence if he makes the statement, promise or forecast or conceals the facts for the purpose of inducing, or is reckless as to whether it may induce, another person (whether or not the person to whom the statement, promise or forecast is made or from whom the facts are concealed) to enter or offer to enter into, or to refrain from entering or offering to enter into, an investment agreement or to exercise, or refrain from exercising, any rights conferred by an investment.

18. Guilty parties are liable to imprisonment 'for a term not exceeding seven years'. Note that mere recklessness is sufficient for a criminal prosecution: fraud does not have to be proven. This somewhat harsh looking measure reflects the long history of situations where prospectuses, inviting the public to subscribe for shares, have contained positively dishonest or wildly optimistic statements.

Liability under contract law

19. The guidance statement 'Professional liability of accountants and auditors' (November 1983) makes the following observations regarding the accountant's duty of care:

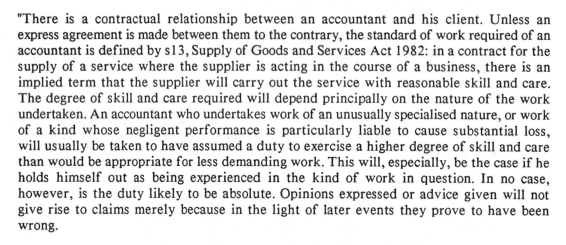

> "There is a contractual relationship between an accountant and his client. Unless an express agreement is made between them to the contrary, the standard of work required of an accountant is defined by s13, Supply of Goods and Services Act 1982: in a contract for the supply of a service where the supplier is acting in the course of a business, there is an implied term that the supplier will carry out the service with reasonable skill and care. The degree of skill and care required will depend principally on the nature of the work undertaken. An accountant who undertakes work of an unusually specialised nature, or work of a kind whose negligent performance is particularly liable to cause substantial loss, will usually be taken to have assumed a duty to exercise a higher degree of skill and care than would be appropriate for less demanding work. This will, especially, be the case if he holds himself out as being experienced in the kind of work in question. In no case, however, is the duty likely to be absolute. Opinions expressed or advice given will not give rise to claims merely because in the light of later events they prove to have been wrong.

> The accountant should ensure that at the time he agrees to perform certain work for the client the scope of his responsibilities is made clear, preferably in writing, and the terms of his contract with his client are properly defined. Wherever possible, a letter of engagement should be prepared setting out in detail the actual services to be performed and the terms of the engagement should be accepted by the client so as to minimise the risk of disputes regarding the duties assumed. It may also be helpful for the avoidance of misunderstanding to indicate any significant matters which are not included in the scope of responsibilities undertaken, although it will rarely be possible to provide a comprehensive list of matters excluded."

20. As regards the auditor, his duties and thus his potential liabilities will clearly be determined by the nature and terms of his appointment – hence the engagement letter is crucial in at least clarifying the 'express terms' of his appointment.

21. The auditor must remember that he has a duty to be aware of relevant statutory or constitutional provisions in relation to a client company. This fact was clearly established by *Astbury J* in the case of *Republic of Bolivia Exploration Syndicate Limited (1914)* where he said:

> "... I think that the auditors of a limited company are bound to know or make themselves acquainted with their duties under the articles of the company, whose accounts they are appointed to audit, and under the Companies Acts for the time being in force...."

22. This need for the auditor to fully acquaint himself with the articles of a client company was stressed by *Lindley L J* in *re Kingston Cotton Mill (No 2) (1896)* where he said:

"... auditors are, however, in my opinion bound to see what exceptional duties, if any, are cast upon them by the articles of the company whose accounts they are called upon to audit. Ignorance of the articles and of exceptional duties imposed by them would not afford any legal justification for not observing them."

23. Although the articles of a company may extend the auditor's responsibilities beyond those envisaged by the Companies Act, they cannot be used so as to restrict the auditor's statutory duties, neither may they place any restriction upon the auditor's statutory rights which are designed to assist him in the discharge of those duties. This point was well made by *Buckley J* in the case of *Newton v BSA Co Limited (1906)* where he said:

"... any regulations which preclude the auditors from availing themselves of all the information to which under the Act they are entitled as material for the report which under the Act they are to make as to the true and correct state of the company's affairs are, I think, inconsistent with the Act."

24. If the auditor is involved in a non-statutory audit then the only 'express terms' will be those which are contained in any specific contract which may exist with the client. An auditor is always likely to be judged on the content of any report which he has issued, and so he should always ensure that his report clearly states the effect of any limitations that there have been upon the extent and scope of his audit work where such limitations exist. The auditor must take special care to ensure that his report does not in any way imply that he has in fact done more work than that required by the terms of his contract. Great care must be taken in the first instance to establish that the client really does require an audit - not an accounting exercise. Remember, the *operational* standard applies whenever an audit is carried out.

25. As well as 'express terms' of an auditor's appointment, we must also consider the question of the 'implied terms' of any such appointment. 'Implied terms' are those which the parties to a contract may have left unstated because they consider them too obvious to express, but which, nevertheless, the law will impart into a contract.

26. The 'implied terms' which the law will impart into a contract of the type with which we are currently concerned are as follows:

(a) the auditor has a duty to exercise reasonable care;
(b) the auditor has a duty to carry out the work required with reasonable expediency;
(c) the auditor has a right to reasonable remuneration.

The most important of these generally implied terms is the auditor's duty to exercise reasonable care which we shall consider in the light of decided cases in the following paragraphs.

The auditor's duty of care

27. As explained above the standard of work of an accountant is generally as defined by the Supply of Goods and Services Act 1982. As regards the auditor of a limited company there are a number of celebrated judgements that give us a flavour of how his duty of care has been gauged at various points in time.

28. Nowhere in the Companies Act does it clearly state the manner in which the auditor should discharge his duty of care; neither is it likely that this would be clearly spelt out in any contract setting out the terms of an auditor's appointment. As *Warrington L J* said in *re City Equitable Fire Assurance Co Limited (1925):*

> "... the Act (Companies Act 1908) does not lay down any rule at all as to the amount of care, or skill, or investigation which is to be brought to bear by the auditors in performing the duties which are imposed upon them. ... That is left to be determined by the general rules which, in point of law, are held to govern the duties of the auditors, whether these rules are to be derived from the ordinary law, or from the terms under which the auditors are to be employed."

29. To identify the 'general rules' to which Warrington L J refers, it is perhaps necessary to consider what the court regard as being the purpose of an audit. To do this we can refer to the opinion of *Lindlay L J* in *re London and General Bank (No 2) (1895)* where he said:

> "...it evidently is to secure to the shareholders independent and reliable information respecting the true financial position of the company at the time of the audit."

30. From the same case we find that Lindley L J provides us with an excellent assessment of how the auditor is to approach this task;

> "... (the auditor's) business is to ascertain and state the true financial position of the company at the time of the audit, and his duty is confined to that.... An auditor, however, is not bound to do more than exercise reasonable care and skill in making inquiries and investigations. He is not an insurer; he does not guarantee that the books do correctly show the true position of the company's affairs; he does not even guarantee that his balance sheet is accurate according to the books of the company... Such I take to be the duty of the auditor; he must be honest, ie he must not certify what he does not believe to be true, and he must take reasonable care and skill before he believes that what he certifies is true. What is reasonable care in any particular case must depend upon the circumstances of that case."

31. When Lopes L J considered the degree of skill and care required of an auditor in *re Kingston Cotton Mill* he declared:

> "... it is the duty of an auditor to bring to bear on the work he has to perform that skill, care and caution which a reasonably competent, careful and cautious auditor would use. What is reasonable skill, care and caution, must depend on the particular circumstances of each case."

32. Both Lindley and Lopes were careful to point out that what constitutes reasonable care depends very much upon the facts of a particular case. One should also note that another criteria by which the courts will determine the adequacy of the auditor's work is by assessing it in relation to the generally accepted auditing standards of the day. The fact that the courts will be very much concerned with accepted advances in auditing techniques was clearly evidenced by *Pennycuick J* in *re Thomas Gerrard & Son Limited (1967)* where he observed:

> "... the real ground on which *re Kingston Cotton Mill* ... is, I think, capable of being distinguished is that the standards of reasonable care and skill are, upon the expert evidence, more exacting today than those which prevailed in 1896."

33. *Lord Denning* in the case of *Fomento (Sterling Area) Limited v Selsdon Fountain Pen Co Limited (1958)* sought to define the auditor's proper approach to his work by saying:

    "... he must come to it with an inquiring mind - not suspicious of dishonesty.... - but suspecting that someone may have made a mistake somewhere and that a check must be made to ensure that there has been none."

34. As regards the auditor's responsibility to keep himself abreast of professional developments, it is perhaps worth noting again what the APC say in the 'Auditing Standards and Guidelines Explanatory Foreword' in relation to the matter of 'Auditing Standards and the Guidelines and the Law':

    "Members are advised that a court of law may, when considering the adequacy of the work of an auditor, take into account any pronouncements or publications which it thinks may be indicative of good practice. Auditing Standards and Guidelines are likely to be so regarded."

35. When the auditor is exercising judgement he must act both honestly and carefully. *Lord Morris of Borth-y-Gest* in the case of *Sutcliffe v Thackrah (1974)* made the following comment in relation to valuers (although it would be equally relevant in relation to auditors):

    "....(a valuer's) carefully and honestly formed opinion would not make him liable to action merely because in the opinion of some other honest and careful valuer it was thought to be wrong. But suppose it was proved that he had been clearly negligent and so given a wrong figure I see no reason why there should not then be liability."

36. Obviously, if an auditor is to be 'careful' in forming an opinion, he must give due consideration to all relevant matters. Provided he does this and can be seen to have done so, then his opinion should be above criticism. But if the opinion reached by an auditor is one that no reasonably competent auditor would have been likely to reach then he would still possibly be held negligent. This is because however carefully an auditor may appear to have approached his work, it clearly could not have been careful enough, if it enabled him to reach a conclusion which would be generally regarded as unacceptable.

37. In order to give his report the auditor must examine each of the items which go to make up the financial statements to which his report relates. In the course of such examination the auditor must reasonably satisfy himself that each item is fairly stated and in doing this he should bear in mind that, as per *Lindley L J* in *re London and General Bank,* his:

    "duty is to examine the books, not merely for the purpose of ascertaining what they do show, but also for the purpose of satisfying himself that they show the true financial position of the company."

38. If an auditor's suspicions are aroused, he must conduct further investigations until such suspicions are either confirmed or allayed. Over the years, there have been many occasions where the courts have had to consider cases in which it has been held, on the facts of those cases, that the auditors ought to have been put upon inquiry.

39. Some of the more common situations in which an auditor should be put upon inquiry, because of the strong possibility of the existence of errors, either clerical or fraudulent, are detailed below:

   (a) knowledge of dishonesty in an employee of the company:
         Todd Motor Co v Gray (1928)
         Nelson Guarantee Corporation Ltd v Hodgson (1958)

   (b) entries made in the books after a relevant date:
         Irish Wool Co Limited v Tyson & Others (1900)

   (c) alterations or erasures in the records:
         re Thomas Gerrard & Son Limited (1967)
         Ross & Co v Wright, Fitzsimmons & Mays (1896)
         Armitage v Brewer and Knott (1936)

   (d) the existence or possibility of deficiencies:
         Brown and Wright v Thomson, Plucknett & Co (1939)

   (e) existence of increasing or unusually large cash balances:
         The London Oil Storage Co Limited v Seear, Hasluck & Co (1904)

   (f) acceptability of explanations of directors or other officers after having been put upon inquiry:
         re Thomas Gerrard & Son Limited (1967)
         Pacific Acceptance Corp Limited v Forsyth (1970)

   (g) need to report suspicious circumstances to directors:
         Tenant's Corporation v Max Rothenburg & Co (1970)

40. By way of summary we can say that it is the duty of the auditor to employ reasonable care in all he does. He must employ generally accepted auditing techniques when seeking to satisfy himself that the matters upon which he reports accurately reflect the true financial state of his client's business. If during the course of his work the auditor comes across any matter which puts him upon inquiry then he has a duty to investigate such matter until he is able to resolve it to his own reasonable satisfaction. It will never be prudent for the auditor to accept any explanation unless he has first carried out such investigations as will enable him properly to assess whether the explanation offered is in fact a reasonable one.

The auditor's responsibility in relation to specific aspects of his work

41. Frequently the courts may have to consider the auditor's responsibility in relation to certain specific aspects of his work. The examples cited here will not of course cover every conceivable aspect of an auditor's work, however, the cases referred to will help to establish some of the more important principles applied by the courts in reaching their judgement.

42. *Securities:* one of the problems which may arise here is whether or not the auditor should insist upon the personal inspection of all the relevant documentation or whether he is entitled to rely upon a certificate obtained from some third party who is perhaps holding such securities on behalf of the client. As a result of the case of *re City Equitable Fire Insurance Co Limited (1925)*, it would appear that the auditor's duty is always to insist on personal inspection of securities held by a third party unless he is satisfied, and can show that he has reasonable

grounds for being so satisfied, that it is proper for such securities to be held by that third party. It follows that such third party must be trustworthy in the opinion of the auditor and that any suggestion that the third party was 'connected' with the client would reduce the reliability of their testimony and necessitate further investigations on the part of the auditor.

43. *Stock and WIP:* there have perhaps been more cases revolving around problems in relation to stock and WIP than any other single item typically appearing in the accounts of a company. Undoubtedly, this is because stock is one of the easiest figures to manipulate in the accounts, and has a direct result upon the profit or loss made by a company. In 1896 *Lindlay L J* held in the *re Kingston Cotton Mill (No 2)* case that:

> "It is no part of an auditor's duty to take stock. No one contends that it is. He must rely on other people for details of the stock in trade on hand."

44. Whilst accepting this judgement, we will see when we go on to study the balance sheet audit that the auditor does have a duty to satisfy himself as to the accuracy and completeness of the client's assessment of the quantity and type of stocks held and the reasonableness of the subsequent valuation of such stocks.

45. As regards the auditor's need to confirm the physical *existence* of stocks, the case of *Henry Squire Cash Chemist Limited v Ball Baker & Co (1911)* held that there was, by the accepted standards of the day, no need for an auditor to gain contact with the client's stocks. However, as a better indication of the likely attitude of the courts today we could perhaps refer to a report of the American Securities and Exchange Commission, following the famous case of *McKesson and Robins (1939)*, which stated:

> "... auditors should gain physical contact with the inventory either by test counts, by observation of the inventory taking, or by a combination of these methods."

46. The Auditing Guideline *Attendance at stocktaking* states that "Where stocks are material in the enterprise's financial statements, and the auditor is placing reliance upon management's stocktake in order to provide evidence of existence, then the auditor *should* attend the stocktaking."

47. In relation to the *valuation* of stocks, the auditor is entitled to rely upon the valuation arrived at by a competent person provided that he has satisfied himself that such valuation has been reasonably given. The auditor cannot of course simply rely upon the certificate of a competent person without carrying out any audit work at all in that area, this principle was established in the case of *Fomento (Sterling Area) Limited v Selsdon Fountain Pen Co Limited (1958)*.

48. *Debtors:* the auditor must consider the debtors from a critical viewpoint so as to ensure that they are not stated in the accounts at a figure in excess of their realisable value; such was the implication in the judgement of Romer L J in the case of *Scarborough Harbour Commissioners v Robinson, Couslon Kirby & Co (1934)*. In the case of *Arthur E Green & Co v The Central Advance and Discount Corporation Limited (1920)*, it was held by Shearman J that the auditors may be held negligent for accepting schedules of bad debts supplied to them by the client where there were reasonable grounds for doubting the realisability of debts against which no provision had been

made. As regards circularisation of debtors, the practice is now so widespread in this country that it is likely that the courts would hold it negligent not to follow it where trade debtors are material.

49. *Cash:* it is likely that the attitude of the courts will be to say that the auditor should always hold a cash count, unless the auditor is satisfied as to the effectiveness of the internal control in respect of cash and has assured himself that the system is operating satisfactorily. Even where controls are deemed to be effective the auditor should consider holding a cash count occasionally, if not every year. As regards cash at bank recognised best practice dictates that as well as examining the underlying records, the auditor should obtain a certificate from the bank.

50. The courts have accepted the basic principle that the auditor may use the technique of random test checking. As always, the amount and nature of test checking required, and considered necessary by the courts, must vary with each audit assignment, the aim always being to ensure that whatever the test relates to appears to be in order. Referring once again to the judgement of Lindley L J in the case of *re London and General Bank:*

"...Where there is nothing to excite suspicion, very little inquiry will be reasonably sufficient, and in practice I believe businessmen select a few cases at random, see that they are right, and assume that others like them are correct also. Where suspicion is aroused, more care is obviously necessary; but, still, an auditor is not bound to exercise more than reasonable care and skill, even in a case of suspicion..."

51. Above we have looked at just some of the cases arising in relation to specific aspects of the auditor's work. The list has not been exhaustive, but is perhaps sufficient for us to see that the general principle applied by the courts has been to see whether the duty to exercise reasonable care has been properly discharged. As always, it is important to remember that each case must be judged on its own merit.

Actions for negligence against auditors

52. There are two methods by which civil proceedings may be taken against auditors for damages occasioned by negligent or unskilful discharge of the duties imposed upon them:
    (a) by way of action for negligence;
    (b) by way of misfeasance summons as discussed in paragraphs 9 and 10.

53. A client who brings a civil claim does so in order to fasten on the auditor the financial responsibility for loss occasioned to them through the failure of the auditor to perform his duty or through his negligence in the manner of performing it.

54. If a client is to bring a successful action against an auditor then they, as the plaintiff, must satisfy the court in relation to three matters, all of which must be established:

    (a) *duty of care:* ie, that there existed a duty of care enforceable at law. Such duty could be found to exist, under:
         (i)   common law;
         (ii) contract;
         (iii) statute;

(b) *negligence:* ie. that in a situation where a duty of care existed, the auditor was negligent in the performance of that duty, judged by the accepted professional standards of the day;

(c) *damages:* ie. that the client has suffered some pecuniary loss as a direct consequence of the negligence on the part of the auditor.

55. A good early example of a client action for negligence is that of *Wilde & Others v Cape & Dalgleish (1897)*. In this case the auditors were held to have been negligent in failing to detect defalcations, the primary reason for this being that they did not examine the bank pass books contrary to generally accepted best practice. An interesting point which arises from this case is that despite any disclaimers concerning the discovery of frauds that may appear in a letter of engagement, where the auditors do not carry out the audit with the due professional diligence expected of auditors they will be liable for losses arising out of their negligence.

56. We have already seen that it is the auditor's duty to take reasonable care. This duty to a client is a contractual one in almost every instance and failure to fulfil that duty can give rise to an action for negligence. However, it is perhaps worth noting that in recent years it has been held that a professional man, such as an auditor, may owe a duty of care to his clients in tort as well as in contract. Lord Denning in the case of *Esso Petroleum v Marden (1976)* said:

> "... in the case of a professional man, the duty to use reasonable care arises not only in contract, but is also imposed by the law apart from contract, and is therefore actionable in tort."

57. Even casual readers of the financial press will be aware that there has been an increase in civil actions against auditors for negligence in the recent past. Some of these are actions by third parties under the law of tort which we will consider in the next section, but many have arisen where there is a contractual duty to the client. It is pertinent therefore to consider whether there are any circumstances in which the accountant or auditor might be able to restrict liability to a client. The following comments are derived from the guidance statement 'Professional liability of accountants and auditors'.

Excluding or restricting liability to a client

58. An agreement with a client designed to exclude or restrict an accountant's liability may not always be effective in law. The following are the main relevant considerations.

59. S310 Companies Act 1985 makes void any provision in a company's articles or any contractual arrangement purporting to exempt the auditor from or to indemnity him against any liability for negligence, default, breach of duty or breach of trust. Although the courts have power in certain circumstances to grant relief either wholly or in part from any of such liabilities, it appears that these powers have seldom been exercised and it would be prudent to assume that an auditor might not be relieved of liability.

60.   The Unfair Contract Terms Act 1977 introduces extensive restrictions upon the enforceability of exclusions of liability for negligence and breaches of contract. S2 of the Act, which applies in England, Wales and Northern Ireland, makes void any contractual exclusion or restriction of liability for negligence, even in a case where the client has agreed to it and where legal consideration exists, unless the person seeking to rely on that exclusion or restriction can show that it was reasonable. Part II of the Act contains somewhat similar provisions applying as part of the law of Scotland.

61.   There is at present, little case law which affords guidance as to what exclusions or restrictions of liability for negligence will be regarded as reasonable. However, unless the work undertaken presents unusual difficulties or is required to be carried out in unusually difficult circumstances, it would be prudent to assume that an exclusion of liability for negligence may be treated by the courts as unreasonable. A limitation of liability for negligence to a particular sum will more readily be treated by the courts as reasonable, particularly if the accountant relying upon it can show that he would have difficulty in obtaining professional indemnity insurance for any greater sum.

62.   An exclusion of restriction of an accountant's liability will not generally avail him against a third party. Avoidance of liability to third parties is dealt with separately in later paragraphs. In summary, we can conclude that the auditor of a limited company cannot limit or exclude liability and that in other circumstances it is probably prudent to assume that an exclusion of liability will be treated by the courts as unreasonable.

Liability to third parties

63.   Recent decisions of the courts, including two important decisions of the House of Lords, have expanded the classes of case in which a person professing some special skill (as an accountant does) may be liable for negligence to someone other than his own client: *Hedley Byrne and Co Limited v Heller and Partners (1964)* and *Anns v Merton London Borough Council (1978)*.

64.   For many years, it was the widely held view of the accounting profession that the auditor could have no legally enforceable duty of care as regards third parties with whom he had no direct contractual or fiduciary relationship. This view appeared to find support in decided cases, particularly that of *Candler v Crane, Christmas & Co 1951*.

65.   The situation with regard to third party liability was, however, changed quite significantly with the decision by the House of Lords in the case of *Hedley Byrne & Co Limited v Heller & Partners Limited (1963)*.

66.   Hedley Byrne & Co Limited were advertising agents and the defendants were merchant bankers. They had a mutual client called Easipower Limited. The agency had contracted to place orders for advertising the company's products with the media, and since this involved extending credit to the company, they asked the company's bankers for a reference as to its credit worthiness. The bank replied that the company was respectably constituted and considered good, though they said that the statement was made without responsibility on their part. The agency, relying on this reply, placed advertisements for the company and in so doing assumed personal responsibility for payment to the television and newspaper companies concerned. Shortly after this, Easipower Limited went into liquidation and the agency lost over £17,000 on the advertising contracts. The

agency then sued the bank for the amount of the loss, claiming that the bank had not informed themselves sufficiently about the company before writing the statement of credit worthiness and were therefore liable in negligence.

67. It was held, in this case, that the bank's disclaimer was sufficient to absolve them from liability, but that, in the absence of the disclaimer, the circumstances would have given rise to a duty of care in spite of the absence of a contractual or fiduciary relationship.

68. The implications of the Hedley Byrne decision appeared at first to be very far reaching, particularly for auditors and accountants. The Institute of Chartered Accountants took legal advice on the effects of the case and issued the following statement:

> "Counsel has advised that the Hedley Byrne decision is much more restricted in its effect than may first appear, and has drawn attention to the development of the law in this sphere overseas, referring particularly to the cases of *Ultramares Corporation v Touche* in the United States, and *Herschel v Mrupi* in South Africa. In this connection the *Ultramares* case is of particular interest. There the court decided that auditors were not liable for negligence to a plaintiff who lent money on the strength of accounts on which the auditors had reported but which they did not know were required for the purposes of obtaining financial assistance or would be shown to the plaintiff. In so deciding the court recognised that it would be quite wrong to expose the auditors to a potential liability 'in an indeterminate amount for an indefinite time to an indeterminate class'.

> In Counsel's view third parties entitled to recover damages under the 'Hedley Byrne' principle will be limited to those who by reason of accountants' negligence in preparing reports, accounts or financial statements on which the third parties place reliance suffer financial loss in circumstances where the accountants knew or ought to have known that the reports, accounts or financial statements in question were being prepared for the specific purpose or transaction which gave rise to the loss and that they would be shown to and relied on by third parties in that particular connection. There is no general principle that accountants may be liable for damages if a report or statement which proves to have been prepared negligently by them is shown casually or in the course of business to third parties who suffer loss through reliance on the report or statement."

69. The question to be considered now is whether or not Hedley Byrne should still be taken as the leading authority, or whether in fact potential liability to third parties has been extended still further since the early 1960s. Initially it may be worth noting the comments of Lord Reid in relation to the *Hedley Byrne* case itself when considering just how far the responsibilities of a professional person issuing a report may go:

> "... I can see no logical stopping place short of all those relationships where it is plain that the party seeking information or advice was trusting the other to exercise such a degree of care as the circumstances required, where it was reasonable for him to do that, and where the other gave the information or advice when he knew or ought to have know that the inquiror was relying on him...."

70. The position since Hedley Byrne can be seen as an unacceptable choice between two diametric opposites. At one extreme, is the pure unqualified test of an auditor's liability based on reasonable foresight; unacceptable because it is felt to render the auditor vulnerable to indeterminate liability and a multiplicity of legal actions. At the other extreme is a test of

liability dependent upon the existence of a 'special relationship' between the parties as conceived in Hedley Byrne; unacceptable because it limits too closely the range of injured parties entitled to bring an action.

71. Until recently, it was therefore hoped that the English Courts might adopt a 'middle of the road view', broader than Hedley Byrne but narrower than the unrestricted view. This position has now, indeed, been confirmed in the *1980 Jeb Fasteners Limited v Marks, Bloom & Co* decision.

72. *The facts*

In April 1975 the defendants, a firm of accountants, prepared an audited set of accounts for a manufacturing company for the year ended 31 October 1974. The company's stock, which had been purchased for some £11,000, was shown as being worth £23,080, that figure being based on the company's own valuation of the net realisable value of the stock. The defendants nevertheless described the stock in the accounts as being 'valued at lower of cost and net realisable value'. On the basis of the inflated stock figure the accounts showed a net profit of £11, whereas if the stock had been included at cost with a discount for possible errors the accounts would have shown a loss of over £13,000.

The defendants were aware when they prepared the accounts that the company faced liquidity problems and was seeking outside financial support from, inter alia, the plaintiffs, who manufactured similar products and were anxious to expand their business. The accounts prepared by the defendants were made available to the plaintiffs, who, although they had reservations about the stock valuation, decided to take over the company in June 1975 for a nominal amount, because they would thereby obtain the services of the company's two directors who had considerable experience in the type of manufacturing carried on by the plaintiffs. In discussions between the plaintiffs and the defendants during the takeover the defendants failed to inform the plaintiffs that the stock had been put in the accounts at an inflated value.

The plaintiff's takeover of the company proved to be less successful than they had anticipated and they brought an action for damages against the defendants alleging that the defendants had been negligent in preparing the company's accounts, that they had relied on the accounts when purchasing the company, and that they would not have purchased the company had they been aware of its true financial position. The plaintiffs contended that an auditor when preparing a set of accounts owed a duty of care to all persons whom he ought reasonably to have seen would rely on the accounts. The defendants contended that if a duty of care existed it was only owed to persons who made a specific request for information.

Action

By a writ issued on 31 May 1978, the plaintiffs, Jeb Fasteners Limited, claimed against the defendants, Marks, Bloom & Co, damage for loss suffered by the plaintiffs following the acquisition of the issued share capital of a company, BG Fasteners Limited, which the plaintiffs claimed to have done in reliance on the accounts of the company negligently prepared by the defendants as accountants and auditors of the company. The facts are set out in the judgement.

Held

1. Whether the defendants owed a duty of care to the plaintiffs in regard to their preparation of the accounts of the company depended on whether they knew or ought reasonably to have foreseen at the time the accounts were prepared that persons such as the plaintiffs might rely on the accounts for the purpose of deciding whether to take over the company and might suffer loss if the accounts were inaccurate. Since the defendants knew at the time the accounts were prepared that the company needed outside financial support and ought reasonably to have foreseen that a takeover was a possible means of obtaining finance and that a person effecting a takeover might rely on those accounts, it followed that the

defendants owed the plaintiffs a duty of care in the preparation of the accounts. The defendants were in breach of that duty by negligently including in the accounts stock at a value of some £13,000 over the discounted cost without appending a note in the accounts to that effect.

2.   However, even though the plaintiffs had relied on the accounts, they would not have acted differently had they known the true position since they knew the company was in financial difficulties, their reason for taking over the company was to obtain the services of its directors and the consideration paid for the company was only nominal. Accordingly, the defendants' negligence in preparing the accounts was not a cause of any loss suffered by the plaintiffs as a result of taking over the company. The plaintiffs action would therefore be dismissed.

73. Jeb Fasteners Limited took the case to the Court of Appeal. In a judgement delivered on July 22 1982 the appeal was unanimously dismissed.

74. The most significant aspect of the Jeb Fasteners decision is, clearly, the finding of the existence of a legal duty of care owed by auditors to a stranger at the time of the audit, and half of the summing up is devoted to this one issue.

75. Mr Justice Woolf considered the liability of auditors: the appropriate test for establishing whether a duty of care exists is whether the defendant auditors knew, or reasonably should have foreseen at the time the accounts were audited, that a person might rely on those accounts for the purpose of deciding whether or not to take over the company, and therefore could suffer loss if the accounts were inaccurate.

76. This approach was said to place a limit on those entitled to contend that there had been a breach of duty owed to them by auditors. First, they must have relied on the accounts; and second, they must have done so in circumstances where either the auditors knew that they would, or ought to have known, that they might so rely.

77. If the situation was one where it would not be reasonable for the accounts to be relied on, then, in the absence of the auditors' express knowledge, the auditor would be under no duty. In any event, there was a limit to the period for which audited accounts can be relied on. The longer the period which elapses prior to the accounts being relied on, from the date on which the auditor makes his report, the more difficult it will be to establish that the auditor ought to have foreseen that his report would, in the circumstances, be relied on.

78. That the decision may be expected to cause some concern among the profession there can be no doubt, since it results in a significantly larger number of potential plantiffs to whom the auditor could be liable in damages, if negligent, than hitherto. Indeed, the decision has already had an influence on the outcome of another case of alleged accountant's negligence.

79. *Twomax Limited and Goode v Dickson McFarlane & Robinson (1983)* SLT98.
      (Gordon v Dickson, McFarlane and Robinson)

This is a Scottish case held before Lord Stewart in the Court of Session.

The facts

Twomax Limited acquired a majority shareholding in a private company, Kintyre Knitwear Limited. Goode was introduced into Kintyre by Twomax, and subsequently became chairman, whereupon he purchased shares in the company. Gordon also took shares in Kintyre and later became a director. The three plaintiffs argued that in making the acquisitions they had relied on the balance sheets and accounts prepared and audited by the defendants.

In particular, the accounts for the year ending 31 March 1973 had much influenced the plaintiffs in that they disclosed a sizeable move from a loss of £12,318 to a profit of £20,346. In subsequent years, the trading position of the company deteriorated to a loss of £87,727 in 1975, whereupon the company went into liquidation and all three plaintiffs lost their entire investment.

It was found that the profit figure for 1973 was incorrect to the extent of an understatement of doubtful debts and an error in agents' commission, thus reducing the profit to £16,779. Lord Stewart also held that the enormous loss in 1975 could only be explained by the fact that two earlier years had been unprofitable, and despite the fact that the plaintiffs were unable to prove what the true figure of profit or loss for 1973 should have been, he concluded that the accounts produced a seriously distorted picture.

Held

The auditors of Kintyre Knitwear Limited, Dickson, McFarlane & Robinson were liable to pay damages to the plaintiffs who had purchased shares on the strength of accounts which had been negligently audited. The level of damages was set at the full amounts paid for the shares on the basis that the shares would not have been purchased at any price had the accounts disclosed the current position.

Summing up

On the question of whether the auditors owed a duty to the plaintiffs, Lord Stewart observed: "The auditors of a company, public or private, must know that reliance is likely to be placed upon their work by a number of persons for a number of purposes. While their contractual and statutory duty may be to the shareholders, their work has repercussions in a wider field. The question is whether that duty extends to persons such as the plaintiffs in the present case, who relied upon the audited accounts, in coming to a decision to acquire shares."

His Lordship was impressed by the decision of the New Zealand Court of Appeal in *Scott Group Limited v McFarlane (1978)* and by the *Jeb Fasteners* decision. In particular, he considered commendable Woolf J's approach for establishing whether a duty of care exists by reference to whether the defendant knew, or reasonably should have foreseen at the time the accounts were audited, that a person might rely on the accounts for the purpose of deciding whether or not to take-over the company. Such an approach combines "the simplicity of the proximity or neighbour principle with a limitation which has regard to the warning against exposing accountants to indeterminate liability."

Lord Stewart held that although auditors did not know of the specific interest of the plaintiffs at the time of the audit they were, nevertheless, aware that Kintyre was short of capital, that the accounts were made available to lenders in that they were lodged with the company's bank, and that a director wanted to sell his shares. The auditors "knew that 'clean' certificates were commonly relied on by shareholders, potential investors and potential lenders. In the whole circumstances, I consider that McFarlane (the auditor) should have foreseen before he certified the accounts that these accounts might be relied on by a potential investor. The situation was such that I would have thought it an inevitable inference that McFarlane should have realised by the time he came to grant his certificate that there would shortly be some dealings in the issued shares of Kintyre'."

Caparo Industries plc v Dickman and Others (1988)

80. The facts as pleaded were that in 1984 Caparo Industries purchased 100,000 Fidelity shares in the open market. On June 12 1984, the date on which the accounts (audited by Touche Ross) were published, they purchased a further 50,000 shares. Relying on information in the accounts, further shares were acquired. On October 25, the plaintiffs announced that they owned or had received acceptances amounting to 91.8% of the issued shares and subsequently acquired the balance. The plaintiffs argued that Touche owed a duty of care to investors and potential investors in respect of the audit. They should have been aware that in March 1984 a press release stating that profits would fall significantly had made Fidelity vulnerable to a takeover bid and that bidders might well rely upon the accounts.

81. The findings were that the auditor's duty does not include potential investors. While the auditors owed a statutory duty to shareholders as a class or body this did not extend to individual investors save as a member of the class in respect of some class activity. The claim of an individual shareholder would, ordinarily, be very hard to establish. The claimant would have to show a failure to exercise the ordinary skill of an ordinary competent man.

82. The conclusion must be that the decision in Caparo v Dickman has once more narrowed the auditor's potential liability. However you should note that this was the judgement of the Appeal Court. At the time of writing, the case has still to be heard by the House of Lords.

Avoiding or disclaiming liability to third parties

83. The cases above establish that a duty of care to a third party may arise when an accountant does not know that his work will be relied upon by a third party, but only knows that it is work of a kind which is liable in the ordinary course of events to be relied upon by a third party. Conversely, an accountant may sometimes be informed, *before* he carries out certain work, that a third party will rely upon the results. An example likely to be encountered in practice is a report upon the business of a client which the accountant has been instructed to prepare for the purpose of being shown to a potential purchaser or potential creditor of that business. In such a case it would be prudent for an accountant to assume that he will be held to owe the same duty to the third party as to his client.

84. One way that the accountant may seek to avoid liability to third parties is to limit access to his work or reports. Another approach might be to include a disclaimer of liability in the relevant documents or reports. To obtain guidance on both these possibilities we can return to the ethical statement 'Professional liability of accountants and auditors':

> *Avoiding liability to third parties:*
> "In many cases there are no steps which an accountant can reasonably take to limit the circulation of his work or the use which is made of it. Some documents, such as the reports of auditors of public companies, are by their nature incapable of being restricted in this way. In other cases, however, there may be steps which an accountant can take to reduce his exposure to the claims of third parties. These cases cannot be exhaustively defined but the following are some of the more important examples of them.
>
> *Documents published generally.* An accountant may publish a document which is prepared neither in response to the instructions of a particular client nor for any statutory or public purpose: eg a text book or a newsletter. In such cases there will often be no circumstances which would enable a third party to assume that it had necessarily been

prepared with all due skill and care, and substantial reliance upon it would not be reasonable. An accountant can reinforce his legal position in relation to documents of this kind by including a disclaimer of liability in the document itself. The form of the disclaimer will depend upon the nature of the document. In many cases a disclaimer along the following lines will be found appropriate: 'While every care has been taken in the preparation of this document, it may contain errors for which we cannot be responsible.'

Work done for special purposes. An accountant may be instructed to prepare or report upon financial material for some particular purpose. He will not usually be liable to a third party who relies on it for any other purpose for which it is or may be unsuitable. In such a case the accountant would usually have no reason to suppose that such reliance would be placed upon it. Moreover, it would be unreasonable for a third party to rely on it for such a purpose. Members would, however, be well advised to make the position clear by including in the document itself a short statement of the purpose for which it was prepared, if that is not apparent.

Confidential reports. Certain reports or statements may appropriately include a rubric specifically restricting its circulation. For example:

"Confidential
This report (statement) has been prepared for the private use of X (the client) only and on condition that it must not be disclosed to any other person without the written consent of Y (the accountant).'

Current practice is that clients will respect a rubric of this kind. Accordingly, when a document is so marked but is nevertheless relied upon by a third party without the accountant's consent, the accountant will as a general rule be able to resist liability on the basis that the third party was not a person whom he should have had in mind as being likely to suffer loss by his negligence. Such a rubric should be introduced only where the circumstances warrant it, as it would tend to be devalued by indiscriminate use in connection with documents which by their nature must receive a wide distribution. Where a document is prepared in the first instance for discussion with or approval by the client or others, and is liable to be altered before it appears in its final form, this fact should be made clear so as to prevent persons from placing undue reliance upon it. This may be done by overstamping the document on each page: 'Unrevised draft'.

Documents intended to be checked; accounts prepared for tax purposes. An accountant may prepare a report or statement to be issued by his client in circumstances where he can reasonably expect his client to check it for fairness or accuracy before any use is made of it involving third parties. Accounts prepared for the purpose of being submitted to the Inland Revenue for the assessment of taxation will frequently, although not invariably, fall within this category. In such cases, the effective cause of any loss suffered by a third party will ordinarily be the negligence of the person in whose name it was issued and who ought to have checked the document, and not that of the accountant."

Disclaimer of liability to third parties

"A disclaimer of liability to third parties may sometimes be made in circumstances where liability would or might otherwise arise. Such a disclaimer might for example, be introduced along the following lines:

'This report is prepared for the use of X (the client) only. No responsibility is assumed to any other person.'

Members should, however, be aware that such a disclaimer will often be inappropriate or ineffective. Disclaimers will be inappropriate in circumstances where their use will tend to impair the status of practising accountants by indicating a lack of confidence in their professional work. It would not, for example, be proper to endorse copies of accounts filed in accordance with s241 Companies Act 1985 with a disclaimer by the auditor of liability to persons other than shareholders.

The following paragraphs deal with those cases in which there are no professional objections to the use of disclaimers, but in which reservation must be made as to their effectiveness.

Information prepared for the client and passed to third parties. Where a statement or report is prepared by an accountant for his client, which is not confidential and can be expected in the ordinary course to be relied upon by third parties, a disclaimer which purports to apply only as against the third parties presents particular difficulties as a matter of law. By it, the accountant seeks in effect to assume a dual standard of care, the one applicable insofar as his work is read by the client and the other insofar as it is read by the third party. Since the third party will normally rely on the report because he expects the accountant to have performed his duty to the client, and since that expectation will normally be reasonable, the attempt to assume such a dual standard is unlikely to succeed.

Information passed directly to third parties. Where an accountant (necessarily with the authority of his client) passes information directly to a third party there is no question of a dual standard of liability because the third party is generally the only person who is intended to rely on the accountant's work. In such a case the effectiveness of a disclaimer will depend upon the nature of the information. For example, when giving references or assurances regarding creditworthiness or similar matters, the normal commercial practice is to state that although the reference or assurance is given in good faith the accountant accepts no financial responsibility for the opinion he expresses. Such disclaimers will generally be effective because such references or assurances are not information of the kind which is expected to be the result of extensive research by the accountant. Sometimes, however, an accountant may supply directly to a third party information of a kind which the third party (unless he is told otherwise) can reasonably expect to be the result of research of a more or less extensive kind. As applied to such information, a disclaimer will generally be ineffective in England because of S 2, Unfair Contract Terms Act 1977 (see the following paragraph).

Unfair Contract Terms Act 1977, S2. The effect of this provision is that where a person is in principle liable for negligence he cannot exclude that liability by a reference to a notice, except where the notice is reasonable. If an accountant prepares a report or statement in circumstances where it can reasonably be expected that a third party may rely on it, a notice excluding liability to him would only exceptionally be regarded as reasonable."

85. A brief summary of the above may be useful:

(a) When publishing documents generally an accountant may find it advantageous to include in the document a clause disclaiming liability.

(b) When submitting unaudited accounts or other unaudited financial statements or reports to the client, an accountant should ensure that any special purpose for which the statements or reports have been prepared is recorded on their face, and in appropriate cases should introduce a clause recording that the report or statement is confidential and has been prepared solely for the private use of the client.

(c) It should be recognised that there are areas of professional work (for example when acting as an auditor under the Companies Act), where it is not possible for liability to be limited or excluded, and that there are other areas of professional work (for example when preparing reports on a business for the purpose of being submitted to a potential purchaser) where although such a limitation or exclusion may be included, its effectiveness will depend on the view which a court may subsequently form of its reasonableness.

86. As the accountant/auditor is so heavily exposed to the possibility of incurring liability for professional negligence, professional firms must clearly have sufficient indemnity insurance. But the recent spate of huge claims has caused a crisis of confidence in the insurance market - cover has been reduced and premiums have soared.

Auditor's liability to detect fraud and irregularities

87. The incidence of financial fraud, particularly in a computer environment, is increasing fast - it has been a central feature in a number of financial scandals in recent years. This fact, together with the increasing sophistication of fraudsters, creates difficult problems for management and auditors. Recently the Minister for Corporate and Consumer Affairs called on the profession to be 'the front line of the public's defences against fraud'.

88. It is against this background that the profession has taken the initiative by publishing a draft auditing guideline on 'The auditor's responsibility for detecting and reporting fraud and other illegal acts' (January 1988).

The draft guideline

89. The purpose of the draft guideline is to provide auditors with guidance on:

(a) the extent of their responsibilities for the detection of fraud, other illegal acts and misstatements in financial statements;

(b) the factors that will influence the auditor's planning and conduct of the audit; and

(c) the extent to which the auditor's findings should be reported to management, shareholders and third parties.

90. The draft guideline sets out some important points of terminology.

(a) The term *error* is used to refer to unintentional misstatements in the accounting records or financial statements.

(b) The term *irregularity* is used to refer to intentional misstatements, and also to missappropriation of the entity's assets.

(c) The terms *fraud* and *fraudulent* are used to refer to irregularities involving the use of criminal deception to obtain an unjust or illegal advantage.

(d) The term *illegal act* is used to refer to an act committed, or a transaction entered into, by or in the name of the auditor's client or on its behalf by its employees, which is contrary to the law. Such acts or transactions may be either intentional or inadvertent. Some illegal acts may also be irregularities.

(e) The term *improprieties* is used to cover irregularities (including fraud), illegal acts and errors.

91. The primary responsibility for the prevention and detection of improprieties rests with management. Management should discharge this responsibility:

(a) by setting up an adequate system of internal control;
(b) by issuing codes of conduct to employees; and
(c) by monitoring and reacting to new legal requirements.

It is appropriate for the auditor to remind management of this responsibility, for example in the engagement letter. The auditor may also wish to receive a written representation relating to the disclosure of any improprieties that have come to the attention of management.

92. Since fraud invariably has an impact on either the accounting records or the financial statements, it is generally accepted that auditors should plan their audits so that they have a reasonable expectation of detecting material misstatements caused by fraud. Other illegal acts may be remote from the accounting records and the auditor would not be held responsible for detecting all such acts. He should design his work so that he has a reasonable expectation of detecting material acts which are contrary to legislation having a direct impact on the form and content of financial statements.

93. Auditors in the public sector generally have wider responsibilities than those set out in the previous paragraph. In addition, statutory requirements sometimes impose wider responsibilities even on private sector auditors; for example, the auditor of a building society is required to report to the Building Societies Commission whether or not the control systems comply with the requirements of the Building Societies Act 1986.

94. The auditor should consider the risk of misstatements arising from improprieties during his audit planning. The procedures he adopts will depend on his judgement as to:

(a) the extent of directly relevant legislation;

(b) the risk that a particular type of irregularity, error or breach of directly relevant legislation could impair the true and fair view;

(c) the risk that such improprieties can occur and remain undetected by the company;

(d) the relative effectiveness of different audit tests.

95. Where doubts exist about the appropriateness of the going concern basis, the auditor should be aware that there is an increased risk of improprieties. He should also be aware that weaknesses in the internal control system may facilitate improprieties. Good internal controls (especially segregation of duties, authorisation procedures, reconciliations and internal audit) are a strong safeguard against improprieties.

96. In carrying out his audit work, the auditor may discover circumstances that could be indicative of improprieties. Examples include:

   (a) lack of records or control breakdowns;
   (b) unsatisfactory explanations;
   (c) unusual payments (penalties, fines, excessive commissions or fees, payments to government officials);
   (d) evidence of unduly lavish life styles by officers and employees.

97. When such circumstances come to the auditor's attention, he should act as follows:

   (a) Unless he can conclude that no material misstatement could arise from the impropriety he should carry out additional tests.

   (b) He should agree with management on any adjustments necessary to the accounts.

   (c) Regardless of materiality, he should discuss the matter with management so as to keep them informed.

   (d) He should critically examine any legal advice received by the client in relation to the impropriety.

   (e) If he suspects that serious financial or legal implications may exist, he should consider taking his own legal advice.

98. The auditor should report formally to management on any improprieties he has discovered. It is important that he reports to a suitably senior level if he suspects that management may be involved in, or are condoning, improprieties. He is not specifically required to mention improprieties in his audit report unless they prevent the financial statements from showing a true and fair view. In certain rare cases he may need to consider reporting the matter to a third party. This might occur:

   (a) if his duty of confidentiality is overridden by consideration of the public interest. In this case he should first seek legal advice;

   (b) if the matter is covered by s109 Financial Services Act 1986 (communications by an auditor with supervisory authorities);

   (c) if the matter is covered by other regulations requiring a report to third parties. For example, the Building Societies Act 1986 defines circumstances in which a report should be made to the Building Societies Commission in order to protect the investments of shareholders or depositors.

Summary of the chapter

99. In order to learn the cases affecting auditor's liability, you may find it useful to list them under the headings given as topics right at the start of the chapter. But remember to test yourself on what points each case illustrates – it is no good simply remembering their names.

100. You should also bear in mind that two very important documents relevant to auditor's liability are the ethical guidance statement *Professional liability of accountants and auditors*, and the draft auditing guideline *The auditor's responsibility for detecting and reporting fraud and other illegal acts*.

TEST YOUR KNOWLEDGE
Numbers in brackets refer to paragraphs in this chapter

1. On what grounds might an accountant defend an action for negligence? (7)

2. When might an auditor be subject to a civil action under statute? (9)

3. Under what statutory provisions is it possible for an auditor to be criminally liable? (11)

4. What Act normally determines the standard of work required of an accountant? (19)

5. Which American case confirmed that normal best practice is for the auditor to 'gain physical contact with the inventory'? (45)

6. What is the relevance of the Unfair Contract Terms Act 1977 to the accountant when attempting to restrict liability to a client? (60)

7. What third parties may be entitled to recover damages under the *Hedley Byrne* judgement? (68)

8. What, in summary form, are the facts of the *Jeb Fasteners* case? (72)

9. What was the judgement in the *Jeb Fasteners* case? (72)

10. What, in summary form, are the facts of the *Twomax* case? (79)

11. What was the judgement in the *Twomax case*? (79)

12. What is the distinction between an 'error' or 'irregularity' and a 'fraud' in the eyes of the APC? (90)

13. What should an auditor do when he discovers an impropriety? (97)

SECTION 2: ILLUSTRATIVE QUESTIONS

1. A practising accountant, in addition to auditing the accounts of a small unincorporated manufacturing business, has also undertaken various additional services of an accounting, taxation and advisory nature for the owners of the business.

    On relinquishing these appointments, what are the main considerations that he should take into account as regards the handing over, or retention, of the following types of records in his possession that relate to this work:

    (a) books and documents relating to:
    - (i)   the business;
    - (ii) the individual owners;

    (b) working papers relating to:
    - (i)   the audit;
    - (ii) other work;

    (c) correspondence with:
    - (i)   the clients;
    - (ii) the Inland Revenue;
    - (iii) other third parties.

2. Although an auditor can incur either civil or criminal liability under various statutes it is far more likely that he will incur liability for negligence under the common law, as the majority of cases against an auditor have been in this area. An auditor must be fully aware of the extent of his responsibilities, together with steps he must take to minimise the danger of professional negligence claims.

    Required:

    (a) Discuss the extent of an auditor's responsibilities to shareholders and others during the course of his normal professional engagement.

    (b) List six steps which an auditor should take to minimise the danger of claims against him for negligent work.

3. The judge in a recent US court ruling drew a distinction between fraud *on behalf* of the company (such as by management) and fraud *against* the company (by a single employee).

    You are required to:

    (a) discuss what responsibility the auditor in the UK has to detect fraud and comment on whether you consider there is a greater expectation for him to detect 'management' fraud or 'employee' fraud.

    (b) outline how the auditor might conduct his audit in the light of this responsibility.

1. In considering which records to hand over, or retain, on relinquishing his appointments the outgoing accountant should consider two fundamental points.
    -   Whether the various records belong to him or to his client.
    -   If any fees are unpaid, whether a right of lien exists over certain records.

    Ownership
    In order to determine whether documents and records belong to the accountant it may be necessary to consider:
    -   the contract between the accountant and his client;
    -   the capacity in which the accountant acts in relation to his client; and
    -   the purpose for which the documents and records exist or are brought into being.

    Clearly, if the records do not belong to the accountant then he has no right to retain them (save perhaps to exercise a right of lien regarding unpaid fees; this point is dealt with below).

    In *Leicestershire County Council v Michael Faraday & Partners Limited (1941)* 2 K.B 205, the Court of Appeal stated that if an agent brings into existence certain documents whilst in the employment of his principal, they are the principal's documents and the principal can claim that the agent should hand them over. Some areas of an accountant's practice involve his acting as agent for his client. Conversely, if the accountant is acting as a principal, then the records will belong to him.

    Applying this principle to the points in the question, and assuming that no specific contracts exist between the accountant and his clients, the position would be as follows:

    (a) Books and documents relating to:
        (i)   the business
        (ii) the individual owners.

        In both these cases the records clearly belong to the business and the individual owners respectively and not to the accountant. They should therefore be returned to the former clients or to their nominee (eg the new accountant). The outgoing accountant should ensure that he obtains a suitable acknowledgement and discharge in relation to these records from the former clients or their nominee.

    (b) Working papers relating to:
        (i)   the audit
        (ii) other work.

        In acting as an auditor, the accountant is acting as a principal, and his working papers are his own property. Similarly his working papers prepared to help him carry out his other work are normally his own property, but the end product of his engagement will belong to the client. For example, if the work is to prepare or write up a set of books for the clients, the completed books belong to the clients, but schedules which he prepares for the purpose of writing up the books will belong to him. This was established in *Chantrey Martin & Co v Martin (1953)*.

    (c) Correspondence with:
        (i)   the clients
              Letters received by the accountant from his client are the accountant's property and may be retained by him. The same situation applies with regard to the accountant's copies of his letters to his client. The accountant is clearly acting as a principal and not as an agent.

(ii) the Inland Revenue

In *Chantrey Martin & Co v Martin* it was held that correspondence between an accountant and the Inland Revenue was the property of the client. This is because the accountant is acting as agent for the client for the purpose of agreeing with the Inland Revenue the client's tax liability.

(iii) other third parties

Communications with third parties are the property of the accountant where the relationship is that of client and professional man and not that of principal and agent.

Lien

It may be that the accountant has not been paid for work carried out for either the business or the owners or both. In this situation he must consider whether he can retain any records which, under the principles established above, do not belong to him but over which he has a right of lien for the unpaid fees. A lien is a right of a person to retain possession of the owner's property until the owner pays what he owes to the person in possession.

In the case of *Woolworth v Conroy 1976* the Court of Appeal held that whilst an accountant possesses no general right of lien over records which pass through his hands in the course of his professional duties he does possess a particular right of lien over certain records.

In order to establish a particular right of lien the following circumstances must exist.
(a) The documents retained must be the property of the client who owns the money and not a third party, no matter how closely connected with the client.
(b) The documents must have come into the possession of the accountant by proper means.
(c) Work must have been done on the documents.
(d) The fees for which the lien is exercised must be outstanding in respect of such work and not in respect of work on other documents belonging to the same client.

Applying the above points to the records in question (ie those records which the accountant, prima facie, does not own):
(a) Books and documents relating to:
(i) the business
(ii) the individual owner.

Provided work has been carried out on the above records for fees which remain unpaid, then the accountant can retain these records, However, if the fee relating to work carried out on the business is unpaid the accountant cannot retain the records relating to the individual owners because:
- they are not the property of the client owing the money; and
- they are not the documents on which work has been done for which the fee is due.

(b) This principle is not relevant to working papers relating to audit or other work as they are owned by the accountant.

(c) Correspondence with:
(i) the Inland Revenue
(ii) other third parties

If the accountant acted as agent in relation to this correspondence then the points mentioned in (a) above will apply.

2. (a) An auditor of a limited company has a responsibility, imposed upon him by statute, to form and express a professional opinion on the financial statements presented by the directors to the shareholders. He must report upon the truth and fairness of such statements and the fact that they comply with the law. In so doing, the auditor owes a duty of care to the company imposed by statute. But such duty also arises under contract and may also arise under the common law (law of tort).

Nowhere in the Companies Act does it clearly state the manner in which the auditor should discharge his duty of care; neither is it likely that this would be clearly spelt out in any contract setting out the terms of an auditor's appointment (ie. the engagement letter). Although the articles of a company may extend the auditor's responsibilities beyond those envisaged by the Companies Act, they cannot be used so as to restrict the auditor's statutory duties, neither may they place any restriction upon the auditor's statutory rights which are designed to assist him in the discharge of those duties.

In summary, the comments of Lopes L J when considering the degree of skill and care required of an auditor in re Kingston Cotton Mill are still relevant:

> "... it is the duty of an auditor to bring to bear on the work he has to perform that skill, care and caution which a reasonably competent, careful and cautious auditor would use. What is reasonable skill, care and caution must depend on the particular circumstances of each case."

Clearly, with the advent of Auditing Standards and Guidelines, a measure of good practice is now available for the courts to take into account when considering the adequacy of the work of the auditor.

The law of tort has established that a person owes a duty of care and skill to "our neighbours" (common and well-known examples of this neighbour principle can be seen in the law of trespass, slander, libel etc). In the context of the professional auditor the wider implications, however, concern the extent to which the auditor owes a duty of care and skill to third parties who rely on financial statements upon which he has reported but with whom he has no direct contractual or fiduciary relationship.

Recent decisions of the courts, including three important decisions of the House of Lords, have expanded the classes of case in which a person professing some special skill (as an auditor does) may be liable for negligence to someone other than his own client: *Hedley Byrne & Co Ltd v. Heller & Partners (1964), Anns v. Merton London Borough Council (1978)* and *Junior Books Ltd v. Veitschi Co Ltd (1982)*. Such liability may arise whenever a professional person does work for his client in circumstances where he knows or ought to know (a) that his work is liable to be relied upon by a third party and (b) that that third party may suffer financial loss if the work in question has been done negligently. Liability will arise when the work in question is of a kind which it was reasonable for the third party to rely on for his particular purpose. If these conditions are satisfied, the third party is a person whom in the eyes of the law the professional man ought to have in mind in applying his skills to the work in question.

It is important to appreciate that a duty of care to a third party may arise when an auditor does not know that his work will in fact be relied upon by a third party, but only knows that it is work of a kind which is liable in the ordinary course of events to be relied upon by a third party. For this purpose it is immaterial whether the third party be identifiable in advance or not. In *Jeb Fasteners v Marks Bloom & Co (1981)*, the plaintiffs, who had acquired a company, contended that they had done so in reliance on accounts which had been negligently audited by the defendant accountants., The judge decided that the appropriate test for establishing whether a duty of care existed was whether the auditors know *or should reasonably have foreseen* at the time when the accounts were audited that a person *might* rely on those accounts for the purpose of deciding whether or not to acquire the company. That was a question which depended principally on the ordinary practice of persons acquiring companies. The same test has more recently been applied in Scotland in *Twomax Ltd v Dickson McFarlance & Robinson (1983)* In both cases it was held that the auditors owed a duty of care to the plaintiff. In the English case, the auditors escaped liability only because on the facts of that case it was proved that the plaintiff would have bought the company even if the accounts had revealed its true financial position. In the Scots case, substantial damages were awarded to the plaintiff.

(b) In order to provide a means of protection for the auditor arising from the comments in (a) above, the following steps should be taken:

    (i) Agreements concerning the duties of the auditor should be
        - clear and precise;
        - in writing;
        - confirmed by a Letter of Engagement, including matters specifically excluded.

    (ii) Audit work should be
        - relevant to the system of internal control, which must be ascertained, evaluated and tested (per the decision in an Australian case *Pacific Acceptance Corporation v Forsyth).* Whilst this decision may be contested by UK auditors using the Operational Standard as their authority, it is still true to say that controls cannot be entirely ignored: for the auditor to have any confidence in an accounting system there must be present and evident the existence of minimum controls to ensure completeness and accuracy of the records;
        - adequately planned before the audit commences;
        - reviewed by a senior member of the firm to ensure quality control of the audit and to enable a decision to be made on the form of audit report.

    (iii) Any queries arising during an audit should be
        - recorded on the current working papers;
        - cleared and filed.

    (iv) A Management Letter should be
        - submitted to the client or the Board of Directors in writing immediately following an audit;
        - seen to be acted upon by the client.

    (v) *All* members of an auditing firm should be familiar with
        - the standards expected throughout the firm;
        - the standards of the profession as a whole by means of adequate training, which should cover the implementation of the firm's Audit Manual and the recommendations of the professional accountancy bodies.

    (vi) Insurance should be taken out to cover the firm against possible claims.

3. The primary responsibility for the prevention and detection of fraud and irregularities rests with management. This responsiblity may be partly discharged by the institution of an adequate system of internal control including, for example, authorisation controls and controls covering segregation of duties.

   The auditor's duties do not require him specifically to search for fraud unless required by statute or the specific terms of his engagement.

   However, the auditor should recognise the possibility of material irregularities or frauds which could, unless adequately disclosed, distort the results or state of affairs shown by the financial statements. The auditor should, therefore, plan his audit so that he has a reasonable expectation of detecting material misstatements in the financial statements resulting from irregularities or fraud.

   Accordingly, in obtaining sufficient appropriate audit evidence to afford a reasonable basis of support for his report, the auditor seeks reasonable assurance, through the application of procedures that comply with Auditing Standards, that frauds or irregularities which may be material to the financial statements have not occurred or that, if they have occurred, they are either corrected or properly accounted for in the financial statements.

   The Auditing Standards do not distinguish 'employee' and 'management' fraud; the auditor must be able to recognise the possibility of either fraud type where the effect of the fraud may be material. The characteristics of the two categories of fraud are as follows:

   Employee fraud: involves theft, misappropriation or embezzlement of the enterprise's funds, usually in the form of cash or other readily realisable assets such as stock or fixed assets. Such frauds are usually perpetrated by employees, but occasionally management may be tempted to 'put their hands in the till'.

   Management fraud: involves the manipulation of the records and the accounts (eg. by 'window dressing'), typically by the enterprise's senior officers with a view to benefitting in some indirect way.

   Employee frauds are more likely to be encountered where internal controls are weak. When evaluating controls the auditor will need to place special emphasis on the following control aspects:
   - segregation of duties
   - authorisation (particularly of expense items and new ledger accounts)
   - completeness and accuracy of accounting data
   - safeguard procedures (eg signing cheques)
   - comprehensiveness of controls (eg including all relevant sub-systems)

   In addition, where accounting procedures are computerised, the auditor should be concerned to ensure that a lack of computer controls cannot be exploited to suppress evidence that an irregularity may exist or indeed to allow an irregularity to occur.

   When carrying out his detailed auditing testing he could discover circumstances that are indicative of employee fraud. Examples of such circumstances include:
   - missing vouchers or documents
   - evidence of falsified documents
   - unsatisfactory explanations
   - figures, trends or results which do not accord with expectations
   - unexplained items on reconciliations or suspense accounts
   - evidence of disputes
   - evidence of unduly lavish life styles by officers and employees

- unusual investment of funds held in fiduciary capacity
- evidence that the system of internal control is not operating as it was believed or intended to.

The auditor's programme of work needs to be sufficiently flexible to follow up any such points arising and any irregularities or frauds detected.

Many substantive tests normally performed by the auditor may assist in isolating employee frauds, if they are occurring. For example, tests performed on the debtors ledger may be aimed at revealing overstatement or bad debts, but the design of such tests also assists with cash understatement objectives and may reveal irregularities such as 'teeming and lading'.

When seeking to evaluate the possibility of management fraud the auditor will need to consider the business environment by identifying:
- circumstances which may exert undue influence on management (eg the desire to retain the confidence of depositors or creditors may encourage overstatement of results)
- company performance (eg the deliberate distortion of the financial statements to meet a profit forecast, to increase profit related remuneration or to avoid the appearance of insolvency).

If the auditor concludes that there is a high risk of management fraud he will concentrate on techniques such as analytical review and review of post balance sheet events (including going concern evaluation) that should reveal any material distortions in the financial statements.

SECTION 3

AUDIT PLANNING AND CONTROL

Chapter 6

THE AUDIT IN OUTLINE

Topics covered in this chapter:

- The chronology of an audit
- The nature of the systems-based audit
- The differences between interim and final audits

The chronology of an audit

1. The chart on the next page shows, in outline, the main stages that are normally followed in a logical sequence to comply with the operational standard. Before examining each stage in detail it is worth reiterating the more important duties of the auditor of a limited company. He must satisfy himself that:

   (a) proper accounting records have been kept;

   (b) the accounts are in agreement with the accounting records;

   (c) the accounts have been prepared in accordance with the Act, and relevant SSAPs;

   (d) the balance sheet shows a true and fair view of the state of the company's affairs and the profit and loss account shows a true and fair view of the results for the period.

   The objects of most other audits will be broadly similar.

2. It follows that a major part of the auditor's work will involve:

   (a) making such tests and enquiries as he considers necessary to form an opinion as to the reliability of the accounting records as a basis for the preparation of accounts;

   (b) checking the accounts against the underlying records; and

   (c) reviewing the accounts for compliance with the Companies Act and SSAPs.

3. When assessing the reliability of the accounting records, the auditor will consider three main points:

   (a) the extent to which it is necessary to find evidence that supports the figures in the records;

   (b) the extent to which he can rely on the controls over the preparation of the records as a means of ensuring their accuracy;

6: THE AUDIT IN OUTLINE

A DIAGRAMMATIC REPRESENTATION OF THE SYSTEMS AUDIT

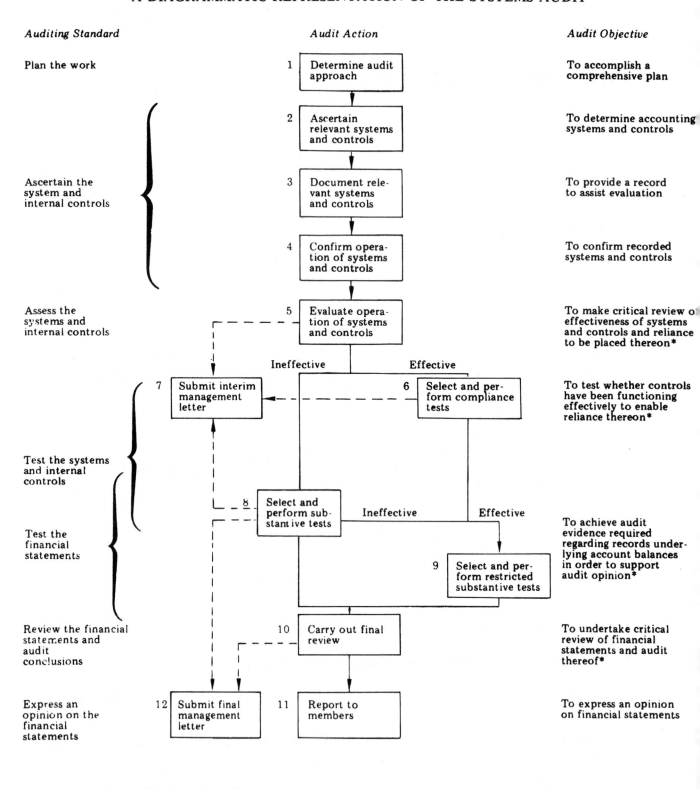

Auditing Standard	*Audit Action*	*Audit Objective*
Plan the work	1 Determine audit approach	To accomplish a comprehensive plan
Ascertain the system and internal controls	2 Ascertain relevant systems and controls	To determine accounting systems and controls
	3 Document relevant systems and controls	To provide a record to assist evaluation
	4 Confirm operation of systems and controls	To confirm recorded systems and controls
Assess the systems and internal controls	5 Evaluate operation of systems and controls	To make critical review of effectiveness of systems and controls and reliance to be placed thereon*
Test the systems and internal controls	7 Submit interim management letter 6 Select and perform compliance tests	To test whether controls have been functioning effectively to enable reliance thereon*
Test the financial statements	8 Select and perform substantive tests 9 Select and perform restricted substantive tests	To achieve audit evidence required regarding records underlying account balances in order to support audit opinion*
Review the financial statements and audit conclusions	10 Carry out final review	To undertake critical review of financial statements and audit thereof*
Express an opinion on the financial statements	12 Submit final management letter 11 Report to members	To express an opinion on financial statements

Ineffective / Effective (after box 5)

Ineffective / Effective (after box 8)

—————▶ Stages in audit procedures

— — — ▶ Contact with management

* A secondary objective of this audit action is to recommend to management improvements in systems and controls and in accounting procedures and practices.

(c) the extent to which the overall view of the accounts derived from the underlying records conforms with the auditor's expectations, based on his knowledge of the enterprise.

4. Points (a) and (b) are complementary in so far as the greater the reliance he can place on the controls, the less he will need to seek direct evidence to substantiate the figures in the accounts. The extent to which he can rely on the controls will depend, among other things on:

(a) their existence and strength in principle;

(b) the effectiveness with which they are performed;

(c) the extent to which their effectiveness can be tested;

(d) the effect on the audit in terms of time spent (and hence cost) and level of confidence of identifying, evaluating and testing the controls as compared with carrying out more extensive tests on the accounting records themselves.

The degree of reliance placed on controls by the auditor is hence a crucial factor in the operational approach. Internal control systems are considered in detail in chapter 8.

5. *Stage 1:* – The first stage in any audit should be to determine its scope and the auditor's general approach. For statutory audits the scope is clearly laid down in the Companies Act as expanded by current best practice. A letter of engagement will be submitted or confirmed before the start of each annual audit.

6. In addition to the letter of engagement it is becoming increasingly common for auditors to prepare an audit planning memorandum to be placed on the audit file. The purpose of this memorandum is to provide a record of the major areas to which the auditors attach special significance and to highlight any particular difficulties or points of concern peculiar to the audit client.

7. The detailed audit planning which arises from the determination of the scope of work is discussed further in chapter 7.

8. *Stages 2 - 4:* The objectives of these stages are:

(a) *Stage 2:* to determine the flow of documents and extent of controls in existence. This is very much a fact finding exercise, achieved by discussing the accounting system and document flow with all the relevant departments - including typically, sales, purchases, cash, stock and accounts personnel. It is good practice to make a rough record of the system during this fact finding tour, which will be converted to a formal record at stage 3 below.

(b) *Stage 3:* to prepare a comprehensive record to facilitate evaluation of the systems. Such a record may include:
   (i) charts; eg organisation charts and records of the books of account;
   (ii) narrative notes;
   (iii) internal control questionnaires (ICQs);
   (iv) flowcharts.

(c) *Stage 4:* to confirm that the system recorded is the same as that in operation. After completion of the preparation (or update) of the systems records the auditor will confirm his understanding of the system by performing 'walk-through' tests - tracing literally a handful of transactions of each type through the system. This procedure will establish that there is no reason to suppose that the accounting system does not operate in the manner ascertained and recorded - the need for this check arises as client's staff will occasionally tell the auditor what they *should* be doing (ie the established procedures) rather than what is actually being done in practice. Stages 2 and 3 as described above will be carried out in detail at the beginning of a new audit assignment and the results of these stages, which will be incorporated in the *permanent file*, will be reviewed and amended each year at the start of the annual audit. As part of this annual review further walk-through tests will be carried out to confirm the system.

9. *Stage 5:* the purpose of evaluating the systems is to gauge their reliability and formulate a basis for testing their effectiveness in practice. Following the evaluation the auditor will be able to recommend improvement to the system and determine the extent of the further tests to be carried out at stages 6 and 8 below.

10. *Stage 6:* given effective controls, the objective is to select and perform tests designed to establish compliance with the system. One of the most important points underlying modern auditing is that, if the controls are strong, the records should be reliable and consequently the amount of detailed testing can be reduced. It is, however, still necessary for the auditor to check that the controls are as effective in practice as they are on paper. The auditor will, therefore, carry out compliance tests. These are like walk through checks in so far as they are concerned with the workings of the system. They differ in that they:

(a) are concerned only with those areas subject to effective control;
(b) cover a representative sample of transactions throughout the period.

11. The conclusion drawn from the results of a compliance test may be either:

(a) that the controls are effective, in which case the auditor will only need to carry out restricted substantive tests; or
(b) that the controls are ineffective in practice, although they had appeared strong on paper, in which case the auditor will need to carry out more extensive substantive tests.

12. It should be noted that stage 6 should only be carried out if the controls are evaluated at stage 5 as being effective. If the auditor knows that the controls are ineffective then there is no point in carrying out compliance tests which will merely confirm what is already known. Instead the auditor should go straight on to carry out his full substantive tests.

13. *Stage 7: interim comments letter.* After evaluating the systems and carrying out compliance tests, it is normal practice to send management a letter identifying weaknesses and recommending improvements.

14. *Stages 8 and 9: substantive tests.* These are not concerned with the workings of the system, but with substantiating the figures in the books of account, and eventually, in the final accounts themselves. The tests are designed for two purposes:

(a) to support the figures in the accounts; and

(b) where errors exist, to assess their effect in monetary terms.

Before designing a substantive test it is essential to consider whether any errors produced by weak systems could lead to material differences. If the answer is 'NO' there is no point in performing a test.

15. *Stages 10-12*

(a) *Stage 10:* the aim of the overall review (including an analytical review) is to determine the overall reliability of the accounts by making a critical analysis of content and presentation.

(b) *Stage 11:* the report to the members is the statutory end product of the audit in which the auditors express their opinion of the accounts.

(c) *Stage 12:* the final letter to management is an important non-statutory end product of the audit. Its purpose is to make further suggestions for improvements in the systems and to place on record specific points in connection with the audit and accounts.

16. Before going on to discuss the distinctions between systems audits and wholly substantive audits, it is worth giving a practical example of the different types of tests discussed above to remove any confusion. If we were considering a material purchases system then the tests would be built up as follows:

(a) *Walk through tests:* taking a few transactions (1 or 2) and following them through every stage of the system from material requisition to settlement of the suppliers invoice. This would take place at stage 4 in the chart;

(b) *Compliance tests:* taking a representative sample of transactions spread over the year - perhaps chosen using random numbers - and testing certain significant controls only. For a purchases system, compliance tests might be applied to the purchase payments routine by checking that purchase invoices have been authorised before payment and checking control account reconciliations to verify the completeness of postings to the purchase ledger;

(c) *Substantive tests:* taking a relatively large sample of transactions - perhaps biased to include high value items - and testing for completeness and accuracy eg testing calculations of purchase invoices and postings, via day book, to purchases account and purchase ledger to confirm validity of purchases figure.

The nature of the systems-based audit

17. The chart that we have used to demonstrate the principal stages in the audit process is headed 'A diagrammatic representation of the *systems audit*. The phrase 'systems audit' is not to be found in the Auditing Standards and Guidelines, yet it is a well established term. The phrase refers to the typical audit approach to medium and large companies and is based on the assumption that such companies have internal control systems which will constitute a reliable base for the preparation of the accounts. In other words, the characteristic of a systems audit is an examination of internal control.

18. Many small companies cannot achieve satisfactory internal control and it is clearly futile for the auditor to seek to rely on controls if they are non-existent or unreliable. For such enterprises the auditor has no alternative but to carry out a so called 'substantive audit' involving extensive verification of transactions, followed by a detailed examination of the balance sheet (verification of assets and liabilities and review of the financial statements).

19. The contemporary audit approach to reasonably sophisticated companies is therefore to carry out a system-based audit during the course of the accounting year, followed by a balance sheet audit at the year end - if the systems audit work is successful, ie the controls prove reliable, the auditor can use his judgement to *reduce* the extent of the balance sheet work. In *no* circumstances will the balance sheet work be eliminated entirely.

The distinction between interim and final audits

20. Whereas the split between the systems and balance sheet audits is concerned with the type of work covered, that between the interim and final audits is concerned with timing. The interim audit will normally take place approximately three-quarters of the way through the financial year.

21. There is an element of similarity between systems/balance sheet work and interim/final audits in as much as the majority of the systems work will be carried out during the interim audit and the majority of the balance-sheet work during the final audit. However, it will be necessary to complete some systems work during the final audit so that transactions between the time of the interim and final audits do not escape the auditor's attention. Similarly, some substantive testing is very likely to be carried out during the interim (eg verifying fixed assets additions to date).

22. With very small audits, it is sometimes considered unnecessary to carry out an interim audit. This means that, as a matter of convenience, all the audit work will be carried out in a single phase commencing typically, a short time before the year-end and continuing into the post balance sheet period.

23. At the other extreme, with large companies it is sometimes necessary to carry out more than one interim audit or, alternatively, adopt a continuous auditing approach. In the case of a continuous audit the auditor's staff will either make several visits to the client spread throughout the year or, as in the case of very large companies, some of the audit staff will be present at the client's premises virtually all the time.

24. There are several important advantages and disadvantages of a continuous audit.

  (a) *Advantages:*
    (i)   the continual or regular attendance of the auditor may act as a deterrent to fraud;
    (ii) weaknesses in the client's systems are noticed earlier and, if they exist, errors and fraud may be discovered more quickly;
    (iii) it is sometimes possible to start the balance sheet work before the year end. This will lead to swifter financial reporting;
    (iv) the auditor's work is spread more evenly throughout the year. This will help to relieve the pressures on staff that arise for many audit firms during the first few months of each year.

(b) *Disadvantages:*
  (i)   audit staff who spend much of their time working on one client may find their independence adversely affected;
  (ii) the auditor's frequent (and sometimes unexpected) visits may cause inconvenience to the client;
  (iii) it is possible that figures may be altered (innocently or fraudulently) after they have been checked;
  (iv) it may be found that outstanding points and queries raised at one visit are forgotten and not followed up at a later stage. Strict control is needed to ensure that this does not happen particularly where the staff assigned to the audit have changed.

Conclusion

25. We have identified twelve stages in a typical systems audit. All audits will pass through stages one to five, and also through stages ten to twelve. Which route the audit takes through stages six to nine depends on the auditor's evaluation of the organisation's controls.

26. Nearly all of the chapters which make up the remainder of this text are devoted to explaining each of the stages in more detail. The next chapter starts at the beginning - with the appointment of an auditor, and the drawing up of an audit plan.

TEST YOUR KNOWLEDGE
Numbers in brackets refer to paragraphs in this chapter

1.   Briefly sketch the typical stages of an audit defined in terms of the audit action required.   (Audit diagram)

2.   What is a 'walk through test'? (8 (c))

3.   Distinguish a compliance test and a walk through test. (10)

4.   What is a 'systems audit'? (17)

5.   Distinguish 'interim' and 'final' audits. (20)

Chapter 7

INITIAL PROCEDURES

Topics covered in this chapter:

- Procedures before accepting nomination
- Procedures after accepting nomination
- Planning the audit
- Controlling the audit
- Recording the audit

Procedures before accepting nomination

1. Before a new audit client is accepted, the auditor concerned must ensure that there are no independence or other ethical problems likely to cause conflict with the ethical code. Furthermore, it is important for the new auditor to ensure that he has been appointed in a proper and legal manner, especially since one auditor's appointment is normally another auditor's removal or resignation.

2. The nominee auditor must take the following steps:

   (a) Ensure that he is professionally qualified to act ie is not disqualified on any of the legal or ethical grounds set out in earlier chapters.

   (b) Ensure that the firm's existing resources are adequate to service the needs of the new client: this will raise questions of staff and time availability and the firm's technical expertise.

   (c) Seek references in respect of the new client company: it may be, as is often the case, that the directors of the company are already personally known to the firm; if not, independent enquiries should be made concerning the status of the company and its directors (agencies such as Dun & Bradstreet might be of assistance together with a formal search at Companies House).

   (d) Communicate with the present auditor.
       (i) The auditing bodies have laid down strict rules of conduct in their ethical statement entitled 'Changes in professional appointments', regarding the purpose and the nature of such a communication. The purpose is primarily to protect the shareholders. The proposed auditor should not accept nomination without first enquiring from the existing auditor whether there is any reason for or circumstances behind the proposed change of which he should be aware. A secondary reason for the communication is as a matter of professional courtesy.

(ii)   The statement requires that the nominee:
    1.   requests the prospective client's permission to communicate with the auditor last appointed. If such permission is refused he should *decline nomination;*
    2.   on receipt of permission, requests in writing of the auditor last appointed all information which ought to be made available to him to enable him to decide whether he is prepared to accept nomination.

The incumbent auditor receiving the request in 2 above should:
-   request permission of the client to discuss the client's affairs freely with the proposed nominee. If this request is not granted the member should report that fact to the proposed nominee, who, if a member, should not accept nomination;
-   discuss freely with the proposed nominee all matters relevant to the appointment of which the latter should be aware, and disclose fully all information which appears to him to be relevant to the client's affairs or which may be reasonably requested of him by the proposed nominee.

(iii)   The following draft indicates the contents of the initial communication:

> To: Retiring & Co
>   Certified Accountants
>
> Dear Sirs
>
>   Re: New Client Co Ltd
>
> We have been asked to allow our name to go forward for nomination as auditors of the above company, and we should therefore be grateful if you would please let us know whether there are any professional reasons why we should not accept nomination....
>
> Acquiring & Co
> Certified Accountants

The following letter would be sent if the nominee has not received a reply to the letter above within a reasonable time.

> To: Retiring & Co
>   Certified Accountants
>
> Dear Sirs
>
>   Re: New Client Co Ltd
>
> As we have been unable to obtain a reply to our letters of the 1 and 14 September we would inform you that, unless we hear from you by 30 September, we shall assume that there are no professional reasons preventing our acceptance of nomination as auditors of the above company and we shall allow our name to go forward. We ourselves are not aware of any reasons why we should not consent to act for this company....
>
> Acquiring & Co
> Certified Accountants.

Having negotiated steps (i) to (iii) the auditor will be in a position to accept the nomination, or not, as the case may be.

7: INITIAL PROCEDURES

Procedures after accepting nomination

3. (a) Ensure that the outgoing auditor's removal or resignation has been properly conducted in accordance with the Companies Act 1985.

    The new auditor should see a valid notice of the outgoing auditor's resignation (under S390 CA 1985), or confirm that the outgoing auditor was properly removed (under S386 CA 1985) at a general meeting of the company.

    (b) Ensure that the new auditor's appointment is valid. The new auditor should obtain a copy of the resolution passed at the general meeting appointing him as the company's auditor.

    (c) Set up and submit a letter of engagement to the directors of the company.

    This important procedure is considered immediately below.

The engagement letter

4. Modern accountancy firms provide a wide range of professional services in addition to audit, but the duties of directors and auditors are very clearly specified by statute. It is the purpose of an engagement letter to define clearly the extent of the auditor's responsibilities and so minimise the possibility of any misunderstanding between the client and the auditor. Further, the engagement letter provides written confirmation of the auditor's acceptance of the appointment, the scope of the audit, the form of his report and the scope of any non-audit services. If an engagement letter is not sent to clients - both new and existing - there is scope for argument about the precise extent of the respective obligations of the client and its directors and the auditor. The contents of an engagement letter should be discussed and agreed with management before it is sent and preferably *prior* to the audit appointment.

5. The engagement letter is a well established audit technique. Guidance is available in the form of the detailed operational guideline 'Engagement letters' issued in May 1984 from which the following comments are derived.

6. The auditor should send an engagement letter to all new clients soon after his appointment as auditor and, in any event, before the commencement of the first audit assignment. He should also consider sending an engagement letter to existing clients to whom no letter has previously been sent as soon as a suitable opportunity presents itself.

7. Once it has been agreed by the client, an engagement letter will, if it so provides, remain effective from one audit appointment to another until it is replaced. However, the engagement letter should be reviewed annually to ensure that it continues to reflect the client's circumstances. If a change has taken place, including a significant change in management, which materially affects the scope or understanding of the audit, the auditor should discuss the matter with management and where appropriate send a revised engagement letter.

8. The letter should explain the principal statutory responsibilities of the client and the statutory and professional responsibilities of the auditor.

9. In the case of a company, it should be indicated that it is the statutory responsibility of the client to maintain proper accounting records, and to prepare financial statements which give a true and fair view and comply with the Companies Act 1985 and other relevant legislation. It should also be indicated that the auditor's statutory responsibilities include making a report to the members stating whether in his opinion the financial statements give a true and fair view and whether they comply with the Companies Act.

10. It should be explained that the auditor has an obligation to satisfy himself whether or not the directors' report contains any matters which are inconsistent with the audited financial statements. Furthermore, it should be indicated that the auditor has a professional responsibility to report if the financial statements do not comply in any material respect with statements of standard accounting practice, unless in his opinion the non-compliance is justified in the circumstances.

11. The scope of the audit should be explained. In this connection, it should be pointed out that the audit will be conducted in accordance with approved auditing standards and have regard to relevant auditing guidelines. It should be indicated that:

   (a) the auditor will obtain an understanding of the accounting system in order to assess its adequacy as a basis for the preparation of the financial statements;

   (b) the auditor will expect to obtain relevant and reliable evidence sufficient to enable him to draw reasonable conclusions therefrom;

   (c) the nature and extent of the tests will vary according to the auditor's assessment of the accounting system and, where he wishes to place reliance upon it, the system of internal control;

   (d) the auditor will report to management any significant weaknesses in, or observations on, the client's systems which come to his notice and which he thinks should be brought to management's attention.

12. Where appropriate, reference should be made to recurring special arrangements concerning the audit. These could include arrangements in respect of internal auditors, divisions, overseas subsidiaries, other auditors and (in the case of a small business managed by directors who are the major shareholders) significant reliance on supervision by the directors.

13. Where appropriate it should be indicated that, prior to the completion of the audit, the auditor may seek written representations from management on matters having a material effect on the financial statements.

14. The responsibility for the prevention and detection of irregularity and fraud rests with management and this responsibility is fulfilled mainly through the implementation and continued operation of an adequate system of internal control. The engagement letter should make this clear. Furthermore, it should explain that the auditor will endeavour to plan his audit so that he has a reasonable expectation of detecting material misstatements in the financial statements resulting from irregularities or fraud, but that the examination should not be relied upon to disclose irregularities and frauds which may exist. If a special examination for irregularities or fraud is required by the client, then this should be specified in the engagement letter, but not in the audit section.

15. The auditor may undertake services in addition to carrying out his responsibilities as auditor. An engagement letter should adequately describe the nature and scope of those services. In the case of accounting services, the letter should distinguish the accountant's and the client's responsibilities in relation to them and to the day-to-day bookkeeping, the maintenance of all accounting records and the preparation of financial statements. Preferably this should be done in a separate letter but such services may form the subject of a section in the audit engagement letter.

16. In the case of the provision of taxation services, the responsibilities for the various procedures such as the preparation of tax computations and the submission of returns to the relevant authorities should be clearly set out, either in a section of the main letter or in a separate letter.

17. Where accounting, taxation or other services are undertaken on behalf of an audit client, information may be provided to members of the audit firm other than those engaged on the audit. If this is the case, it may be appropriate for the audit engagement letter to indicate that the auditor is not to be treated as having notice, for the purposes of his audit responsibilities, of the information given to such people.

18. Mention should normally be made of fees and of the basis on which they are computed, rendered and paid.

19. The engagement letter should include a request to management that they confirm in writing their agreement to the terms of the engagement. It should be clearly understood that when agreed the letter will give rise to contractual obligations, and its precise content must therefore be carefully considered. In the case of a company, the auditor should request that the letter of acknowledgement be signed on behalf of the board.

20. The principles contained in the guideline should also be followed in the case of non-audit engagements. In such a case, if purely accounting services are being provided to a client such as a sole trader or partnership, the engagement letter should make it clear that these services will be performed without any audit work being carried out.

21. A form of wording is set out below appropriate for a limited company audit - it is *not* a 'standard' wording as it must be tailored to specific circumstances. It can also be used as the basis of an engagement letter for unincorporated clients.

SPECIMEN ENGAGEMENT LETTER

To the directors of...

The purpose of this letter is to set out the basis on which we (are to) act as auditors of the company (and its susidiaries) and the respective areas of responsibility of the company and of ourselves.

Audit

1.1 As directors of the above company, you are responsible for maintaining proper accounting records and preparing financial statements which give a true and fair view and comply with the Companies Act 1985. You are also responsible for making available to us, as and when required, all the company's accounting records and all other records and related information, including minutes of all management and shareholders' meetings.

1.2 We have a statutory responsibility to report to the members whether in our opinion the financial statements give a true and fair view of the state of the company's affairs and of the profit or loss for the year and whether they comply with the Companies Act 1985 (or other relevant legislation). In arriving at our opinion, we are required to consider the following matters, and to report on any in respect of which we are not satisfied:

(a) whether proper accounting records have been kept by the company and proper returns adequate for our audit have been received from branches not visited by us;

(b) whether the company's balance sheet and profit and loss account are in agreement with the accounting records and returns;

(c) whether we have obtained all the information and explanations which we think necessary for the purpose of our audit; and

(d) whether the information in the directors' report is consistent with that in the audited financial statements.

In addition, there are certain other matters which, according to the circumstances, may need to be dealt with in our report. For example, where the financial statements do not give full details of directors' remuneration or of transactions with the company, the Companies Act requires us to disclose such matters in our report.

1.3 We have a professional responsibility to report if the financial statements do not comply in any material respect with statements of standard accounting practice, unless in our opinion the non-compliance is justified in the circumstances.

1.4 Our audit will be conducted in accordance with the auditing standards issued by the accountancy bodies and will have regard to relevant auditing guidelines. Furthermore, it will be conducted in such a manner as we consider necessary to fulfil our responsibilities and will include such tests of transactions and of the existence, ownership and valuation of assets and liabilities as we consider necessary. We shall obtain an understanding of the accounting system in order to assess its adequacy as a basis for the preparation of the financial statements and to establish whether proper accounting records have been maintained. We shall expect to obtain such relevant and reliable evidence as we consider sufficient to enable us to draw reasonable conclusions therefrom. The nature and extent of our tests will vary according to our assessment of the company's accounting system, and where we wish to place reliance on it the system of internal control, and may cover any aspect of the business operations. We shall report to you any significant weaknesses in, or observations on, the company's systems which come to our notice and which we think should be brought to your attention.

1.5 As part of our normal audit procedures, we may request you to provide written confirmation of oral representations which we have received from you during the course of the audit.

1.6 In order to assist us with the examination of your financial statements, we shall request sight of all documents or statements, including the chairman's statement and the directors' report, which are due to be issued with the financial statements. We are also entitled to attend all general meetings of the company and to receive notice of all such meetings.

1.7 *(Where appropriate).* We appreciate that the present size of your business renders it uneconomic to create a system of internal control based on the segregation of duties for different functions within each area of the business. In the running of your company we understand that the directors are closely involved with the control of the company's transactions. In planning and performing our audit work we shall take account of this supervision. Further we may ask additionally for confirmation in writing that all the transactions undertaken by the company have been properly reflected and recorded in the accounting records, and our audit report on your company's financial statements may refer to this confirmation.

1.8 The responsibility for the prevention and detection of irregularities and fraud rests with yourselves. However we shall endeavour to plan our audit so that we have a reasonable expectation of detecting material misstatements in the financial statements or accounting records resulting from irregularities or fraud, but our examination should not be relied upon to disclose irregularities and frauds which may exist.

1.9 *(Where appropriate).* We shall not be treated as having notice, for the purposes of our audit responsibilities, of information provided to members of our firm other than those engaged on the audit (eg information provided in connection with accounting, taxation and other services).

Accounting and other services, and taxation services (either included here or set out in a separate letter.)

It was agreed that we should carry out the following services as your agents and on the basis that you will make full disclosure to us of all relevant information.

Accounting and other services

We shall:

2.1 prepare the financial statements based on accounting records maintained by yourselves;

2.2 provide assistance to the company secretary by preparing and lodging returns with the Registrar of Companies;

2.3 investigate irregularities and fraud upon receiving specific instructions.

Taxation services

3.1 We shall in respect of each accounting period prepare a computation of profits, adjusted in accordance with the provisions of the Taxes Acts, for the purpose of assessment to corporation tax. Subject to your approval, this will then be submitted to the Inspector of Taxes as being the company's formal return. We shall lodge formal notice of appeal against excessive or incorrect assessments to corporation tax where notice of such assessments is received by us. Where appropriate we shall also make formal application for postponement of tax in dispute and shall advise as to appropriate payments on account.

3.2 You will be responsible, unless otherwise agreed, for all other returns, more particularly: the returns of advance corporation tax and income tax deducted at source as required on Forms CT61, returns relating to employee taxes under PAYE and returns of employee expenses and benefits on form P11D. Your staff will deal with all returns and other requirements in relation to value added tax.

3.3 We shall be pleased to advise you on matters relating to the company's corporation tax liability, the implications of particular business transactions and on other taxation matters which you refer to us, such as national insurance, income tax deducted at source, employee benefits, value added tax and inheritance tax.

Fees

Our fees are computed on the basis of the time spent on your affairs by the partners and our staff, and on the levels of skill and responsibility involved. Unless otherwise agreed, our fees will be charged separately for each of the main classes of work described above, will be billed at appropriate intervals during the course of the year and will be due on presentation.

Agreement of terms

Once it has been agreed, this letter will remain effective, from one audit appointment to another, until it is replaced. We shall be grateful if you could confirm in writing your agreement to the terms of this letter, or let us know if they are not in accordance with your understanding of our terms of appointment.

Yours faithfully,

Certified Accountants

Acquiring knowledge of the business

22. The first audit of any client is exceptional - there is certain setting-up work necessary that will not be required in such depth in subsequent years. Sufficient work must be carried out to enable the auditor to gain a sound knowledge of the client's background, operations, accounting procedures and internal controls to allow him properly to plan the strategy and scope of his audit work. The following are some of the factors relating to the client environment that might need to be investigated and recorded:

(a) The historical background of the company.

(b) The characteristics of the company's business, including:
(i) the economic climate of the industry;
(ii) the factors affecting the industry;
(iii) the position of the company in the industry;
(iv) the main competitors;
(v) the marketing methods;
(vi) the methods of distribution;
(vii) the production functions;
(viii) labour relations.

(c) The structure of the organisation including the following:
(i) the organisation chart of the company showing the names, responsibilities and authority of the officials;
(ii) the location of the main operating accounting and custodian centres;

(iii)   whether an internal audit department exists;

(iv)   the flow of documentation including budgets and reports;

(v)   the books of account and ancillary records (in summary, not necessarily detailed form at this stage).

(d) Statutory information including:

    (i)   unusual clauses in the Memorandum and Articles of Association;

    (ii)   directors' interests in other businesses;

    (iii) charges on assets of the company;

    (iv) extent of distributable reserves.

(e) Accounts, accounting policies including:

    (i)   copies of last five years' (say) statutory accounts, management accounts and forecasts;

    (ii)   review for consistency of accounting policies including dates and effects of recent changes.

(f) Previous auditors:

    (i)   weaknesses in controls noted by previous auditors (if available);

    (ii)   reports of irregular transactions (if any).

(g) Taxation:

    (i)   bases of computations and agreements with HMIT;

    (ii)   letter of authority to Inland Revenue.

(h) Bankers:

    letter of authority to bankers to provide information concerning the client.

23. The auditor is effectively establishing above so called 'permanent file' information. The significance of the permanent file is discussed further below. Once sufficient background information has been accumulated, and all the procedural niceties described in the earlier paragraphs have been satisfied then the auditor will be in a position to determine the audit approach and establish his comprehensive plan. There is, however, one particular problem associated with the first year audit that warrants consideration before we look at planning in detail - this is the problem of figures derived from the previous year's accounts.

Amounts derived from the preceding financial statements

24. In expressing an opinion on the accounts of a new client the auditor accepts responsibility not only for the accounts of the year being reported on, but also:

(a) the consistency of the application of accounting policies;

(b) the reliability of the opening balances (which have an effect on the results for the current year, ie the profit or loss and source and application of funds);

(c) the appropriateness of the comparative figures included in the accounts, in as much as they may render the current year's figures misleading.

25. Clarification of the auditor's responsibility for amounts taken from the preceding period's financial statements is provided in the detailed operational guideline 'Amounts derived from the preceding financial statements' issued in November 1982. The following selected comments are extracted from this guideline.

26. Financial statements of companies incorporated under the provisions of the Companies Act 1985 are required to disclose corresponding amounts for all items in a company's balance sheet and profit and loss account. In other cases, financial statements usually contain corresponding amounts as a matter of law, regulation or good practice. Their purpose, unless stated otherwise, is to complement the amounts relating to the current period and not to re-present the complete financial statements for the preceding period. The auditor is *not* required to express an opinion on the corresponding amounts as such. His responsibility is to ensure that they are the amounts which appeared in the preceding period's financial statements or, where appropriate, have either been properly restated to achieve consistency and comparability with the current period's amounts, or have been restated due to a change of accounting policy or a correction of a fundamental error as required by SSAP6.

27. In these special circumstances the new auditor will have to satisfy himself as to the matters identified in paragraph 24, but his lack of prior knowledge of the preceding period's financial statement will require him to apply additional procedures in order to obtain the necessary assurance.

28. The additional procedures that should be performed by the auditor may include any of the following:

    (a) consultations with the client's management;

    (b) review of the client's records, working papers and accounting and control procedures for the preceding period, particularly in so far as they affect the opening position;

    (c) audit work on the current period, which will usually provide some evidence regarding opening balances; and

    (d) in exceptional circumstances, substantive testing of the opening balances, if he does not consider the results of procedures (a) to (c) to be satisfactory.

29. In addition, the auditor may be able to hold consultations with the previous auditor. Whilst outgoing auditors can normally be expected to afford reasonable co-operation to their successors, neither ethical statements nor the law place them under a specific obligation to make working papers or other information available to their successors. Consultations would normally be limited to seeking information concerning the previous auditor's examination of particular areas which are important to his successor, and to obtaining clarification of any significant accounting matters which are not adequately dealt with in the client's records. If, however, such consultations are not possible or alternatively, if the preceding period's financial statements were unaudited, the only evidence about the opening position available to the auditor will be that generated by procedures such as those set out in paragraph 28 above.

30. Under normal circumstances the auditor will be able to satisfy himself as to the opening position by performing the work set out in paragraphs 28 and 29. If he is not able to satisfy himself in any material respect he will need to qualify his report for the possible effect on the financial statements.

Planning the audit

31. The Auditor's Operational Standard requires that 'the auditor should adequately plan, control and record his work'. The associated guideline stresses that audits, irrespective of their size, must be properly planned, controlled and recorded at each stage of their progress if they are to be efficiently and effectively carried out. It is convenient to consider planning, controlling and recording separately although, as already stated, they are not mutually exclusive.

32. The guideline 'planning, controlling and recording' under the heading 'planning' makes the following broad observations regarding the scope and objectives of audit planning:

     "The form and nature of the planning required for an audit will be affected by the size and complexity of the enterprise, the commercial environment in which it operates, the method of processing transactions and the reporting requirements to which it is subject. In this context the auditor should aim to provide an effective and economic service within an appropriate time-scale.

     Adequate audit planning:
     (a) establishes the intended means of achieving the objectives of the audit;
     (b) assists in the direction and control of the work;
     (c) helps to ensure that attention is devoted to critical aspects of the audit; and
     (d) helps to ensure that the work is completed expeditiously.

     In order to plan his work adequately the auditor needs to understand the nature of the business of the enterprise, its organisation, its method of operating and the industry in which it is involved, so that he is able to appreciate which events and transactions are likely to have a significant effect on the financial statements."

33. With regard to specific planning procedures and decisions the guideline states:

     "The auditor should consider the outline audit approach he proposes to adopt, including the extent to which he may wish to rely on internal controls and any aspects of the audit which need particular attention. He should also take into account in his planning any additional work which he has agreed to undertake.

     Preparatory procedures which the auditor should consider include the following:

     (a) reviewing matters raised in the audit of the previous year which may have continuing relevance in the current year;

     (b) assessing the effects of any changes in legislation or accounting practice affecting the financial statements of the enterprise;

     (c) reviewing interim or management accounts where these are available and consulting with the management and staff of the enterprise. Matters which should be considered include current trading circumstances, and significant changes in:

        (i)   the business carried on;

        (ii) the enterprise's management;

(d)   identifying any significant changes in the enterprise's accounting procedures, such as a new computer based system.

The auditor should also consider:

- the timing of significant phases of the preparation of the financial statements;
- the extent to which analyses and summaries can be prepared by the enterprise's employees;
- the relevance of any work to be carried out by the enterprise's internal auditors.

The auditor will need to determine the number of audit staff required, the experience and special skills they need to possess and the timing of their audit visits. He will need to ensure that all audit staff are briefed regarding the enterprise's affairs and the nature and scope of the work they are required to carry out. The preparation of a memorandum setting out the outline audit approach may be helpful."

It should be noted that the guideline is written in the context of the established audit engagement rather than the first time audit. As we have seen earlier, planning the first audit raises special problems due to the auditor's relative lack of knowledge and precedent.

34.   To appreciate better the significance of certain of the comments above it is useful to establish some prerequisites for effective organisation of an accounting office. Efficient organisation is necessary so that a firm can provide a competent service to clients in compliance with auditing standards, and of course, be profitable.

35.   Efficient organisation may be achieved by ensuring that the following procedures are used.

(a)   Efficient time recording and costing methods.

(b)   Preparation of time and cost budgets for audit (and other work); audits being performed by an efficient team of assistants (juniors, semi-seniors and seniors, typically) working under the supervision of competent managers who are responsible to their partners.

(c)   Experience and knowledge used to the maximum advantage of clients when providing audit, accounting, taxation and other services. This *may* lead to the creation of separate departments - for instance, a taxation department, management consultancy department, secretarial services department. Not all firms adopt this approach, however, some preferring to retain a 'general practice' approach. Whatever the organisation structure, there must be adequate numbers of staff who are knowledgeable and experienced in the areas of professional expertise provided by the firm.

(d)   Consistent practices within the firm including provision of an audit procedures manual, a system for preparation and retention of audit working papers and a degree of standardisation regarding check-lists, standard forms and certain audit procedures eg sampling techniques.

36.   The objectives and preparatory procedures outlined in paragraphs 32 and 33 provide a satisfactory overview of the planning function. To appreciate a little more fully how the planning objectives in paragraph 32 are achieved it is helpful to look at three practical aspects of planning in greater detail:

    (a)   audit risk evaluation;
    (b)   materiality;
    (c)   use of analytical review techniques.

Audit risk evaluation

37.   The term 'audit risk' does not appear in the guideline 'planning, controlling and recording' but is alluded to in the phrase 'adequate audit planning ... helps to ensure that attention is devoted to critical aspects of the audit'. Audit risk is a combination of:

    (a)   the risk that the accounts under review may contain material errors (ie do not give a true and fair view);

    (b)   the risk that the errors will not be detected by the auditor's procedures; this itself is a combination of (i) sampling risk and (ii) the risk that the auditor might apply the wrong procedures (this is very much a quality control problem). Sampling risk can be quantified where statistical sampling techniques are utilised - this aspect of risk analysis is considered further in a later chapter.

38.   Evaluating risk in the context of category (a) above is an important consideration when determining the nature and scope of audit work. Where there is *no* indication that *material* errors may be present, the auditor may be justified in carrying out the minimum amount of work consistent with reasonable caution. Conversely, where it appears from the auditor's knowledge of the business, past experience of the company or analytical review procedures that there could be material errors, the auditor will need to investigate further until he has determined the extent of error or satisfied himself that the accounts are materially correct. Hence, the auditor in practice tends to evaluate his audits as a 'normal risk' or 'higher than normal risk' - prudence dictates that there is no such situation as a 'less than normal risk'.

39.   At the planning stage the auditor should assess the risk of material errors:
    (a)   in the accounts as a whole; and
    (b)   in each transaction stream (eg purchases, sales, cash).

This assessment will be kept under continuous review as the audit progresses. It should be appreciated that material errors could arise intentionally, or unintentionally, and the auditor must hence be alive to circumstances that could give rise to errors arising through either cause.

40.   In reaching his decision as to the areas to be tested and the number of balances and transactions to be examined, the auditor will need to consider information available from prior experience, where available, and knowledge of the client's business and accounting systems. More specifically, the procedures adopted by the auditor for the purpose of detecting material errors and irregularities in conducting an audit will depend on his judgement as to:

    (a)   the types of errors or irregularities that are likely to occur (or have occurred previously);
    (b)   the relative risk of their occurrence;
    (c)   the likelihood that a particular type of error or irregularity could have a material effect on the financial statements; and
    (d)   the relative effectiveness of different audit tests.

41. An audit might be assessed as high risk as a result of the evaluation approach outlined above. Conversely, a normal risk decision might be justified if some of the following 'positive' factors are identified:

    (a) the company is private and financially stable, without excessive debt, and is likely to remain so in the foreseeable future;
    (b) the proprietor takes an active role in the business;
    (c) the company's history with the regulatory bodies has been good;
    (d) internal controls are strong and the company's accounting personnel competent;
    (e) the company is profitable;
    (f) past audit experience has provided evidence of good accounting controls with no major audit problems.

42. In summary the benefit of evaluating audit risk is that it aids recognition of the types of error and irregularity that are most likely to occur. The audit work can consequently be planned to investigate the risk areas thoroughly.

43. Audit risk should be evaluated and documented in the audit plan. Some larger firms have developed comprehensive risk questionnaires which interrogate the client's financial and management environment in considerable detail; other firms prefer a less stylised approach.

Materiality

44. The main purpose of an audit is to express an opinion on the truth and fairness of the results and financial position shown by the accounts. The first way in which the concept of materiality affects the audit is that it is one of the factors which influences the nature and size of audit tests; the auditor needs to design audit procedures to verify only those items which could be materially wrong and he need only do sufficient work to satisfy himself that balances and transactions do not contain material errors. Hence, if an auditor sets a materiality level of £50,000, he does not direct much, if any, audit work towards verifying prepayments totalling £10,000. The second way in which the concept of materiality affects audit work is when deciding whether to seek adjustment for errors found. The auditor is concerned that adjustments are made for *material* errors - not immaterial errors.

45. It is becoming increasingly common practice for the auditor to set a materiality level at the initial planning stage of the audit to act as a guideline for determining the extent of audit testing and for deciding whether to seek adjustment for errors or whether to qualify his audit report.

46. To set the materiality level the auditor needs to decide the level of errors which would distort the view given by the accounts. Because many users of accounts are primarily interested in the profitability of the company, the level is often expressed as a proportion of its profits (typically 5%). Some argue, however, that it is more sound to think of materiality in terms of the size of the business and hence recognise that, if the company remains a fairly constant size, the materiality level should not change; similarly if the business is growing, the level of materiality *will* increase from year to year.

47. The size of a company can be measured in terms of turnover and total assets before deducting any liabilities (sometimes referred to in legislation as 'the balance sheet total') both of which tend not to be subject to the fluctuations which may affect profit. As a guide, between ½% and 1% of turnover and between 1% and 2% of total assets are often taken as as a measure of what is material. These figures, based on the *latest* available information (the previous year's accounts if nothing else is available) hence form the basis of the materiality levels set and evidenced in the planning memorandum.

48. The APC in 1984 published a discussion paper by Professor Tom Lee in the Audit Brief series entitled 'Materiality, a review and analysis of its reporting significance and auditing implications'. It is not possible to reproduce the whole paper here, but the following extract under the heading 'Audit considerations' is relevant:

> "The concept of materiality is an accounting matter of much relevance to the auditor. Its nature and main features do not alter when they are being considered by him. However, the concept brings specific implications for the auditor's work, and these should be considered separately.
>
> The auditor is concerned essentially with collecting and evaluating sufficient evidence to conclude whether or not a true and fair view has been given in the financial statements. In this respect, because of the close relationship between a true and fair view and materiality, the auditor's task is to evaluate whether or not the available evidence reveals accounting errors which have exceeded a tolerable materiality level and thus damaged a true and fair view.
>
> The need for the auditor to consider accounting materiality decisions of management and the preparer of financial statements must affect all aspects of the audit - that is, in terms of planning, testing, evaluating and reporting on it. But it is at the planning stage where a consideration of materiality has its greatest impact on the work of the auditor. In broad terms, what he is seeking is assurance that the monetary and non-monetary errors existing in the audited financial statements do not exceed levels which are deemed to be material in accordance with the needs of report users and the specific circumstances of the reporting entity. In particular, he must review what management and the preparer of financial statements have determined as tolerable levels of error.
>
> Much will depend on his review of the materiality decisions of management and the preparer of financial statements, and the specific circumstances of the reporting entity (for example, the nature of its business, the strength of its internal controls, and the integrity of its management). The level of precision set by the auditor in his sampling will be equivalent to what he judges to be sufficient to derive a sample which will provide evidence of whether or not the total error is greater than the materiality level concerned. In other words, a quantification of what is material for accounting and disclosure purposes should provide an upper limit of the tolerable error to be used as a basis for statistical sampling. This upper limit of materiality may have to be reduced to a precision level for sampling to minimise the risk of undetected error and to allow for the level of error expected to be discovered.
>
> If from an examination of the actual errors detected by means of sampling, coupled with an estimate of the total errors therefore likely to exist, the total error is found to be in excess of the tolerable materiality level, then the auditor will be concerned either to see that management and the preparer of financial statements make some suitable correcting of the data or, that failing, he will make a suitable qualification in his audit report.

Analytical review

49. Analytical review has been used by auditors in practice for many years, but it is only recently that formal guidance has been given by the APC in the form of a detailed operational guideline entitled 'Analytical review' issued in April 1988. The guideline aims to explain the underlying principles of the technique and sets out the factors which the auditor should consider when performing analytical review. It does not deal with the specific methods to be applied; this is a matter which the auditor must judge in the light of the particular circumstances of the audit. The following comments are derived from this guideline.

50. Analytical review is defined as audit procedures which systematically analyse and compare related figures, trends, ratios and other data with the aim of providing evidence to support the audit opinion on the financial statements. As such, it is a substantive technique that can be used at various stages in the audit.

51. The data used in the review may be financial or non-financial data, and may originate from within or outside the client organisation. The procedures used can include:

    (a) comparison of current with prior year's figures, or ratios;
    (b) comparison of financial information with anticipated results, such as budgets, or with similar industry information;
    (c) comparison of data using advanced statistical techniques, and computer audit software.

52. Analytical review can be used at several stages in the audit, including as part of the review procedures at the end of the audit, in the context of reviewing the financial statements (Stage 10 of our audit diagram). The guideline envisages the adoption of the procedure at the following different stages:

Stage	Objectives
● Planning	- to improve the auditor's understanding of the enterprise; - to identify areas of potential risk or significant change.
● Detailed testing	- to obtain assurance as to the completeness, accuracy and validity of transactions and balances.
● Review of financial statements and formulation of the opinion	- to support conclusions from other audit work; - to assess the overall reasonableness of the financial statements.

53. In determining the extent of the auditor's use of analytical review, consideration should be given to:

    (a) the nature of the enterprise and its operations;
    (b) knowledge of the client, problems which have arisen in the past and the inherent risk;
    (c) the availability of financial and non-financial information;
    (d) the reliability, relevance, comparability and independence of available information; and
    (e) cost effectiveness.

54. The audit staff who perform analytical review should possess experience, judgement and a thorough knowledge of the enterprise, and the factors that might affect it. In addition, the risk of relying on analytical review is heightened in areas of the audit which are subject to a high degree of management discretion.

55. Analytical review can be used to evaluate:
    (a) financial information of individual enterprises or particular activities, and
    (b) individual account areas (eg debtors, stock or depreciation charges).

56. The application of analytical review is basically a four stage process as follows:

    (a) identify the factors likely to have a material effect on the items in the financial statements;
    (b) ascertain the probable relationships between these factors and such items;
    (c) predict the likely range of values of individual items; and
    (d) compare the prediction with the actual recorded amounts. This will indicate the extent to which any further audit work may be required.

57. The auditor should consider the implications of any significant fluctuations, unusual items or those which are inconsistent with audit evidence obtained from other sources. Management should be requested to provide explanations for these significant fluctuations. However, before placing full reliance on such explanations, the auditor should try and corroborate them by independent evidence, or examine them critically in the light of other audit evidence.

58. Obviously, the auditor's reaction to significant fluctuations will depend upon the stage in the audit that has been reached, and the explanations so far received:

    (a) At the planning stage, the auditor will react by deciding the extent, nature and direction of other audit tests. Where explanations reveal changes in the enterprise or its activities, the auditor will need to ensure that the audit approach takes these changes into account.

    (b) At the detailed testing stage, where the explanations received cannot be substantiated, the auditor will need to obtain sufficient evidence using alternative methods.

    (c) At the review of financial statements stage, the auditor would not normally expect to find material fluctuations of which he had no prior knowledge. If such fluctuations are found at this late stage, and alternative forms of evidence are not available, the auditor will need to consider qualifying his audit opinion.

59. The extent of the auditor's reliance on analytical review will be based on his assessment of the risk of failing to detect material error. Where certain items are not individually significant to the financial statements, the auditor may rely largely or even entirely on analytical review.

60. In assessing the risk of failure to detect material error, the following factors should be considered:

    (a) the relevance, reliability, comparability and independence of the data being used;

    (b) for internally generated data, the adequacy of controls over the preparation of financial and non-financial information;

    (c) the accuracy with which the figures being examined by analytical review procedures can be predicted; and

    (d) the materiality of the items.

61. Analytical review, like other audit procedures, needs to be properly recorded. The documentation should show:

    (a) the information examined, its sources and reliability;
    (b) extent and type of fluctuations found;
    (c) explanations for significant fluctuations;
    (d) the verification of those explanations;
    (e) the conclusions drawn by the auditor; and
    (f) any further action taken.

In addition, a client profile may be built up in the permanent file detailing key ratios and trends from year to year, for use in subsequent years.

The planning memorandum

62. We have now established that audit planning is a complex but vital stage in the audit process. If we return briefly to paragraph 33, the final sentence of the excerpt from the guideline 'planning, controlling and recording' reads:

"The preparation of a memorandum setting out the outline audit approach may be helpful"

This emphasises that it is one thing to make intelligent planning decisions, but another to ensure that they are satisfactorily recorded for the benefit of the audit team. The preparation of a memorandum is therefore established best practice.

Controlling the audit

63. Having established that it is essential to the effectiveness and efficiency of an audit for an appropriate degree of planning to be carried out prior to the commencement of the work, the guideline outlines the various procedures needed to control an audit.

64. The guideline identifies three key elements of control: *the direction of audit staff, their supervision* and a *review of the work* they have done. The degree of supervision required will depend on the complexity of the assignment and the experience and proficiency of the audit staff. It is important to appreciate that, as it is the reporting partner who forms the audit opinion, he above all needs to be satisfied that the audit work is being performed to an acceptable standard.

65. The guideline notes that management structures vary between firms of auditors. It is also true that audits vary in size and complexity: some will require a small audit team, while others will require considerable manpower resources. One factor is constant - there will always be a reporting partner.

66. Control procedures should therefore be designed and applied to ensure the following:

    (a) that work is allocated to audit staff who have appropriate training, experience and proficiency;
    (b) that audit staff of all levels clearly understand their responsibilities, the objective of the procedures which they are required to perform, and the channels of communication should any significant problems be encountered during the audit;
    (c) that working papers provide adequate evidence of the work that has been carried out; and
    (d) that the work performed by each member of the audit staff is reviewed by more senior persons in the audit firm to ensure that it was adequately performed and to enable a proper assessment to be made of the results of the work and the audit conclusions drawn therefrom.

67. During the final stages of an audit special care needs to be taken as pressures are greatest. Hence control is particularly important to ensure that mistakes and omissions do not occur. The use of an audit completion checklist, with sections to be filled in by the reporting partner and his staff, in particular the audit manager, helps to provide such control. The use of such a checklist is discussed further in chapter 13.

68. One further technique that aids control is consultation. Where matters of principle or contentious matters arise which may affect the audit opinion the partner should consider consulting another experienced accountant. Such an accountant may be a fellow partner or senior colleague, or another practitioner. If an independent practitioner is consulted, care must be taken to ensure confidentiality of the client's affairs.

69. Finally, it should be appreciated that the guideline is concerned only with control of specific audits. The closing line of the guideline states 'The auditor should also consider how the overall quality of the work carried out within the firm can best be monitored and maintained.' This is control in a broader sense ie quality control. This important aspect of control - which is the subject of a detailed operational guideline - is discussed in chapter 13.

Recording the audit

70. It is essential that *all* audit work is documented - the working papers are the *tangible* evidence of the work done in support of the audit opinion.

71. The guideline identifies the reasons for preparing audit working as follows.

    (a) The reporting partner needs to be able to satisfy himself that work delegated by him has been properly performed. The reporting partner can generally only do this by having available to him detailed working papers prepared by the audit staff who performed the work.

(b) Working papers provide for future reference, details of problems encountered, together with evidence of work performed and conclusions drawn therefrom in arriving at the audit opinion.

(c) The preparation of working papers encourages the auditor to adopt a methodical approach.

72. The exact form that working papers should take cannot be prescribed: each firm will have its own disciplines. Whatever form the papers take, however, they must achieve the main objectives set out above.

73. The guideline stresses that 'Audit working papers should always be sufficiently complete and detailed to enable an experienced auditor with no previous connection with the audit subsequently to ascertain from them what work was performed and to support the conclusions reached.' It also emphasises the special care needed to record difficult questions of principle or of judgement. The auditor should record all relevant information known to him at the time, the conclusions to be reached based on that information and the views of management.

74. Although the guideline does not attempt to define precisely the *form* of working papers it does indicate what might typically be contained therein as follows:

(a) information which will be of continuing importance to the audit (eg Memorandum and Articles of Association);

(b) audit planning information;

(c) the auditor's assessment of the enterprise's accounting system and, if appropriate, his review and evaluation of its internal controls;

(d) details of the audit work carried out, notes of errors or exceptions found and action taken thereon, together with the conclusions drawn by the audit staff who performed the various sections of the work;

(e) evidence that the work of the audit staff has been properly reviewed;

(f) records of relevant balances and other financial information, including analysis and summaries supporting the financial statements;

(g) a summary of significant points affecting the financial statements and the audit report, showing how these points were dealt with.

75. Working papers are conventionally subdivided into *current* and *permanent* files for convenience and control. The characteristic of current working papers is that they relate specifically to the audit of a particular set of accounts whereas permanent papers comprise matters of *continuing* importance affecting the client. Hence items (a) and (c) above are typically retained on the permanent file.

76. The guideline does not use the terms permanent and current working papers, but these terms do appear in UEC Statement 3 entitled 'The auditor's working papers'. This statement not only contains a more comprehensive list than above of typical working papers but also classifies them into permanent and current. This listing is reproduced here in full.

77. The *permanent audit file* might include, inter alia:

(a) a copy of the enterprise's statutes and other legal or statutory documents governing the enterprise's existence;

(b) other important legal documents and agreements;

(c) description of the business, its operations, together with the address of its locations. This section might also include details of specific matters relating to the industry or activity in which the enterprise is involved and which might affect the audit;

(d) an organisation chart showing the (top) management functions and the division of responsibilities;

(e) details of the system of accounting, including, where applicable, details of computer applications;

(f) an internal control questionnaire, memorandum or other means of assessing the adequacy of the internal control system, including those areas where information is processed by means of a computer;

(g) a letter of engagement defining the auditor's understanding of the work to be performed and his responsibilities, together with confirmation from the client that the letter sets out the position as the client also understands it;

(h) correspondence, or notes of discussions with the client on internal control matters;

(i) in the case of group companies details of all companies in the group including names and addresses of the auditors of the subsidiaries; this section might also contain a record of all information concerning other auditors on whose work reliance is placed for the purpose of the audit of group accounts;

(j) the principal accounting policies followed, key ratios, history of capital, profits and reserves;

(k) a reasoned description of the audit approach adopted;

(l) details of important matters arising from each audit, and a record of what decisions were taken and how they were arrived at.

78. The *current audit file* might include inter alia:

(a) a copy of the audited financial statements and any report prepared as a result of the audit work carried out;

(b) an annual audit programme detailing the audit steps to be taken and recording the audit steps carried out;

(c) details of the audit plan, including time budgets, staffing and statement of the scope and level of tests;

(d) schedules showing an analysis of the individual items in the financial statements, the notes thereto and the management's report; the schedules should also show comparative figures and state how the auditor has verified the existence, ownership and the amounts at which they are stated in the financial statements; there should also be evidence that the fairness of the presentation of items in the financial statements has been considered. These schedules should contain the auditor's conclusions, and should be cross-referenced to supporting schedules and external documentary evidence, as appropriate;

(e) notes of meetings and all correspondence relating to the audit, including all certificates and other third party audit confirmations;

(f) extracts from meetings of shareholders, management, directors and other relevant bodies;

(g) records of detailed audit tests carried out, the reasons for the timing and level of the tests, together with the conclusions drawn from those tests;

(h) the information received from the other auditors regarding the financial statements audited by them;

(i) records of queries raised by the auditors and how such queries have been dealt with;

(j) a letter or a statement from the management representing that they have supplied the auditors with all the information and explanations relevant to the audit and disclosed in the financial statements all matters required by statute and accounting standards;

(k) a review of post balance sheet date events up to the date of signing the audit report;

(l) names and initials of the audit staff.

Standardisation

79. The APC guideline states:

"The use of standardised working papers may improve the efficiency with which they are prepared and reviewed. Used properly they help to instruct audit staff and facilitate the delegation of work while providing a means to control its quality.

However, despite the advantages of standardising the routine documentation of the audit (eg checklists, specimen letters, standard organisation of the working papers) it is never appropriate to follow mechanically a 'standard' approach to the conduct and documentation of the audit without regard to the need to exercise professional judgement."

80. On balance, there should be a degree of standardisation of working papers and practically all firms recognise this need. Finally, it should be noted that working papers are the property of the auditor and he should adopt procedures to ensure their safe custody and confidentiality.

Summary

81. This chapter covers certain key audit areas that are favourites of the examiner:
    (a) legal, ethical and operational considerations on appointment;
    (b) the engagement letter;
    (c) planning the *new* audit;
    (d) planning the *established* audit;
    (e) permanent and current working papers;

More novel areas that may feature in forthcoming exams include:
(f) audit risk; and
(g) materiality.

TEST YOUR KNOWLEDGE
Numbers in brackets refer to paragraphs in this chapter

1. Summarise procedures that the potential new auditor of a limited company should take before accepting nomination. (2)

2. What is the purpose of an engagement letter? (4)

3. When should an engagement letter be sent? (6)

4. What are the principal contents of the engagement letter (in summary form only)? (21)

5. What is the nature of the background information with which the newly appointed auditor should concern himself to acquire sufficient knowledge of the business? (22)

6. When expressing an opinion on the accounts of a new client what relevance do the preceding period's financial statements have to the auditor? (24)

7. What additional procedures should be performed by the new auditor regarding the preceding period's financial statements? (28)

8. What is the purpose of audit planning? (32)

9. What preparatory procedures should the auditor carry out when planning his audit work? (33)

10. What is audit risk? (37)

11. What specific factors may indicate a higher than normal risk audit? (40)

12. Why does the concept of materiality affect the auditor? (44)

13. What are the three key elements of control in the context of planning, controlling and recording? (64)

14. What are the reasons for preparing audit working papers? (71)

15. Distinguish 'permanent' and 'current' working papers. (75)

SECTION 3: ILLUSTRATIVE QUESTIONS

1. An audit has five basic stages:
    (i)   planning;
    (ii)   reviewing systems of accounting and internal control;
    (iii)   obtaining audit evidence;
    (iv)   reviewing financial statements; and
    (v)   reporting findings.

    In the case of an audit where you have acted for a number of years, state briefly the work carried out at each of the above five stages.

    You are not required to draft an audit programme.

2. Mr J R Evans is the managing director of Removals Limited presently audited by Tickers, Certified Accountants. He has informed you that his Board of directors wishes to appoint your firm as auditors to the company in place of Tickers, but he considers that Tickers will not be willing to resign.

    You are required to write formally to Mr Evans, setting out the statutory and other procedures that will have to be adopted by both the company and your firm and which may be adopted by Tickers, in connection with your proposed appointment.

3. Your client, Adam plc owns and operates three large departmental stores in London, Birmingham and Manchester. Each store has more than 22 departments.

    You are at present preparing your audit plan and you are considering carrying out detailed audit tests on a rotational basis. You consider that all departments within the stores should be covered over a period of five years but that more frequent attention should be given to those where the 'audit risk' demands it.

    You are required to detail the factors which you would consider in order to evaluate the audit risk attaching to each department.

4. You have been invited to give a short presentation to some new students in your office on the subject of audit working papers.

    You are required to prepare your notes for this presentation setting out:

    (a)   the reasons for preparing working papers;
    (b)   the contents of working papers; and
    (c)   the criteria you would use to judge the quality of working papers.

SECTION 3: SUGGESTED SOLUTIONS

1. (a) Planning

    Audit work: the auditor must establish any critical areas to which particular attention will need to be paid. Experience gained from previous audits should help him to identify those parts of the audit which are likely to cause problems requiring professional judgement to resolve. To achieve this he will carry out:

    (i)   a review of the continuing relevance of matters raised during previous audits;

    (ii) a review of interim and management accounts;

    (iii) an assessment of the effects on the enterprise's financial statements of any changes in legislation or accounting practice;

    (iv) a review of the relevance of the work carried out by the internal auditors (if any);

    (v)   a review of any significant changes in the activities of the company or in key personnel.

    Timing: the auditor will need to prepare a time budget showing the dates of all the significant stages of the audit work. For example, it will be necessary to find out when the management want the accounts finalised, the locations and dates when stock counts will be taken etc. Arrangements will be made with the client for them to make available relevant summaries and analyses prepared by the client's staff.

    Staff: the partner or manager in charge of the audit must make sure that the proper numbers of suitably experienced staff are available at the times required. Furthermore, all staff must be properly briefed as to the nature of the client's business, and the scope of the audit work to be carried out.

    (b) Reviewing systems of accounting and internal control

    (i)   The accounting system (as recorded in the permanent file) should be reviewed and updated. Walk through tests should be carried out to ensure that the system functions as recorded. The auditor must form an opinion as to the adequacy of the accounting system as a basis for preparing the financial statements.

    (ii) If applicable the system of internal control (as recorded in the permanent file) should be reviewed (normally by means of an ICEQ) and updated. A programme of compliance tests should be carried out to ensure the proper functioning of all key controls. (Note the auditor will review the system of internal control only if he wishes to place reliance thereon as a basis for restricting the level of substantive tests.)

    (iii) Weaknesses in the systems of accounting and internal control should be reported to the client in a management letter. Desirably weaknesses should first be discussed with the client's staff. The management letter should identify the effect of each weakness and recommend *practical* improvements to the system to remedy the weaknesses.

(c) Obtaining audit evidence

(i) The review of the systems of accounting and internal control will form the basis of the nature and level of the substantive tests to be carried out. These are designed to provide evidence as to the completeness, accuracy and validity of the information contained in the accounting records or in the financial statements. In particular the tests will involve:
- verifying transactions for each major transaction cycle (sales, purchases etc)
- inspection procedures (reviewing or examining records, documents or tangible assets);
- observation (eg stocktake attendance);
- enquiry of persons inside or outside the business (particularly third party confirmations for debtors and banks);
- computation;
- checking financial statements to the accounting records.

(ii) Sufficient audit evidence must be obtained such that reasonable conclusions can be drawn therefrom.

(d) Reviewing financial statements

(i) Review of the accounting policies adopted by the enterprise to determine whether such policies:
- comply with statements of standard accounting practice or, in the absence thereof, are otherwise acceptable;
- are consistent with those of the previous period;
- are consistently applied throughout the enterprise;
- are disclosed in accordance with the requirements of SSAP 2 *Disclosure of accounting policies* and, if applicable, Companies Act 1985.

(ii) Review of the financial statements to ensure consistency with the auditor's knowledge of the underlying circumstances of the business. Analytical review techniques (including ratio analysis) would normally be appropriate.

(iii) Review of the financial statements in order to ensure compliance with the disclosure and other requirements of statute, statements of standard accounting practice and other applicable regulations.

(iv) Carrying out post balance sheet review up to the date of the audit report to ensure that post balance sheet events and contingencies have been properly accounted for and application of the going concern concept to the accounts is valid.

(e) Reporting findings

(i) To client
- Discussing systems weaknesses found during audit and report by means of second management letter.
- Discussing any matters which may lead to a qualification in the audit report and, if appropriate, discuss changes to the financial statements.
- Discussing proposed wording of audit report, ensuring that wording and format is in compliance with the Audit Report standard.
- Obtaining letter of representation from directors.

(ii) To members
- Checking final draft of financial statements and ensuring these incorporate agreed audit report. Submit to client.

SECTION 3: SUGGESTED SOLUTIONS

2. J R Evans Esq   30 Montpelier Road
    Managing Director   Acton
    Removals Limited   London W3A 1BX
    20 Commercial Road
    Bristol BS90 7PY   30 June 19X1

Dear Sir,

Proposed replacement of existing auditors

We thank you for your letter informing us that your Board of Directors wishes to appoint us as auditors to the company in place of Messrs Tickers. In this connection we set out below the various procedures that will have to be adopted by your company and by us, and also those which may be adopted by Messrs Tickers.

(a) *Powers of directors*

First, we must stress that only in the case of the first audit or of a casual vacancy can directors of a company appoint the auditors. In all other cases, power of appointment lies with the members of the company.

(b) *Statutory removal provisions*

It is not clear whether it is wished to appoint new auditors as soon as possible or wait until the next general meeting at which accounts will be laid before the members of the company.

Normally the term of the auditors' appointment runs from the date of the meeting at which the appointment is made until the completion of the next meeting at which audited accounts are presented for approval. At each such general meeting a specific ordinary resolution must be passed appointing auditors. This applies whether or not it is proposed to reappoint the existing auditors. However, the Companies Act 1985 also provides that auditors may be removed *before* the expiry of their term of office, notwithstanding any agreement between the auditors and the company. This can be done by means of an ordinary resolution (of which special notice of 28 days has been given) passed at any general meeting of the company. Notification of any resolution to remove the auditors must be given to the Registrar of Companies within fourteen days of the passing of it.

(c) *The statutory rights of the existing auditors*

(i) *Removal*

Whether it is intended to remove the present auditors at the expiry of their term of office or at a general meeting convened before that time, the auditors have the right to receive notice of the relevant resolutions and to make written representations to the company in which they can set out any matters which they feel to be relevant to the proposal to remove them. Unless received too late, copies of the representations must be sent to every member to whom notice of the meeting is sent. If a copy is not sent to all members, the auditors may request that the representations should be read out at the general meeting. There is one proviso to this right of making written representations in so far as application may be made to the Court for the representations neither to be circulated to, nor read out at the meeting, if in the view of the company the right to make representations is being abused to secure needless publicity for defamatory matter.

It must be stressed that the right to make written representations is in addition to the auditors' normal right under the Companies Act 1985 to be heard at any general meeting which he attends on any part of the business which concerns him as auditor.

If it is proposed to seek the removal of the auditors before the expiry of their term of office by convening a general meeting for the purpose, then they have the right to receive all notices and other communications which a member is entitled to receive relating to such meetings and to attend and speak not only at that meeting but also at the general meeting at which their appointment would normally have expired.

(ii) *Resignation*

You have indicated that, in your opinion, Messrs Tickers will not be willing to resign. However, the Companies Act 1985 does contain special provisions relating to circumstances in which auditors decide that their position is untenable. The auditors may resign office at a date of their own choosing by depositing a notice to that effect at the registered office of the company. This notice must include a statement of any circumstances which the auditors consider should be brought to the attention of members or creditors or a statement to the effect that no such circumstances exist. In cases where the notice does contain details of circumstances to be brought to the company's attention the auditors may require the Directors to convene an extraordinary general meeting at which the circumstances can be discussed. The auditors have the same rights of making written representations, and of attending and speaking at such a meeting, as have been outlined above.

(d) *Ethical considerations*

There are strict rules which must be observed by members of the accountancy profession when a change of auditors is being proposed. These are a matter of professional ethics, and are quite separate from the statutory provisions outlined in (a) to (c) above. We should require the consent of your Board to communicate with Messrs Tickers and to request from them all information which we consider necessary before we could decide whether or not to allow our name to go forward for nomination as auditors.

(e) *Purpose of the procedures*

You will appreciate that all the procedures which we have outlined above - cumbersome though they may seem to be - are designed to protect the interests of shareholders. It is vital that the auditors holding office should be in an independent position, and that they are protected from the possibility of being removed without the assent of members, or with the assent of members but without those members being aware of all the relevant circumstances.

We shall be grateful if, in due course and in the light of the contents of this letter, you will let us know how you wish to proceed.

Yours faithfully,

Arthur Daley & Co
Certified Accountants.

SECTION 3: SUGGESTED SOLUTIONS

3. Risk may be evaluated by considering:
    - the probability of an event
    - the potential size of the event

In the case of an audit the event concerned is material error or fraud.

In evaluating risk in the context of the audit of a company owning and operating three large department stores the factors to be considered are:

(a) *Factors influencing probability*

    (i) Strengths and weaknesses in system of internal control, overall and for each individual store and department in the following respects:

Organisation of staff
- definition of responsibilities
- plan of organisation in each department
- decision-making
- communication, both within and between departments
- numbers in each department

Segregation of duties
- avoidance of one person being able to combine
    - authorisation
    - execution
    - custody
    - recording
- must be part of routine system
- work of one person should be independent of, yet complementary to, work of another

Physical controls
- custody of assets themselves
- custody of records relating to them
- the more valuable, the more important
- importance of an inventory, especially of stock in a retail store

Authorisation and approval
- applicable to all transactions
- clearly-defined limits of responsibility
- lists of specimen signatures, kept up to date

Arithmetic and accounting
- checks within the recording functions itself that all transactions are included
- correctly recorded
- properly authorised
- accurately processed

Personnel
- are staff capable of fulfilling their responsibilities?
- adequate safeguards in recruitment and training
- effect of personalities

Supervision
- day-to-day supervision by responsible officials of regular transactions and their recording ensures that
    - impression is given of management's concern
    - staff are kept on their toes
    - particularly important *within* retail departments

Management
- controls outside routine
- comparison of results with budgets and previous years
- noticing and acting upon exceptions and variances

(ii) Existence or otherwise of effective internal audit, and consideration of internal audit reports where they exist.

(iii) Experience derived from previous audits

(iv) Whether the prices of goods sold are fixed by head office or variable by local store or departmental managers

(v) Extent of local purchasing for each store or department

(vi) The nature of the stock (eg high unit value, attractiveness)

(vii) Effectiveness of cash-handling systems.

(b) *Factors influencing size*

(i) Relative size of department in terms of:
- turnover
- number of transactions
- average value of stock

(ii) Internal statistics of losses through shoplifting and staff pilferage.

(c) *Other general factors*

(i) Comparison among stores and among like departments in the three stores, using ratio analysis

(ii) Risk of deterioration or obsolescence of stocks

(iii) Rate of turnover of store staff.

4 Notes for presentation to new students on their introductory course

(a) Reasons for preparing working papers

The main reasons for preparing audit working papers include the following:

(i) The reporting partner needs to be able to satisfy himself that work delegated by him has been properly performed. The reporting partner can generally only do this by having available to him detailed working papers prepared by the audit staff who performed the work.

(ii) Working papers provide, for future reference, details of problems encountered, together with evidence of work performed and conclusions drawn therefrom in arriving at the audit opinion.

(iii) The preparation of working papers encourages the auditor to adopt a methodical approach.

The Auditing Guideline 'Planning, controlling, and recording' stresses that "Audit working papers should always be sufficiently complete and detailed to enable an experienced auditor with no previous connection with the audit subsequently to ascertain from them what work was performed and to support the conclusions reached."

(b) Contents of working papers

(i) General considerations:
- Timing
  Audit working papers should be prepared as the audit progresses. This will ensure that the contents are sufficiently complete and detailed to assist a review of the progress of the audit at any time by a senior member of staff, or the reporting partner.
- Standardisation of working papers
  Many firms of accountants use standardised working papers. Whilst it is recognised that some standardisation can improve the efficiency of preparation and review of the working papers and is advantageous for routine documentation (eg. check lists,

specimen letters, standard organisation for working papers), it must be remembered that each audit is different and that the mechanical adoption of a 'standard' approach is no substitute for professional judgement.

(ii) Classification

It is usual for the audit working papers to be divided into:
- a *current* file prepared for each annual audit and containing information relating primarily to the particular audit.
- a *permanent* file containing information of continuing importance.

Examples of the contents of each file are set out below:

Current file:
- copy of the accounts, signed by the directors;
- index to all working papers;
- details of the audit plan;
- audit programme particulars and dates of work carried out and precise details of audit tests, their results and conclusions drawn;
- schedules supporting each item in the balance sheet; showing make-up and how existence etc, has been verified, suitably cross-referenced to documents arising from external verification;
- as above for all items in profit and loss account;
- check list for compliance with statutory disclosure requirements and SSAPs;
- record of queries raised and the way in which they were resolved;
- schedule of important statistics and working ratios together with explanations received of any significant variations (analytical review);
- records or extracts of directors' and shareholders' minutes, cross-referenced where appropriate to working papers;
- copy of management letter(s) and client's response;
- letter of representation;
- matters which, though not of permanent importance, will require attention during subsequent periods.

Permanent file:
- copy of the engagement letter, whether a statutory or non-statutory audit;
- Memorandum and Articles of Association;
- copies of minutes and other documents;
- short description of business and places of business;
- lists of accounting records and responsible officials and plan of organisation (constantly updated);
- statements showing a note of any accounting matters of importance and bases of accounting adopted;
- clients internal accounting instructions (including where appropriate, stocktaking);
- systems notes, flowcharts and internal control questionnaires.

(c) Criteria used to judge the quality of working papers

The working papers must support the audit opinion. The following criteria would be applied to measure the quality of the working papers:

Structures of files

A methodical and consistent structure is an essential requirement for the organisation of each client's working papers. The schedules appropriate to each section of the files should be indexed and cross-referenced in accordance with the standard method employed.

Where a standard format is instituted for the presentation of schedules commonly used, these should be examined to ensure consistency in layout (preprinted forms are designed to assist members of staff in this respect and should be used where appropriate).

Working paper discipline
Whatever the detailed content and purpose of a working paper, certain basic information must be shown. This information is:
- the name of the client
- the balance sheet date
- the reference of the working paper
- the name (initials) of the auditor preparing the working paper
- the date of preparation
- the subject, purpose or content of the working paper
- the name (initials) of the person reviewing the working paper and
- the date of review.

In addition the following must be indicated:
- the source of the information included in the working paper (e.g. figures from the nominal ledger, from the payroll journal for a particular month, or information from a particular month, or information from a particular member of the client's staff), if this is not otherwise apparent;
- the nature of the balance or amount dealt with in the working paper, if this is not otherwise apparent;
- the scope of the audit tests which are recorded on the working paper;
- a legend describing the audit tick marks used, or an explanation of the audit procedures carried out (if this is not evident from the audit programme itself);

Completeness
The schedules should be scrutinised to ensure that:
- all relevant and material facts and their source are shown in respect of information and evidence obtained in the audit;
- the nature, extent and timing of the audit procedures undertaken by the members of staff is shown;
- summaries of evidence are shown and where this is not readily apparent from the information, notes etc, the basis for arriving at the conclusion is set out clearly.

SECTION 4

AUDIT PROCEDURES

Chapter 8

ACCOUNTING SYSTEMS AND INTERNAL CONTROLS

Topics covered in this chapter:

- The requirements of an accounting system
- Ascertaining, recording and confirming an accounting system
- Internal controls
- Reliance on internal audit
- The management letter

Introduction

1. As part of his audit planning, in particular in determining the nature and timing of his audit tests, the auditor needs to consider the effectiveness of the accounting system in providing a timely and methodical capture of accounting information and the adequacy of the accounting records from which the accounts are prepared. The auditor will hence retain a record of the accounting system in order to:

    (a) provide evidence of the system upon which the subsequent audit tests were based; and
    (b) act as a base for the planning of future audits.

2. Paragraph 3 of the Operational Standard states:

    "The auditor should ascertain the enterprise's system of recording and processing transactions and assess its adequacy as a basis for the preparation of financial statements".

    Paragraph 3 applies *irrespective of whether the auditor seeks to rely on internal controls*. Hence stages 2-5 of our audit diagram are mandatory. In the case of a limited company audit, the auditor has a concurrent but distinct responsibility to form an opinion as to whether proper accounting records have been kept in compliance with the Companies Act 1985. We look at the nature of an accounting system and the techniques for ascertaining, recording and confirming in this chapter.

3. Depending on the size and nature of a business, the accounting system will frequently need to incorporate internal controls. The evaluation of internal controls is dealt with in the separate guideline 'Internal controls', but in practice the auditor carries out his work of recording and evaluating controls in unison with his assessment of the accounting system. We examine the nature of internal controls, their significance to management and the auditor, and the auditor's evaluation techniques.

4. Two particular aspects of internal controls and the auditor are the subject of detailed operational guidelines - the external auditor's reliance on the internal audit function and the technique of the management letter. These guidelines are discussed in the final sections of this chapter.

The requirements of an accounting system

5. Before any audit tests can be designed and performed, it is necessary to understand the accounting records kept and the manner in which transactions are processed through the accounting system. As mentioned, this is necessary whether or not internal controls are likely to be relied on.

6. The management of a company require complete and accurate accounting and other records to assist it in:

   (a) controlling the business;
   (b) safeguarding the assets;
   (c) preparing financial statements; and
   (d) complying with statutory requirements.

7. Clearly accounting systems vary enormously in their sophistication. To quote from the guideline 'Accounting systems':

   "What constitutes an adequate accounting system will depend on the size, nature and complexity of the enterprise. In its simplest form for a small business dealing primarily with cash sales and with only a few suppliers the accounting system may only need to consist of an analysed cash book and a list of unpaid invoices. In contrast, a company manufacturing several different products and operating through a number of dispersed locations may need a complex accounting system to enable information required for financial statements to be assembled."

8. Many accounting systems are of course computerised. This does not alter the audit principles and approach. It may mean, however, that specialist assistance is required to record and assess the system - this is a requirement that should be identified at the initial planning stage of the audit.

9. It is important to appreciate that an accounting system embraces not merely the recording function but all the stages leading up to recording for each transaction stream. Unless the source documents of all authentic transactions are completely and accurately captured and recorded for processing, the account balance to which the transaction stream is posted is unlikely to be materially correct. By way of illustration let us look at the purchases cycle (we

will assume that the purchases are of goods not services). When ascertaining the purchases accounting system the auditor will typically need to concern himself with the following functions, departments and documents:

Function	Department	Document raised internally (I) or received from outside (O)
Initiation	Warehouse	Requisition (I)
Authorisation/ execution	Buying or ordering	Purchase order (I)
Custody	Goods inwards	Goods inwards or received note -GIN or GRN (I) Delivery note (O)
Invoice approval	Purchase ledger	Purchase invoice (O)
Recording	Computer/accounting machine etc (accounting records)	Purchase invoice in form suitable for posting (I or O)
Cash settlement	Cashier	Cheque/giro (I) Remittance advice (I) Statement (O)

10. This is just a brief summary of some of the documents involved and of the departments through which they pass; it is how such documents flow, and are controlled, that will determine whether the records completely and accurately record purchases and trade creditors. What it does demonstrate is that the auditor when ascertaining a system will need to determine the flow of documents within and between the appropriate departments for all the transaction streams, from initiation through to recording. The term 'from cradle to grave' is sometimes used to describe the life cycle of a transaction.

Accounting records: statutory requirements

11. The responsibility for installing and maintaining a satisfactory accounting system rests, of course, with the directors. Four objectives have been defined in paragraph 6 emphasising why management require an accurate system. We must now look at objective (d) a little more closely for it directly affects the auditor as well as the directors.

12. All companies are required to keep proper accounting records and moreover the auditor must form an opinion as to whether proper records have been kept. These provisions were introduced by the 1967 Companies Act but it was not until the 1976 Act that legislation attempted to define what these records should comprise. The regulations are now contained in sections 221 and 222 Companies Act 1985. These sections are reproduced in part below and must be borne in mind when considering the auditor's procedures necessary to satisfy his statutory obligations (S237 (1)(a) CA 1985):

> "221 (1) Every company shall cause accounting records to be kept in accordance with this section.

(2) The accounting records shall be sufficient to show and explain the company's transactions and shall be such as to:
(a) disclose with reasonable accuracy, at any time, the financial position of the company at that time; and
(b) enable the directors to ensure that any balance sheet and profit and loss account prepared under this Part comply with the requirements of this Act as to the form and content of company accounts and otherwise.

(3) The accounting records shall in particular contain:
(a) entries from day to day of all sums of money received and expended by the company, and the matters in respect of which the receipt and expenditure takes place; and
(b) a record of the assets and liabilities of the company.

(4) If the company's business involves dealing in goods, the accounting records shall contain:
(a) statements of stock held by the company at the end of each financial year of the company;
(b) all statements of stocktakings from which any such statement of stock as is mentioned in paragraph (a) has been or is to be prepared; and
(c) except in the case of goods sold by way of ordinary retail trade, statements of all goods sold and purchased, showing the goods and the buyers and sellers in sufficient detail to enable all these to be identified.

222 (1) A company's accounting records shall be kept at its registered office or such other place as the directors think fit, and shall at all times be open to inspection by the company's officers.

13. Where a company holds stocks that are material in value the requirements of section 221 (4) are clearly important. We shall return to this sub-section in chapter 10 when we investigate the balance sheet audit of stock in detail.

14. Officers of a company are liable to imprisonment or a fine (or both) if found guilty of failing to comply with sections 221, 222 (1), (2) or (4).

15. Although sections 221 and 222 are extremely important in that they impose a modicum of accounting discipline on all companies, there is no requirement here – or indeed elsewhere in the Companies Act 1985 – for a company to implement internal controls.

16. Some other enterprises, such as building societies, *are* required by statute to supplement their accounting systems in certain respects with controls. Many commentators argue that it is high time that corporate legislation imposed similar disciplines on certain classes, or a certain size, of company, if not all companies.

17. The Operational Standard requires the auditor to ascertain and record a client's accounting system, and such a system may be very simple or highly complex. We will now identify and compare the techniques that the auditor may employ to record the system.

Ascertaining, recording and confirming an accounting system

18. To set the scene we can return to the guideline 'Accounting systems'. Under the heading 'procedures' paragraphs 8 and 9 read as follows:

> "The auditor will need to obtain an understanding of the enterprise as a whole and how the accounting system reflects assets and liabilities and transactions.
>
> The auditor will need to ascertain and record the accounting system in order to assess its adequacy as a basis for the preparation of financial statements. The extent to which the auditor should record the enterprise's accounting system and the method used will depend on the complexity and nature of the system and on the degree of reliance he plans to place on internal controls. Where the auditor plans to rely on internal controls, the accounting system needs to be recorded in considerable detail so as to facilitate the evaluation of the controls and the preparation of a programme of compliance and substantive tests. The record may take the form of narrative notes, flowcharts or checklists or a combination of them."

19. The final sentence above identifies the three principal recording techniques:
    (a)   narrative notes;
    (b)   flowcharts;
    (c)   checklists (ie internal control questionnaires).

20. In practice it is (a) and (b) above that are the favoured methods; the internal control questionnaire's (ICQ's) main purpose is to evaluate a system *not* to describe it. We will hence encounter the ICQ later as part of our review of internal controls and the auditor. Occasionally, however, it may be found that in answering the questions in an ICQ the auditor will discover more detail about the system than is already recorded in the flowcharts and/or narrative notes, and this will hence help him in ascertaining and recording the system.

21. Flowcharts are the best way of recording any system which involves the movement of documents from one person to another. They are *vital* when the auditor wishes to rely on any controls in the system. Narrative notes are preferable for very simple systems where all the paperwork is handled by only one or two people - they are also helpful to amplify particular procedures on flowcharts. Really complex systems may only be adequately documented by a combination of all three techniques in paragraph 19.

22. Whatever method of recording the system is used, the record will be retained on the *permanent* file. With established clients, it is of course only necessary for the auditor to update the records on the permanent file year by year. For a new client, or a client whose systems have changed substantially, the auditor will be required to set up a comprehensive record from scratch. Occasionally, clients may have their own in-house procedural manuals - in such circumstances the auditor may be able to save time by obtaining copies of these manuals. Care must be taken however to ensure that such manuals achieve the *auditor's* objective; often clients use them more as a means of instructing their staff in a particular area rather than to give a complete description of the system. Let us now examine the techniques of narrative notes and flowcharts in more detail.

Narrative notes

23. Narrative notes have the advantage of being simple to record but are awkward to change. The purpose of the notes is to describe and explain the system, at the same time making any comments or criticisms which will help to demonstrate an intelligent understanding of the system. For each system they need to deal with the following questions:

    (a) what functions are performed and by whom?
    (b) what documents are used?
    (c) where do the documents originate and what is their destination?
    (d) what sequence are retained documents filed in?
    (e) what books are kept and where?

24. Narrative notes can be used to support flow charts. They can effectively explain error procedures or uncomplicated alternatives to standard procedures and may also be used to provide additional information on operations or checks.

Flowcharts

25. There are two methods of flowcharting in regular use:
    (a) document flowcharts; and
    (b) information flowcharts.

26. Document flowcharts are more commonly used because they are relatively easy to prepare. *All* documents are followed through from 'cradle to grave' and *all* operations and controls are shown.

27. Information flowcharts are prepared in the reverse direction from the flow – they start with the entry in the general/nominal ledger and work back to the actual transaction. They concentrate on significant information flows and ignore any unimportant documents or copies of documents. They are subsequently more compact than document flowcharts and are intended to highlight key controls. They are easy to understand but require skill and experience to compile them. We shall concentrate on document flowcharts in the remainder of this chapter.

28. The golden rules of flowcharting are as follows.

    (a) A flowchart should only be used when the system being reviewed cannot be readily understood in words. The purpose of a flowchart is to help the understanding of a complex system, but the price is that the complexity of the system is replaced by using a 'foreign' diagrammatic language in preference to English. It follows that where a system is readily understood in English, it need not be charted.

    (b) Flowcharts should be kept simple, so that the overall structure or flow is clear at first sight. In keeping a flowchart simple the following points should be noted:

        (i) there must be absolute conformity of symbols, with each symbol representing one and only one thing;

    (ii)   the direction of the flowchart should be from top to bottom and from left to right. There must be no loose ends and the main flow should finish at the bottom right hand corner, not in the middle of the page;

    (iii) connecting lines should cross only where absolutely necessary to preserve the chart's simplicity.

29. The major advantages of using flowcharts include:

    (a)   after a little experience they can be prepared quickly. It is often found that an auditor can draw a draft chart as the client describes the system;

    (b)   as the information is presented in a standard form, they are fairly easy to follow and to review;

    (c)   they generally ensure that the system is recorded in its entirety, as all document flows have to be traced from beginning to end and any 'loose ends' will be apparent from a cursory examination;

    (d)   they eliminate the need for *extensive* narrative and can be of considerable help in highlighting the salient points of control and any weaknesses in the system.

Their major disadvantages are that:

    (a)   they are only really suitable for describing standard systems. Procedures for dealing with unusual transactions will normally have to be recorded using narrative notes;

    (b)   they are useful for recording the flow of documents, but once the records or the assets to which they relate have become static they can no longer be used for describing the controls (eg over fixed assets);

    (c)   *major* amendment is difficult without redrawing;

    (d)   time can be wasted by charting areas that are of no audit significance (a criticism of *document* not *information* flowcharts).

30. It is possible that an examination question may require interpretation and evaluation of a document flowchart. It is unlikely in the *auditing* paper that *production* of a flowchart will be required. However, it is futile to try to understand and review a flowchart without an appreciation of the drafting techniques. The following notes are intended to (re)familiarise students with basic flowcharting conventions for manual systems.

31. Basic symbols will be used for the charting of all systems, but where the client's system involves mechanised or computerised processing, then further symbols may be required to supplement the basic ones. The basic symbols used are shown overleaf:

Document (eg purchase order)

3-part document

Document sequentially numbered

Account book or ledger

File - letter in centre denotes
arrangement of file

A	=	alphabetical order
N	=	numerical order
D	=	date order
T	=	temporary
TA	=	temporary alphabetical etc.

An operation (but not a check),
whether manual or automated.
A narrative description of the
operation will always be necessary.

A check function

A connector - number in centre
refers to the continuation
(eg. page 3)

$\longrightarrow$ Document flow

$- - - - \rightarrow$ Information flow

32. *Preparation of a basic flowchart*
    (a) *Document flow*
        The document flow is basically from top to bottom of the chart, the basic symbols being used to represent the various operations applied to a document during the processing cycle. Those symbols showing the sequence of operations taking place within the one department are joined by a vertical line as illustrated in the figure below.

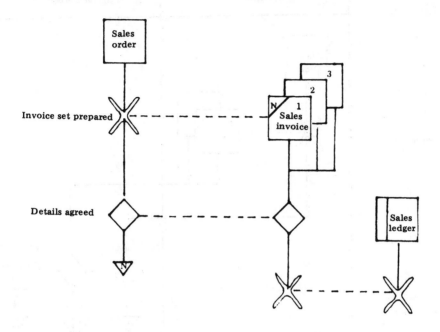

    (b) *Information flow*
        During the course of the processing cycle it will often be found that information is transferred from one document to another. This would occur as in the situation illustrated in the figure above, where a sales invoice set is produced using information obtained from a sales order. Such information flow may also arise where a document is used to update a book of account, the document being used as the posting media, or where the content of two documents is being compared. These latter two situations are also demonstrated in the figure above and you will observe that, in all cases, information flow is represented by a broken horizontal line.

        Note: it is possible to trace the processing history of any document individually, simply by following down the appropriate vertical line and reading the processing steps which occur.

    (c) *Division of duties*
        One of the key features of any good system of internal control is that there should be a system of 'internal check'. Internal check is the requirement for a division of duties amongst the available staff so that one person's work is independently reviewed by another, no one person having complete responsibility for all aspects of a transaction.

        Since the main purpose of a flow chart is to record the controls operating within a company's system, it would clearly be advantageous if the structure of the chart itself could indicate the division of duties. With this method of flow charting this is achieved by dividing the chart into vertical columns. In a smaller enterprise there would be one column to show the duties of each individual, whereas in a large company the vertical columns would show the division of duties amongst the various departments.

The figure below shows, in a small company, the division of duties between Mr Corbett and Mr Barker.

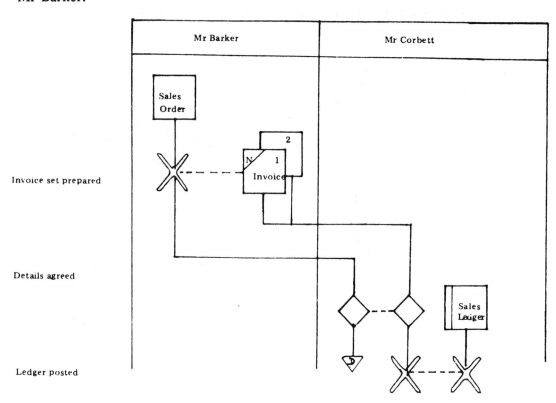

(d) *Sequence and description of operations*

To facilitate ease of reference each operation shown on the chart is numbered in sequence on the chart, a separate column being used for this purpose, as shown below. Note carefully that the operation number is set on the same horizontal plane as the symbols representing the process being described and that every operation, including check functions and filing must be given a number. It is essential that care is taken when drawing the chart to ensure that no two unconnected operations appear on the same horizontal plane.

Finally, the chart will be completed by the inclusion of a narrative column which will describe significant operations. Narrative should be kept to a minimum and only included where in fact it is required, for example filing of documents would frequently not need any narrative.

NB: where the chart indicates a check function, some narrative will always be required.

(e) *Chart organisation*

Any flowchart will basically comprise the symbols described but a critical factor in good flowcharting is chart organisation. The following may provide some useful hints:

(i) On the whole you should aim to chart the flow of documents etc from top left down, in stages, towards bottom right. Reversal of flow from right to left may be necessary at times. However, if reverse flow occurs too frequently the chart will be that much more difficult to read.

(ii) Don't use diagonal lines: all document flow lines should be either horizontal or vertical. There is a convention that a vertical document flow line represents a 'movement in time', whereas a horizontal document line represents a 'movement in space'.

(iii) Where an intersection of flow lines on the chart is unavoidable, there being no intention to suggest a merge. The continual direction of flow is most clearly shown by having a 'bridge' on the crossing line.

(iv) Don't try to get too much detail onto one chart. It is much better to split a system into logical sections, and then chart each section separately. Where several charts are used each chart should be given an identifying number. Continuation between charts is achieved by use of the connector symbol.

(v) Make sure that the flow line showing the life of a document is complete eg don't end a document flow line in a temporary file or at an operation symbol, unless of course the operation involves sending the document out of the business, as where an invoice copy is mailed to a customer.

(vi) Use the technique of 'ghosting' where it is necessary to show a document symbol a second time at some later stage in the chart. This will arise where a document has been carried forward to another chart, or when it is eventually necessary to split up a document set which has previously been processed as though it were a single document (below).

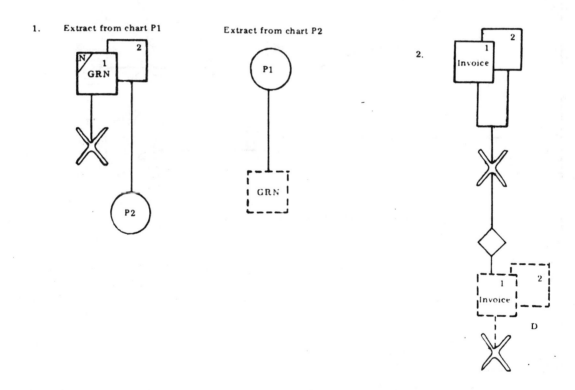

33. On the following pages you will find two charts which illustrate typical procedures in a company's purchasing system:
(a) ordering and receiving of goods;
(b) approval of invoices.

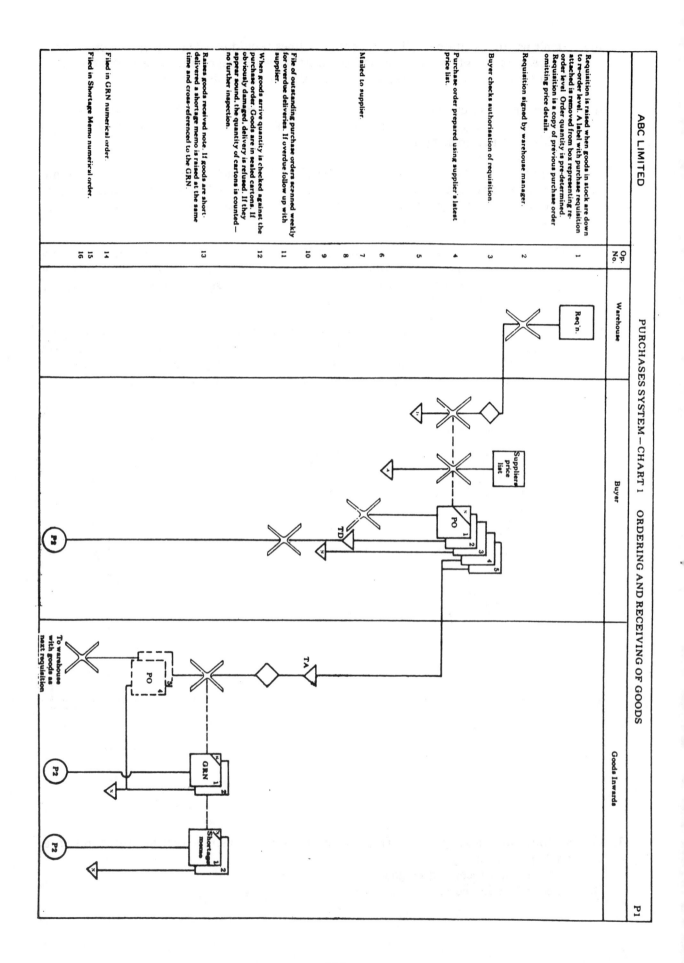

ABC LIMITED — PURCHASES SYSTEM—CHART 1 — ORDERING AND RECEIVING OF GOODS — P1

Op. No.		Warehouse	Buyer	Goods Inwards

1. Requisition is raised when goods in stock are down to re-order level. A label with purchase requisition attached is removed from box representing re-order level. Order quantity is pre-determined. Requisition is a copy of previous purchase order omitting price details.

2. Requisition signed by warehouse manager.

3. Buyer checks authorisation of requisition.

4. Purchase order prepared using supplier's latest price list.

7. Mailed to supplier.

11. File of outstanding purchase orders scanned weekly for overdue deliveries. If overdue follow up with supplier.

12. When goods arrive quantity is checked against the purchase order. Goods are in sealed cartons. If obviously damaged, delivery is refused. If they appear sound, the quantity of cartons is counted — no further inspection.

13. Raises goods received note. If goods are short-delivered a shortage memo is raised at the same time and cross-referenced to the GRN.

14. Filed in GRN numerical order.

15. Filed in GRN numerical order.

16. Filed in Shortage Memo numerical order.

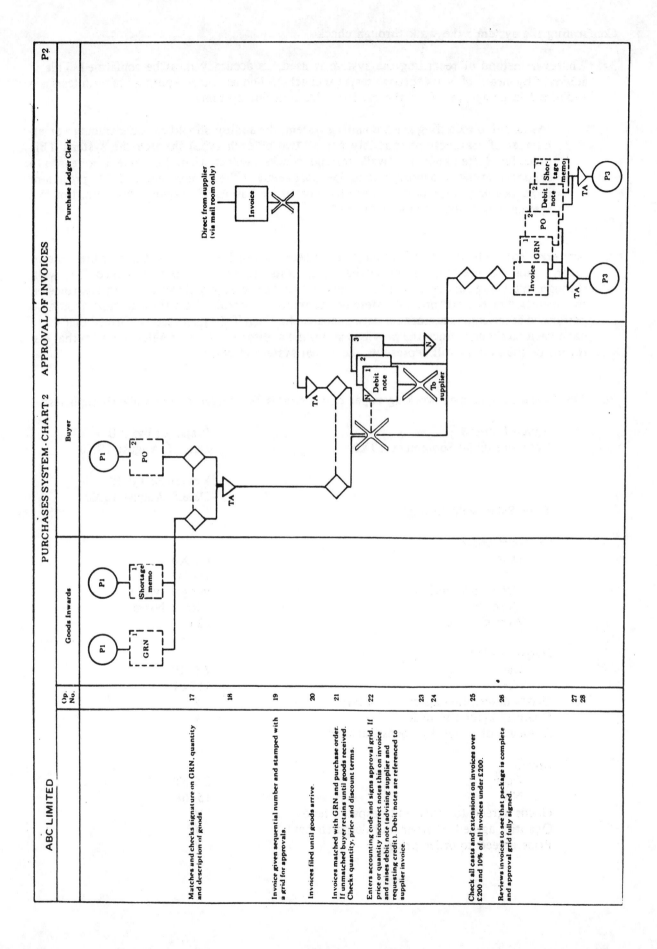

ABC LIMITED

PURCHASES SYSTEM - CHART 2   APPROVAL OF INVOICES

Op. No.	Description
17	Matches and checks signature on GRN, quantity and description of goods
18	Invoice given sequential number and stamped with a grid for approvals.
19	Invoices filed until goods arrive.
20	
21	Invoices matched with GRN and purchase order. If unmatched buyer retains until goods received. Checks quantity, price and discount terms.
22	Enters accounting code and signs approval grid. If price or quantity incorrect notes this on invoice and raises debit note (advising supplier and requesting credit). Debit notes are referenced to supplier invoice.
23	
24	
25	Check all casts and extensions on invoices over £200 and 10% of all invoices under £200.
26	
27	Reviews invoices to see that package is complete and approval grid fully signed.
28	

Confirming the system : the walk through check

34. Whatever method of recording the system is used, its accuracy must be confirmed. This is achieved by means of 'walk through tests (or checks).' The nature and purpose of such tests are explained in paragraph 10 of the guideline 'Accounting systems'.

> "As an aid to recording the accounting system, the auditor should consider tracing a small number of transactions (possibly one or two of each type) through the system. This procedure (often known as 'walk-through checks') will confirm that there is no reason to suppose that the accounting system does not operate in the manner recorded. The procedure is particularly appropriate where the enterprise has itself prepared the record of the system which the auditor is to use."

35. Any error may indicate that the system has not been recorded correctly, and clearly the systems records must be amended *before* detailed audit tests are designed and conducted. The walk through test, being confined to so few items, does not provide any significant audit reliance on the operation of the accounting system or the internal controls. Walk through tests should be performed at the commencement of each annual audit. Even if the client has confirmed that there have been no changes since the previous audit, the auditor must nevertheless confirm that *his* record of the system still represents the actual system in operation.

36. The following specimen working paper demonstrates the nature of the walk through test:

Anyco Limited	Prepared by: AB
Year ended: 30 September 19X0	Date: 1 August 19X0
	Reviewed by: BC
	Date:8 August 19X0

Title: Sales walk through test

Customer order

Date:	4.6.X0
No:	16450
Goods description:	widget type 6
Quantity:	600 (2 boxes)
Agreed price:	£25

Despatch note

Date:	7.6.X0
No:	15943
Goods description agreed to order	√
Quantity agreed to order	√
Evidence of check by goods outwards	√

Invoice

Date:	8.6.X0
No:	15468
Goods agreed to order and despatch note	√
Quantity agreed to order and despatch note	√
Price agreed to order price	√

Posting
Invoice correctly entered in:
sales day book ✓
sales ledger ✓
Conclusion: The credit sales system is correctly
recorded on our flowchart

Internal controls

37. All companies should have a satisfactory accounting system and, as regards accounting records, must comply with the requirements of the Companies Act 1985. Returning briefly to the guideline 'Accounting systems' paragraph 6 reads as follows:

     "Depending upon the size and nature of the business concerned an accounting system will frequently need to incorporate internal controls to provide assurance that:

     (a) all the transactions and other accounting information which should be recorded have in fact been recorded;
     (b) errors or irregularities in processing accounting information will become apparent;
     (c) assets and liabilities recorded in the accounting system exist and are recorded at the correct amounts."

38. The purpose of internal controls is clear from the above paragraph. They supplement the accounting system, providing management with greater assurance regarding the integrity of the accounting environment. We can now turn to the guideline 'Internal controls' which in its initial paragraphs emphasises management's responsibility for internal control.

39. First, an internal control system is defined as being:

     '...the whole system of controls, financial and otherwise, established by the management in order to carry on the business of the enterprise in an orderly and efficient manner, ensure adherence to management policies, safeguard the assets and secure as far as possible the completeness and accuracy of the records. The individual components of an internal control system are known as 'controls' or 'internal controls'.

40. Second, management's responsibility is defined in the following terms:

     "It is a responsibility of management to decide the extent of the internal control system which is appropriate to the enterprise. The nature and extent of controls will vary between enterprises and also from one part of an enterprise to another. The controls used will depend on the nature, size and volume of the transactions, the degree of control which members of management are able to exercise personally, the geographical distribution of the enterprise and many other factors. The choice of controls may reflect a comparison of the cost of operating individual controls against the benefits expected to be derived from them.

     The operating procedures and methods of recording and processing transactions used by small enterprises often differ significantly from those of large enterprises. Many of the internal controls which would be relevant to the larger enterprise are not practical, appropriate or necessary in the small enterprise. Managements of small enterprises have less need to depend on formal internal controls for the reliability of the records and other information, because of their personal contact with, or involvement in, the operation of enterprise staff."

41. An appendix to the guideline describes the main types of internal controls which may be found.

TYPES OF INTERNAL CONTROLS

"The following is a description of some of the types of controls which the auditor may find in many enterprises and on some or a combination of which he may seek to place some degree of reliance.

1. *Organisation.* Enterprises should have a plan of their organisation, defining and allocating responsibilities and identifying lines of reporting for all aspects of the enterprise's operations, including the controls. The delegation of authority and responsibility should be clearly specified.

2. *Segregation of duties.* One of the prime means of control is the separation of those responsibilities or duties which would, if combined, enable one individual to record and process a complete transaction. Segregation of duties reduces the risk of intentional manipulation or error and increases the element of checking. Functions which should be separated include those of authorisation, execution, custody, recording and, in the case of a computer-based accounting system, systems development and daily operations.

3. *Physical.* These are concerned mainly with the custody of assets and involve procedures and security measures designed to ensure that access to assets is limited to authorised personnel. This includes both direct access and indirect access via documentation. These controls assume importance in the case of valuable, portable, exchangeable or desirable assets.

4. *Authorisation and approval.* All transactions should require authorisation or approval by an appropriate responsible person. The limits, for these authorisations should be specified.

5. *Arithmetical and accounting.* These are the controls within the recording function which check that the transactions to be recorded and processed have been authorised, that they are all included and that they are correctly recorded and accurately processed. Such controls include checking the arithmetical accuracy of the records, the maintenance and checking of totals, reconciliations, control accounts and trial balances, and accounting for documents.

6. *Personnel.* There should be procedures to ensure that personnel have capabilities commensurate with their responsibilities. Inevitably, the proper functioning of any system depends on the competence and integrity of those operating it. The qualifications, selection and training as well as the innate personal characteristics of the personnel involved are important features to be considered in setting up any control system.

7. *Supervision.* Any system of internal control should include the supervision by responsible officials of day-to-day transactions and the recording thereof.

8. *Management.* These are the controls exercised by management outside the day-to-day routine of the system. They include the overall supervisory controls exercised by management, the review of management accounts and comparison thereof with budgets, the internal audit function and any other special review procedures."

---

42. Management, within their resources, should introduce appropriate controls to prevent or substantially reduce intentional *and* unintentional errors in the accounting system. The possibility of intentional errors (or fraud) is restricted by ensuring an effective segregation of duties. There are three elements to most transactions:

    (a) authority to initiate the transaction, committing the company to carry out the contract (referred to as 'authorisation' and 'execution' in paragraph 41 above);
    (b) control over recording the transaction in the company's records;
    (c) custody of assets and determination of their release.

    Each of these elements should therefore ideally be carried out by separate individuals within each transaction cycle. As we shall see later, this control type is of considerable significance to the auditor, and his evaluation techniques are therefore designed to identify any lack of segregation of duties in the client's system.

Limitations on the effectiveness of internal controls

43. The guideline warns us that no internal control system is foolproof. Paragraph 6 reads:

    "No internal control system, however elaborate, can by itself guarantee efficient administration and the completeness and accuracy of the records, nor can it be proof against fraudulent collusion, especially on the part of those holding positions of authority or trust. Internal controls depending on segregation of duties can be avoided by collusion. Authorisation controls can be abused by the person in whom the authority is vested. Whilst the competence and integrity of the personnel operating the controls may be ensured by selection and training, these qualities may alter due to pressure exerted both within and without the enterprise. Human error due to errors of judgement or interpretation, to misunderstanding, carelessness, fatigue or distraction may undermine the effective operation of internal controls."

    The auditor will need to be aware of the possibility that even the best looking system can break down; hence, as we have established, his reliance on internal controls (confirmed by compliance testing) is only part of his audit evidence - some substantive work will *always* be carried out!

Types of control for each transaction cycle

44. Before we consider the auditor's use of internal controls and the procedures he adopts in relation to controls, it is useful to identify some of the more important control considerations for each of the conventional transaction streams. In other words, we will examine how management might apply the techniques available from paragraph 41 to achieve satisfactory control for the following cycles:

    (a) purchases and creditors;
    (b) sales and debtors;
    (c) cash at bank and in hand;
    (d) wages and salaries;
    (e) stock and work in progress;
    (f) fixed assets;
    (g) investments.

45. *Purchases and creditors*
The three separate elements into which accounting controls may be divided clearly appear in the consideration of purchase procedures. They are buying ('authorisation'), receipt of goods ('custody') and accounting ('recording').

46. *Buying:* factors to be considered include:

(a) the procedure to be followed when issuing requisitions for additions to and replacement of stocks, and the persons to be responsible for such requisitions;
(b) the preparation and authorisation of purchase orders (including procedures for authorising acceptance where tenders have been submitted or prices quoted);
(c) the institution of checks for the safe-keeping of order forms and safeguarding their use;
(d) as regards capital items, any special arrangements as to authorisations required (for a fuller description of this aspect see the section dealing with fixed assets below).

47. *Goods inwards:* factors to be considered include:

(a) arrangements for examining goods inwards as to quantity, quality and condition; and for evidencing such examination;
(b) the appointment of a person responsible for accepting goods, and the procedure for recording and evidencing their arrival and acceptance;
(c) the procedure to be instituted for checking goods inwards records against authorised purchase orders.

48. *Accounting:* factors to be considered include:

(a) the appointment of persons so far as possible separately responsible for:
    (i) checking suppliers' invoices;
    (ii) recording purchases and purchase returns;
    (iii) maintaining suppliers' ledger accounts or similar records;
    (iv) checking suppliers' statements;
    (v) authorising payment;

(b) arrangements to ensure that before accounts are paid:
    (i) the goods concerned have been received, accord with the purchase order, are properly priced and correctly invoiced;
    (ii) the expenditure has been properly allocated; and
    (iii) payment has been duly authorised by the official responsible.

49. *Sales and debtors*
The separation of authorisation, custody and recording functions described above in respect of purchases and trade creditors applies similarly to sales and trade debtors.

50. *Selling:* considerations include the following:

(a) what arrangements are to be made to ensure that goods are sold at their correct price and to deal with and check exchanges, discounts and special reductions including those in connection with cash sales;
(b) who is to be responsible for, and how control is to be maintained over, the granting of credit terms to customers;

(c) who is to be responsible for accepting customer's orders and what procedure is to be adopted for issuing production orders and despatch notes;

(d) who is to be responsible for the preparation of invoices and credit notes and what controls are to be instituted to prevent errors and irregularities (for instance, how selling prices are to be ascertained and authorised, how the issue of credit notes is to be controlled and checked, what checks there should be on prices, quantities, extensions and totals shown on invoices and credit notes, and how such documents in blank or completed form are to be protected against loss or misuse);

(e) what special controls are to be exercised over the despatch of goods free of charge or on special terms.

51. *Goods outwards:* factors to be considered include:

(a) who may authorise the despatch of goods and how is such authority evidenced;

(b) what arrangements are to be made to examine and record goods outwards (preferably this should be done by a person who has no access to stocks and has no accounting or invoicing duties);

(c) the procedure to be instituted for agreeing goods outwards records with customers' orders, despatch notes and invoices.

52. *Accounting:* so far as possible sales ledger staff should have no access to cash, cash books or stocks, and should not be responsible for invoicing and other duties normally assigned to sales staff. The following are amongst matters which should be considered:

(a) the appointment of persons as far as possible separately responsible for:
   (i) recording sales and sales returns;
   (ii) maintaining customers's accounts;
   (iii) preparing debtors' statements;

(b) the establishment of appropriate control procedures in connection with sales returns, price adjustments and similar matters;

(c) arrangements to ensure that goods despatched but not invoiced (or vice versa) during an accounting period are properly dealt with in the accounts of the periods concerned (ie cut-off procedures);

(d) the establishment of arrangements to deal with sales to companies or branches forming part of the same group;

(e) what procedures are to be adopted for the preparation, checking and despatch of debtors' statements and for ensuring that they are not subject to interference before despatch;

(f) how discounts granted and special terms are to be authorised and evidenced;

(g) who is to deal with customers' queries arising in connection with statements;

(h) what procedure is to be adopted for reviewing and following up overdue accounts;

(i) who is to authorise the writing off of bad debts, and how such authority is to be evidenced;

(j) the institution of a sales control account and its regular checking preferably by an independent official against customers' balances on the sales ledger.

53. *Cash at bank and in hand*

Receipts
Receipts by post and cash sales: considerations involved in dealing with cash and cheques received by post include:

(a) instituting safeguards to minimise the risk of interception of mail between its receipt and opening;

    (b) wherever possible, appointing a responsible person, independent of the cashier, to open, or supervise the opening of, mail;

    (c) ensuring that cash and cheques received are:

        (i) adequately protected (for instance, by the restrictive crossing of all cheques, money orders and the like on first handling); and

        (ii) properly accounted for (for instance, by the preparation of post-lists of moneys received for independent comparison with subsequent records and book entries).

54. In establishing an adequate *system of control over cash sales and collections* it should be decided:

    (a) who is to be authorised to receive cash and cash articles (ie whether such items are to be received only by cashiers or may be accepted by sales assistants, travellers, roundsmen, or others);

    (b) how sales and the receipt of cash and cash articles are to be evidenced, and what checks may be usefully adopted as regards such transactions (for instance, by use of serially numbered receipt forms or counterfoils, or cash registers incorporating sealed till rolls).

55. *Custody and control of money received:* money received should be subject to adequate safeguards and controls at all stages up to lodgement in the bank. Amongst the matters which may require consideration are the following:

    (a) the appointment of suitable persons to be responsible at different stages for the collection and handling of money received, with clearly defined responsibilities;

    (b) how, by whom, and with what frequency cash offices and registers are to be cleared;

    (c) what arrangements are to be made for agreeing cash collections with cash and sales records (preferably this should be carried out by a person independent of the receiving cashier or employee);

    (d) according to the nature of the business, what arrangements are to be made for dealing with, recording and investigating any cash shortages or surpluses.

56. *Recording:* incoming cash and cheques should be recorded as soon as possible. Means of recording include, as appropriate, receipt forms and counterfoils, cash registers and post lists. Matters for consideration include the following.

    (a) Who is to be responsible for maintaining records of money received?

    (b) What practicable limitations may be put on the duties and responsibilities of the receiving cashier particularly as regards dealing with such matters as other books of account, other funds, securities and negotiable instruments, sales invoices, credit notes and cash payments?

    (c) Who is to perform the receiving cashier's functions during his absence at lunch, on holiday, or through sickness?

    (d) In what circumstances, if any, receipts are to be given, whether copies are to be retained; the serial numbering of receipt books and forms; how their issue and use are to be controlled; what arrangements are to be made, and who is to be responsible for checking receipt counterfoils against:

        (i) cash records; and

        (ii) bank paying-in slips and how alterations to receipts are to be authorised and evidenced?

57. *Paying into bank:* it is desirable that cash and cheques received should be lodged with the bank with the minimum of delay. Adequate control over bank lodgements will involve rules as to:

    (a) how frequently payments are to be made into the bank (preferably daily);

(b) who is to make up the bank paying-in slips (preferably this should be done by a person independent of the receiving and recording cashier) and whether there is to be any independent check of paying-in slips against post-lists, receipt counterfoils and cash book entries;

(c) who is to make payments into the bank (preferably not the person responsible for preparing paying-in slips);

(d) whether all receipts are to be banked intact; if not, how disbursements are to be controlled.

58. *Cash and bank balances:* questions to be decided in connection with the control of cash balances include:

(a) what amounts are to be retained as cash floats at cash desks and registers, whether payments out of cash received are to be permitted;

(b) what restrictions are to be imposed as to access to cash registers and offices;

(c) rules regarding the size of cash floats to meet expenses, and their methods of reimbursement;

(d) the frequency with which cash floats are to be checked by independent officials;

(e) what arrangements are to be made for safeguarding cash left on the premises outside business hours;

(f) whether any special insurance arrangements (such as fidelity guarantee and cash insurance) are judged desirable having regard to the nature of the business, the sums handled, and the length of time they are kept on the premises;

(g) what additional independent checks on cash may be usefully operated (for instance, by periodic surprise cash counts);

(h) what arrangements are to be made for the control of funds held in trust for employees, both those which are the legal responsibility of the company and, as necessary, those which are held by nominated employees independent of the company's authority (for instance, sick funds or holiday clubs).

59. Regular reconciliation of bank accounts by a responsible official is an essential element of *control over bank balances.* Considerations involve deciding to whom bank statements may be issued, how frequently reconciliations should be performed, by whom, and the detailed procedure to be followed. Special factors include the treatment of long-standing unpresented cheques, stop-payment notices, examination of the sequence of cheque numbers and comparison of cheque details with details recorded in the cash book. So far as possible the person responsible for carrying out the bank reconciliation should not normally be concerned with handling cash and cheques received or with arrangements for disbursements.

60. *Payments*
Cheque and cash payments: the arrangements for controlling payments will depend to a great extent on the nature of business transacted, the volume of payments involved and the size of the company.

61. *Cheque payments:* amongst the points to be decided in settling the system for payments by cheque are the following:

(a) what procedure is to be adopted for controlling the supply and issue of cheques for use, and who is to be responsible for their safe-keeping;

(b) who is responsible for preparing cheques and traders' credit lists;

(c) what documents are to be used as authorisation for preparing cheques and traders' credit lists, rules as to their presentation to cheque signatories as evidence in support of payment, and the steps to be taken to ensure that payment cannot be made twice on the strength of the same document;

(d) the names, number and status of persons authorised to sign cheques, limitations as to their authority; the minimum number of signatories required for each cheque; if only one signatory is required, whether additional independent authorisation of payments is desirable - if more than one signatory is required, how it is to be ensured that those concerned will operate effective independent scrutiny (for instance, by prohibiting the signing by any signatory of blank cheques in advance); limitations, if any, as to the amount permissible to be drawn on one signature - whether cheques drawn in favour of persons signing are to be prohibited;

(e) safeguards to be adopted if cheques are signed mechanically or carry printed signatures;

(f) the extent to which cheques issued should be restrictively crossed; and the circumstances, if any, in which blank or bearer cheques may be issued;

(g) arrangements for the prompt despatch of signed cheques and precautions against interception;

(h) arrangements for obtaining paid cheques; whether they are to be regarded as sufficient evidence of payment or whether receipts are to be required; and the procedure to be followed in dealing with paid cheques returned as regards examination and preservation;

(i) the arrangements to be made to ensure that payments are made within discount periods.

62. *Cash payments:* factors to be considered include the following:

(a) nomination of a responsible person to authorise expenditure, the means of indicating such authorisation and the documentation to be presented and preserved as evidence;

(b) arrangements to ensure that the vouchers supporting payments cannot be presented for payment twice;

(c) whether any limit is to be imposed as regards amounts disbursed in respect of individual payments;

(d) rules as to cash advances to employees and officials, IOUs and the cashing of cheques.

The 'imprest system' may be used to advantage, whereby the expenditure incurred during the period of the imprest (ie. fixed sum advance) is independently checked before refund of the amount expended.

63. *Cheque and cash payments generally:* arrangements should be such that so far as practicable the cashier is not concerned with keeping or writing-up books of account other than those recording disbursements nor should he have access to, or be responsible for the custody of, securities, title deeds or negotiable instruments belonging to the company.

Similarly, so far as possible the person responsible for preparing cheques or traders' credit lists should not himself be a cheque signatory - cheque signatories in turn should not be responsible for recording payments.

On the other hand, it must be recognised that in the circumstances of smaller companies, staff limitations often make it impossible to divide duties in this manner and in such cases considerable responsibility falls on the adequacy of managerial supervision.

64. *Wages and salaries*
While in practice separate arrangements are generally made for dealing with wages and salaries, the considerations involved are broadly similar and for convenience the two aspects are here treated together.

65. *General arrangements:* responsibility for the preparation of pay sheets should be delegated to a suitable person, and adequate staff appointed to assist him. The extent to which the staff responsible for preparing wages and salaries may perform other duties should be clearly defined. In this connection full advantage should be taken where possible of the division of duties, and checks available where automatic wage-accounting systems are in use. Inter alia provision should be made as to:

(a) who may authorise the engagement and discharge of employees;
(b) who may authorise general and individual changes in rates of pay;
(c) how notification of changes in personnel and rates of pay are to be recorded and controlled to prevent irregularities and errors in the preparation and payment of wages and salaries;
(d) how deductions from employees' pay other than for income tax and national insurance are to be authorised;
(e) what arrangements are to be made for recording hours worked (in the case of hourly paid workers) or work done (in the case of piece workers) and for ensuring that the records are subject to scrutiny and approval by an appropriate official before being passed to the wages department; special supervision and control arrangements may be desirable where overtime working is material;
(f) whether advances of pay are to be permitted, if so, who may authorise them, what limitations are to be imposed, how they are to be notified to and dealt with by wages and salaries departments, and how they are to be recovered;
(g) how holiday pay is to be dealt with;
(h) who is to deal with pay queries.

66. *Preparation of payroll:* the procedure for preparing the payroll should be clearly established. Principal matters for consideration include the following:

(a) matters such as: what records are to be used as bases for the compilation of the payroll and how they are to be authorised;
(b) who is responsible:
    (i) for preparing pay sheets;
    (ii) for checking them; and
    (iii) for approving them (preferably separate persons) and by what means individual responsibility at each stage is to be indicated.
(c) what procedures are to be laid down for notifying and dealing with non-routine circumstances such as an employee's absence from work or employees leaving at short notice in the middle of a pay period.

67. *Payment of wages and salaries:* where employees are paid in cash the following matters are amongst those that require decisions.

(a) What arrangements are to be made to provide the requisite cash for paying out (eg by encashment of a cheque for the total amount of net wages) and what steps are to be taken to safeguard such monies during collection and transit and until distributed?

    (b)   What safeguards against irregularities are to be adopted (eg by arranging for pay packets to be filled by persons other than those responsible for preparing pay sheets, providing them with the exact amount of cash required and forbidding their access to other cash) and what particulars are to be given to payees?

    (c)   Who is to pay cash wages over to employees (preferably a person independent of those engaged in the preparation of pay sheets and pay packets) how payees' identities are to be verified; what officials are to be in attendance, and how distribution is to be recorded (eg by recipient's signature or by checking off names on the pay list)?

68.   Where wages and salaries are paid by cheque or bank transfer the matters to be decided include:

    (a)   which persons are:
       (i)   to prepare; and
       (ii)   to sign cheques and bank transfer lists (preferably these persons should be independent of each other and of those responsible for preparing pay sheets).

    (b)   whether a separate wages and salaries bank account is to be maintained, what amounts are to be transferred to it from time to time (preferably on due dates the net amount required to meet pay cheques and transfers) and who is to be responsible for its regular reconciliation (preferably someone independent of those responsible for maintaining pay records).

69.   *Deductions from pay:* appropriate arrangements should be made for dealing with statutory and other authorised deductions from pay, such as national insurance, PAYE, pension fund contributions, and savings held in trust. A primary consideration is the establishment of adequate controls over the records and authorising deductions.

70.   *Additional checks on pay arrangements:* in addition to the routine arrangements and day-to-day checks referred to above, use may be made as judged desirable, of a number of independent overall checks on wages and salaries. Amongst those available may be listed the following:

    (a)   the maintenance, separate from wages and salaries departments, of employees' records, with which pay lists may be compared as necessary;

    (b)   the preparation of a reconciliation to explain changes in total pay and deductions between one pay day and the next;

    (c)   surprise counts of cash (and any other valuables) held by wages and salaries departments;

    (d)   the comparison of actual pay totals with independently prepared figures such as budget estimates or standard costs and the investigation of variances;

    (e)   the agreement of gross earnings and total tax deducted for the year to 5 April with PAYE returns to the Inland Revenue.

71.   *Stock and work in progress*
     Stocks may be as susceptible to irregularities as cash and, indeed, in some circumstances the risks of loss may be materially higher. Arrangements for the control of stocks should be framed with this in mind.

72.   The stock control procedures should ensure that stocks held are adequately protected against loss or misuse, are properly applied in the operations of the business, and are duly accounted for. According to the nature of the business separate arrangements may be necessary for different categories of stocks, such as raw materials, components, work in progress, finished goods and consumable stores.

73. Amongst the main considerations may be listed the following:

   (a)   what arrangements are to be made for receiving, checking and recording goods inwards (see also purchases and trade creditors above);

   (b)   who is to be responsible for the safeguarding of stocks and what precautions are to be taken against theft, misuse and deterioration;

   (c)   what arrangements are to be made for controlling (through maximum and minimum stock limits) and recording stocks (eg by stock ledgers, independent control accounts and continuous stock records such as bin cards), who is to be responsible for keeping stock records (preferably persons who have no access to stocks and are not responsible for sales and purchase records); and what procedure is to be followed as to the periodic reconciliation of stock records with the financial accounts;

   (d)   how movements of stock out of store (or from one process or department to another) are to be authorised, evidenced and recorded, and what steps are to be taken to guard against irregularities;

   (e)   what arrangements are to be made for dealing with and accounting for returnable containers (both suppliers' and own);

   (f)   what arrangements are to be made for dealing with and maintaining accounting control over company stocks held by others (for instance goods in warehouse, on consignment or in course of processing) and goods belonging to others held by the company (eg how withdrawals are to be authorised and evidenced, and how goods belonging to others are to be distinguished from own goods);

   (g)   what persons are to be responsible for physically checking stocks, at what intervals such checks are to be carried out, and what procedures are to be followed (for instance, if continuous stocktaking procedures are in use, arrangements should ensure that all categories of stock are counted at appropriate intervals, normally at least once a year; counts should preferably be conducted by persons independent of storekeepers; how stock counts are to be recorded and evidenced, and what cut-off procedures are to be operated to ensure that stocks are adjusted to take proper account of year-end sales and purchases invoiced);

   (h)   what bases are to be adopted for computing the amount at which stocks are to be stated in the accounts (these should be in accordance with SSAP9 and should be applied consistently from year to year), and which persons are to perform and check the calculations;

   (i)   what arrangements are to be made for the periodic review of the condition of stocks, how damaged, slow-moving and obsolete stocks are to be dealt with and how write-offs are to be authorised;

   (j)   what steps are to be taken to control and account for scrap and waste, and receipts from the disposal of such items.

74.   *Fixed assets*
Some of the principal matters to be decided in connection with controls relating to fixed assets are as follows:

   (a)   who is to authorise capital expenditure and how such authorisation is to be evidenced;

   (b)   who is to authorise the sale, scrapping or transfer of fixed assets, how such authorisation is to be evidenced, and what arrangements are to be made for controlling and dealing with receipts and disposals;

   (c)   who is to maintain accounting records in respect of fixed assets and how it is to be ensured that the proper accounting distinction is observed between capital and revenue expenditure;

   (d)   what arrangements are to be made for keeping plant and property registers and how frequently they are to be agreed with the relevant accounts and physically verified;

(e) what arrangements are to be made to ensure that fixed assets are properly maintained and applied in the service of the company, (eg by periodic physical checks as to their location, operation and condition);

(f) where fixed assets are transferred between branches or members of the same group, what arrangements in respect of pricing, depreciation and accounting are to be made;

(g) how depreciation rates are to be authorised and evidenced, and which persons are to be responsible for carrying out and checking the necessary calculations.

75. *Investments*
Arrangements for dealing with investments will involve, inter alia, determining:

(a) who is to be responsible for authorising purchases and sales of investments, and how such authorisations are to be evidenced (those responsible should preferably have no concern with cash or the custody of documents of title);

(b) what arrangements should be made for maintaining a detailed investment register, and who should be responsible for agreeing it periodically with the investment control account and physically verifying the documents of title;

(c) what arrangements are to be made for checking contract notes against authorised purchase or sale instructions and for ensuring that charges are correctly calculated: for dealing with share transfers, and for ensuring that share certificates are duly received or delivered and that bonuses, rights, capital repayments and dividends or interest are received and properly accounted for.

Documents of title: adequate arrangements should be made for the scheduling and safe custody of property deeds, share certificates and other documents of title, with the object of protecting them against loss and irregularities. Preferably they should be deposited in a secure place under the authority and control of at least two responsible persons, and access to or withdrawal of such documents should be permissible only on the authority of such persons acting jointly.

Control problems of small enterprises

76. Paragraphs 45-75 identify the main control considerations applicable to the types of transaction encountered in most, if not all, companies. In paragraph 40 we have established that:

"The operating procedures and methods of recording and processing transactions used by small enterprises often differ significantly from those of large enterprises. Many of the internal controls which would be relevant to the larger enterprises are not practical, appropriate or necessary in the small enterprise."

77. The most effective form of internal control for small enterprises is generally the close involvement of the directors or proprietors. With reference to the types of control identified in paragraph 41 it will be appreciated that a small company will find it very difficult, or well nigh impossible, to achieve adequate segregation of duties. Similarly, it will not have the resources to implement management controls such as an internal audit function. The lack of these controls, and others, will be compensated for in the small company environment by the supervision exercised by the directors/proprietors.

78. This involvement of the directors will however enable them to override controls and purposely to exclude transactions from the records. This possibility can give rise to problems for the auditor, not because there is a lack of controls but because of insufficient evidence as to

their operation and the completeness of the records. The solution for the auditor is to carry out a predominantly substantive audit, with extensive testing of transactions and balances, supported by analytical review.

79. The operational and reporting approach to the audit of small companies is, however, a controversial area. We shall return to this topic in detail in chapter 15.

Evaluation of internal controls

80. Paragraph 5 of the Auditing Standard *The auditor's operational standard* states:

> "If the auditor wishes to place reliance on any internal controls, he should ascertain and evaluate those controls and perform compliance tests on their operation."

81. Returning to the guideline 'Internal controls' we should re-establish why the auditor may wish to place reliance on internal controls. Paragraph 7 states:

> "The auditor's objective in evaluating and testing internal controls is to determine the degree of reliance which he may place on the information contained in the accounting records. If he obtains reasonable assurance by means of compliance tests that the internal controls are effective in ensuring the completeness and accuracy of the accounting records and the validity of entries therein, he may limit the extent of his substantive testing."

82. The auditor needs to ascertain and record the internal control system in order to make a preliminary evaluation of the effectiveness of its component controls and to determine the extent of his reliance on these controls. This recording will normally be carried out concurrently with the recording of the accounting system; the use of flowcharting techniques is a simple yet effective way of achieving this dual objective. It should be appreciated that the purchases system charted in paragraph 33 demonstrates this point - the system contains many internal control features, including segregation of duties, arithmetical checks and authorisation and approval controls: these are easy to identify as one follows the document flow.

83. Having documented the system, including internal controls, and confirmed its operation by means of walk through tests, the auditor will then commence his evaluation. We can return to the guideline 'Internal controls' to establish the two principal techniques available to him.

"The evaluation of internal controls will be assisted by the use of documentation designed to help identify the internal controls on which the auditor may wish to place reliance. Such documentation can take a variety of forms but might be based on questions asking either:

(a) whether controls exist which meet specified control objectives; or
(b) whether they are controls which prevent or detect particular specified errors or omissions."

84. The two documents referred to in terms of their objectives in (a) and (b) are more recognisable to the auditor as the Internal Control Questionnaire (ICQ) and Internal Control Evaluation Questionnaire or Form (ICEQ or ICEF) respectively. The ICQ has been around longer than the ICEQ so we will give it pride of place and examine its approach first.

Internal control questionnaires

85. The major question which internal control questionnaires are designed to answer is "How good is the system of controls?" Where strengths are identified, the auditor will perform work in the relevant areas. If, however, weaknesses are discovered he should then ask:

    - what errors or irregularities could be made possible by these weaknesses?
    - could such errors or irregularities be material to the accounts? and hence
    - what substantive audit tests will enable such errors or irregularities to be discovered and quantified?

86. Although there are many different forms of ICQ in practice, they all conform to the following basic principles:

    - they comprise a list of questions designed to determine whether desirable controls are present; and
    - they are formulated so that there is one to cover each of the major transaction cycles.

87. Since it is the primary purpose of an ICQ to evaluate the system rather than describe it, one of the most effective ways of designing the questionnaire is to phrase the questions so that all the answers can be given as 'YES' or 'NO' and a 'NO' answer indicates a weakness in the system. An example would be:

Are purchase invoices checked to goods received notes before being passed for payment?	YES/NO

A 'NO' answer to that question clearly indicates a weakness in the company's payment procedures.

88. A specimen ICQ is provided on the following pages covering the purchases cycle. The questions follow as closely as possible the sequence of the accounting system. As regards the questions themselves they cover in rather more detail the various desirable checks and controls considered earlier in the chapter. A column is provided for referring to the audit programme and for making comments. The auditor's comments will record the extent to which he considers any weakness material. He may be able to point to other controls which compensate for a particular weakness. In any event, his conclusions will form the basis for determining the nature and extent of his subsequent testing.

89. The strengths of ICQs are that they facilitate the orderly evaluation of controls present in a system - important matters should not be overlooked, which may be possible if the auditor attempts his evaluation without an aide-memoire such as the ICQ. They provide tangible evidence of the basis of the audit approach for the benefit of the manager and partner.

SECTION A - PURCHASES AND TRADE CREDITORS

	YES/NO	Comments and audit programme reference

Introduction

1. Is accounting control established over the purchase of goods and services when they are first requested?

Buying

2. Are requisitions to the buying department for supplies or services issued only by authorised personnel within strict laid down limits?

3. (a) Are official orders issued showing suppliers' names quantities ordered and prices?

   (b) Are copies retained?

   (c) If goods are supplied or services rendered without the issue of an official order, are there suitable controls to ensure that all such purchases are duly authorised?

4. Are orders made only by duly authorised persons within laid down limits?

5. Are persons who make orders independent of those who issue requisitions?

6. Is a proper record kept of orders placed but not yet fulfilled and is it periodically examined by a responsible official?

Goods inward

7. Are supplies examined on arrival as to quantity and quality?

8. Is such examination evidenced in some way?

9. Is the receipt of supplies recorded e.g. by means of goods inwards notes?

10. Are receipt records prepared by a person independent of those responsible for:-

   (a) ordering functions;

   (b) the processing and recording of invoices.

11. Are goods inwards records controlled to ensure that invoices are obtained for all goods received and to enable the liability for unbilled goods to be determined (eg. by pre-numbering the records and accounting for all serial numbers)?

SECTION A - PURCHASES AND TRADE CREDITORS

	YES/NO	Comments and audit programme reference

12. (a) Are goods inward records regularly reviewed for items for which no invoices have been received?

   (b) Are any such items investigated?

13. Are these records reviewed by a person independent of those responsible for the receipt and control of goods?

Goods returned

14. Are suitable records of documents prepared:-

   (a) when goods are returned to suppliers?

   (b) when claims are made in respect of short deliveries or incorrect prices?

15. Are these records prepared by a person independent of those responsible for:-

   (a) ordering functions?

   (b) the processing and recording of invoices?

16. Are goods returned records controlled to ensure that credit notes are obtained for all returns and claims (eg. by pre-numbering the records and accounting for all serial numbers)?

17. (a) Are goods returned records regularly reviewed for items for which no credit notes have been received?

   (b) Are any such items investigated?

18. Are these records reviewed by a person independent of those responsible for the receipt and control of goods?

Reconciliation of purchases

19. In respect of raw materials and supplies, are reconciliations made of quantities and/or values received, as shown by purchase invoices, with receipts into stock records?

20. Are the reconciliations prepared by a person independent of those responsible for:-

   (a) the receipt and control of goods?

   (b) maintaining the stock records?

21. Is there evidence that such reconciliations are regularly prepared?

SECTION A - PURCHASES AND TRADE CREDITORS

YES/NO   Comments and audit programme reference

Purchase invoices

22. Are all copies of invoices received except the original, stamped to indicate that they are duplicates?

23. Are invoices received:-

 (a) compared with copy orders?

 (b) compared with goods inwards records?

 (c) checked for prices (where not quoted on order)?

 (d) checked for extensions and additions?

24. Are these functions carried out by a person independent of those responsible for:-

 (a) ordering functions?

 (b) the receipt and control of goods?

25. Are credit notes received:-

 (a) compared with goods returned records or other substantiating evidence?

 (b) checked for extensions and additions?

26. Are these functions carried out by a person independent of those responsible for:-

 (a) ordering functions?

 (b) the receipt and control of goods?

27. Is suitable action taken to investigate differences disclosed by the comparisons in 23 and 25 above?

28. Are differences reported to a responsible official?

29. Are invoices and credit notes signed or initialled as evidence that the work in 23, 25 and 27 above has been carried out?

30. Is there a proper procedure for the allocation of charges and credits to nominal and cost accounts?

31. Is the cost allocation shown on invoices?

32. Are invoices and credit notes finally approved for payment?

33. Is the authority for approval restricted to responsible officials up to specific limits?

SECTION A - PURCHASES AND TRADE CREDITORS

YES/NO   Comments and audit programme reference

34. Is final approval evidenced on the invoice?

35. Are those authorised to give final approval independent of those responsible for:-

 (a) ordering functions?

 (b) the receipt and control of goods?

 (c) the processing and recording of invoices?

36. Does the system ensure that all invoices and credit notes received are duly processed?

37. Is this function carried out by a person independent of those responsible for the processing and recording of invoices?

Purchase ledger and control accounts

38. Is the purchase ledger:-

 (a) handwritten?

 (b) mechanised?

 (if mechanised, state the system).

39. Are the purchase ledger personnel independent of those responsible for:-

 (a) passing invoices and credit notes?

 (b) cheque payments functions?

40. Does the system ensure that all authorised transactions, and only those transactions, are recorded in the purchase ledger (eg. by pre-listing the authorised invoices and credit notes and determining a total for posting to an independent control account before they are processed by the ledger/cheque payments personnel)?

41. Is the purchase ledger balanced regularly against a control account?

42. Is the person who maintains the control account and performs the reconciliations independent of the purchase ledger personnel?

General

43. Are there proper systems for controlling and recording inter-company or inter-branch purchases, where

90. The weakness of ICQs is that they can promote a somewhat standardised approach to evaluation. The answering of the questions becomes an end in itself, rather than the means to an end. The auditor is concerned whether the controls do or do not prevent the possibility of material errors occurring. This is not always easy to determine with an ICQ where the questions are notionally of equal weight. In many systems a particular 'No' answer - say, referring to a lack of segregation of duties - may cancel the apparent value of a string of 'Yes' answers. Each situation must be judged on its own merits and hence, although the ICQs are a standard pre-printed pack, they should be used with imagination. As using ICQs is a skilled and responsible task, the evaluation should be performed by a senior member of the audit team. They should be completed by that member of the audit team; not, as sometimes happened in the past, by the client!

Internal control evaluation questionnaires

91. ICQs have been in use in the UK since the 1960s. In recent years many auditing firms have developed and implemented an evaluation technique more concerned with assessing whether specific errors (or frauds) are possible rather than establishing whether certain desirable controls are present. This is achieved by reducing the control criteria for each transaction stream down to a handful of *key questions* (or *control questions*) whose characteristic is that they concentrate on the significant errors or omissions that could occur at each phase of the appropriate cycle if controls are weak.

92. The nature of the key questions may best be understood by reference to the examples on the following pages.

Internal control evaluation questionnaire - control questions

The sales (revenue) cycle
1. Is there reasonable assurance that sales are properly authorised?
2. Is there reasonable assurance that all goods despatched are invoiced?
3. Is there reasonable assurance that all invoices are properly prepared?
4. Is there reasonable assurance that all invoices are recorded?
5. Is there reasonable assurance that invoices are properly supported?
6. Is there reasonable assurance that all credits to customers' accounts are valid?
7. Is there reasonable assurance that cash and cheques received are properly recorded and deposited?
8. Is there reasonable assurance that slow payers will be chased and that bad and doubtful debts will be provided against?
9. Is there reasonable assurance that all transactions are properly accounted for?
10. Is there reasonable assurance that cash sales are properly dealt with?
11. Is there reasonable assurance that sundry sales are controlled?
12. Is there reasonable assurance that at the period end the system will neither overstate nor understate debtors?

The purchases (expenditure) cycle
1. Is there reasonable assurance that goods or services could not be received without a liability being recorded?
2. Is there reasonable assurance that receipt of goods or services is required in order to establish a liability?
3. Is there reasonable assurance that a liability will be recorded:
   (a) only for authorised items; and
   (b) at the proper amount?

4. Is there reasonable assurance that all payments are properly authorised?
5. Is there reasonable assurance that all credits due from suppliers are received?
6. Is there reasonable assurance that all transactions are properly accounted for?
7. Is there reasonable assurance that at the period end liabilities are neither overstated nor understated by the system?
8. Is there reasonable assurance that the balance at the bank is properly recorded at all times?
9. (a) Is there reasonable assurance that unauthorised cash payments could not be made?
   (b) And that the balance of petty cash is correctly stated at all times?

Wages and salaries
1. Is there reasonable assurance that employees are only paid for work done?
2. Is there reasonable assurance that employees are paid the correct amount;
   (a) gross?
   (b) net?
3. Is there reasonable assurance that the right employees actually receive the right amount?
4. Is there reasonable assurance that accounting for payroll costs and deductions is accurate?

Stock
1. Is there reasonable assurance that stock is safeguarded from physical loss (eg fire, theft, deterioration)?
2. Is there reasonable assurance that stock records are accurate and up to date?
3. Is there reasonable assurance that the recorded stock exists?
4. Is there reasonable assurance that the cut off is reliable?
5. Is there reasonable assurance that the costing system is reliable?
6. Is there reasonable assurance that the stock sheets are accurately compiled?
7. Is there reasonable assurance that the stock valuation is fair?

Fixed tangible assets
1. Is there reasonable assurance that recorded assets actually exist and belong to the company?
2. Is there reasonable assurance that capital expenditure is authorised and reported?
3. Is there reasonable assurance that disposals of fixed assets are authorised and reported?
4. Is there reasonable assurance that depreciation is realistic?
5. Is there reasonable assurance that fixed assets are correctly accounted for?

Investments
1. Is there reasonable assurance that recorded investments:
   (a) belong to the company?
   (b) are safeguarded from loss?
2. Is there reasonable assurance that all income, rights or bonus issues are properly received and accounted for?
3. Is there reasonable assurance that investment transactions are made only in accordance with company policy and are appropriately authorised and documented?
4. Is there reasonable assurance that the carrying values of investments are reasonably stated?

Management information and general controls
1. Is the nominal ledger satisfactorily controlled?
2. Are journal entries adequately controlled?
3. (a) Does the organisation structure provide a clear definition of the extent and limitation of authority?
   (b) Are the systems operated by competent employees adequately supported?
   (c) If there is an internal audit function, is it adequate?

4. Are financial planning procedures adequate?
5. Are periodic internal reporting procedures adequate?

93. Each key control question is supported by detailed control points to be considered in the context of the system being evaluated. An example of a complete ICEQ form follows incorporating the detailed control points. It is extracted from the expenditure cycle pack and covers the first key control question:

Is there reasonable assurance that goods or services could not be received without a liability being recorded?

INTERNAL CONTROL EVALUATION QUESTIONNAIRE (continued)
B   EXPENDITURE CYCLE

	Yes	No	Reference
I IS THERE REASONABLE ASSURANCE THAT GOODS OR SERVICES COULD NOT BE RECEIVED WITHOUT A LIABILITY BEING RECORDED?			

Reasoning

Specify key controls, if any

*Programmed functions and general controls
(if any of the above key controls depend upon programmed functions, discuss
here our approach to general controls)

	19	19	19	19
Prepared/updated by	....	....	....	....
Date	....	....	....	....
Reviewed by	....	....	....	....

160

INTERNAL CONTROL EVALUATION QUESTIONNAIRE (continued)
B   EXPENDITURE CYCLE

**I   IS THERE REASONABLE ASSURANCE THAT GOODS OR SERVICES COULD
         NOT BE RECEIVED WITHOUT A LIABILITY BEING RECORDED? (continued)**

	Yes	No	Remarks

Consider the following questions:

1   Is segregation of duties satisfactory?

*2   Are controls over relevant master files satisfactory?

+3   Are (pre-numbered) purchase orders all compared to invoices received,
      missing numbers being accounted for?

      * — in a computerized invoice approval system, is there a sequence
          number control on purchase orders to see that they all get into the
          system?

      * — are rejects controlled and promptly re-input?

4   Is the record or print-out or orders placed but not yet filled periodically
      examined by a responsible person?

+5   Are all goods received recorded, to show what was received and when?

      — on pre-numbered goods received notes which are then compared with
        invoices, missing numbers being accounted for?

      * — in a computerized invoice approval system, is the sequence control
          used to see that they all get into the system?

      * — are there print-outs of goods received notes not matched by invoices?

      * — which are examined by a responsible person?

*6   Are all mis-matches in a computerized invoice approval system printed out and
      examined by a responsible person where all three elements are present (order,
      GRN, invoice) but they are not equal ('equal' within pre-determined tolerances
      of minor discrepancies)?

+7   Is there an invoice register showing when received, to whom passed for
      approval, and when received back again for payment?

      * — where this is computerized, is there a sequence number control on all
          invoices put into the system?

      * — is it regularly checked that the items dropped from this system are the
          ones input to the bought ledger control account (including
          reconciliation of those that never got into this system)?

      * — are rejects from the system printed out, controlled and promptly re-
          input?

      * — is there a periodic print-out of long outstanding items which are
          regularly chased and cleared?

*8   In a computerized invoice approval systems, is the invoice register (computer
      or manual) regularly cleared to see that all invoices received get into this
      system? (If this works properly, batch control over invoices may be
      unnecessary.)

INTERNAL CONTROL EVALUATION QUESTIONNAIRE (continued)
B   EXPENDITURE CYCLE

I   IS THERE REASONABLE ASSURANCE THAT GOODS OR SERVICES COULD NOT BE RECEIVED WITHOUT A LIABILITY BEING RECORDED? (continued)

	Yes	No	Remarks

Consider the following questions:

*9   In computerized systems, if some or all of the data are input under batch control, are all rejects controlled and promptly re-input?

— if some or all of the data are input from terminals, are rejects immediately corrected and re-input (ie no outstanding items)?

*10   Are sensible control totals produced of items dropped from a computerized invoice approval system which can be, and are, regularly reconciled with items input to the stock system (eg hash-totals, money values, sequence numbers of GRN's processed)?

— is the reconciliation put to good use?

+ 11   Are suppliers' statements regularly reconciled to the ledger or to payments?

— are copies of the reconciliations retained?

+ 12   Is there evidence that the purchase ledger control account is regularly agreed with a list of balances?

— and that this is checked periodically by an independent person?

*13   In a computerized invoice approval system, is the print-out of invoices dropped from the system regularly agreed in total with the corresponding input to the bought ledger control account?

*14   In a computerized creditors' ledger system:

— is it ensured that all transactions submitted for processing are *completely* input (eg register of pre-added batch values agreed with print out of accepted and rejected items)?
— are rejects continuously controlled on money values to see they do not get lost (at whatever point in the system rejects can arise)?
— are rejects corrected and re-input promptly, with the same validity tests as apply to original transactions?

*15   Computer ledger control account
(NB This is not the 'control account' that the computer prints out; it is another *real* control account (which may be in the nominal ledger) that predicts what balance the computer ought to have. It *controls* by enabling one to see whether the computer balance is right.)

a   Does every entry in this real control account come from a source independent of the computer?
b   If not, because only accepted transactions are posted to this control account, is there a further real control account on unprocessed or rejected items, so that effective control *is* exercised over all the original data?
c   If not, because data output from another computerized application (eg goods received) are input to this system, is the input total or output entry in the *real* control account of the transferor system agreed manually to the input entry in the *real* control account of this system?
d   If not, because the computer itself generates some of the entries in the ledger, is the control of these shown by relevant later questions of this ICEQ satisfactory?
e   Is (are) the real control account(s) regularly reconciled to:
— the computer ledger balance?
— the nominal ledger balance (if separate)?

INTERNAL CONTROL EVALUATION QUESTIONNAIRE (continued)
B   EXPENDITURE CYCLE

**I   IS THERE REASONABLE ASSURANCE THAT GOODS OR SERVICES COULD
NOT BE RECEIVED WITHOUT A LIABILITY BEING RECORDED? (continued)**

	Yes	No	Remarks

Consider the following questions:

*16   For computer-generated liability (eg rents due, hire purchase, deposit interest):

—   is there a satisfactory analysis of output (eg by regions, categories of customer) so that discrepancies between periods and categories etc can be (and are) identified and explained?

—   is there an overall manual reasonableness check on the result?

—   are amounts computed as due compared with details supplied by the creditor (where he does this?)

17   Is there evidence that debits on the periodic list of balances are enquired into by an independent person?

18   Are direct purchases (ie going straight from supplier to customer) controlled?

19   Is the liability for goods sold from consignment stocks held duly set up in the records?

Other relevant controls in the system

94. The following notes explain how the forms are completed:

   - The main concern is with the answers to the control questions, but they need not be answered where the relevant accounting information is *immaterial*. The purpose of answering the control questions is to enable the auditor to identify key controls upon which he may rely and to identify (and subsequently to investigate) material weaknesses.

   - The 'Yes/No' pattern is set up in the same manner as for an ICQ in this particular ICEQ format; some firms reverse the pattern, and the desirable answer is therefore 'No'- eg 'can goods or services be received without a liability being recorded?'

   - The answers to the control objective questions require consideration in the light of the answers to the detailed supporting questions which will normally be factual rather than subjective. The supporting questions are of two types. First there are those that *must* be answered representing basic business controls - these are marked by a plus (+). Secondly there are those which need not be answered but which may be found helpful when reviewing a system and trying to find out how it is controlled and which, if any, are the key controls. Some supporting questions are marked with asterisks(*). These questions only apply to computerised systems and are therefore ignored if the system under review is a manual one. A very few questions are marked with a T; this indicates that tact is required!

   - The first supporting question asks 'is segregation of duties satisfactory?' Detailed questions relating to segregation of duties are listed on a separate form for the revenue, expenditure and wages and salaries cycles, as many of the questions are relevant to several control objectives. The form for the expenditure cycle is provided by way of illustration.

   - The reference to be placed opposite each answered control objective question is to the part of the systems description (normally in flowchart form) that describes the operations and controls relevant to the objective.

Consideration of risk of irregularities at the evaluation stage

95. (a) We have established that the auditor at the planning stage of the audit will assess audit risk, including the possibility of material errors arising due to irregularities or fraud. Where the auditor has decided to seek to rely on internal controls and is therefore required to evaluate and test the controls, he will be concerned whether the system prevents irregularities. Both the ICQ and the ICEQ assist him in identifying areas where there may be a high risk of irregularities occurring. The draft guideline on fraud and other illegal acts recommends that special emphasis should be placed on the following control aspects when considering the risk of irregularities at the evaluation stage:
   - segregation of duties
   - authorisation (particularly of expense items and new ledger accounts)
   - completeness and accuracy of accounting data
   - safeguard procedures (eg signing cheques)
   - comprehensiveness of controls (eg including all relevant sub-systems)
   - adequacy of internal audit.

   (b) In addition, where accounting procedures are computerised, the auditor should be concerned to ensure that a lack of computer controls cannot be exploited to suppress evidence that an irregularity may exist or indeed to allow an irregularity to occur.

(c) Internal audit, when present and effective, is an important element of a system of internal control and should be a deterrent to irregularities. If he intends to place reliance on the internal audit function, the auditor will need to assess its effectiveness and degree of independence. This will involve reviewing reports made by the internal audit department for evidence of possible irregularities and assessing the extent to which management takes action based upon such reports. (We consider the guideline 'Reliance on internal audit' immediately below.)

96. Although the likelihood of irregularities by employees can be evaluated by concentrating on the above areas (in particular, segregation of duties) the possibility of distortion by senior officials/management will not be readily determined by questionnaires. This may, however, be revealed during the course of evaluation by observing whether management appear under pressure.

Reliance on internal audit

97. Internal audit is an example of a management control exercised outside the day-to-day routine of the accounting system. In the case of a limited company it exists because of a management decision; in the public sector it may arise because of a statutory requirement. Where an enterprise's internal control system includes internal audit the external auditor may be able to place reliance on that internal audit function. In order to establish in what circumstances such reliance may be justified and to determine the procedures that need to be followed by the external auditor we can turn to the detailed operational guideline 'Reliance on internal audit' issued in November 1984. The following comments are derived from this guideline.

98. Certain of the objectives of internal audit may be similar to those of external audit, and procedures similar to those carried out during an external audit may be followed. Accordingly, the external auditor should make an assessment of the internal audit function in order to be able to determine whether or not he wishes to place reliance on the work of internal audit. An external auditor may be able to place reliance on internal audit as a means of reducing the work he performs himself in:

(a) the documentation and evaluation of accounting systems and internal controls;
(b) compliance and substantive testing.

99. The scope of internal audit's work will generally be determined in advance and a programme of work will be prepared. Where reliance is placed on the work of internal audit, the external auditor will need to take into account this programme of work and amend the planned extent of his own audit work accordingly. In addition, the external auditor may agree with management that internal audit may render him direct assistance by performing certain of the procedures necessary to accomplish the objectives of the external audit but under the control of the chief internal auditor, who would then have to consider the effect on his department's programme of work.

100. The guideline does not deal with those cases where internal audit staff are seconded to work under the direct supervision and control of the external auditor. This is because the guideline addresses reliance on internal audit as a function, rather than reliance on individuals within that function. The work of seconded internal audit staff should be controlled by the external auditor in accordance with the auditing guideline 'Planning, controlling and recording', having regard to the position of internal audit staff as employees of the enterprise.

Scope and objectives of the internal audit function

101. The scope and objectives of internal audit vary widely and are dependent upon the responsibilities assigned to it by management, the size and structure of the enterprise and the skills and experience of the internal auditors. Normally, however, internal audit operates in one or more of the following broad areas:

   (a) review of accounting systems and related internal controls;
   (b) examination of financial and operating information for management, including detailed testing of transactions and balances;
   (c) review of the economy, efficiency and effectiveness of operations and of the functioning of non-financial controls;
   (d) review of the implementation of corporate policies, plans and procedures;
   (e) special investigations.

102. Where internal audit staff carry out routine tasks such as authorisation and approval or day-to-day arithmetical and accounting controls, they are not functioning as internal auditors and these tasks are not dealt with in this guideline: this is because these tasks are recognised as other types of internal controls by the Appendix to the Auditing Guideline 'Internal controls'. Moreover, objectivity may be impaired when internal auditors audit any activity which they themselves carried out or over which they had authority. The possibility of impairment should be considered when deciding whether to place reliance on internal audit.

The relationship between external and internal audit

103. Unlike the internal auditor who is an employee of the enterprise or a related enterprise, the external auditor is required to be independent of the enterprise, usually having a statutory responsibility to report on the financial statements giving an account of management's stewardship.

104. Although the extent of the work of the external auditor may be reduced by placing reliance on the work of internal audit, the responsibility to report is that of the external auditor alone, and therefore is indivisible and is not reduced by this reliance.

105. As a result, all final judgements relating to matters which are material to the financial statements or other aspects on which he is reporting, must be made by the external auditor.

Procedures

106. Before any decision is taken to place reliance on internal audit, it is necessary for the external auditor to make an assessment of the likely effectiveness and the relevance of the internal audit function. The criteria for making this assessment should include the following.

   (a) *The degree of independence.* The external auditor should evaluate the organisational status and reporting responsibilities of the internal auditor and consider any constraints or restrictions placed upon him. Although an internal auditor is an employee of the enterprise and cannot therefore be independent of it, he should be able to plan and carry out his work as he wishes and have access to the highest level of management. He should also be free of any responsibilities which may create a conflict of interest when he attempts to discharge his internal audit function, or of a situation where middle management on whom he is reporting is responsible for his or his staff's appointment, promotion or remuneration. Furthermore, an internal auditor should be free to communicate fully with the external auditor, who should be able to receive copies of all internal audit reports that he requires.

(b) *The scope and objectives of the internal audit function.* The external auditor should examine the internal auditor's formal terms of reference and should ascertain the scope and objectives of internal audit assignments. In most circumstances, the external auditor will regard assignments as likely to be relevant where they are carried out in the areas described in paragraphs 101 (a) and (b) above. He will also be interested in internal audit's role in respect of specialist areas and those described in paragraphs 101 (c),(d) and (e) above, when it has an important bearing on the reliability of the financial statements or other matters being reported on.

(c) *Due professional care.* The external auditor should consider whether the work of internal audit generally appears to be properly planned, controlled, recorded and reviewed. Examples of the exercise of due professional care by internal audit are the existence of an adequate audit manual, general internal audit plans, procedures for supervising individual assignments, and satisfactory arrangements for ensuring adequate quality control, reporting and follow-up.

(d) *Technical competence.* The external auditor should ascertain whether the work of internal audit is performed by persons having adequate training and proficiency as auditors. Indications of technical competence may be membership of an appropriate professional body or the possession of relevant practical experience, such as computer auditing skills.

(e) *Internal audit reports.* The external auditor should consider the quality of reports issued by internal audit and ascertain whether management considers, responds to and, where appropriate, acts upon internal audit reports, and whether this is evidenced.

(f) *Level of resources available.* The external auditor should consider whether internal audit has adequate resources, eg in terms of staff and of computer facilities.

107. The external auditor's assessment of the likely effectiveness and the relevance of the internal audit function will influence his judgement as to whether he wishes to place reliance on internal audit. Consequently, the external auditor should document his assessment and conclusions in this respect, and he should update his assessment year by year. Where the external auditor concludes that the internal department is weak or ineffective, then it should not be relied on. Furthermore, the external auditor should inform management in writing of the significant weaknesses in the internal audit function, his reasons for not placing reliance on their work and his recommendations for improvement.

108. Where the external auditor decides that he may be able to place reliance on internal audit, he should consider in determining the extent of that reliance:

(a) the materiality of the areas or the items to be tested or of the information to be obtained;
(b) the level of audit risk inherent in the areas or items to be tested or in the information to be obtained;
(c) the level of judgement required;
(d) the sufficiency of complementary audit evidence;
(e) specialist skills possessed by internal audit staff.

109. The external auditor should be involved in the audit of all material matters in the financial statements particularly in those areas where there is significant risk of misstatement. High audit risk does not preclude placing some reliance on internal audit, but the external auditor should ensure that the extent of his involvement is sufficient to enable him to form his own conclusions.

110. Having decided that he may be able to place reliance on the work of internal audit, the external auditor should agree with the chief internal auditor the timing of internal audit work, test levels, sample selection and the form of documentation to be used.

111. The external auditor should record in his working papers the extent to which he intends to place reliance on internal audit, and the reasons for deciding that extent. Furthermore, the external auditor should consider confirming with management the overall arrangements that have been agreed, either in the engagement letter or in a separate letter.

112. Where the external auditor places reliance on the work of internal audit, he should review that work and satisfy himself that it is being properly controlled. In this connection the external auditor should:

   (a) consider whether the work has been appropriately staffed and properly planned, supervised and reviewed;
   (b) compare the results of the work with those of the external auditor's staff on similar audit areas or items, if any;
   (c) satisfy himself that any exceptions or unusual matters that have come to light as a result of the work have been properly resolved;
   (d) examine reports relating to the work produced by internal audit and management's response to those reports.

113. In addition, the external audit should determine whether internal audit will be able to complete, on a timely basis, the programme that it has agreed to undertake and, if it will not, he should make appropriate alternative arrangements.

114. At the conclusion of the audit, the external auditor should review the economy, efficiency and effectiveness of the basis of working and discuss with the chief internal auditor the significant findings and any means of improving the approach.

115. The external auditor will need to ensure that all work relating to his audit, whether performed by internal audit or the external auditor, is properly recorded. He should satisfy himself that the working papers relating to the work of internal audit upon which he is placing reliance are up to an acceptable standard. Consideration should be given to the method of recording so that relevant working papers are available and are of use to both the external auditor and internal audit.

116. Where the external auditor places reliance on internal audit, whether by means of direct assistance or otherwise, he should satisfy himself that sufficient evidence is obtained to afford a reasonable basis for the conclusions reached by internal audit, and that those conclusions are appropriate to the circumstances and are consistent with the results of the work performed. This may involve him in performing supplementary procedures. The extent of these

procedures will depend on his assessment of the internal audit function, the materiality of the area or item to be tested and the risk of misstatement in the financial statements (see paragraph 109). The procedures may include re-examining transactions or balances that internal audit have tested, examining similar transactions or balances, or the performance of analytical review procedures, as well as discussing with internal audit the work they have performed.

117. Where the work of internal audit reveals weaknesses in internal controls, the external auditor should consider whether it is enough to draw management's attention to a report from internal audit or whether he should also report to management himself, particularly where he considers management response to internal audit reports is inadequate or where the weaknesses are significant. The external auditor should consider whether his own programme should be amended because of those weaknesses.

Communication with management: the management letter

118. We have reached the conclusion of stage 5 of the audit as depicted in our diagrammatic approach. At stage 6, the auditor performs compliance tests to obtain reasonable assurance that the controls on which he wishes to rely have been functioning properly; where the preliminary evaluation has disclosed weaknesses in, or the absence of controls, such that material errors or omissions could arise he will move directly to designing and carrying out substantive tests. We will consider how the auditor designs his audit tests in the next chapter. For the moment we will concentrate on stage 7 of the audit - the management letter.

119. Paragraphs 21 and 22 of the Auditing Guideline 'Internal controls' state:

"It is important that the auditor should report, as soon as practicable, significant weaknesses in internal controls which come to his attention during the course of an audit to an appropriately senior level of management of the enterprise. Any such report should indicate that the weaknesses notified are only those which have come to the attention of the auditor during the course of his normal audit work and are not necessarily, therefore, all the weaknesses which may exist.

The fact that the auditor reports weaknesses in internal controls to management does not absolve:

(a) management from its responsibility for the maintenance of an adequate internal control system;
(b) the auditor from the need to consider the effect of such weaknesses on the extent of his audit work and on his audit opinion."

120. The technique of the management letter is well-established in practice but it is only recently that formal guidance has been provided by the APC in the form of a detailed operational guideline entitled 'Reports to management' issued in December 1986. The following comments are derived from this guideline.

Form of the report to management

121. Reports to management are known by various names, for example management letters, post audit letters and letters of weaknesses. The report should preferably take the form of a letter. Occasionally, the volume or nature of the auditor's comments may be such that this form of report is either unnecessary or inappropriate. In these circumstances the report will consist of

a record of a discussion with management forming part of the auditor's working papers. The principles outlined in the guideline should be followed whatever method is used to report to management on matters which have arisen during the audit.

122. The auditor's primary duty is to express an opinion on the financial statements and this responsibility is not reduced by any reports made to management.

Purpose

123. The principal purpose of a report to management is to enable the auditor to give his comments on the accounting records, systems and controls that he has examined during the course of his audit. Significant areas of weakness in systems and controls that might lead to material errors should be highlighted and brought to management's attention.

124. There is usually no requirement for the auditor to make a report to management where no significant weaknesses have come to his attention. However, the auditor should be aware that in certain cases, for example in local authority, Stock Exchange firm and housing association audits, there is a specific requirement to make a report to management.

125. As a secondary purpose, a report to management may also be used to provide management with other constructive advice. The auditor might, for example, be able to suggest areas where economies could be made or where resources could be used more efficiently.

126. A report to management is also a useful means of communicating matters that have come to the auditor's attention during the audit that might have an impact on future audits.

Timing

127. A report to management will normally be a natural by-product of the audit, and the auditor should incorporate the need to report in the planning of the audit.

128. To be effective, the report should be made as soon as possible after completion of the audit procedures giving rise to comment. Where the audit work is performed on more than one visit, it will often be appropriate to report to management after interim audit work has been completed as well as after the final visit. If there are procedures that need to be improved before the financial year end the auditor should raise them in a letter or in discussion at an interim stage. As soon as an accounting breakdown is identified or serious weaknesses are apparent senior management should be informed without delay.

Contents

129. Generally the following matters, arising out of the audit, will be included in a report to management:
    (a) weaknesses in the structure of accounting systems and internal controls;
    (b) deficiencies in the operation of accounting systems and internal controls;
    (c) unsuitable accounting policies and practices;
    (d) non-compliance with accounting standards or legislation.

130. An auditor may have a specific duty to form an opinion as to whether proper accounting records have been kept. For example, this duty is laid upon the auditor of a company by s 237 (1)(a) Companies Act 1985. In such a case, if a qualified audit report is necessary because of (b) above, a report to management is no substitute for a qualified audit report.

131. Reports to management should explain clearly the risks arising from internal control weaknesses. The use of specific examples discovered in the audit to illustrate the potential effects of weaknesses helps readers to understand the nature of the problems which require rectification.

132. The auditor may also include comments on inefficiencies as well as weaknesses which have come to his attention.

133. It is normally helpful for the auditor to make recommendations for improvements so that weaknesses can be eliminated. This should not however delay the issuing of any report. It should be borne in mind that determination of appropriate improvements in systems and the assessment of the cost-effectiveness of additional controls may be complex issues that in any event are management's responsibility.

134. Points made in previous years' reports should be reviewed. Where they have not been dealt with effectively the auditor should enquire why appropriate action has not been taken. If the auditor considers the points still to be significant, they should be included again in his current report. In addition, recommendations made by internal audit which have not been implemented by management may need to be included.

Format and presentation

135. The report should be clear, constructive and concise. Careful presentation will help the recipient to understand the significance of the comments and devise corrective actions. The following factors should therefore be borne in mind.

136. It is important that matters of concern should be discussed and recorded as they arise to ensure that the auditor has properly understood the situation. These discussions may take place with members of staff at an operating level as well as with executives concerned solely with finance and accounting. When the points in the report are drafted they should be cleared for factual accuracy with the client's staff concerned.

137. The auditor should explain in his report to management that it only includes those matters which came to his attention as a result of the audit procedures, and that it should not be regarded as a comprehensive statement of all weaknesses that exist or all improvements that might be made.

138. The report may contain matters of varying levels of significance and thus make it difficult for senior management to identify points of significance. The auditor can deal with this by giving the report a 'tiered' structure so that major points are dealt with by the directors and minor points are considered by less senior personnel. Alternatively, by agreement with the client, this objective might best be achieved by preparing separate reports for different levels of management, and reporting that this has been done.

139. Where different members of management are responsible for different regions, branches or functions, the report may have separate sections relating to the various areas of responsibility.

140. When submitting his report the auditor should use his best endeavours to ensure that its contents reach those members of management who have the power to act on the findings. It is usually appropriate to address the report, or that part of the report containing the major points, to the Board of Directors or equivalent body even if the receipt of a report of less important points is delegated by the Board.

141. If the auditor chooses not to send a formal letter or report but considers it preferable to discuss any weaknesses with management, the discussion should be minuted or otherwise recorded in writing. Management should be provided with a copy of the note to ensure the discussion has been fairly reflected. The written record of any such discussions should be filed with the audit working papers.

Management response

142. The auditor should request a reply to all the points raised, indicating what action management intends to take as a result of the comments made in the report. It should be made clear in the report that the auditor expects at least an acknowledgement of the report or, where he considers it appropriate, the directors' discussion of the report to be recorded in the board minutes.

143. Where weaknesses have been discussed with client staff as and when they arise, the responses made by staff should be embodied where possible in the final form of a report. This will be particularly useful where, say, senior management receive the report and need to be informed of the action taken by their staff.

144. Where the report to management takes the form of a record of the auditor's discussion with management this record should include management's response and intended action.

Third parties interested in reports to management

145. Any report made to management should be regarded as confidential communication. The auditor should therefore not normally reveal the contents of the report to any third party without the prior written consent of the management of the company.

146. In practice, the auditor has little control over what happens to the report once it has been despatched. Occasionally management may provide third parties with copies of the report, for example, their bankers or certain regulatory authorities. Therefore care should be taken to protect the auditor's position from exposure to liability in negligence to any third parties who may seek to rely on the report. Accordingly, the auditor should state clearly in his report that it has been prepared for the private use of his client. However, the auditor should recognise that the report may be disclosed by management to third parties, and in certain cases it may be appropriate for the auditor to request that the report is not circulated to any third parties without his prior consent.

147. Reports to management may contain comments which are critical of members of the client's management or staff, and could lay the auditor open to a charge of defamation. The auditor should therefore ensure that his comments are factually accurate, and do not include any gratuitous remarks of a personal nature.

Specimen management letter

148. A specimen letter is provided below which demonstrates how the principles described in the previous paragraphs are put into practice. The following points should be noted.

(a)	*Timing:* (see paragraph 128)	This particular letter is submitted after the conclusion of the interim audit, ie after completion of stage 5 (evaluation) and stage 6 (compliance testing) in our diagrammatic representation. This is the conventional approach where a separate interim audit has been performed. A further letter may be submitted at the conclusion of the audit. If no separate interim audit is carried out, one letter will be sent after all audit work has been completed.
(2)	*Format:* (see paragraph 137)	The letter contains a caveat, advising the directors that it only contains those matters which have come to the auditor's attention as a result of his audit procedures and is hence not to be regarded as a comprehensive statement of all the weaknesses that may exist.
(3)	*Contents:* (see paragraphs 129,131 & 132)	The letter identifies specific weaknesses but also the risk arising from those weaknesses and *practical* recommendations for improvements.
(4)	*Response:* (see paragraph 142)	In the penultimate paragraph the auditor emphasises that he requires a response to the points made in the letter, preferably in the form of management's action programme.

SPECIMEN MANAGEMENT LETTER

AB & Co
Certified Accountants
29 High Street
London, N10 4KB

The Board of Directors,
Manufacturing Co Limited,
15 South Street
London, S20 1CX

1 April 198X

Gentlemen,

Financial statements for the year ended 31 May 198X

1. In accordance with our normal practice we set out in this letter certain matters which arose as a result of our review of the accounting systems and procedures operated by your company during our recent interim audit.

173

2. We would point out that the matters dealt with in this letter came to our notice during the conduct of our normal audit procedures which are designed primarily for the purpose of expressing our opinion on the financial statements of your company. In consequence our work did not encompass a detailed review of all aspects of the system and cannot be relied on necessarily to disclose defalcations or other irregularities or to include all possible improvements in internal control.

Purchases - ordering procedures

3. *Present system*
   During the course of our work we discovered that it was the practice of the stores to order certain goods from X Limited orally without preparing either a purchase requisition or purchase order.

4. *Implications*
   There is therefore the possibility of liabilities being set up for unauthorised items and at a non-competitive price.

5. *Recommendations*
   We recommend that the buying department should be responsible for such orders and, if they are placed orally, an official order should be raised as confirmation.

Purchase ledger reconciliation

6. *Present system*
   Although your procedures require that the purchase ledger is reconciled against the control account on the nominal ledger at the end of every month, this was not done in December or January.

7. *Implications*
   The balance on the purchase ledger was short by some £2,120 of the nominal ledger control account at 31 January 198X for which no explanation could be offered. This implies a serious breakdown in the purchase invoice and/or cash payment batching and posting procedures.

8. *Recommendations*
   It is important in future that this reconciliation is performed regularly by a responsible official independent of the day to day purchase ledger, cashier and nominal ledger functions.

Sales ledger - credit control

9. *Present system*
   As at 28 February 198X debtors account for approximately 12 weeks sales, although your standard credit terms are cash within 30 days of statement - equivalent to an average of about 40 days (6 weeks) of sales.

10. *Implications*
    This has resulted in increased overdraft usage and difficulty in settling some key suppliers accounts on time.

11. *Recommendations*
    We recommend that a more structured system of debt collection be considered using standard letters and that statements should be sent out a week earlier if possible.

Preparation of payroll and maintenance of personnel records

12. *Present system*

Under your present system, just two members of staff are entirely and equally responsible for the maintenance of personnel records and preparation of the payroll. Furthermore, the only independent check of any nature on the payroll is that the chief accountant confirms that the amount of the wages cheque presented to him for signature agrees with the total of the net wages column in the payroll. This latter check does not involve any consideration of the reasonableness of the amount of the total net wages cheque or the monies being shown as due to individual employees.

13. *Implications*

It is a serious weakness of your present system, that so much responsibility is vested in the hands of just two people. This situation is made worse by the fact that there is no clearly defined division of duties as between the two of them. In our opinion, it would be far too easy for fraud to take place in this area (eg by inserting the names of 'dummy workmen' into the personnel records and hence on to the payroll) and/or for clerical errors to go undetected.

14. *Recommendations*

   (i) Some person other than the two wages clerks be made responsible for maintaining the personnel records and for periodically (but on a surprise basis) checking them against the details on the payroll;

   (ii) The two wages clerks be allocated specific duties in relation to the preparation of the payroll, with each clerk independently reviewing the work of the other;

   (iii) When the payroll is presented in support of the cheque for signature to the chief accountant, that he should be responsible for assessing the reasonableness of the overall charge for wages that week.

15. Our comments have been discussed with your finance director and the chief accountant and these matters will be considered by us again during future audits. We look forward to receiving your comments on the points made. Should you require any further information or explanations do not hesitate to contact us.

16. We should like to take this opportunity of thanking your staff for their co-operation and assistance during the course of our interim audit.

Yours faithfully

Summary of the chapter

149. This chapter embraces some of the key operational features of the audit in practice and unearths a rich vein of examination question topics.

150. Note the distinction between an accounting system, which must be ascertained, recorded and assessed, and an internal control system which is desirable but not normally mandatory. Appreciate that the walk through test is an aid to recording the system not an evaluation tool.

151. Be prepared for very general questions on the nature of internal controls and their audit significance but also more precise questions concerned with controls applicable to particular transaction types (paragraphs 45 to 74 should be studied in detail). Questions in the latter category may be constructed in such a way that evaluation of a flowchart (provided in the question) is required.

152. The nature of the internal audit function, a comparison with the external audit role and reliance that may be placed on internal audit by the external auditor, are all well established question areas based on the guideline 'Reliance on internal audit'.

153. Questions invoking the principles of the management letter are usually of a case study variety. The requirements are typically to evaluate part of a system (perhaps, as mentioned in paragraph 151, presented in flowchart form) and then draft a letter to management identifying the weaknesses, their significance and recommendations for improving the system.

TEST YOUR KNOWLEDGE
Numbers in brackets refer to paragraphs in this chapter

1. Why does management require a complete and accurate accounting system? (6)

2. What are the principal statutory requirements regarding a company's accounting records? (12)

3. What are the three main recording techniques used by the auditor? (19)

4. What objectives should be achieved by narrative notes regarding functions, documents and accounting records? (23)

5. What are the principal advantages and disadvantages of flowcharts? (29)

6. What is a walk through test? (34)

7. What is the definition of an internal control system? (39)

8. What are the eight main types of internal control? (41)

9. What control considerations arise in respect of:
   (a) goods inwards? (47)
   (b) accounting for sales? (52)
   (c) receipts by post? (53)
   (d) paying into bank? (57)
   (e) preparation of payroll? (66)
   (f) fixed assets? (74)

10. Why should the auditor wish to place reliance on internal controls? (81)

11. What is the distinction between an ICQ and an ICE(Q)? (83 & 84)

12. What are the inherent weaknesses of ICQs? (90)

13. What are the possible key control questions relevant to the purchases cycle? (92)

14. In what broad areas might internal audit operate? (101)

15. What are the principal criteria for making an assessment of the effectiveness and relevance of the internal audit function? (106)

16. Where the external auditor places reliance on the work of internal audit, how should he ensure that it is being properly controlled? (112)

17. What audit matters may be included in a report to management? (129)

18. If the auditor chooses not to send a formal management letter how should he otherwise report to management? (141)

19. How may the auditor protect himself from exposure to liability to third parties who may seek to rely on his management letter? (146)

Chapter 9

TESTING THE ACCOUNTING RECORDS

Topics covered in this chapter:

- Techniques of audit testing
- Design of compliance tests
- Design of substantive tests
- Directional testing
- Audit sampling techniques

Introduction

1. After the system of internal controls has been evaluated (stage 5 in our diagrammatic representation of the systems audit) the next stage is to design audit tests. If the controls have been assessed as effective, the auditor will design compliance tests to check how well they operate in practice; if the controls are considered to be weak, he will move directly to substantive testing to obtain direct assurance that transactions have been recorded completely and correctly.

Techniques of audit testing

2. The types of evidence relied upon by an auditor can be divided on the basis of the way in which they are obtained. The guideline identifies the following techniques of audit testing:

   "(a) *Inspection* - reviewing or examining records, documents or tangible assets. Inspection of records and documents provides evidence of varying degrees of reliability depending upon their nature (see reliability presumption (b) in paragraph 8 above). Inspection of tangible assets provides the auditor with reliable evidence as to their existence, but not necessarily as to their ownership, cost or value.

   (b) *Observation* - looking at an operation or procedure being performed by others with a view to determining the manner of its performance. Observation provides reliable evidence as to the manner of the performance at the time of observation, but not at any other time.

   (c) *Enquiry* - seeking relevant information from knowledgeable persons inside or outside the enterprise, whether formally or informally, orally or in writing. The degree of reliability that the auditor attaches to evidence obtained in this manner is dependent on his opinion of the competence, experience, independence and integrity of the respondent.

(d) *Computation* - checking the arithmetical accuracy of accounting records or performing independent calculations.

(e) *Analytical review* - these procedures include studying significant ratios, trends and other statistics and investigating any unusual or unexpected variations. The precise nature of these procedures and the manner in which they are documented will depend on the circumstances of each audit.

The comparisons which can be made will depend on the nature, accessibility and relevance of the data available. Once the auditor has decided on the comparisons which he intends to make in performing his analytical review, he should determine what variations he expects to be disclosed by them.

Unusual or unexpected variations, and expected variations which fail to occur, should be investigated. Explanations obtained should be verified and evaluated by the auditor to determine whether they are consistent with his understanding of the business and his general knowledge. Explanations may indicate a change in the business of which the auditor was previously unaware in which case he should reconsider the adequacy of his audit approach. Alternatively they may indicate the possibility of misstatements in the financial statements; in these circumstances the auditor will need to extend his testing to determine whether the financial statements do include material misstatements."

3. In conducting his tests, the auditor should inspect original documents wherever possible. When it appears that the original document is not readily available, the auditor should consider the following points in deciding whether he may rely on a copy as evidence of the document's contents:

(a) the reason why the original is not available. The auditor might, for example, consider it suspicious that the original of one document is not available when those of other similar documents are;
(b) the controls over the process of making the copy;
(c) the extent to which other evidence supports the contents of the copy;
(d) whether the document was internally generated or derived from an external source.

4. It is generally considered that, provided there are adequate controls over the copying process, copies of internally generated documents are satisfactory evidence for audit purposes. Indeed, the original may well be in the hands of third parties (eg sales invoices). The auditor will normally, however, seek additional evidence to support that obtained from the copies (eg in the case of sales, direct confirmation from the debtors).

5. In the case of external documents, it is agreed that, no matter how good the control procedures are, internally produced copies are not satisfactory as audit evidence. The reasons for this include:

(a) that the original may have been altered in a way that is not apparent from the copy;
(b) that the copy may not contain all relevant information, eg. that on the back of the original.

The auditor should, therefore, consider insisting on the retention of the originals, at least until after the audit has been completed.

6. To obtain audit evidence the auditor will carry out his audit tests classified as 'substantive' or 'compliance' according to their primary purpose, applying a combination of the techniques identified in paragraph 2. Both such purposes are sometimes achieved concurrently. Before we return to our audit in progress and the testing of the transactions, let us refresh our memories as to the formal definitions of compliance and substantive tests.

    (a) *Compliance tests* are those tests which seek to provide audit evidence that internal control procedures are being applied as prescribed.

    (b) *Substantive tests* are those tests of transactions and balances, and other procedures such as analytical review, which seek to provide audit evidence as to the completeness, accuracy and validity of the information contained in the accounting records or in the financial statements.

Design of compliance tests

7. Where the preliminary evaluation described in chapter 8, using ICQs or ICEQs as the case may be, indicates that there are key controls which meet the objective which the auditor has identified he should design and carry out compliance tests if he wishes to rely on them. Where the evaluation discloses weaknesses, or the absence of internal controls, such that material error or omission could arise in the accounting records or the financial statements, the auditor will move directly to designing and carrying out substantive tests.

8. It should be noted that it is the control which is being tested by a compliance test, and not the transaction which may be the medium used for the test. For this reason the auditor should record and investigate all exceptions revealed by his compliance testing, regardless of the amount involved in the particular transaction. (An 'exception' in this context is where a control has not been operated correctly whether or not a quantitative error has occurred.)

9. If compliance tests disclose no exceptions the auditor may reasonably place reliance on the effective functioning of the internal controls tested. He can, therefore, limit his substantive tests on the relevant information in the accounting records.

10. If the compliance tests have disclosed exceptions which indicate that the control being tested was not operating properly in practice, the auditor should determine the reasons for this. He needs to assess whether each exception is only an isolated departure or is representative of others, and whether it indicates the possible existence of errors in the accounting records. If the explanation he receives suggests that the exception is only an isolated departure, then he must confirm the validity of the explanation, for example by carrying out further tests. If the explanation or the further tests confirm that the control being tested was not operating properly throughout the period, then he cannot rely on that control. In these circumstances the auditor is unable to restrict his substantive testing unless he can identify an alternative control on which to rely. Before relying on that alternative control he must carry out suitable compliance tests on it.

11. If reliance is to be placed on the operation of controls, the auditor should ensure that there is evidence of the effectiveness of those controls throughout the *whole period* under review. This is an important point, for we are presently engaged in the interim audit - at a date prior to the year end. The compliance tests carried out at the interim stage will therefore need to be supplemented by further tests for the remainder of the financial year. These additional tests will be carried out during the final audit.

12. Alternatively, the auditor will need to carry out other procedures to enable him to gain adequate assurance as to the reliability of the accounting records during the period which has not been subject to compliance tests. In determining the alternative procedures which are necessary he should consider:

    (a) the results of earlier compliance tests;
    (b) whether, according to enquiries made, controls have remained the same for the remaining period;
    (c) the length of the remaining period;
    (d) the nature and size of the transactions and account items involved; and
    (e) the substantive tests which he will carry out irrespective of the adequacy of controls.

13. Where the internal control system has changed during the accounting period under review, the auditor will have to evaluate and test the internal controls on which he wishes to rely, both before and after the change.

14. The main aim of any compliance test is to discover whether there are any deviations from the prescribed system which may have a material effect on the reliability of the records as a basis for the accounts. The auditor is hence only concerned with those controls ('key controls') whose failure could lead to material misstatement and are not compensated for by other controls. Controls which are not key should not be tested nor should they be relied on as they cannot give any audit assurance. Also the auditor will only seek to rely on internal controls where it is cost effective, ie:

    (a) the reliance on internal controls enables the auditor to reduce specific substantive tests; and
    (b) the time costs of identifying key controls and carrying out the compliance testing is less than the time costs saved by reducing the substantive testing.

Examples of compliance tests

15. The types of key control that the auditor will be looking out for during his evaluation and testing will, of course, be derived from those classified in the Appendix to the guideline Internal Controls. But it should be appreciated that the nature of the compliance test will vary with the type of control.

16. The normal compliance philosophy is to test only for evidence of the control being performed; for example, completion of an invoice grid stamp on a purchase invoice. Strictly a control can only be tested, and subsequently relied upon, if there is some evidence of its performance. This evidence might typically be a signature or initials on a document indicating authorisation or checking of computation. The testing technique being applied here is clearly 'inspection' - see paragraph 2(a).

17. However, there is a problem where a control does not leave permanent evidence of its performance. It may be possible to test it by observing its performance (see paragraph 2 (b)) or by attempting to defeat it. For example, controls over the opening of post and the distribution of wages may be observed on a surprise basis. Password controls on computer terminals may be tested by attempting to defeat this control and by examining the record of passwords issued and password changes.

18. Where a compliance test is carried out on a sample basis the auditor should consider whether the same sample can be used for any substantive tests on the same documents - clearly, where practicable, compliance and substantive tests should be carried out simultaneously. Some compliance tests can be achieved by perusing the whole of the population rather than by sampling - for example, if purchase invoices are being tested for proper completion and initialling of a grid stamp, the test may be effectively and simply achieved by flicking through invoice files or batches to ensure that all invoices appear to carry the completed stamp.

19. To demonstrate the nature of compliance tests a little more precisely there follow some possible examples based on a selection of ICEQ control questions for the sales cycle:

   (a) Control question 1: Is there reasonable assurance that all goods despatched are invoiced?

Possible key controls	*Possible compliance tests*
Checks of credit limits etc before goods are despatched	For sample of despatches, check for evidence of credit check.

   (b) Control question 2: Is there reasonable assurance that all goods despatched are invoiced?

Possible key controls	*Possible compliance tests*
Reconciliation on regular basis of stock per physical count to records, investigating differences	Check for evidence of regular reconciliations ensuring that they appear reasonable with no unexplained differences
Goods despatch note and invoice part of same set, or cross-referenced to each other. Filed together sequentially with regular sequence checks.	For sample of despatch notes, check cross-reference to invoice and check for evidence of sequence test.

   (c) Control question 3: Is there reasonable assurance that all invoices are properly prepared?

Possible key controls	*Possible compliance tests*
Evidence on invoice, for example grid stamp, to indicate checks of quantities, prices and calculations (including value added tax).	For sample of invoices, check for initials/grid stamp (it may be feasible to check all invoices - see paragraph 18).

   (d) Control question 4: Is there reasonable assurance that all invoices are recorded?

Possible key controls	*Possible compliance tests*
Evidence on invoice, eg grid stamp to indicate posted to sales day book.	For sample of invoices, check for initials/grid stamp.
Sequence check on sales day book to ensure all invoices are entered	Check for evidence of sequence check
Regular reconciliations of balances per sales ledger accounts and sales ledger control account	Examine sample of reconciliations and ensure they appear reasonable with no differences brought or carried forward.

20. The auditor's compliance programme will embrace all material transaction types where key controls have been identified at the evaluation stage. The tests, results of the tests and conclusions must be recorded in the audit working papers - normally such information is retained on the current file, but some firms prefer to record the compliance tests on schedules which are effectively extensions of the ICEQs, in which case they may be considered part of the permanent file information.

Design of substantive tests of transactions

21. The principal objective of our transaction work is to determine:

    (a) whether all income and expenses have been recorded; and
    (b) whether the recorded income and expense transactions did in fact occur.

    In short, we are concerned with completeness, accuracy and validity.

22. Some audit comfort in terms of satisfying this objective will be gained from successful compliance testing, but it will always be necessary to perform substantive work. Broadly speaking the tests will fall into two categories:

    (a) tests to discover errors (resulting in *over* or *under* statement);
    (b) tests to discover omissions (resulting in *under* statement).

23. Tests designed to discover errors will start with the records in which the transactions are recorded and check from the entries to supporting documents or other evidence. Such tests should detect any *over* statement and also any *under* statement through causes *other than omission*.

24. Tests designed to discover omissions must start from outside the accounting records and then check back to those records. For example, if the test is designed to discover whether all raw material purchases have been properly processed the test would start, say, with goods received notes and check them to the stock records or purchase ledger. Understatements through omission will never be revealed by starting with the account itself as there is clearly no chance of selecting items that have been omitted from the account.

25. For most systems it is desirable to include tests designed to discover both errors and omissions and it is important that the type of test, and direction of the test, is recognised before selecting the test sample. If the sample which tested the accuracy and validity of the sales ledger were chosen from a file of sales invoices then it would not substantiate the fact that there were no errors in the sales ledger. The approach known as 'directional testing' which is discussed below, applies this testing discipline in an even more rigorous and logical manner as we shall discover.

26. When designing his programme the auditor will invoke the techniques described in paragraph 2 as he thinks fit; many transaction tests are likely to fall within categories (a) and (d) - inspection and computation.

Transactions audit programme

27. We have ascertained that a practical approach to the transactions audit is to combine as far as possible the compliance and substantive tests in a single programme. In the case of an established audit, the programme can be drafted at the planning stage of the audit, based on previous experience but reflecting any known changes in the accounting system. Clearly amendments will be necessary as the field work progresses.

28. On the following pages a transactions programme is illustrated incorporating compliance and substantive tests. It is entitled 'Standard audit programme' - this is something of a misnomer, for in practice the transactions programme must of course, be tailored to test the particular client's accounting and control systems.

29. The conclusions drawn from the interim audit tests will form the basis for amendments to the balance sheet audit programme. Interim notes should be prepared linking the interim and final visits. Such notes should identify the following matters:

    (a) work outstanding from the interim audit;
    (b) proposals for reduction in work at final visit (where parts of the system have been evaluated and tested as strong);
    (c) problems identified during the interim audit and effect on final audit work;
    (d) advance planning matters, for example, date for setting up debtors circularisation, date of stocktake.

    In addition, the interim management letter will be drafted, approved and submitted.

30. Finally, a few points on audit terminology. We concentrate in this text on terminology emanating from the Auditing Standards and Guidelines, hence there are references to 'walk through checks', 'compliance tests' and 'substantive texts'. There are however, a number of terms that one may still encounter in the context of the interim audit that pre-date the Standards and Guidelines. These include:

    (a) *procedural tests:* these are basically the same as *compliance tests;*
    (b) *weakness tests:* these are basically the same as *substantive tests* of transactions;
    (c) *depth tests:* these are *compliance tests* but conducted rather like a walk-through test. Tests on different control features are strung together so they become in effect a walk-through test. Unlike a walk-through test, however, the sample must be representative of the population to achieve the compliance objectives;
    (d) *vouching tests:* vouching may be defined as the examination by the auditor of all the documentary evidence which is available to support the authenticity of transactions entered in the client's records. It is therefore a *substantive test* invoking the technique of 'inspection'.

STANDARD AUDIT PROGRAMME   APPENDIX VIII

PART I - INTERIM

SECTION A - CASH	Extent	Schedule Ref	Initials

Cash receipts

1. Remittances received by post

(a) confirm that the official procedures for opening the post are being followed;

(b) confirm that cheques etc. received by post are immediately crossed in favour of the company;

(c) select items entered in the rough cash book (or other record of cash, cheques etc. received by post), and trace entries to:
   (i) cash book
   (ii) paying-in book
   (iii) counterfoil or carbon copy receipts

   verify amounts entered as received with remittance advices or other supporting evidence.

2. Cash sales, branch takings

   Select a sample of cash sale summaries/branch from different locations and check as follows:-

(a) with till rolls or copy cash sale notes;

(b) if branch takings are banked locally, check with paying-in slip date-stamped and initialled by the bank. Verify that takings are banked intact daily;

(c) if payments are made out of takings, vouch expenditure paid thereout.

3. Collections by travellers, salesmen etc.

   Select a sample of items from the original collection records and verify as follows:-

(a) trace amounts to cash book via collectors' cash sheets or other collection records;

(b) check entries on cash sheets or collection records with collectors' receipt books;

(c) verify that goods delivered to travellers/salesmen have been regularly reconciled with sales and stocks in hand.

4. Receipts cash book

(a) select several days throughout the period and check in detail as follows:-

STANDARD AUDIT PROGRAMME   APPENDIX VIII

PART I - INTERIM

SECTION A - CASH	Extent	Schedule Ref	Initials

   (i) with entries in rough cash book, receipts, branch returns or other records;

   (ii) non-trade receipts with satisfactory documentary evidence;

   (iii) with paying-in slips obtained direct from the bank, observing that there is no delay in banking monies received. Check additions of paying-in slips;

   (iv) check additions of cash book;

   (v) check postings to the Sales Ledger;

   (vi) check postings to the Purchase Ledger;

   (vii) check postings to the Nominal Ledger, including Control accounts.

(b) scrutinise periods not covered by the foregoing audit tests and examine items of a special or unusual nature.

Cash payments

5. Select a sample of payments and check in detail as follows:-

(a) with paid cheques, noting that cheques are signed by the persons authorised to do so within their authority limits;

(b) if payments are effected by means of traders' credits, trace the selected items to the detailed lists of suppliers to be credited, duly stamped by the bank. Agree total with paid cheques drawn in favour of the banks concerned;

(c) with suppliers' invoices for goods and services. Verify that supporting documents are signed as having been checked and passed for payment and have been stamped 'paid';

(d) with suppliers' statements;

(e) with other documentary evidence, as appropriate- agreements, authorised expense vouchers, wages/ salaries records, petty cash books etc.

6. Payments cash book.

(a) select a sample of weeks and check as follows:-

   (i) with paid cheques, noting that the cheques are signed only by duly authorised persons within their authority limits;

185

PART I - INTERIM

SECTION A - CASH

Extent   Schedule Ref   Initials

(ii) check the sequence of the cheque numbers and enquire into missing numbers;

(iii) trace transfers to other bank accounts, petty cash books or other records, as appropriate;

(iv) check additions, including extensions, and balances forward at the beginning and end of the months covering the periods chosen;

(v) check postings to the Sales Ledger;

(vi) check postings to the Purchase ledger;

(vii) check postings to the Nominal ledger, including the control accounts.

(b) where practicable, scrutinise periods not covered by the preceding tests and examine items which appear to be of a special or unusual nature.

Bank reconciliations

7. Select a period which includes a reconciliation date and check as follows:

(a) compare cash book(s) and bank statements in detail, clearing both records for the period chosen. Simultaneously check items outstanding at the reconciliation date to bank reconciliations concerned;

(b) verify contra items appearing in the cash books or bank statements;

(c) note and obtain satisfactory explanations for all items in the cash book for which there are no corresponding entries in the bank statement and vice versa;

(d) examine all lodgements in respect of which payment has been refused by the bank and ensure that they are cleared on representation or that other appropriate steps have been taken to effect recovery of the amount due.

8. Verify that reconciliations have been prepared at regular intervals throughout the year.

PART I - INTERIM

SECTION A - CASH

Extent   Schedule Ref   Initials

Petty cash

9. Select a sample of payments, and check with supporting vouchers, noting that they are properly approved. See that vouchers and other supporting documents have been marked paid and initialled by the cashier to prevent their re-use.

10. Select a sample of weeks and check as follows:

(a) trace amounts received to cash books;

(b) additions and balances carried forward;

(c) postings to the nominal ledger.

Conclusions

11. Write conclusions covering any errors or weaknesses discovered during the above tests and noting any possible management letter points.

PART I - INTERIM

SECTION B - PURCHASES

	Extent	Schedule Ref	Initials

1. Select a sample of invoices representative of all types of transactions and check as follows:-

   (a) Invoices for capital expenditure, services, office supplies, expenses:

      (i) with appropriating supporting evidence;

      (ii) see approval by duly authorised officials and verify that authority limits are being observed;

      (iii) check entries in plant register etc.

   (b) Invoices for goods, raw materials:

      (i) with purchase requisitions and purchase orders signed by duly authorised officials;

      (ii) with goods received notes and inspection notes;

      (iii) check entries in stock records;

      (iv) see that partial deliveries are properly accounted for to ensure there is no duplicate payment;

      (v) with quotations, price lists to see the price is in order.

      (vi) if an invoice has not been passed due to some defect in the goods, weight or price discrepancy. trace entry in record of goods returned etc. and see credit note duly received from the supplier;

   (c) check calculations and additions;

   (d) check entries in Purchase Day Book and verify that they are correctly analysed,

   (e) check posting to Purchase Ledger.

2. Select a sample of credit notes and verify the correctness of credit received with correspondence etc. and:

   (a) check entries in stock records;

   (b) check entries in record of returns;

   (c) check entries in Purchase Day Book and verify that they are correctly analysed;

   (d) check postings to Purchase Ledger.

3. Select a sample of items from record of returns and verify credit notes are duly received from the suppliers.

PART I - INTERIM

SECTION B - PURCHASES

	Extent	Schedule Ref	Initials

4. Test numerical sequence and enquire into missing numbers;

   (a) Purchase requisitions;

   (b) Purchase orders;

   (c) goods received notes;

   (d) return notes;

   (e) suppliers' invoices.

5. Examine file of unmatched purchase requisitions, purchase orders, goods received notes (ie. those for which invoices do not appear to have been received) and obtain satisfactory explanations for items outstanding for an unreasonable time.

6. Examine file of unprocessed invoices and obtain satisfactory explanations for items outstanding for an unreasonable time.

Purchase day book

7. (a) select entries at random and examine invoices - verify that they are initialled for prices, calculations and extensions and cross-referenced to purchase orders, goods received notes etc. See that they have been duly authorised for payment;

   (b) make a similar test check of credit notes;

   (c) test check additions and cross-casts and check postings to Nominal Ledger accounts and Control Account;

   (d) test check postings of entries to Purchase Ledger.

Purchase ledger

8. (a) select a sample of accounts and:

      (i) test check entries back into books of prime entry;

      (ii) test check additions and balances forward;

      (iii) note and enquire into all contra entries;

   (b) see that Control Account balancing has been regularly carried out during the year;

   (c) examine Control Account for unusual entries.

Conclusions

9. Write conclusions covering any errors or weaknesses discovered during the above tests and noting any possible management letter points.

STANDARD AUDIT PROGRAMME

APPENDIX VII

PART I - INTERIM

SECTION C - SALES

	Extent	Schedule Ref	Initials

1. Select a sample of items from the goods despatched records and check as described below.

2. Non-routine sales (scrap, fixed assets, etc.):
   (a) with appropriate supporting evidence;
   (b) see approval by duly authorised officials;
   (c) check entries in plant register etc.;

3. Other sales:
   (a) with customers' orders;
   (b) with internal sales orders approved by duly authorised officials;
   (c) with sales invoices:
   (i) quantities;
   (ii) prices charged with official price lists;
   (iii) see that trade discounts have been properly dealt with;
   (iv) check calculations and additions;
   (v) check entries in Sales Day Book and verify that they are correctly analysed. See that VAT where chargeable, has been properly dealt with;
   (vi) check postings to Sales Ledger. Generally scrutinise accounts arising in this test to see whether credit limits have been observed;
   (d) check entries in stock records.

4. Select a sample of credit notes and check as follows:
   (a) with correspondence or other supporting evidence;
   (b) see approval by duly authorised officials.
   (c) check entries in stock records;
   (d) check entries in record of goods returned;
   (e) check calculations and additions;
   (f) check entries in day book and verify they are correctly analysed. See that VAT where charge-able, has been properly dealt with;
   (g) check postings to Sales Ledger.

5. Test numerical sequence of Despatch notes and enquire into missing numbers.

6. Test numerical sequence of invoices and credit notes, enquire into missing numbers and inspect copies of those cancelled.

STANDARD AUDIT PROGRAMME

APPENDIX VIII

PART I - INTERIM

SECTION C - SALES

	Extent	Schedule Ref	Initials

Sales day book

7. (a) test check entries with invoices and credit notes respectively;
   (b) test check additions and cross casts and test check postings to Nominal Ledger and Control Account;
   (c) test check postings to Sales Ledger.

Sales ledger

8. Select a sample of accounts and:
   (a) test check entries back into books of prime entry;
   (b) test check additions and balances carried down;
   (c) note and enquire into contra entries.

9. See that control account balancing has been regularly carried out during the year.

Conclusions

10. Write conclusions covering any errors or weaknesses discovered during the above tests and noting any possible management letter points.

188

PART I - INTERIM

SECTION D - PAYROLL

	Extent	Schedule Ref	Initials

Industrial wages and weekly salaries

1. Arrange to attend the pay-out of wages to confirm that the official procedures are being followed.

Industrial wages

2. In respect of a number of weeks select a sample of employees at random and check as follows:

   (a) with personnel records. See that written authorities have been completed in respect of the engagement of new employees and discharges;

   (b) check calculation of gross pay with:

   (i) authorised rates of pay;

   (ii) production records. See that production bonuses have been authorised and properly calculated;

   (iii) with clock cards, time sheets or other evidence of hours worked. Verify that overtime has been authorised.

   (c) examine receipts given by employees; trace unclaimed wages to Unclaimed Wages Book;

   (d) trace gross wages earned to tax deduction cards and, where appropriate, to holiday pay records; check calculations of deductions for PAYE and National Insurance;

   (e) check other deductions to appropriate records. In respect of voluntary deductions, see authority therefor completed by the employees concerned.

3. In respect of the weeks selected above:

   (a) test check additions of payroll sheets;

   (b) check totals of wages sheets selected in (a) to summary;

   (c) check additions and cross-casts of summary;

   (d) check postings of summary to Nominal ledger (including control accounts);

   (e) check total of net pay column to cash book;

   (f) verify that the wages summary has been signed as approved for payment;

   (g) verify that reconciliations have been made with:

   (i) the previous week's payroll;

PART I - INTERIM

SECTION D - PAYROLL

	Extent	Schedule Ref	Initials

   (ii) clock cards with time sheets/job cards (hours);

   (iii) gross wages with costing analyses, production budgets.

Unclaimed wages

4. Test check entries in the Unclaimed Wages book with the entries on the wages sheets. Select any sample of entries in the Unclaimed Wages book and see that the payments have been authorised and receipts obtained from the employees.

5. See that unclaimed wages are banked regularly.

Holiday pay

6. Select a sample of payments in respect of holiday pay and verify with the underlying records and agreements the correctness of the amounts paid.

Salaries - weekly and monthly

7. In respect of a number of weeks/months select a sample of employees at random and check as follows:

   (a) with personnel records. See that written authorities have been completed in respect of the engagement of new employees and discharges;

   (b) verify that gross salaries and bonuses are in accordance with personnel records, letters of engagement etc. and that increases in pay have been properly authorised;

   (c) verify that overtime has been properly authorised;

   (d) trace gross salaries to tax deduction cards and check calculations of deductions for PAYE and National Insurance;

   (e) verify that other deductions have been correctly made and accounted for;

   (f) check calculation of net pay;

   (g) see receipts from employees paid in cash;

   (h) examine paid cheques or certified copy of bank list for employees paid by cheque or bank transfer;

APPENDIX VIII

STANDARD AUDIT PROGRAMME

PART I - INTERIM

SECTION D - PAYROLL

Extent | Schedule Ref | Initials

8. In respect of a number of weeks/months

(a) test check additions and cross-casts of payroll sheets;

(b) check totals of salaries sheets selected in (a) to summary;

(c) check additions and cross-casts of summary;

(d) check postings of summary to Nominal ledger (including control accounts);

(e) check total of net pay column to cash book;

(f) verify that the summary has been signed as approved for payment;

(g) verify that the total salaries has been reconciled with the previous week/month or standard payroll.

9. Compare the total of wages and salaries paid from week to week/month to month throughout the year to ascertain whether there have been any large fluctuations and obtain explanations therefor.

Deductions

10. Scrutinise the control accounts maintained for various deductions. Test check to see that the employer's contribution for national insurance has been correctly calculated. Test check to see that the payments to the Inland Revenue and other bodies are correct.

Conclusions

11. Write conclusions covering any errors or weaknesses discovered during the above tests and noting any possible management letter points.

APPENDIX VIII

STANDARD AUDIT PROGRAMME

PART I - INTERIM

SECTION E - NOMINAL LEDGER AND JOURNAL

Extent | Schedule Ref | Initials

Nominal Ledger

1. Agree opening balances with last year's accounts and audit file.

2. Check additions and carry forwards.

3. Test postings from books of prime entry.

4. Ensure that the ledger is being regularly balanced.

5. Scrutinise the ledger for an extended period and note any large or unusual items for follow-up.

Journal

6. Check additions of individual entries.

7. Vouch entries with authorised journal voucher and other source documents.

8. Scrutinise for an extended period and note any large or unusual items for follow up.

Conclusions

9. Write conclusions covering any errors or weaknesses discovered during the above tests and noting any possible management letter points.

SECTION F - MISCELLANEOUS

Extent | Schedule Ref | Initials

1. Complete work on permanent file.

2. Draft possible management letter, cross-referencing to working papers.

3. Amend final audit programme in the light of the results to the interim audit tests.

4. Schedule outstanding points for completion at the final audit.

5. Write summary notes on the interim audit for the manager and partner;

190

Directional testing

31. As discussed above, audit objectives can be related to five attributes:
    - completeness
    - existence
    - ownership
    - valuation
    - disclosure

    The technique that a number of the larger accounting practices use to test the first four of these attributes is referred to as 'directional testing'. The fifth attribute - disclosure - is tested as part of the review of financial statements.

32. The concept of directional testing derives from the principle of double-entry bookkeeping, ie for every debit there is a corresponding credit, and vice versa. (This of course presupposes that the double entry is complete and that the accounting records balance.) Therefore, any mis-statement of a debit entry will result in either a corresponding mis-statement of a credit entry or a mis-statement in the opposite direction, of another debit entry. By designing audit tests carefully the auditor is able to use this principle in drawing audit conclusions, not only about the debit or credit entries that he has directly tested, but also about the corresponding credit or debit entries that are necessary to balance the books.

33. Tests are therefore designed in the following way:
    Debit items (expenditure or assets) are tested for *overstatement*. This is done by selecting debit entries recorded in the nominal ledger and ensuring that they represent valid entries in terms of value, existence and ownership.

    For example, if a fixed asset entry in the nominal ledger of £1,000 is selected, it would be overstated if it should have been recorded at anything less than £1,000 or if the company did not own it, or indeed if it did not exist (eg it had been sold or the amount of £1,000 in fact represented a revenue expense).

    Credit items (income or liabilities) are tested for *understatement*. This is done by selecting items from appropriate sources independent of the nominal ledger and ensuring that they result in the correct nominal ledger entry.

    For example, the auditor might select a goods despatched note and ensure that the resultant sale has been recorded in the nominal ledger sales account. Sales would be understated if the nominal ledger did not reflect the transaction at all (completeness) or reflected it at less than full value (eg if goods valued at £1,000 were recorded in the sales account at £900, there would be an understatement of £100).

34. The matrix set out below demonstrates how directional testing is applied to give assurance on all account areas in the financial statements:

Type of account	Purpose of primary test	Primary test also gives comfort on:			
		Assets	Liabilities	Income	Expenses
Assets	Overstatement (O)	U	O	O	U
Liabilities	Understatement (U)	U	O	O	U
Income	Understatement (U)	U	O	O	U
Expense	Overstatement (O)	U	O	O	U

35. Thus, a test for the overstatement of an asset simultaneously gives comfort on understatement of other assets, overstatement of liabilities, overstatement of income and understatement of expenses.

36. It can be seen from the matrix that assets can only be understated by virtue of:
    - other assets being overstated; or
    - liabilities being understated; or
    - income being understated; or
    - expenses being overstated.

37. Similarly, liabilities can only be overstated by virtue of:
    - assets being overstated; or
    - other liabilities being understated; or
    - income being understated; or
    - expenses being overstated.

38. So, by performing the primary tests shown in the matrix, the auditor obtains audit assurance in other audit areas. Successful completion of the primary tests will, therefore, result in his having tested all account areas both for overstatement and understatement.

39. The major advantage of the directional audit approach, testing assets and expense for overstatement only, and liabilities and income for understatement only, is its cost-effectiveness. This arises because items are not tested for both overstatement and understatement. It also audits directly the more likely types of transactional mis-statement, ie unrecorded income and improper expense (whether arising intentionally or unintentionally).

Audit sampling techniques

40. The APC have recognised the need for guidance on the important topic of audit sampling, and a draft guideline was finally published in April 1987. At the same time a draft audit brief was also published in order to provide more explanation of the background to some common audit sampling techniques, together with further guidance on practical aspects of their implementation. The following comments are taken from the draft detailed operational guideline entitled 'Audit Sampling'.

41. Audit tests may be carried out using various techniques which fall into the broad categories of inspection, observation, enquiry or computation. The auditor may apply such tests to an entire set of data (100% testing) or he may choose to draw conclusions about the entire set of data ('the population') by testing a representative sample of items selected from it; this latter procedure is 'audit sampling'.

42. Audit sampling is defined as the application of a compliance or substantive test to less than 100% of the items within an account balance, class of transactions or other population, as representative of that population, to enable the auditor to obtain and evaluate evidence of some characteristic of that population and to assist in forming a conclusion concerning that characteristic.

43. Audit sampling does not include audit procedures where the auditor tests only those individual items within a population which have a particular significance (eg all items individually over a certain amount or those which the auditor believes are particularly prone to error); in such cases the auditor is simply testing part of the population in its entirety and cannot use the results to draw conclusions about the rest of the population. Such procedures may, however, be used in conjunction with audit sampling as a further source of evidence. Similarly, the auditor is not sampling in the context of the guideline when he examines certain items solely to gain an understanding of the nature of an enterprise's activities or to understand its systems of accounting and internal control ('walk-through checks').

44. Because the auditor does not examine all the items in the population when applying audit sampling, there is a risk that the conclusion that he draws will be different from that which he would have drawn had he examined the entire population; this is 'sampling risk'. The auditor should use a rational basis for planning, selecting and testing the sample and for evaluating the results so that he has adequate assurance that the sample is representative of the population, and that sampling risk is reduced to an acceptable level. A rational basis can be achieved using either non-statistical or statistical sampling, provided in either case it is properly carried out in accordance with the guideline.

45. Both non-statistical and statistical sampling require the use of professional judgement in planning, testing and evaluating the sample. Statistical sampling, however, requires the use of random selection and uses probability theory to determine the sample size, evaluate quantitatively the sample results and measure the sampling risk. Non-statistical sampling may use non-random sample selection methods, does not rely on probability theory and requires more subjectivity in making sampling decisions. Statistical sampling provides a measure of sampling risk to assist the auditor in drawing his conclusion regarding the total population; the auditor using non-statistical sampling will also need to consider whether the sample provides a reasonable basis for making an inference about the total population.

46. The auditor needs to decide which audit tests and procedures should be used to obtain the audit evidence he requires. His decision will be influenced by the materiality of, and inherent risk of error in, the account balance or class of transactions and the number and relative sizes of items in the population, the relevance and reliability of the evidence produced by each of the audit tests and procedures, and by the cost and time involved in carrying out the audit tests. He will weigh the relative costs against the benefits to determine the best combination of audit tests and procedures to obtain the overall level of assurance required. He may decide to rely solely on substantive tests or on a combination of compliance and substantive tests.

Stages of audit sampling

47. Audit sampling can be divided into four basic stages:

    Stage one - planning the sample

    Having decided to use audit sampling the auditor needs to plan the sample properly. The factors to consider include:

    - the audit objectives;
    - the population and sampling unit;
    - the definition of error (in substantive tests) or deviation (in compliance tests);
    - the sample size, which will be influenced by:
      - the assurance required (or risk accepted) having regard to other sources of evidence available;
      - the tolerable error/deviation rate;
      - the expected error/deviation rate;
      - the stratification.

    Consideration of these factors will collectively influence the choice of sampling method and the sample size. The number of items in the population does not have a significant impact on sample size except where there are few items in the population.

48. The auditor needs to consider his specific audit objective to enable him to determine the nature of the evidence he is seeking and the best audit procedures to be applied. This will assist in defining the population and the conditions that will be regarded as errors or deviations.

49. The population should be carefully identified so as to include all the items about which it is desired to draw a conclusion in a particular audit test. In particular, in the case of classes of transactions, the auditor must clearly define the period of time covered by the population. The results of the sample can only be evaluated and a conclusion drawn on the actual population from which the sample was selected. Furthermore, sampling from a population does not establish its completeness.

50. The sampling unit is any of the individual items that constitute the population. For example, in substantive tests the sampling unit may be the individual balances making up an account balance, the underlying transactions or monetary units. In compliance tests the sampling unit depends on the way in which the control is exercised; for example if a control is performed on each sales invoice then the sales invoice is the sampling unit.

51. Before performing tests on the sample the auditor should define clearly those test results and conditions that will be considered errors or deviations by reference to the audit objective.

52. The sample size may be affected by the following four related factors, which all require the auditor's judgement.

    (i)   *Assurance required (or risk accepted)*
'Audit risk' (or 'ultimate risk') is the term given to the risk accepted by the auditor that an invalid conclusion will be drawn after completion of all audit procedures. The risk that the auditor may draw an invalid conclusion that no material errors exist when in fact they do, is composed of:

- the risk that material errors may occur (sometimes called 'inherent risk');
- the risk that the internal controls may fail to prevent or correct such material errors (sometimes called 'control risk'); and
- the risk that the auditor's substantive tests may fail to detect any remaining material errors (sometimes called 'detection risk').

Sampling risk, which is one component of audit risk, is the converse of assurance required by the auditor. Absolute assurance that the sample is representative of the population is never possible from a sampling procedure. The auditor therefore has to accept a risk ('sampling risk') that he may reach a different conclusion by sampling than he would if he examined the entire population. The degree of assurance the auditor plans to obtain from the results of the sample has a direct effect on the sample size. The greater the degree of assurance required the larger will be the required sample size.

Non-sampling risk, which exists with any audit procedure, should not be ignored. It can be reduced by appropriate planning, direction, supervision and review of audit procedures.

    (ii) *Tolerable error/deviation rate*
Tolerable error or tolerable deviation rate is the maximum error or deviation rate the auditor is prepared to accept in the population and still conclude that his audit objective has been achieved. Tolerable error is not the same as materiality relating to the financial statements: tolerable error is an audit planning measure and is used at the level of individual audit procedures whereas materiality relates to the financial statements and can only be finally determined when complete financial statements are available.

For substantive tests tolerable error is likely to be expressed as a monetary amount and is the maximum error acceptable in respect of the individual audit test such that when the auditor considers the results of all audit procedures together he is able to conclude, with reasonable assurance, that the financial statements do not contain a material error.

For compliance tests tolerable deviation is the maximum rate of failure of an internal control that the auditor is prepared to accept and still be satisfied that he does not need to alter his planned reliance on that control.

The larger the tolerable error or deviation rate, the smaller need be the sample size.

(iii) *Expected error/deviation rate*

If the auditor expects errors or deviations to be present before performing tests, for example, because of the results of a previous year's tests or his evaluation of internal controls, he will need to take this into account in selecting an efficient sampling method and determining the sample size. Errors increase the imprecision of results from sampling and therefore where errors occur a larger sample size is required in order to be able to draw a conclusion within tolerable error and with the required assurance. If a high error rate is anticipated it may not be efficient for the auditor to obtain his evidence from audit sampling although sampling techniques do exist which are aimed at estimating the amount of error in populations with high error rates.

(iv) *Stratification*

Stratification is the process of dividing a population into sub-populations (or 'strata') so that items within each sub-population are expected to have similar characteristics in certain respects, such as monetary value. This reduces the degree of variation between items. By stratifying, the auditor can devote more of his attention to those items considered most vulnerable to material error. Accordingly, the more efficient the stratification the smaller need be the sample size. Stratification is more important in substantive testing of monetary amounts than in compliance testing where adherence to control procedures is likely to be relevant to all the items in the population.

Stage two - Selecting the items to be tested

53. The purpose of audit sampling is to draw a conclusion about the entire population from which the sample was selected. Thus it is necessary that the sample items should be selected in such a way that they can be expected to be representative of the population as a whole. A sample cannot be relied on to be representative unless it is drawn from the whole of the population. The aim is to ensure that within each stratum all sampling units should have a quantifiable (often an equal) chance of being selected.

54. Representative selection methods commonly in use include random, value weighted, systematic or haphazard selection. Sampling one or a few blocks of items in sequence will not generally be representative.

Stage three - Testing the items

55. Having selected the sample items the auditor should carry out the pre-determined audit tests for each item. If this is not possible for particular sample items, alternative procedures which provide equivalent evidence should be carried out on the same selected items. If it is not possible to carry out alternative procedures on those items the auditor should consider the effect on his conclusions of assuming the items to be in error. The auditor may eventually have to accept that the test was inconclusive if sufficient evidence cannot be found, in which case he will seek alternative audit evidence from other tests.

Stage four - Evaluating the results of the tests

56. Having tested the items in the sample, the auditor should perform the following steps to evaluate the results of his tests:

(a) *Analysis of errors or deviations*

When planning the sample, the auditor defines the conditions which constitute an error or deviation by reference to his audit objective. He should confirm that detected errors or deviations fulfil the defined conditions for the particular audit procedures. Whether the errors or deviations are those for which the auditor was looking or not he should consider their nature and cause and their possible impact on the financial statements and on other phases of the audit. He may, for example, need to consider whether his planned reliance on internal control is still appropriate.

In assessing any errors or deviations discovered, the auditor may conclude that many have a common and potentially significant feature, in which case he may decide to identify all items in the population which possess that common feature, thereby producing a sub-population on which he may carry out further tests. He should then perform separate evaluations for each sub-population.

(b) *Projection of errors*

The auditor should estimate the expected error or deviation rate in the whole population by projecting the results of the sample to the population from which it was selected. This is undertaken to obtain a broad view of the scale of the possible error or deviation rate for comparison with tolerable error and is not meant to imply that the precise amount or rate of error in the whole population is known. Accordingly projected errors should be used with great caution.

If the auditor has previously stratified the population into sub-populations, he would normally project the results within each sub-population and combine the results to form a conclusion on the whole population. The projected error or deviation rate from sampling procedures should be added to known errors or deviations from non-sampling procedures to give the total estimated error in the account balance or class of transactions.

(c) *Assessing the risk of an incorrect conclusion*

The auditor cannot in general expect the projected error or deviation rate to be a precise measure of the actual error or deviation rate present in the population. Actual error may be greater or smaller than projected error. The auditor must therefore consider, on the basis of his sample results and relevant evidence obtained from other audit procedures, the possible level(s) which the actual error or deviation rate might take and in particular the likelihood that the actual error or deviation rate may exceed tolerable error or deviation rate.

When using statistical sampling, this will mean comparing the maximum probable error or deviation rate, that is the upper error limit at the required level of assurance, with the tolerable error. If non-statistical sampling is used the auditor must rely on his judgement in assessing the likelihood that the actual error exceeds tolerable error.

If the auditor is not able to obtain the required degree of assurance that the actual error or deviation rate in the population is within his tolerable error, he should consider:

- requesting the client to investigate the errors and potential for further errors and to make any necessary adjustments to the financial statements;
- extending his own audit procedure (for example to a larger sample); or
- performing alternative procedures;

with a view to obtaining sufficient evidence to enable him to draw reasonable conclusions on which to base his opinion on the financial statements, including any adjustments which may have been agreed upon.

Summary of results

57. The auditor should consider, by reference to the amount which is ultimately considered to be material to the financial statements, the results from all audit procedures, both sampling and other, and the total estimated unadjusted error, to determine whether he has obtained sufficient appropriate audit evidence for each account balance or class of transactions. He should then aggregate these results to consider whether he has obtained sufficient evidence for the financial statements as a whole.

Controlling and recording

58. The auditor should adequately control and record the work involved in planning, selecting, testing and evaluating audit samples. The work should be carried out or supervised by audit staff who have appropriate training, experience and proficiency in audit sampling. The auditor's working papers should contain details of each stage of audit sampling and in particular, they should record:

- the audit objectives;
- the definition of the population and sampling unit;
- the definition of error or deviation;
- the means of determining the sample size;
- the selection method used;
- details of the items selected;
- the tests carried out;
- the errors or deviations noted and the explanations as to their causes;
- the projection of errors or deviations;
- the auditor's assessment of the assurance obtained as to the possible size of actual error or deviation rate;
- the nature and details of the conclusions drawn from the sample results; and
- details of further action taken where required.

Audit brief – audit sampling

59. This brief gives more detailed guidance to the auditor on the contents of the draft auditing guideline 'Audit sampling'. It follows a similar plan to the guideline, but simply takes the discussion of certain topics further. It is not possible to reproduce the whole paper here, but the following extract under the heading 'Approaches to audit sampling' contains a useful precis of the advantages and disadvantages of various sampling methods.

Statistical and non-statistical sampling

60. 'Sampling procedures can be carried out using statistical methods or non-statistical methods. The use of non-statistical methods is often referred to as 'judgement sampling' but this does not mean that professional judgement is not required when using a statistical method. Judgement is used to set the objectives for the sample and to evaluate the results of the tests.

61. Statistical sampling differs from non-statistical sampling however, in that it uses probability theory to measure sampling risk and to evaluate the sample results. In making the choice between a statistical and a non-statistical sampling procedure, the auditor weighs up the benefits against the costs of the two methods for the particular circumstances.

62. The more obvious benefits of statistical sampling are as follows:

    (a) *It imposes on the auditor a more formal discipline as regards planning the audit of a population.* He cannot perform the mechanics of selecting a statistical sample until he has decided on the tolerable error in respect of the population and the amount of audit assurance that he wishes to obtain from the sample.

    (b) *The required sample size is determined objectively.* Once the auditor has used his judgement to decide subjectively on the tolerable error and the level of assurance required, the statistical method determines the sample size required to satisfy his objectives.

    (c) *The evaluation of test results* is made more precisely and the sampling risk is quantified.

63. The auditor may decide that these benefits outweigh the main disadvantage of statistical sampling which is the costs associated with implementing the technique. Alternatively he may decide that cost benefit considerations justify the use of only some of the insights of techniques (eg random sampling) provided by statistical theory. Statistical sampling will not always be more expensive to apply than non-statistical sampling. However, there may be additional costs due to the need to design the sample to meet the statistical requirements of the technique and due to the method by which the items have to be selected.

64. The ease of selection of the items will hinge on whether the statistical method proposed is compatible with how the population is organised. For example, if the statistical method requires the auditor to add cumulatively through monetary values and the population is not priced or extended, then it may be impracticable to use the statistical method. Alternatively, the population to be tested may be computerised and in this instance, and if computer-assisted techniques are to be used, it may be as quick and cost-effective to select a statistical sample as it would be to select a non-statistical sample.

65. In addition to the particular costs pertaining to the individual sampling procedures, there are also global costs associated with statistical sampling such as staff training costs. Also, some statistical methods are fairly complex to apply and are not really feasible without the use of computer facilities.

66. A reason sometimes put forward for not using statistical sampling is that it produces sample sizes that are too large. However, if the sample size specified by statistical sampling, given the assurance level and tolerable error, is larger than a non-statistical sample size this may not be a criticism of statistical sampling. What in fact it may imply is that the size of the non-statistical sample is not sufficiently large to satisfy the original objectives and that, in fact, those original objectives are not being met. It can be argued that, other factors being constant, the same degree of assurance can be provided by a smaller sample computed using statistical techniques rather than using non-statistical methods.

67. With compliance tests, the qualitative characteristics of errors discovered, taken together with the auditor's judgement of the organisation's internal controls, are often far more important than the mere presence or absence of errors. Statistical analysis of compliance tests is usually confined to this latter aspect. The more important qualitative aspects of errors and their possible consequences for the accounting system are not generally susceptible to statistical analysis but require the exercise of the auditor's judgement and experience. This limits the statistical sampling when applied to compliance testing.

68. The main types of statistical sampling approaches used in auditing can be categorised either as attribute sampling or as variables sampling.

69. *Attribute sampling* is concerned with sampling units which can only take one of two possible values (eg 0 or 1) and is generally used to provide information about either the rate of occurrence of an event or of certain characteristics in a population. It can thus be used to measure what proportion of items in a population have a particular property and what proportion of items do not have that property. Attribute sampling was the first of the statistical methods to be used by auditors because it is easier to apply. In more recent years its limitations have been more fully recognised in that it deals only with rates of occurrence of events not monetary amounts and it is now primarily used in compliance testing. In attribute sampling, each occurrence of, or deviation from, a prescribed control procedure is given equal weight in the evaluation of the results, regardless of the monetary amount of the transaction. However, despite the fact that attribute sampling is generally used to reach a conclusion about a population in terms of a rate of occurrence, one statistical sampling approach, monetary unit sampling, uses attribute sampling theory to express a conclusion in monetary amounts.

70. *Variables sampling* is concerned with sampling units which can take a value within a continuous range of possible values and is used to provide conclusions as to the monetary value of a population. The auditor can use it to estimate the value of a population by extrapolating statistically the value of a representative sample of items drawn from the population. He can also use it to determine the accuracy of a population that has already been ascribed a value (generally described as 'hypothesis testing'). Thus, he can use variables sampling both in an auditing context to test the amounts of populations such as debtors, payroll expense and fixed assets additions, and also in an accounting context to value populations such as stock by counting and pricing only a proportion of the items in the population.

Monetary unit sampling

71. The most commonly used statistical technique in auditing for substantive procedures is now monetary unit sampling ('MUS'). MUS has two main characteristics: items are selected for testing by weighting the items in proportion to their value and inferences are drawn based on 'attribute sampling' concepts. The main advantages and disadvantages of MUS are described in the following paragraphs.

Advantages
(a) It is generally easier to use than variables sampling. Because it is based on attribute sampling theory the auditor can design and evaluate the sample manually with little difficulty. He can also select samples in a relatively straightforward way, either manually or by computer.

(b) It will stratify the population by monetary value (that is, the probability each item has of being selected will be proportional to the monetary amount of the item). In addition, it will automatically stratify the population to ensure that the auditor selects all items over a certain size (the sampling interval), even though they do not form part of the sample but are separately evaluated.

(c) If the auditor expects to find few if any errors in his sample, he will generally obtain a lower sample size that he would if he used variables sampling.

Disadvantages

(a) MUS does not cope easily with errors of understatement or where there are negative-valued items in the population. Consequently, practical non mathematically based methods have been evolved.

(b) MUS sampling can be over-conservative in evaluating errors, and this may cause the auditor to reject an acceptable population.

(c) Where the auditor cannot use computerised sample selection, adding cumulatively through the population (the most common means of sample selection for MUS) by hand can be time-consuming. This disadvantage will be offset where the auditor decides he wishes to check the addition of the population anyway.

(d) Where there are likely to be numerous errors, the sample size needed in order to obtain an acceptable result can become larger than the corresponding sample size using variables sampling.

(e) As sample selection is based on every nth £ in the population, if the sample needs to be extended this must be done by dividing the sampling interval by a whole number and using the same random start in order that the original sample items could all be selected again. This means the new sample will be at least twice the size of the original sample.

72. MUS will normally prove to be a useful procedure for the auditor where:
    - he is primarily concerned with tests for overstatement and where significant understatements are not expected (debtors, fixed assets and some stock tests are common examples; and
    - he will be able to select the sample relatively easily (most computer-held records, because computer selection is normally easy, or where there is a small number of items in the population and manual selection can be made).

Variables sampling

73. Variables sampling has the following advantages and disadvantages:

Advantages

(a) Variables sampling will generally be more efficient than MUS if there is likely to be a large number of differences between recorded value and audited value.

(b) The auditor can increase the sample size more easily if he uses variables sampling than if he uses MUS.

(c) He can more easily cope with zero and negative value items in the population when he uses variables sampling.

Disadvantages

(a) Variables sampling is far more complicated to use than MUS. The auditor generally needs to use a computer program to design an efficient application. He will also need to attain a reasonable level of mathematical sophistication to avoid potential misapplications.

(b) The size of the sample depends largely on the value of the standard deviation of the population. Because this value is unknown, the auditor can at best estimate its value. This makes it difficult for him to quantify in advance the sample size required and could lead either to an initial sample that is larger than is absolutely necessary or to a later requirement to increase the sample size further.

74. From the above advantages and disadvantages, it can be seen that an MUS sample is:

(a) Easier to design and evaluate. This means that the auditor is less likely to make clerical mistakes and so even with limited mathematical ability, he can more easily use MUS sampling.

(b) More practical, in that the auditor can commence at an interim stage, and then extend it up to the reporting date.

(c) Efficient when the population is likely to contain few errors.

If a substantial number of errors is expected, variables sampling is likely to prove more helpful.

75. The auditor will generally use MUS only to test populations for overstatement. As with other sampling approaches, it is extremely difficult to use MUS to test populations directly for understatement. There are two reasons for this. Firstly, items that are omitted completely from the population will have no probability at all of being selected. Secondly, items whose monetary amount is understated will have too low a probability of being selected. To illustrate, if a £1,000 item is recorded as £1, its probability of being selected will be negligible.

76. There are also circumstances in which it is not practicable to use MUS because the population being audited does not contain monetary amounts. A common example is despatch notes. In this instance, the auditor may decide to take out a numerical statistical sample based on the number of items in the population. However, he can evaluate a numerical statistical sample only in terms of the rate of occurrence of errors, not in monetary terms. Therefore, he may decide that a numerical statistical sample has few, if any, advantages over a non-statistical sample.'

Summary of the chapter

77. Great care must be taken with this chapter in distinguishing the core examination topics and the more peripheral areas.

78. The following are fertile examination areas:

(a) nature and design of compliance tests;
(b) design of substantive transaction tests on an audit area basis.

79. Try and understand *objectives* of the tests in (a) and (b): it makes the design of detailed audit tests so much easier and negates the tendency to learn audit programmes by heart. Be prepared to design a programme incorporating both compliance and substantive tests for a prescribed transaction cycle.

80. Directional testing is of relatively low priority, but appreciate that the technique is no more than a logical extension of the principles developed in the preceding sections of the chapter.

81. The topic of Audit Sampling includes certain areas of examination impact. Expect questions that require a basic understanding of sample selection. The examiner's stock statistical sampling question requires a comparison with judgement sampling - advantages and disadvantages. You will probably *not* be required to demonstrate a detailed knowledge of statistical sampling methods but appreciate the scope of the applications.

TEST YOUR KNOWLEDGE
Numbers in brackets refer to paragraphs in this chapter

1. What are the five principal audit evidence techniques available to the auditor? (2)

2. How are substantive tests defined? (6)

3. What key controls might the auditor expect to find to be able to give an affirmative answer to the sales cycle control question 'Is there reasonable assurance that all invoices are recorded?' (19 (d))

4. How does the auditor test for omissions from the accounting records? (24)

5. What is:
   (a) a depth test?
   (b) a vouching test? (30)

6. How are directional tests designed in terms of income, expenditure, assets and liabilities? (33)

7. If certain assets are understated what effect does this have on other assets, liabilities, income or expenses in terms of over or understatement? (36)

Chapter 10

THE BALANCE SHEET AUDIT: ASSETS

Topics covered in this chapter:

- Timing of the balance sheet audit
- Reliance on other specialists
- Stocks and work in progress
- Intangible and tangible fixed assets
- Investments
- Debtors and prepayments
- Bank and cash

Introduction

1. The interim audit will have established whether the accounting and internal control systems provide reasonable assurance that the accounting records form a reliable base for the preparation of the financial statements for the period under review. Attention now turns to the financial statements themselves. From a company's viewpoint, relatively soon after the year end they will extract a trial balance from the accounting records and prepare the first draft of the accounts. For this draft to be meaningful it is of course important that the accounting records are substantially complete - hence the debtors and creditors ledgers will have been closed off and generally all routine transactions will have been posted. Certain post-trial balance adjustments will normally be necessary to ensure completeness of the assets and liabilities - typically, these will include adjustments to purchases and sales to ensure proper cut-off, provision for sundry accruals and prepayments and the incorporation of the closing stock figure.

2. The auditor's balance sheet ('final audit') work is motivated by the requirement of the operational standard for him to 'obtain relevant and reliable evidence sufficient to enable him to draw reasonable conclusions therefrom'. More detailed objectives have already been highlighted, but they merit repeating here:

    (a)   Have all of the assets and liabilities been recorded?
    (b)   Do the recorded assets and liabilities exist?
    (c)   Are the assets owned by the enterprise and are the liabilities properly those of the enterprise?
    (d)   Have the amounts attributed to the assets and liabilities been arrived at in accordance with the stated accounting policies, on an acceptable and consistent basis?

    (e)   Have the assets, liabilities and capital and reserves been properly disclosed?

    (f)   Have the income and expenses been measured in accordance with the stated accounting policies, on an acceptable and consistent basis?

    (g)   Have income and expenses been properly disclosed where appropriate?

3.   Much of the sweat and toil of the balance sheet audit is expended in relation to objectives (a) - (d) above, or, to use our previously established shorthand, the completeness, existence, ownership and valuation of the assets and liabilities. Objectives (e) - (g) are principally concerned with disclosure and will be considered by the auditor as part of his review of the financial statements. The approach of this chapter and the next is therefore to establish for each major balance sheet category how the auditor might obtain audit evidence to confirm its completeness, existence, ownership and valuation - any *special* accounting or disclosure problems are also highlighted. It should be recalled, however, that as regards 'completeness', the auditor is heavily reliant on the effectiveness of the internal control system in ensuring that all data is satisfactorily captured in the accounting records. If internal control is very weak the auditor may not be able to obtain sufficient evidence as regards completeness, and hence may have to qualify his audit report.

Timing of the balance sheet audit

4.   The work discussed in this chapter will commence on or very soon after the year-end of the client. Judicious planning will of course have determined in advance the precise timetable that the client is adopting for the preparation of the accounts and hence when the individual elements of accounting information will be available to the auditor. The auditor will also be concerned with the timing of any physical stocktaking - this could well take place literally on the last day of the financial year.

5.   The assets and liabilities verification work will proceed well into the so called 'post balance sheet period'. The auditor will take advantage of the fact that he has access to information arising subsequent to the year end when forming his opinion in respect of the assets and liabilities at the balance sheet date. This is an important accounting as well as auditing principle embraced by SSAP17 and 18. The accounting and auditing implications in general of the post balance sheet period are considered further later and, as we shall see, certain procedures are performed right up to the date of signing the audit report. Clearly, as the post balance sheet period progresses, the auditor will devote more time to his detailed review of the financial statements.

6.   Nevertheless, it is the verification work that requires the major time and manpower resources in the post balance sheet period. Finally, it must be recalled that the auditor may also need to perform certain work outstanding from the interim audit - this is likely to include further compliance testing in respect of the period of the financial year not covered by his earlier transactions audit work.

Reliance on other specialists

7.   Much emphasis has been placed in this text on the responsibilities of the directors concerning accounting records and the accounts. It will be appreciated that, although these responsibilities cannot legally be delegated, the directors will from time to time regard it as necessary to consult experts within, or independent of, the company on matters affecting the accounts. Where such consultation has taken place, the auditor will need to consider the authority and independence of such experts where their judgements materially affect the

accounts. In some instances it may be the auditor himself who recognises the need for an expert opinion. Reliance on other specialists is the subject of an APC detailed operational guideline of that title, issued in May 1986. Many of the circumstances likely to give rise to the requirement for expert evidence crystallise during the balance sheet audit. The comments that follow are derived from the guideline.

8.   For the purpose of the guideline, a specialist is a person or firm possessing special skills, knowledge and experience in a discipline other than accounting or auditing.

9.   The guideline does *not* however, apply to specialists in the employment of the auditor as, under the Explanatory Foreword to Auditing Standards and Guidelines, they fall within the definition of the auditor himself. Reliance on the work of other auditors, both external and internal, is dealt with in separate guidelines. Additional detailed guidance on the relationship of auditors and actuaries of long-term insurance funds is also given separately and, because of their specialist nature separate guidance has also been developed on the audit of pension schemes.

Examples of specialist evidence

10.   During the course of an audit, the auditor may need to consider evidence in the form of statistical data, reports, opinions, valuations or statements from specialists such as valuers, architects, engineers, actuaries, geologists, lawyers, stockbrokers and quantity surveyors. Examples include:

(a)   valuations of fixed assets, including freehold and leasehold property, plant and machinery, works of art and antiques;

(b)   the measurement of work done on long-term contracts;

(c)   valuations of certain types of stocks and consumable materials, including the determination of their quantity and composition;

(d)   geological determination of mineral reserves and characteristics;

(e)   the legal interpretation of agreements, statutes or regulations;

(f)   legal opinions on the outcomes of disputes and litigation; and

(g)   actuarial advice for the purpose of assessing the cost of pension provision and its disclosure in the employer's financial statements.

11.   The guideline is presented in the context of reliance on the work of a particular specialist. Where the nature of the business of an enterprise is such that a number of specialists produce reports routinely for management purposes, (for example, regular site valuation reports by quantity surveyors in a contracting company) the scope of the work performed by the auditor will need to take account of the frequent and systematic way that reports are produced and his previous experience of the reliability and objectivity of such information.

Considerations for the auditor

12.   When planning the audit, the auditor should consider whether specialist evidence may be necessary in order to form his opinion.

When determining the need for specialist evidence regarding information contained in, or relevant to, the financial statements, the auditor should consider:

(a) the materiality of, and the likelihood of significant error in, the information being examined;

(b) the complexity of the information, together with his knowledge and understanding of it and of any specialism relating to it; and

(c) whether there are any alternative sources of audit evidence.

13. Requests for specialist evidence should be made either by the management of the client, or by the auditor, after obtaining the consent of management.

14. Where management is unable or unwilling to obtain specialist evidence, the auditor does not have a responsibility to seek that evidence independently by engaging his own specialist. If there is insufficient alternative audit evidence to enable the auditor to draw reasonable conclusions, then he can properly discharge his responsibilities by qualifying his audit report.

15. The auditor should satisfy himself that the specialist is competent to provide the audit evidence he requires. Normally this will be indicated by technical qualifications or membership of an appropriate professional body. Exceptionally, in the absence of any such indications of his competence, the specialist's experience and established reputation may be taken into account.

16. The auditor should consider the relationship between the specialist and the client; whether, for example, the specialist or any of his partners or co-directors are closely related to the client, or are directors or employees of the client or its associates. In particular, the auditor should consider whether the specialist's objectivity is likely to be impaired by such a relationship. This may be the case if the specialist has a significant financial interest in the client. He should also consider the extent to which the specialist is bound by the disciplines of his professional body or by statutory requirements to act responsibly, notwithstanding his relationship to the client.

17. The auditor's assessment of the specialist's competence and objectivity will influence his evaluation of the evidence provided by the specialist, and his decision on the extent to which he can place reliance on that evidence. If the auditor believes that the specialist may not be sufficiently competent or objective to provide the audit evidence which is needed, he should discuss his reservations with the management of the client.

18. It is desirable that, where the evidence of a specialist is to be provided, there should be consultation between the auditor, the client and the specialist, in order to establish the specialist's terms of reference. This should take place as soon as is practicable after the specialist has been appointed. The terms of reference should be documented, reviewed annually where applicable, and preferably confirmed in writing, and should include the following:

(a) the objectives, scope and subject matter of the specialist's work;

(b) the sources of information to be provided to the specialist;

(c) the identification of any relationship which may affect the specialist's objectivity;

(d) the assumptions upon which the specialist's report depends, and the bases to be used, and their compatibility with the assumptions and bases used in preparing the financial statements;

(e) where appropriate, a comparison of the assumptions and bases to be used with those used in preceding periods, together with explanations for any changes;

      (f)   the use to be made of the specialist's findings in relation to the financial statements or other financial information on which the auditor is required to report;

      (g)   the form and content of the specialist's report or opinion that would enable the auditor to determine whether or not the findings of the specialist constitute acceptable audit evidence.

19. Where it is not practicable for consultation to take place before the specialist carries out his work, the auditor will nevertheless need to obtain an understanding of the specialist's terms of reference and of the work he has been instructed to carry out.

20. The auditor will need to evaluate the audit evidence provided by the specialist to determine whether it is sufficient, relevant and reliable enough for him to draw reasonable conclusions from it. The procedures which the auditor will apply will depend upon the nature of the evidence, the circumstances necessitating its preparation, the materiality of the items to which it relates and the auditor's assessment of the specialist's competence and objectivity.

21. The auditor should make a detailed examination of the specialist's evidence including ascertaining whether:

      (a)   the data provided by management to the specialist is compatible with that used for the preparation of the financial statements;

      (b)   the assumptions and bases used by the specialist are compatible with those used in preparing the financial statements, and consistent with earlier years;

      (c)   the information supplied by the specialist has been prepared and presented in accordance with his terms of reference;

      (d)   the specialist has qualified his opinion, or expressed any reservations;

      (e)   the effective date of the specialist's findings is acceptable;

      (f)   the details of the specialist's findings are fairly reflected in the financial statements.

22. The specialist is responsible for ensuring that he uses assumptions and bases which are appropriate and reasonable. Where the skills applied by the specialist involve highly complex, technical considerations, then it may be that the level of the auditor's understanding of them can be no higher than that of the informed layman. However, the auditor should obtain a general understanding of the assumptions and bases used by the specialist, and consider whether they appear reasonable, given his knowledge of the client's business, and consistent with other audit evidence.

23. Where specialist evidence is obtained on a recurring basis, comparison of the key features of the findings with those of prior years may indicate to the auditor whether there are any grounds for doubting the reasonableness of the evidence.

24. If the auditor considers that the specialist's evidence is not relevant or reliable enough to assist him in forming an opinion on the financial statements, or that the specialist may not have acted within his terms of reference, the auditor should endeavour to resolve the matter by discussion with the management of the client and with the specialist and by further examination of the specialist's findings. In rare circumstances it may be necessary to obtain the opinion of another specialist. However, a second opinion might only relate to part of the original specialist's evidence, for example, the appropriateness of the bases used.

25. The auditor should not ordinarily refer in his report to any specialist on whose evidence he has relied. Such a reference might be misunderstood as either a qualification of his opinion or a division of responsibility, when neither of these is intended.

26. Where the auditor is unable to satisfy himself regarding the specialist's evidence, or where no such evidence is available, and there is no satisfactory alternative source of audit evidence, he should consider qualifying his audit report. The situations in which this may be necessary include:

   (a) where management is unable or unwilling to obtain specialist evidence;
   (b) where the relevance and reliability of the specialist's evidence remains uncertain;
   (c) where management refuses to accept and make use of specialist evidence which is relevant, reliable and material to the financial statements; and
   (d) where management refuses to agree to the appointment of another specialist when the auditor considers that a second opinion is needed.

Stocks and work in progress

27. No balance sheet audit area creates more potential problems for the auditor than that of stock. Stock is often a material figure in the context of the profit and loss account and the balance sheet and as regards bases of valuation it is one of the more subjective areas. Closing stock does not normally form an integrated part of the double entry bookkeeping system and hence a misstatement (under or overstatement) may not be detected from tests in other audit areas.

28. The four main elements of the stock audit - completeness, existence, ownership and valuation - require careful consideration. Typically, the auditor will adopt the following broad approach to the audit of the four elements:

   (a) Existence and apparent ownership will be verified by observing the stocktake (whether year-end or continuous).
   (b) Raw material costs and further comfort on ownership will be verified by checking invoice prices (cost ascertainment may require evaluation of a standard costing system). Cost in the case of work in progress and finished goods will involve consideration of overhead absorption bases.
   (c) Completeness is checked by observing the stocktake, checking that stocktaking records are correctly processed, applying analytical review procedures and occasionally relying on stock records where internal control has been evaluated and tested as strong.
   (d) Valuation is checked by comparing cost with net realisable value. A working knowledge of SSAP9 *Stocks and long-term contracts* is an audit essential.

29. It is logical to commence our review of stock audit procedures with 'existence' as this is usually the element where audit assurance is obtained first.

Existence: attendance at stocktaking

30. In October 1983 the APC issued a detailed operational guideline entitled 'Attendance at stocktaking' which is primarily concerned with 'existence' verification. The following comments are derived from the guideline.

31. It is the responsibility of the management of an enterprise to ensure that the amount at which stocks are shown in the financial statements represents stocks physically in existence and includes all stocks owned by the enterprise. Management satisfies this responsibility by carrying out appropriate procedures which will normally involve ensuring that all stocks are subject to a count at least once in every financial year. Further, where the auditor attends any physical count of stocks in order to obtain audit evidence, this responsibility will not be reduced.

32. In the case of a company, management has responsibilities to maintain proper accounting records and to include all statements of stocktakings in those records.

33. It is the responsibility of the auditor to obtain audit evidence in order to enable him to draw conclusions about the validity of the quantities upon which are based the amount of stocks shown in the financial statements. The principal sources of this evidence are stock records, stock control systems, the results of any stocktaking and test-counts made by the auditor himself. By reviewing the enterprise's stock records and stock control systems, the auditor can decide to what extent he needs to rely upon attendance at stocktaking to obtain the necessary audit evidence.

34. Where stocks are material in the enterprise's financial statements, and the auditor is placing reliance upon management's stocktake in order to provide evidence of existence, then the auditor should attend the stocktaking. This is because attendance at stocktaking is normally the best way of providing evidence of the proper functioning of management's stocktaking procedures, and hence of the existence of stocks and their condition.

35. Evidence of the existence of work in progress will frequently be obtained by a stocktake. However, the nature of the work in progress may be such that it is impracticable to determine its existence by a count. Management may place substantial reliance on internal controls designed to ensure the completeness and accuracy of records of work in progress. In such circumstances there may not be a stocktake which could be attended by the auditor. Nevertheless, inspection of the work in progress will assist the auditor to plan his audit procedures, and it may also help on such matters as the determination of the stage of completion of construction or engineering work in progress.

36. Physical verification of stocks may be by means of a full count (or measurement in the case of bulk stocks) of all the stocks at the year end or at a selected date before or shortly after the year end, or by means of a count of part of the stocks in which case it may be possible to extrapolate the total statistically. Alternatively, verification may be by means of the counting or measurement of stocks during the course of the year using continuous stock-checking methods. Some business enterprises use continuous stock-checking methods for certain stocks and carry out a full count of other stocks at a selected date.

37. Paragraphs 38 and 39 set out some special considerations in circumstances where the count is carried out at a date which is not the same as that of the financial statements or where it takes place throughout the year. The principal procedures which the auditor would normally carry out in relation to his attendance at any count of stocks are set out in paragraphs 41 to 53.

38. The evidence of the existence of stocks provided by the stocktake results is most effective when the stocktaking is carried out at the end of the financial year. Stocktaking carried out before or after the year end may also be acceptable for audit purposes provided records of stock movements in the intervening period are such that the movements can be examined and substantiated. The auditor should bear in mind that the greater the interval between the stocktaking and the year end the greater will be his difficulties in substantiating the amount of stocks at the balance sheet date. Such difficulties will, however, be lessened by the existence of a well developed system of internal control and satisfactory stock records.

39. Where continuous stock-checking methods are being used, the auditor should perform tests designed to confirm that management:

    (a) maintains adequate stock records that are kept up-to-date;
    (b) has satisfactory procedures for stocktaking and test-counting, so that in normal circumstances, the programme of counts will cover all stocks at least once during the year; and
    (c) investigates and corrects all material differences between the book stock records and the physical counts.

40. The auditor needs to do this to gain assurance that the stock-checking system as a whole is effective in maintaining accurate stock records from which the amount of stocks in the financial statements can be derived. It is unlikely that he will be able to obtain such assurance if the three matters above are not confirmed satisfactorily, in which circumstances a full count at the year end may be necessary.

41. The following paragraphs set out the principal procedures which may be carried out by an auditor when attending a stocktake, but are not intended to provide a comprehensive list of the audit procedures which the auditor may find it necessary to perform during his attendance.

42. *Before the stocktaking: planning*
    The auditor should plan his audit coverage of a stocktake by:

    (a) reviewing his working papers for the previous year, where applicable, and discussing with management any significant changes in stocks over the year;
    (b) discussing stocktaking arrangements and instructions with management;
    (c) familiarising himself with the nature and volume of the stocks, the identification of high value items and the method of accounting for stocks;
    (d) considering the location of the stock and assessing the implications of this for stock control and recording;
    (e) reviewing the systems of internal control and accounting relating to stocks, so as to identify potential areas of difficulty (for example cut-off);
    (f) considering any internal audit involvement, with a view to deciding the reliance which can be placed on it;
    (g) ensuring that a representative selection of locations, stocks and procedures are covered, and particular attention is given to high value items where these form a significant proportion of the total stock value;
    (h) arranging to obtain from third parties confirmation of stocks held by them, but if the auditor considers that such stocks are a material part of the enterprise's total stock, or the third party is not considered to be independent or reliable, then arranging where appropriate either for him or for the third party's auditor to attend a stocktake at the third party's premises; and

(i) establishing whether expert help needs to be obtained to substantiate quantities or to identify the nature and condition of the stocks, where they are very specialised.

43. The auditor should examine the way the stocktaking is organised and should evaluate the adequacy of the client's stocktaking instructions. Such instructions should preferably be in writing, cover all phases of the stocktaking procedures, be issued in good time and be discussed with those responsible for carrying out the stocktaking to ensure that procedures are understood and that potential difficulties are anticipated. If the instructions are found to be inadequate, the auditor should seek improvements to them.

44. The draft version of the guideline 'Attendance of stocktaking' contained, as an appendix, a listing of matters that the auditor should have regard to when reviewing a client's stocktaking instructions. Although this appendix did not find its way into the authorised version of the guideline that we are reviewing, its contents are useful to the auditor in the light of his responsibilities in paragraph 43, and are hence reproduced here in full:

(a) supervision of the planning and execution of the stocktake by sufficient senior and qualified personnel drawn from various departments: at least some of the officials should not normally be involved with the custody of stocks;

(b) tidying and marking stock to facilitate counting of items of stock. The whole of the stock-taking area should be divided into sections for control purposes;

(c) the serial numbering and control of the issue and return of all the rough count records, and their retention as required by the Companies Act 1985 S221;

(d) systematic carrying out of counts to ensure coverage of the whole stock;

(e) arrangements for the count to be conducted by at least two people, with one counting and the other primarily to check the count, or alternatively for two independent counts to be carried out; and for any differences arising to be investigated and resolved;

(f) stock sheets being completed in ink and being signed by those who carried out and checked the count;

(g) information to be recorded on the count records. (Normally this will include the location and identity of the stock items, the unit of count, the quantity counted, the condition of the items and the stage reached in the production process);

(h) restriction and control of the production process and stock movements during the count;

(i) identification and segregation of damaged, obsolete, slow moving, third parties' stocks and returnable stocks, so that these can be properly accounted for and recorded;

(j) recording the quantity, condition and stage of production of all the work in progress for subsequent checking with the costing and stock records;

(k) co-ordination of the count with cut off procedures so that documentation concerned with the flow of goods can be reconciled with the financial records. For this purpose, last numbers of goods inwards and outward records and of internal transfer records should be noted; and

(l) reconciliation with the stock records, if any, and identification and correction of differences.

45. *During the stocktaking*
During the stocktaking, the auditor should ascertain whether the client's staff are carrying out their instructions properly so as to provide reasonable assurance that the stocktaking will be accurate. He should make test counts to satisfy himself that procedures and internal controls relating to the stocktaking are working properly. If the manner of carrying out the stocktaking or the results of the test-counts are not satisfactory, the auditor should immediately draw the matter to the attention of the management supervising the stocktaking and he may have to request a recount of part, or all of the stocks.

46. When carrying out test-counts, the auditor should select items both from count records and from the physical stocks and check one to the other to gain assurance as to the completeness and accuracy of the count records. In this context, he should give particular consideration to those stocks which he believes, for example from the stock records or from his prior year working papers, to have a high value either individually or as a category of stock. The auditor should include in his working papers items for subsequent testing, such as photocopies of (or extracts from) rough stocksheets and details of the sequence of stocksheets.

47. The auditor should ensure that the procedures for identifying damaged, obsolete and slow moving stock operate properly. He should obtain (from his observations and by discussion eg with storekeepers) information about the stocks' condition, age, usage and in the case of work in progress, its stage of completion. Further, he should ascertain that stock held on behalf of third parties is separately identified and accounted for.

48. The auditor should consider whether management has instituted adequate cut-off procedures, ie procedures intended to ensure that movements into, within and out of stocks are properly identified and reflected in the accounting records. The auditor's procedures during the stocktaking will depend on the manner in which the year end stock value is to be determined. For example, where stocks are determined by a full count and evaluation at the year end, the auditor should test the arrangements made to segregate stocks owned by third parties and he should identify goods movement documents for reconciliation with financial records of purchases and sales. Alternatively, where the full count and evaluation is at an interim date and the year end stocks are determined by updating such valuation by the cost of purchases and sales, the auditor should perform those procedures during his attendance at the stocktaking and in addition should test the financial cut-off (involving the matching of costs with revenues) at the year end.

49. In addition, the auditor should:

    (a) conclude whether the stocktaking has been properly carried out and is sufficiently reliable as a basis for determining the existence of stocks;
    (b) consider where any amendment is necessary to his subsequent audit procedures; and
    (c) try to gain from his observations an overall impression of the levels and values of stocks held so that he may, in due course, judge whether the figure for stocks appearing in the financial statements is reasonable.

50. The auditor's working papers should include details of his observations and tests, the manner in which points that are relevant and material to the stocks being counted or measured have been dealt with by the client, instances where the client's procedures have not been satisfactorily carried out and the auditor's conclusions.

51. *After the stocktaking*
    After the stocktaking, the matters recorded in the auditor's working papers at the time of the count or measurement should be followed up. For example, details of the last serial numbers of goods inwards and outwards notes and of movements during the stocktaking should be used in order to check cut-off. Further, photocopies of (or extracts from) rough stocksheets and details of test-counts, and of the sequence of rough stocksheets, may be used to check that the final stocksheets are accurate and complete.

52. The auditor should ensure that continuous stock records have been adjusted to the amounts physically counted or measured and that differences have been investigated. Where appropriate, he should ensure also that management has instituted proper procedures to deal with transactions between stocktaking and the year end, and also test those procedures. In addition, he should check replies from third parties about stocks held by or for them, follow up all queries and notify senior management of serious problems encountered during the stocktaking.

53. After the three audit phases of the stocktake have been completed the auditor should have gained sufficient assurance regarding existence and some assurance as regards completeness and ownership. The auditor will now concern himself with valuation verification - which may also provide him with some further assurance in respect of completeness and ownership.

Valuation: assessment of cost and net realisable value

54. The audit objective will be to determine that stocks have been properly and consistently valued at cost, or where stocks are excess, slow-moving, obsolete or defective, reduced to net realisable value. Different considerations will apply to raw materials and components, work in progress and finished goods.

55. It is important that the auditor understands how the company determines the cost of an item for stock valuation purposes. Cost, for this purpose, should include an appropriate proportion of overheads, in accordance with SSAP 9. There are several ways of determining cost (eg FIFO, actual invoice price, latest invoice price, average cost, selling price less the gross profit percentage). He must ensure that the company is applying the method consistently and that each year the method used gives a fair approximation to cost. He may need to support this by procedures such as reviewing price changes near the year end, ageing the stock held, and checking gross profit margins to reliable management accounts.

56. Raw materials and bought in components:

    (a) *Valuation derived from actual costs.* The auditor should check that the correct prices have been used to value items by referring to suppliers' invoices. If any stock was purchased at varying prices he should ensure that the stock valuation reflects this fact. The stock valuation may include unrealised profit if stock is valued at the latest invoice price. Reference to suppliers' invoices will also provide the auditor with assurance as regards ownership.

    (b) *Valuation derived from standard costs.* When stock is valued at standard cost rather than actual cost the auditor must be satisfied that there is no overall material difference between the valuations obtained using the two bases. This may be achieved by:

        (i) comparing the actual and standard costs of specific items included in the year-end stock valuation. In doing this, he should check actual cost with supporting documentation. Significant differences between actual and standard costs may indicate that an alternative valuation, based on actual costs, may need to be made for inclusion in the financial statements.
        (ii) reviewing the price variance account, noting the size and trend of the variance towards the year end. Significant variances arising during the last month or so before the year end may indicate the need to adjust the valuation from standard to actual.

It is important to remember that the balance on a variance account represents the cumulative effect of all variances throughout the year. Thus an insignificant balance on the account at the year end does not necessarily imply that there are no significant variances between actual and standard costs of the year end stock. The specific variances may have swung round from large debit variances to large credit variances during the course of the year.

The company should analyse the price variance account between the variance applicable to the cost of sales for the year, and that applicable to the year-end valuation. The year end valuation at standard cost is then adjusted by the latter portion of the variance account (if material). The auditor must satisfy himself that the adjustment to the valuation at standard cost results in a valuation approximating to actual cost. He will need to review the price variance account and the basis upon which the allocations to cost of sales and stocks have been made.

Valuation of work in progress and finished goods
(other than long-term contract work in progress)

57. SSAP 9 defines 'cost' as comprising the cost of purchase plus the cost of conversion. The cost of conversion comprises:
    - costs specifically attributable to units of production;
    - production overheads;
    - other overheads attributable to bringing the product or service to its present location and condition.

58. The auditor should ensure that the client includes a proportion of overheads appropriate to bringing the stock to its present location and condition. The basis of overhead allocation should be consistent with prior years and should be calculated on the normal level of production activity. Thus, overheads arising from reduced levels of activity, idle time or inefficient production should be written off.

59. There are many methods of allocating overheads and consequently different audit approaches to reviewing the proportion of overheads added to cost. It is not practicable to discuss these in detail in this text. The auditor should ascertain the particular method used by the client and ensure that the overhead element included in stocks is reasonable and consistent.

60. Difficulty may be experienced if the client operates a system of total overhead absorption. It will be necessary for those overheads that are of a general, non productive nature to be identified and excluded from the stock valuation.

61. The value of work in progress comprises the value of the materials, expenses, direct labour and overheads that have brought the item to its present condition and location.

62. The audit procedures will depend on the methods used by the client to value work in progress and finished goods, and on the adequacy of the system of internal control.

    (a) *Valuation derived from actual costs.* The auditor should ensure that the unit costs are properly prepared by checking to supporting documentation such as suppliers' invoices, payroll summaries (to ascertain direct labour rates), production reports and time summaries (to ascertain actual hours worked on specific projects). He can either test the system generally in this way, and then test the valuation of specific items by referring to cost records, or he can select individual items of work in progress and examine the documentation supporting their actual costs.

(b) *Valuation derived from standard costs.* The objective is to determine that standard cost approximates to actual cost. The approach used is similar to that discussed under 56(b) above in that the auditor should compare the actual and standard costs of items included in the year-end valuation. In addition to reviewing the price variance account, he needs to review the material usage and labour variance accounts in order to determine if significant variances have arisen towards the year-end.

When he reviews the material usage variance, he should determine the extent to which the variance arises from wastage, pilferage etc, and the extent to which it arises from out-of-date standards. The former part of the variance should be written off to expense, whilst the latter part should be further analysed to determine how much of it relates to work in progress and how much to cost of sales.

A similar review should be applied to the labour variance accounts. Work in progress should be adjusted by the variances that represent out-of-date standard times and standard rates. Variances resulting from wasted or non-productive time should be written off to the profit and loss account.

63. The auditor should consider what tests he can carry out to check the reasonableness of the valuation of stocks and work in progress. Ratio analysis techniques may assist - comparisons being made with stock items and stock categories from the previous year's stock summaries. If the client has a computerised stock accounting system, the auditor may be able to request an exception report, listing, for example, all items whose value has changed by more than a specified amount. A reasonableness check will also provide the auditor with assurance regarding completeness.

64. Wherever possible cost and net realisable value should be compared for each item of stock. Where this is impracticable, the comparison may be done by stock group or category - surpluses from one category should not be set off against deficits from another in making this comparison.

65. The auditor should review and test the client's system for identifying slow-moving, obsolete or damaged stock. This will necessitate following up any such items that were identified at the stocktaking and ensuring that the client has made adequate provision to write down the items to net realisable value (see paragraph 47).

66. Where the company has stock records, these should be examined to identify slow-moving items. This kind of check can often be made easier if the company has a computerised stock system. It may be possible to incorporate into a computer audit program certain tests and checks such as listing items whose value or quantity has not moved over the previous year, and listing work in progress job numbers which have not had any significant value added over the previous six months.

67. An important procedure is to examine the *prices* at which finished goods have been sold after the year-end. This enables the auditor to ascertain whether any finished goods items need to be reduced below cost. When making this judgement, the auditor should ensure that the selling price takes account of any trade discounts that the client gives, and has been reduced by costs of disposal. This adjusted price is compared with the carrying value of the finished goods.

68. *Quantities* of goods sold after the year end should also be reviewed to determine that year end stock has, or will be, realised. If significant quantities of finished goods stock remain unsold for an unusual time after the year-end, the auditor should consider the need to make appropriate provision.

69. For *work in progress*, the ultimate selling price should be compared with the carrying value at the year end plus costs to be incurred after the year end to bring work in progress to a finished state.

70. If *raw material* costs have been *reduced* after the year-end, it may be necessary to consider the net realisable value of final products incorporating the relevant raw materials to determine if write-down is needed in respect of those raw materials. This is a possibility, albeit remote, in sectors such as food and confectionery. A dramatic decrease in costs of a volatile commodity such as coffee or cocoa could affect the retail price of products based on these commodities in the short term, justifying a write down in the raw material cost. Conversely, a fall in the realisable value of finished goods should not *alone* be considered a justification for writing down raw material costs.

Valuation and audit of long-term contract work in progress

71. *Valuation - attributable profit.* This is a *highly* subjective area, and hence one fraught with difficulty for the auditor.

72. A long-term contract is defined in the new revised SSAP9 as 'a contract entered into for the design, manufacture or construction of a single substantial asset or the provision of a service (or of a combination of assets or services which together constitute a single project) where the time taken substantially to complete the contract is such that the contract activity falls into different accounting periods.'

73. There can be no profit taken on a contract ('attributable profit') until the outcome of the contract can reasonably be foreseen. The calculation of attributable profit should be based on the work performed to date (in other words, matching costs and revenue as far as possible). The value of work performed to date will normally be determined by reference to architects' or surveyors' certificates.

74. In computing the attributable profit, it is first necessary to estimate the profit on the whole contract. This estimate should take account of all further costs necessary to complete, including any rectification and guarantee work that may be called for under the contract. Furthermore, the estimation of the costs to complete should also take into account any likely escalation of these costs due to inflation, penalty clauses imposed etc. The determination of *cost* for a long-term contract is the same as for other work in progress discussed in paragraphs 54-62.

75. *Substantive audit procedures*
The following audit procedures would be relevant.

    (a) Ensure that the classification of contracts into long and short term is in accordance with SSAP9 and consistently applied;

    (b) For each material long-term contract summarise:
-   type of contract
-   contract price
-   terms of payment and progress payments
-   cancellation terms and penalties
-   cost increase provisions
-   insurance requirements
-   equipment and materials supplied
-   renegotiation provisions
-   retentions

    (c) Obtain/prepare summary of contract work in progress, showing costs to date, valuation to date, progress payments applied for and received, costs to complete, contract price (including agreed variations), expected profit margin etc.

    (d) Verify cost figures with contract cost records.

    (e) Check basis and calculation of overhead additions; verify that:
        (i)   the calculation is based on actual expenditure (or else close estimates) and on actual levels of activity;
        (ii) the elements of expenses included are appropriate and consistent from year to year.

    (f) Check the basis of including profit/loss in WIP valuations. Verify that:
        (i)   profit is recognised on long-term contracts only (a) if the outcome of the contract can be foreseen with reasonable accuracy and (b) to the extent that it can be reasonably attributable to the work done;
        (ii) losses (to the end of the contract) are recognised as soon as they can be reasonably foreseen.

    (g) Verify that progress payments (received and receivable) and loss provisions are correctly allocated between WIP and creditors/provisions (ie total WIP should not include negative balances on individual contracts).

Intangible and tangible fixed assets

76. The auditor's substantive work in respect of intangible and tangible fixed assets may involve the two important techniques highlighted earlier in this chapter – third party confirmations and reliance on specialists. The former may be used in the context of verification of title (ownership) and the latter in circumstances where selective revaluation of tangible fixed assets has taken place in the year under review carried out by an internal or external professional valuer. It is, however, the subjective area of depreciation and amortisation that may cause the greatest audit headache. We shall start by considering intangible fixed assets.

Intangible fixed assets

77. The types of asset we are likely to encounter under this heading include patents, licences, trade marks, development costs and goodwill. Development costs and goodwill are subject to specific accounting discipline (SSAP 13 and SSAP 22 respectively). Goodwill *cannot* be revalued upwards (SSAP22 - para 34). *All* intangibles have a finite economic life and should hence be amortised.

78. The following substantive procedures might be performed in respect of intangible assets.

    (a) *General:* Prepare analyses of movements on both cost and amortisation accounts. Note the nature of the assets and the periods of amortisation.

    (b) *Patents and trade marks:* In respect of patents and trade-marks and similar items acquired during the period, inspect the purchase agreements, assignments and other supporting evidence. Where patents have been developed by the company, verify the amount capitalised with supporting costing records.

    (c) Where patents or trade-marks are maintained by a patent agent, obtain confirmation of all patents and trade-marks in force. Verify the payment of annual renewal fees.

    (d) *Goodwill:* Where goodwill has been purchased during the period ensure that it reflects the difference between the fair value of the consideration given and the aggregate of the fair values of the separable net assets acquired. Such goodwill should normally be eliminated from the accounts immediately on acquisition against reserves. It may however, be eliminated from the accounts by amortisation through the profit and loss account systematically over its useful economic life.

    (e) Ensure that any *existing* purchased goodwill is being amortised; again it is preferable that it is written off at the earliest possible opportunity (purchased goodwill should not, in any circumstances, be carried as a permanent item in the balance sheet - SSAP 22 para 31).

    (f) Ensure that no amount has been attributed to *non-purchased* goodwill in the balance sheet.

    (g) *Amortisation:* Review amortisation rates used and determine by enquiry that they are reasonable in the circumstances. Check computation of amortisation charge for the year and trace to profit and loss account. Determine the effect of and reason for any change in rates compared to prior year.

    (h) Ascertain that the unamortised balances on intangible asset accounts represent continuing value, which are proper charges to future operations (including, if applicable, goodwill).

    (i) *Income from intangibles:* Review sales returns and statistics to verify the reasonableness of income derived from patents, trademarks, licences etc.

    (j) Where applicable, examine audited statements of third party sales covered by a patent, licence or trademark owned by the company.

Tangible fixed assets

79. *Internal control considerations*

    In order to ascertain whether the amounts of fixed assets are properly stated in the financial statements it is highly desirable that the client maintains proper fixed asset registers to facilitate identification of those assets. Where such registers are not maintained the auditor must record in his working papers the movements that have taken place in the fixed assets during the year. He should ensure that the company has proper controls over substantial expenditure on capital assets and over any disposals. Such controls may include capital expenditure proposals suitably authorised, disposal of asset forms, and authorisation in Board Minutes. Any lack of control should be referred to in the management letter.

80. *Ownership and existence: freehold and leasehold properties*
The verification of the client's title to property shown in the accounts is strictly a matter for a solicitor, although for normal audit purposes prima facie evidence of title is acceptable. If the deeds are held on the client's premises the auditor should inspect them at or near the balance sheet date; if held by an independent third party, and that third party is a bank, solicitor, insurance company or another recognised depository, it will normally be sufficient to obtain a certificate stating whether or not the deeds are held in safe custody or as security. Where there is doubt about the status of the third party, he should seek to inspect the deeds himself at the party's premises.

81. When deeds are inspected the auditor would normally expect to see either:
    (a) for registered land; the Land Registry Certificate, ensuring that the land is registered in the client's name. Charges are also recorded on the certificate, together with subsequent discharges. This Certificate is conclusive evidence of title and where it is seen, there is normally no need to examine conveyances and other deeds; in cases of doubt or if the certificate is on deposit at the Land Registry because of current dealings a search may be carried out, preferably through the company's solicitors, at the Land Registry;
    (b) for unregistered land: the latest conveyance, ensuring that the title is conveyed to client; or
    (c) for leasehold property, the assignment of a lease and/or the lease itself, ensuring that the lease is current and that the client is named as the lessee.

82. Where a certificate is obtained from a third party the certificate should state in what capacity and on what terms the deeds are held, together with an adequate description. If the certificate is couched in unsatisfactory terms, such as "... an envelope purporting to contain..." the auditor should arrange physically to inspect the deeds. In future years he should request confirmation that the deeds examined have not been withdrawn from the depository during the year; if they have, a further inspection will be necessary.

83. The examination of title deeds does not itself verify the actual *existence* of buildings, even if the deeds refer to them. They may have been subsequently demolished (perish the thought) - the auditor should consider a physical inspection of any buildings whose existence may be in doubt.

84. Occasionally in groups of companies, deeds may be in the name of one company, whereas the property is carried in the books of another company. In such cases written acknowledgement should be seen that the deeds are held by the first company in capacity as nominees; if necessary legal advice should be sought on this subject.

85. *Ownership and existence: other tangible assets*
Ownership of assets such as plant, machinery and motor vehicles is usually relatively easy for the auditor to verify by examining relevant purchase documents, such as invoices but care must be taken with assets purchased under hire purchase and finance lease arrangements (SSAP21). Existence verification will be facilitated if the company maintains a plant register - assets can be selected at random from the register and physically inspected. The register should also help identify old assets which may no longer be in use.

86. *Valuation: land and buildings*

In a year in which property is revalued, a copy of the valuation should be obtained and placed on the permanent file. The auditor should ensure that the valuation has been prepared on an acceptable basis, which, in most cases, will be the open market value of the property reflecting its existing use. The auditor will also of course, be concerned with the competence and independence of the specialist performing the valuation. Such a specialist may be an employee of the client or a third party. The auditor will have regard to the considerations of the guideline 'Reliance on other specialists' discussed in section 4 earlier, when assessing the integrity of the valuation.

87. Where a surplus on revaluation has been incorporated in the accounts by crediting revaluation reserve, the auditor should confirm whether provision has been made against the reserve for the tax that would arise if the surplus were subsequently realised. The client may consider that, applying the recommendations of SSAP15, no provision is necessary - in particular where the property is to continue to be required for the business (eg a factory or office site).

In these circumstances it will be necessary to disclose the potential amount of deferred tax by way of note.

88. *Future capital expenditure*

Board minutes, capital expenditure proposals and any other relevant company documents should be scrutinised in order to verify or ascertain the extent of:

(a) capital expenditure for which the company has contracted and for which provision in the financial statements has not been made;

(b) capital expenditure authorised by the directors but for which no contracts have been placed.

The extent of authorised and contracted for capital expenditure may be confirmed in the letter of representation.

89. *Depreciation.* This is a somewhat subjective area - the auditor must have due regard to the accounting principles and disclosure requirements of SSAP12 and the Companies Act 1985. It is worthwhile summarising the more important matters.

(a) The standard and the Act set out the principles that all fixed assets (including buildings as distinct from the land they are on) having a finite useful life must be depreciated by allocating the cost (or revalued amount) less estimated residual values of the assets as fairly as possible to the periods expected to benefit from their use.

(b) No particular methods of depreciation are laid down - companies should adopt depreciation methods appropriate to the particular assets they use.

(c) Where there is a revision of the estimated useful life of an asset or a change from one method of depreciation to another, the remaining unamortised cost of the asset should be written off over the remaining useful life.

(d) If at any time there is a permanent diminution in the value of an asset and the net book amount is considered not to be recoverable in full, it should be written down immediately to the estimated recoverable amount.

(e) Where assets are revalued, the depreciation charge should be based on the revalued amount and current estimate of remaining useful life.

(f) The depreciation methods used, and the useful lives or depreciation rates used must be disclosed.

90. Special considerations apply in respect of investment properties (SSAP19) – these are discussed later in the chapter.

91. *Summary of audit procedures*
The following series of tests summarise the substantive procedures that the auditor may perform in respect of tangible fixed assets.

1. *General*
   (a) Obtain or prepare a summary of tangible fixed assets under categories, showing how the figures of gross book value, accumulated depreciation and net book value appearing in the trial balance/draft accounts reconcile with the opening position.

   (b) Obtain or prepare a list of additions during the year and verify by inspection of architects' certificates, solicitors' completion statements, suppliers' invoices etc. Make physical inspection of any item over £..... and random selection of others.

   (c) Where the client has used his own labour force to construct assets, ensure that materials, labour and overheads, if appropriate, have been correctly analysed and are properly charged to capital.

   (d) Enquire into the availability of regional development grants for any of the expenditure. Ensure that appropriate claims have been made and grants received and receivable properly accounted for in accordance with SSAP4.

   (e) Obtain or prepare a list of disposals and scrappings from fixed assets during the year. Reconcile original cost with sale proceeds and verify book profits and losses.

2. *Buildings*
   (a) Verify title to land and buildings by inspection of title deeds, land registry certificates or leases. Check that all deeds link up with the draft balance sheet.

   (b) Obtain a certificate from solicitors temporarily holding deeds, stating the purpose for which they are being held and that they hold them free from any mortgage or lien. Where deeds are held by bankers, obtain a similar certificate stating also that the deeds are held for safe custody only.

3. *Plant and equipment/motor vehicles*
   (a) Examine the fixed asset register and ensure that all additions and disposals are entered therein. Confirm that the major items in the register are in existence, in use, and appear in good condition. Prepare a schedule of the items inspected and file on the current audit file.

   (b) Check the reconciliation of the fixed asset register to the trial balance/draft accounts.

   (c) Examine documents of title (eg invoices) for assets purchased during year including, if applicable, hire purchase agreements and operating lease agreements.

(d) Confirm that the company physically inspects all the items in the fixed asset register each year.

(e) Inspect vehicle registration books or verify sale proceeds if sold since the balance sheet date and reconcile opening and closing vehicles by numbers as well as amounts. Confirm that all vehicles are used for the purposes of the company's business.

(f) If a fixed asset register is not kept, obtain a schedule for the permanent file of the major items of fixed assets showing the original cost and estimated present depreciated value, or update the existing schedule. Reconcile both the total cost and total depreciated value with the figures appearing in the balance sheet. Confirm that the major items on the schedule are in existence, in use, and in good condition. Prepare a schedule of the items inspected and file on the current audit file.

(g) Obtain confirmation from a responsible official that all movements on fixed assets have been included in the draft accounts (including scrappings).

4. *Depreciation*
   (a) Review depreciation rates applied in relation to:
       (i)   asset lives;
       (ii)   replacement policy;
       (iii)   past experience of gains and losses on disposal;
       (iv)   consistency with prior years and accounting policy;

   (b) For revalued assets, ensure that the charge for depreciation is based on the revalued amount.

   (c) Compare ratios of depreciation to fixed assets (by category) with:
       (i)   previous years;
       (ii)   depreciation policy rates.

   (d) Ensure no further depreciation provided on fully depreciated assets.

5. *Charges and commitments*
   (a) Review for evidence of charges in statutory books and by company search.

   (b) Review leases of leasehold properties to ensure that company has fulfilled covenants therein.

   (c) Examine invoices received after year-end, orders and minutes for evidence of capital commitments.

6. *Insurance*
   Review insurance policies in force for all categories of tangible fixed assets and consider the adequacy of their insured values and check expiry dates.

Development costs

92. The Companies Act 1985 states that development costs may be included in the balance sheet (that is to say - capitalised) only in 'special circumstances' (Sch 4 Para 20). This term is not defined in the Act. Where development costs are capitalised they must be amortised; the reasons for capitalisation and the period over which they are being written off, or are to be written off, must be disclosed in a note to the accounts.

93. To interpret 'special circumstances' we can turn to the guidance of SSAP13 *Accounting for research and development* (revised January 1989). The provisions of SSAP13 are considered to be compatible with those of the Act.

94. SSAP13 defines two categories of expenditure on research:

   (a) Pure (or basic) research - experimental or theoretical work undertaken primarily to acquire new scientific or technical knowledge for its own sake rather than directed towards any specific aim or application.

   (b) Applied research - original or critical investigation undertaken in order to gain new scientific or technical knowledge and directed towards a specific practical aim or objective.

95. 'Development' is defined as 'the use of scientific or technical knowledge in order to produce new or substantially improved materials, devices, products or services, to install new processes or systems prior to the commencement of commercial production or commercial applications, or to improving substantially those already produced or installed.'

96. Expenditure on *pure* and *applied research (other than on fixed assets)* is required to be written off in the year of expenditure.

97. The special circumstances which must be satisfied to justify deferral of development expenditure are:
   (a) there is a clearly defined project; and
   (b) the related expenditure is separately identifiable; and
   (c) the outcome of such a project has been assessed with reasonable certainty as to:
      (i) its technical feasibility; and
      (ii) its ultimate commercial viability considered in the light of factors such as likely market conditions (including competing products), public opinion, consumer and environmental legislation; and
   (d) the aggregate of the deferred development costs, any further development costs, and related production, selling and administration costs is reasonably expected to be exceeded by related future sales or other revenues; and
   (e) adequate resources exist, or are reasonably expected to be available, to enable the project to be completed and to provide any consequential increases in working capital.

98. From the audit viewpoint, criteria (a) and (b) in paragraph 97 should be relatively easy to establish. In examining criterion (c) the auditor will need to examine feasibility studies, market research reports and other documents, which may give an indication of each project's technical and commercial viability. He will also need to consult with technical experts employed by the client (this is another example of reliance on specialists). In testing the fourth criterion the auditor should examine, or if necessary perform, calculations of all future cash flows of the project and assess its overall economic viability. The last criterion is best tested by examining the overall cash flow forecasts for the company, which should anyway be part of his going concern review, together with the cash flow requirements of the project.

99. Once the auditor is satisfied that certain expenditure should justifiably be deferred he should, in subsequent years, review the deferred expenditure to ensure that the justifying criteria are still satisfied. If they are not the expenditure should be written off.

100. Finally, the auditor should ensure that the amortisation of deferred expenditure commences with the commercial production of the product or process and he should check that amortisation is charged on a systematic basis by reference either to the sale or use of the product or process or the period over which the product or process is expected to be sold or used.

101. The good news for the auditor in this audit area is that many companies adopt a prudent approach and write off research *and* development expenditure in the year it is incurred. The auditor's concern in these circumstances is whether the profit and loss account charge for research and development is complete, accurate and valid.

Investments

102. This section applies to companies where dealing in investments is secondary to the main objectives of the company. Under the general heading of 'investments' four distinct items are considered:
    (a) investment properties;
    (b) investments in companies, whether listed or unlisted, fixed interest or equity;
    (c) income arising from the investments in (b); and
    (d) investment in subsidiary and associated companies.

103. We shall start with investment properties.

Investment properties

104. Investment properties falling within the ambit of SSAP19 are exempted from SSAP12 requirements and are required to be included in the balance sheet at open market value. SSAP19 *Accounting for investment properties* finally saw the light of day as a separate standard rather than as a rider to SSAP12 in November 1981 after a couple of years of heated debate. Broadly speaking, the auditor's responsibilities as regards SSAP19 may be considered under three main headings.

    (a) *Is SSAP19 applicable?* ie deciding whether the standard is applicable to the client and, where it is, properly identifying all investment properties.

    (b) *The valuation of investment properties,* ie giving careful consideration as to whether the client's investment properties, and details of their valuation, have been adequately disclosed in the financial statements and whether any changes in the value of investment properties have been properly accounted for.

    (c) *Disclosure and accounting treatment,* ie. giving careful consideration as to whether the client's investment properties, and details of their valuation, have been adequately disclosed in the financial statements and whether any changes in the value of investment properties have been properly accounted for.

Chart for determination of application of SSAP 19

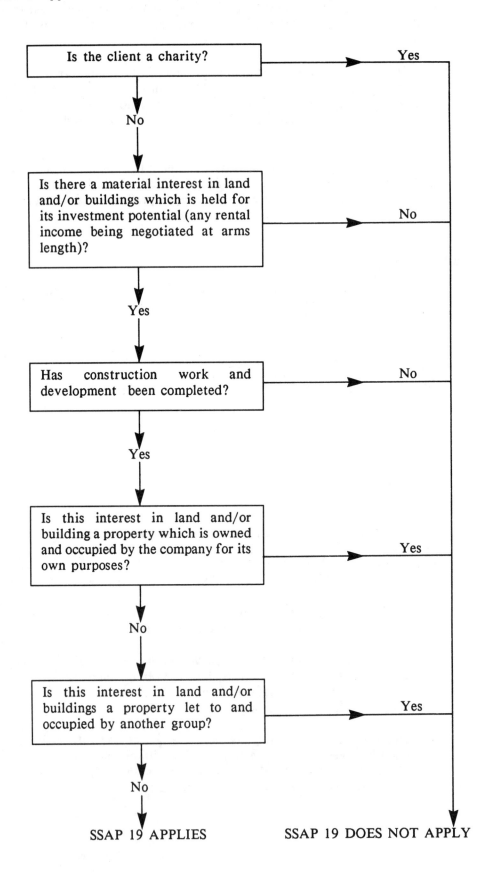

105. So far as the determination of whether or not SSAP19 is applicable is concerned, this will perhaps most readily be achieved by the use of the chart on the following page. The auditor's work in respect of *completeness, existence* and *ownership* will be broadly similar to that carried out for other freehold and leasehold properties discussed earlier.

106. The consideration of the valuation of investment properties is potentially the most problematical area for the auditor. The main responsibility of the auditor will be to determine whether the open market value of the investment properties has been properly arrived at. In order to do this, he will have to ascertain:

  (a) whether the valuation has been determined at the balance sheet date;
  (b) who has carried out the valuation;
  (c) whether the valuer has relevant qualifications and experience;
  (d) the instructions given to the valuer as to the bases of valuation to be used;
  (e) whether the bases of valuation used are appropriate and whether they have been properly applied. Guidance notes have been issued by the Royal Institution of Chartered Surveyors which prove useful in this respect.

107. In a situation where a company is not run by, or does not employ, suitably qualified or experienced persons the auditor will have less assurance that the valuations of property have been carried out, unless an external valuer has been appointed. However, where the valuation has been arrived at by the directors, the auditor should ascertain what interpretation has been used as the basis for the valuation, and whether it is relevant to the properties concerned. Underlying the audit approach will be the considerations outlined in the guideline 'Reliance on other specialists' discussed earlier.

108. However, para 6 of SSAP19 states that where investment properties represent a *substantial* proportion of the total assets of a major enterprise (eg a listed company) the valuation thereof should normally be carried out:

  (a) *annually* by persons holding a *recognised professional qualification* and having recent post-qualification experience in the location and category of the properties concerned; and
  (b) at least every five years by an *external* valuer.

109. Nevertheless, in practice, there are likely to be many situations where directors can arrive at an estimate of open market value with sufficient accuracy to meet the requirements of the standard. Some examples of this may be seen as:

  (a) where the properties can be directly compared with recent sales; or
  (b) where open market value can be computed by reference to rental income received on an arms length basis; or
  (c) where the properties are a small part of the company's assets.

NB: Even in cases such as the above, however, a periodic external valuation will be useful to the auditor as it will provide him with additional evidence as to whether the valuation is appropriate.

110. As regards the disclosure and accounting treatment of investment properties, SSAP19 requires investment properties to be included in the balance sheet at open market value. It does not specify who should make the valuation. However, paragraph 12 of the Standard calls for the disclosure of the names or qualifications of the valuers, the bases used by them and whether the person making the valuation is an employee or officer of the company.

111. Although it is the general approach of this chapter to concentrate on completeness, existence, ownership and valuation, not detailed disclosure requirements, certain further accounting and disclosure points in respect of investment properties must be emphasised:

   (a)   the accounting treatment of changes in the value of investment properties (SSAP19 paragraphs 13 and 14) - the use of the revaluation reserve;

   (b)   the manner in which investment properties and the investment revaluation reserve are displayed in the financial statements (SSAP19 paragraph 15);

   (c)   the need for properties held on leases to be depreciated on the basis set out in SSAP12 when the unexpired term is 20 years or less (SSAP19 paragraph 10); and

   (d)   Section 228 Companies Act 1985 requires certain disclosures to be made in the notes to the accounts where SSAP19 is applied. This is because the application of SSAP19 will usually be a departure, for the overriding purpose of giving a true and fair view, from the otherwise specific requirement of the Act to provide depreciation on any fixed asset which has a finite economic life.

112. As regards the point made in (d) above, the auditor should ensure that, as appropriate, a note such as the following is included in the notes to the accounts:

"INVESTMENT PROPERTIES

In accordance with SSAP19:

(a)   investment properties are revalued annually and the aggregate surplus or deficit is transferred to a revaluation reserve; and

(b)   no depreciation or amortisation is provided in respect of freehold investment properties and leasehold investment properties with over 20 years to run.

The directors consider that this accounting policy results in the accounts giving a true and fair view. Depreciation or amortisation is only one of many factors reflected in the annual valuation and the amount which might otherwise have been shown cannot be separately identified or quantified."

NB: The text of the above note has been reviewed by the DTI and meets with their approval.

Investments in companies

(NB The following comments apply equally to investments treated as 'fixed' or 'current')

113. *Internal control considerations.*
As with all other material assets, the person responsible for recording the purchase and sale of investments should not also have custody of the assets themselves. In practice, it is common for a bank to have custody of the title documents in which case the person with authority to deposit or withdraw securities should be independent of the person responsible for recording investment transactions. As an investment may be misappropriated by being pledged as collateral, it is also important that those responsible, directly or indirectly, for the custody of assets should not have access to cash.

114. Authority for controlling investment dealing should be at a high level, usually the board, but this may be delegated to an investment manager or company secretary provided all transactions are later sanctioned by the board.

115. *Existence and ownership.*
Stockbrokers should not normally be entrusted with the safe custody of share certificates on a *continuing* basis since they have ready access to The Stock Exchange. It is not, therefore, acceptable to rely on a certificate from a broker stating that he holds the company's securities; if securities are being transferred over the year-end the auditor should obtain a broker's certificate but the transaction should be further verified by examining contract notes, and in the case of purchases, examination of the title documents after the year-end.

116. *Profit or loss on disposal of investments.*
In computing the profit or loss on sale of investments the auditor should consider the following specific aspects:
(a) bonus issues of shares;
(b) consistent basis of identifying cost of investment sold (eg FIFO, LIFO, or average cost);
(c) rights issues;
(d) accrued interest;
(e) taxation.

Extel or Stubbs data should be examined for details of bonus and rights issues and to ensure that investment records are appropriately updated.

117. *Valuation.*
The auditor should establish that the company's policy on valuing investments has been correctly applied and is consistent with previous years, eg cost (as identified in 116 (b) above) or market value.

118. A permanent diminution in value should be reflected in the accounts. Stock market fluctuations are normally temporary, but the value of unlisted investments should be reviewed by reference to:
(a) net asset value and income dividend yield according to the latest accounts (audited accounts provide better quality evidence);
(b) any restrictions on realisation or on the remittance of income (particularly for foreign investments);
(c) audit qualifications (if any) in respect of the accounts.

119. Investments should be valued individually, not on a portfolio basis - the latter treatment is discouraged by the Companies Act 1985 (Sch 4 para 14). If the value of an individual investment is difficult to determine because it is not included on the Stock Exchange Daily Official List, a stockbroker may be contacted.

120. *Substantive procedures - investments*
The following tests are suggested.

(a) Obtain or prepare a statement to be placed on the current file reconciling the book value of listed and unlisted investments at the last balance sheet date and the current balance sheet date. The schedule or supporting list should include the title and particulars of the holding, cost and the market value or valuation at the balance sheet date.

(b) Examine certificates of title to investments listed in investment records, at year-end or certificates from any bank authorised to hold the documents in safe custody, ensuring that they are held for the company free from any charges or lien. Inspect blank transfers and declarations of trust where the investment is registered in the name of a nominee. Certificates of shares held for safe custody must not be accepted from stockbrokers.

(c) Verify purchases and sales recorded in the investment records by examining agreements, contract notes, correspondence and the minute book.

(d) Check with Stubbs, Extel cards or appropriate financial statements that all bonus and rights issues are properly accounted for.

(e) Ensure that the investments are properly categorised in the financial statements into listed and unlisted.

(f) Review for evidence of charges and pledging in minutes and other statutory books.

(g) Consider whether there are likely to be any restrictions on realisation of the investment or remittance of any income due (especially for investments abroad) and ensure these are properly disclosed in the financial statements.

(h) In the case of listed investments, confirm the value by reference to the Stock Exchange Daily Lists or the quotations published in the Financial Times or Times. The middle market value should be used.

(i) In the case of unlisted investments, obtain a copy of the accounts of the company or companies concerned and:
(i) - calculate the net assets value of the shares; and
  - value the investment on a yield basis;
(ii) ensure that the value at which the investment is stated in the accounts or valued by the directors is reasonable in the light of the net assets value and yield value.
(iii) see directors' minutes expressing the board's opinion as to the value of such investments, or obtain management representations.

(j) Ascertain that no substantial fall in the value of the investments has taken place since the balance sheet date.

Investment income

121. The basis of recognising income may vary from company to company particularly for dividends, eg:
    (a) credit taken only when received (cash basis);
    (b) credit taken when declared; or
    (c) credit taken only after ratification of the dividend by the investee's shareholders in general meeting.

    A consistent basis must be applied from year to year.

122. Suggested substantive procedures are as follows:

    (a) Check that all income due has been received, by reference to Stubbs or Extel cards for listed investments, and appropriate (audited) financial statements for unlisted investments.
    (b) Review investment income account for irregular or unusual entries, or those not apparently pertaining to investments held (particular attention should be paid to investments bought and sold during the year).
    (c) Ensure that the basis of recognising income is consistent with previous years.
    (d) Compare investment income with prior years and explain any significant fluctuations.

Investment in subsidiary and associated companies

123. First, it should be made quite clear that we are dealing here with investment by a holding company as reflected in its own balance sheet - not the treatment on consolidation of such an investment. Furthermore, we are *not* concerned with inter-group balances comprising current accounts or loans - these we shall consider under debtors and creditors later. The audit work to verify existence and ownership of investments in subsidiary and associated companies and completeness of any income derived therefrom, will be covered by the procedures described in paragraphs 113-122 above. Special considerations, however, apply to valuation and, as a consequence, disclosure.

124. Investments in subsidiaries and investments in associated companies are normally accounted for at cost. SSAP1 *Accounting for associated companies*, states that:

    "Unless shown at a valuation, the amount at which the investing company's interests in associated companies should be shown in the investing company's own financial statements is the cost of the investment less any amounts written off."

    Similar considerations apply to subsidiary companies (SSAP 14).

125. The auditor should review the value at which each subsidiary and associated company is carried in the accounts at the year end in relation to its net asset value. In the case of a subsidiary company, assuming identical year ends, the auditor can make this assessment based on the (draft) accounts for the year under review. For investment in an associated company the auditor should check changes in reserves to *audited* accounts made up to a date not more than six months before the client's year end. The auditor should ensure that any necessary provision against cost is made and that the accounts disclose how the carrying value has been computed.

126. For subsidiaries and associated companies ('related companies' as they are referred to in the Companies Act 1985) the aggregate amount of investment in share capital *must* be distinguished from all other indebtedness or liabilities.

Debtors and prepayments

127. For most commercial and industrial enterprises trading on credit terms, debtors will be a material figure in the balance sheet. The auditor must hence give due weight to this important audit area when designing and conducting his balance sheet tests. Returning to our key objectives of completeness, existence, ownership and valuation, the auditor should normally have obtained valuable audit assurance on the completeness of debtors from his earlier sales cycle work. It is convenient to redefine existence, ownership and valuation in terms of rather more specific objectives for trade debtors:

   (a) Do debtors represent bona fide amounts due to the company? (Existence and ownership)
   (b) Is there a satisfactory cut-off between goods despatched and goods invoiced, so that sales and debtors are recognised in the correct year? (Ownership)
   (c) Has adequate provision been made for bad debts, discounts and returns? (Valuation)

   The auditor will also be concerned with other debtors, such as inter company current and loan account balances and prepayments (where material).

Debtors' listing and aged analysis

128. Much of the auditor's detailed work will be based on a selection of debtors' balances chosen from the sales ledger at the balance sheet date. To assist the auditor, a listing is normally prepared by the client. If this is not the case, the auditor will have to extract the list of balances himself. Assuming that the client has prepared the list, the following substantive procedures are necessary:

   (a) check the balances from the individual sales ledger accounts to the list of balances *and* vice versa;
   (b) check the total of the list to the sales ledger control account; and
   (c) cast the list of balances and the sales ledger control account.

129. The determination of whether the company has made reasonable provision for bad and doubtful debts, objective (c) in paragraph 127, will be facilitated if the company produces a breakdown of the debtors' listing, indicating the age of each debt. This 'aged analysis' is sometimes used as the basis for any general doubtful debt provision by applying a specific formula (eg X% of debts over 3 months, Y% of debts over 2 months etc). Where the sales ledger function is computerised, production of an aged analysis as a regular routine is clearly a simple and desirable procedure, enhancing credit control.

The debtors' circularisation

130. *Strength of circularisation - relevance and reliability*
   The verification of trade debtors by direct communication is the normal means of providing audit evidence to satisfy objective (a) in paragraph 127 - 'Do debtors represent bona fide amounts due to the company'? The circularisation of debtors is best considered as a standard procedure which will only be omitted in special circumstances. Such circumstances might be where overall objectives can, or, occasionally, have to be achieved cost effectively by other means or where

the debtors are immaterial. The circularisation will produce for the current audit file a written statement from each respondent debtor that the amount owed at the date of the circularisation is correct - this is, prima facie, reliable audit evidence, being from an independent source *and* in 'documentary' form.

131. *Timing*

Ideally the circularisation should take place immediately after the year-end and hence cover the year-end balances to be included in the balance sheet. However, time constraints may make it impossible to achieve this ideal. In these circumstances it may be acceptable to carry out the circularisation prior to the year-end provided that:

(a) the balances circularised are not more than, say, 2-3 months prior to the year-end; and

(b) the internal control system is such that the circularisation plus an investigation and reconciliation of the movements in the sales ledger balances in the intervening period between the circularisation date and the balance sheet date will provide the auditor with reasonable assurance. (Paragraph 143 below outlines the further work that may be necessary in respect of the intervening period.)

132. *Client's mandate*

Circularisation is essentially an act of the client, who alone can authorise third parties to divulge information to the auditors. If a suitable approach is made, the client's agreement will generally be forthcoming. Should the client refuse this will inevitably lead the auditors to consider whether they should qualify their report, as they may not be able to satisfy themselves, by means of other audit checks, as to the validity and accuracy of the debtor balances. In general, the weaker the internal control the more important it is to obtain external confirmation of debtor balances. The circularising of debtors on a test basis should not be regarded as replacing other normal audit checks, such as the testing in depth of sales transactions, but the results may influence the scope of such tests.

133. *Positive v negative circularisation*

When circularisation is undertaken the method of requesting information from the debtor may be either 'positive' or 'negative'. Under the positive method the debtor is requested to confirm the accuracy of the balance shown or state in what respect he is in disagreement. Under the negative method the debtor is requested to reply if the amount stated is disputed. In either case, the debtor is requested to reply direct to the auditor. Both methods may be used in conjunction.

134. Weak internal control, the suspicion of irregularities or that amounts may be in dispute, or the existence of numerous book-keeping errors are circumstances which indicate that the positive method is preferable as it is designed to encourage definite replies from those circularised. However, it will almost certainly be found in practice that certain classes of debtors, eg overseas customers and government departments (see paragraph 142) either cannot or will not respond. Nevertheless, it is desirable, where the auditors judge it appropriate, to attempt verification, preferably by the positive method, but this should always be carried out in conjunction with such other audit tests as may be appropriate.

135. Good internal control, with a large number of small accounts, would suggest the negative method as likely to be appropriate. However, in some circumstances, eg where there is a small number of large accounts and a large number of small accounts, a combination of both methods, as noted above, may be appropriate.

136. The following is a specimen 'positive' confirmation letter:

MANUFACTURING CO LIMITED
15 South Street
London

Messrs . . . . (debtor)   Date . . . .

In accordance with the request of our auditors, Messrs Arthur Daley & Co, we ask that you kindly confirm to them directly your indebtedness to us at (insert date) which, according to our records, amounted to £. . . . . as shown by the enclosed statement.

If the above amount is in agreement with your records, please sign in the space provided below and return this letter direct to our auditors in the enclosed stamped addressed envelope.

If the amount is not in agreement with your records, please notify our auditors directly of the amount shown by your records, and if possible detail on the reverse of this letter full particulars of the difference.

Yours faithfully,

For Manufacturing Co Limited

Serial No: . . . .

The amount shown above is in agreement with our records as at . . . .

Account No . . . .   Signature . . . .

Date . . . .   Title or position . . . .

---

137. The statements will normally be prepared by the client's staff, from which point the auditors, as a safeguard against the possibility of fraudulent manipulation, must maintain strict control over the checking and despatch of the statements. Precautions must also be taken to ensure that undelivered items are returned, not to the client, but to the auditors' own office for follow-up by them.

138. *Sample selection*
It is seldom desirable to circularise all debtors and it is therefore necessary to establish an adequate sample, but if this sample is to yield a meaningful result it must be based upon a complete list of all debtor accounts. In addition, when constructing the sample, the following classes of account should receive special attention:

(a) old unpaid accounts;
(b) accounts written off during the period under review; and
(c) accounts with credit balances.

Similarly, the following should not be overlooked:
(d) accounts with nil balances; and
(e) accounts which have been paid by the date of the examination.

139. It may be convenient to apply stratification techniques to reflect the primarily substantive objective of a circularisation. This could be applied as follows to the main population (the selection of items within categories (a) to (e) above will be biased).

(a) The list of balances would be scrutinised to establish the size of the largest balances and the size and approximate frequency of the smallest balances and then four or five class intervals selected (ie ranges within which the balances will fall on the following basis:
    (i) the highest interval (eg over £100,000) which will embrace a limited number of exceptionally large balances;
    (ii) the lowest interval (eg under £1,000) which will embrace individually immaterial accounts;
    (iii) two or three intervals of equal size between these two extremes (eg £1,001 to £35,000; £35,001 to £65,000; £65,001 to £100,000) which will collectively cover the substantial number of balances of an average size.

    The number of balances falling within each class interval should *not* be counted.

(b) A selection at random from each class would be made, probably 3 or 4 accounts would suffice. Further accounts may be selected from higher value classes in order to bring the selection up to the pre-determined monetary target if necessary.

140. *Follow up procedures*
When the positive request method is used the auditors must follow up by all practicable means those debtors who fail to respond. Second requests should be sent out in the event of no reply being received within two or three weeks (except in the case of overseas customers to allow for longer delivery periods) and if necessary this may be followed by telephoning the customer, *with the client's permission*. After two, or even three, attempts to obtain confirmation, a list of the outstanding items will normally be passed to a responsible company official, preferably independent of the sales accounting department, who will arrange for them to be investigated. This does not, of course, absolve the auditors from satisfying themselves that the clearance procedure is properly carried out and from examining the results. Where there is any limitation in the follow-up procedure it is all the more important to apply other auditing tests to establish that there existed a valid debt from a genuine customer at the date of the verification.

141. If it proves impossible to get confirmations from individual debtors, alternative procedures include the following:

(a) check receipt of cash after date;
(b) verify valid purchase orders if any;
(c) examine the account to see if the balance outstanding represents specific invoices;
(d) obtain explanations for invoices remaining unpaid after subsequent ones have been paid;
(e) see if the balance on the account is growing, and if so, why;
(f) test company's control over the issue of credit notes and the write-off of bad debts.

142. *Non purchase ledger accounting*

Certain companies, government departments and local authorities operate systems - often computerised - which make it impossible for them to confirm the balance on their account. Typically in these circumstances their 'purchase ledger' is merely a list of unpaid invoices in *date order*. However, given sufficient information the debtor will be able to confirm that any given *invoice* is outstanding. Hence the auditor *can* circularise such enterprises, but he will need to break down the total on the account into its constituent outstanding invoices. It is good practice for such confirmation letters nevertheless to state the full balance so that the debtor has the option of confirming the balance and also has the opportunity to object if he thinks the total appears incorrect.

143. *Additional procedures where circularisation is carried out before year-end*

The auditor will need to carry out the following procedures where his circularisation is carried out before the year-end (see paragraph 131).

(a) Review and reconcile entries on the sales ledger control account for the intervening period.

(b) Select sales entries from the control account and verify by checking sales day book entries, copy sales invoices and despatch notes.

(c) Select goods returned notes and other evidence of returns/allowances and check that appropriate credit entries have been posted to the sales ledger control account.

(d) Select a sample from the cash received records and ensure that receipts have been credited to the control account.

(e) Review the list of balances at the circularisation date and year end and investigate any unexpected movements or lack of them (it may be prudent to send further confirmation requests at the year end to material debtors where review results are unsatisfactory).

(f) Carry out analytical review procedures, comparing debtors ratios at the confirmation date and year-end.

(g) Carry out year end cut-off tests, in addition to any performed at the date of the confirmation (see paragraphs 145 & 146).

144. *Evaluation and conclusions*

All circularisations, regardless of timing, must be properly recorded and evaluated. All balance-disagreements and non-replies must be followed up and their effect on total debtors evaluated. Differences arising that merely represent invoices or cash in transit (ie normal timing differences) generally do not require adjustment, but disputed amounts, and errors by the client, may indicate that further substantive work is necessary to determine whether material adjustments are required.

Sales cut-off

145. We can now turn to objective (b) identified in paragraph 127 - the requirement to confirm that sales cut-off is satisfactory. During the stocktake the auditor will have obtained details of the last serial numbers of goods outward notes issued before the commencement of the stocktaking.

146. The following suggested substantive procedures are designed to test that goods taken into stock are not also treated as sales in the year under review and, conversely, goods despatched are treated as sales in the year under review and not also treated as stock.

(a) Check goods outwards and returns inwards notes around year-end to ensure:
    (i)   invoices and credit notes are dated in the correct period; and
    (ii) invoices and credit notes are posted to the sales ledger and nominal ledger in the correct period.

(b) Reconcile entries in the sales ledger control around the year-end to daily batch invoice totals ensuring batches are posted in correct year.

(c) Review sales ledger control account around year-end for unusual items.

(d) Review material after-date invoices and ensure that they are properly treated as following year sales.

Provision for bad and doubtful debts, discounts and returns

147. Objective (c) in paragraph 127 is concerned with the familiar concept of reducing the carrying value of an asset to net realisable value where prudence so demands. The following procedures are suggested:

(a) Debts against which specific provision has been made (and debts written off) should be examined in conjunction with correspondence, solicitors'/debt collection agencies' letters, liquidators' statements etc, and their necessity or adequacy confirmed. A general review of relevant correspondence may reveal debts where a provision is warranted, but has not been made.

(b) Where specific and/or general provisions have been determined using an aged analysis, the auditor should ensure that the analysis has been properly prepared. He should check the reasonableness and consistency of any formulae used to calculate general provisions.

(c) Additional tests that should be carried out on individual balances will include the ascertainment of the subsequent receipt of cash, paying particular attention to, and noting, round sum payments on account, examination of specific invoices and, where appropriate, goods received notes, and enquiry into any invoices which have been omitted from payments.

(d) Excessive discounts should be examined, as should journal entries transferring balances from one account to another and journal entries that clear debtor balances after the year end.

(e) Credit notes issued after the year end should be reviewed and provisions checked where they refer to current period sales.

(f) The collectibility of material debtor balances other than those contained in the sales ledger must also be confirmed and similar considerations to those set out above will apply. Certificates of loan balances at the end of the year should be requested from employees and others to whom loans have been extended, and where considered necessary, the authority should be seen.

Goods on sale or return/goods sold subject to reservation of title

148. Care should be exercised to ensure that goods on sale or return are properly treated in the accounts. Except where the client has been notified of the sale of the goods they should be reflected in the accounts as stock at cost and not as debtors, otherwise profits may be incorrectly anticipated.

149. Enquiries should be made concerning the supply of goods subject to reservation of title. If the client trades on terms whereby such a reservation of title exists the auditor must determine whether the accounting treatment is satisfactory. In reaching this decision it is considered that the commercial substance of the relevant transactions should take precedence over the legal form where they conflict. In most circumstances it is likely that sales of such goods should be construed as a normal commercial transaction and hence be treated as purchases in the accounts of the customer and a sale in the books of the client.

Inter-company indebtedness

150. Where significant trading occurs between group companies the auditor should have ascertained as a result of his transactions audit work whether trading has been at arm's length. As regards the balances at the year end, the following substantive procedures are suggested:

(a) confirm balances owing from group and associated companies (current and loan accounts) with the other companies' records. This can be achieved directly where the auditor also audits the other companies; in other cases direct confirmation will be obtained from the companies' auditor;

(b) ensure that cut-off procedures have operated properly regarding inter company transfers;

(c) determine realisability of amounts owing;

(d) ascertain the nature of the entries comprised in the balances at the year end. Ensure that any management charges contained therein have been calculated on a reasonable and consistent basis and have been acknowledged by the debtor companies.

Prepayments

151. The extent of audit testing will be consistent with the materiality of the amounts involved. Suggested procedures are:

(a) Obtain or prepare a schedule of items paid in advance, including prior year's comparative figures.

(b) Verify the detailed items by reference to the cash book, expense invoices, correspondence etc.

(c) Review the detailed profit and loss account to ensure that all likely prepayments have been provided for.

(d) Review the prepayments for reasonableness by comparing with prior years and using analytical review techniques where applicable.

Bank and cash

152. The objectives of the balance sheet audit work will be confined to determining whether:

(a) the amounts stated for bank balances, cash in transit and cash in hand are complete and properly described; and

(b) proper cut-off has been applied in the recording of cash transactions demonstrated by adequate reconciliations.

The day-to-day recording of cash book transactions is an integral part of the sales, purchases and wages/salaries cycles considered in chapter 9. Other receipts and payments relating to, for instance, purchase and sale of fixed assets are considered in this chapter under their appropriate headings.

Bank balances

153. The audit of bank balances will need to cover completeness, existence, ownership and valuation. All of these elements can be audited directly through the device of obtaining third party confirmations from the client's banks and reconciling these with the accounting records, having regard to cut-off.

154. *The bank letter*
The technique of the bank confirmation letter is the subject of a detailed operational guideline issued by the APC in June 1982 entitled 'Bank reports for audit purposes'. This is a somewhat more prescriptive guideline than most, for, as a result of consultation with the committees of the English & Scottish clearing banks, a standard audit request letter has been approved and prepared. On the following pages a specimen letter is reproduced. It should be noted, however, that in the case of institutions other than the clearing banks it will often be more appropriate for the auditor to make a specific request for the information he requires rather than to use the standard letter.

AB & Co
Accountants
29 High Street
London N10

The Manager
Clearing Bank Ltd City Branch

Dear Sir,

.... (Name of customer)
STANDARD REQUEST FOR BANK REPORT
FOR AUDIT PURPOSES FOR THE YEAR ENDED ....

In accordance with your above-named customer's instructions given

(1) hereon	)	
(2) in the attached authority	)	Delete as appropriate
(3) in the authority dated .... already held by you	)	

please send to us, as auditors of your customer for the purpose of our business, without entering into any contractual relationship with us, the following information relating to their affairs at your branch as at the close of business on .... and, in the case of items 2, 4 and 10 during the period since .... For each item, please state any factors which may limit the completeness of your reply; if there is nothing to report, state 'none'.

We enclose an additional copy of this letter, and it would be particularly helpful if your reply could be given on the copy letter in the space provided (supported by an additional schedule stamped and signed by the bank where space is insufficient). If you find it necessary to provide the information in another form, please return the copy letter with your reply.

It is understood that any replies given are in strict confidence.

Information requested   *Reply*

Bank accounts

(1) Please give full titles of all accounts whether in sterling or in any other currency together with the account numbers and balances thereon, including NIL balances:

    (a) where your customer's name is the sole name in the title;

    (b) where your customer's name is joined with that of other parties;

    (c) where the account is in a trade name.

    NOTES

    (i) Where the account is subject to any restriction (eg a garnishee order or arrestment), this information should be stated.

    (ii) Where the authority upon which you are providing this information does not cover any accounts held jointly with other parties, please refer to your customer in order to obtain the requisite authority of the other parties. If this authority is not forthcoming please indicate.

(2) Full titles and dates of closure of all accounts closed during the period.

(3) The separate amounts accrued but not charged or credited at the above date, of:

    (a) provisional charges (including commitment fees); and

    (b) interest.

(4) The amount of interest charged during the period if not specified separately in the bank statement.

Information requested   *Reply*

(5)   Particulars (ie date, type of document
      and accounts covered) of any written
      acknowledgement of set-off, either by
      specific letter of set-off, or incor-
      porated in some other document or
      security.

(6)   Details of:

   (a)   overdrafts and loans repayable on
         demand, specifying dates of
         review and agreed facilities;

   (b)   other loans specifying dates of
         review and repayment;

   (c)   other facilities.

Customer's assets held as security

(7)   Please give details of any such assets
      whether or not formally charged to the
      bank.

      If formally charged, give details of
      the security including the date and
      type of charge. If a security is
      limited in amount or to a specific
      borrowing, or if there is to your know-
      ledge a prior, equal or sub-ordinate
      charge, please indicate.

      If informally charged, indicate nature
      of security interest therein claimed by
      the bank.

      Whether or not a formal charge has been
      taken, give particulars of any under-
      taking given to the bank relating to
      any assets.

Customer's other assets held

(8)   Please give full details of the cus-
      tomer's other assets held, including
      share certificates, documents of title,
      deed boxes and any other items in your
      Registers maintained for the purpose of
      recording assets held.

Information requested   *Reply*

Contingent liabilities

(9) All contingent liabilities, viz:

    (a) total of bills discounted for your customer, with recourse;

    (b) date, name of beneficiary, amount and brief description of any guarantees, bonds or indemnities given to you by the customer for the benefit of third parties;

    (c) date, name of beneficiary, amount and brief description of any guarantees, bonds or indemnities given by you, on your customer's behalf, stating where there is recourse to your customer and/or to its parent or any other company within the group;

    (d) total of acceptances;

    (e) total sterling equivalent of outstanding forward foreign exchange contracts;

    (f) total of outstanding liabilities under documentary credits;

    (g) others - please give details.

Other information

(10) A list of other banks, or branches of your bank, or associated companies where you are aware that a relationship has been established during the period.

Yours faithfully,

. . . .
(Official stamp of bank)

. . . .
(Authorised signatory)

. . . .
(Position)

155. There is nothing particularly complicated in the procedure involved but because of the obvious importance of the confirmation it is essential that the following points are appreciated.

   (a) The banks will require explicit written authority from their client to disclose the information requested.

   (b) The auditor's request must refer to the client's letter of authority and the date thereof. Alternatively it may be countersigned by the client or it may be accompanied by a specific letter of authority.

   (c) In the case of joint accounts, letters of authority signed by all parties will be necessary.

   (d) Such letters of authority may either give permission to the Banks to disclose information for a specific request or grant permission for an indeterminate length of time.

   (e) The request should reach the branch manager at least two weeks in advance of the client's year end and should state both that year end date and the previous year end date.

   (f) The auditor should himself check that the bank answers all the questions and where the reply is not received direct from the bank be responsible for establishing the authenticity of the reply.

   (g) The standard letter should always be used in its complete form. Where further information is required a separate (preferably accompanying) letter specifying the additional information should be sent. Note that the letter should only be used for audit purposes and not for the routine preparation of accounts.

   (h) Note from the principal headings of the letter that the confirmations sought cover more than just the bank accounts - information is also requested concerning:
   - customer's assets held as security;
   - customer's other assets held (as custodian);
   - contingent liabilities; and
   - other banks and branches that the respondent bank is aware have a relationship with the client.

156. It is, of course, essential that all points disclosed in the bank's reply should be followed up. For example, if question 10 in the specimen letter elicits a positive response, then unless the auditor has already sent a request for a report to the other banks concerned he should now do so.

157. *Reconciliation procedures*
Bank reconciliations should be prepared by a person independent of those who handle receipts and payments. The reconciliations should be checked by the auditor to the cash book and bank statements and cross-checked to the bank confirmation letter(s).

158. Care must be taken to ensure that there is no window-dressing, by checking cut-off carefully. Window dressing in this context is usually manifested as an attempt to *overstate* the liquidity of the company by:

   (a) keeping the cash book open to take credit for remittances actually received after the year end - thus enhancing the balance at bank and reducing debtors; and/or

(b) recording cheques paid in the period under review which are not actually despatched until after the year end - thus decreasing the balance at bank and reducing creditors.

A judicious combination of (a) and (b) can contrive to present an artificially healthy looking current ratio.

159. With the possibility of (a) above in mind, where lodgements have not been cleared by the bank until the new period the auditor should examine the paying-in slip to ensure that the amounts were actually paid into the bank on or before the balance sheet date. As regards (b) above, where there appears to be a particularly large number of outstanding cheques at the year, the auditor should check whether these were cleared within a reasonable time in the new period. If not, this may indicate that despatch occurred after the year end.

Cash balances

160. Cash balances/floats are often individually immaterial but they may require some audit emphasis because of the opportunities for irregularities that could exist where internal control is weak and because in total they may be material. In enterprises such as hotels, the amount of cash in hand at the balance sheet date could indeed be considerable; the same goes for retail organisations.

161. Where the auditor determines that cash balances are potentially material he will conduct a cash count ideally at the balance sheet date. Rather like attendance at stocktaking, the conduct of the count falls into three phases - planning, the count itself and follow up procedures. Planning is an essential element, for it is an important principle that all cash balances are counted at the same time as far as possible. Cash in this context may include inter alia, unbanked cheques received, IOUs and credit card slips, in addition to notes and coins. Physical verification of any securities should also take place at the same time. As part of his planning procedures the auditor will hence need to determine the locations where cash is held and which of these locations warrant a count. Planning decisions will need to be recorded on the current audit file including:
- the *precise* time of the count(s) and location(s);
- the names of the audit staff conducting the counts; and
- the names of the client staff intending to be present at each location.

Where a location is not visited it may be expedient to obtain a letter from the client confirming the balance.

162. The following matters of discipline apply to the count itself:

(a) all cash/petty cash books should be written up to date in ink (or other permanent form at the time of the count;
(b) all balances must be counted at the same time;
(c) all negotiable securities must be available and counted at the time the cash balances are counted;
(d) at no time should the auditor be left alone with the cash and negotiable securities;
(e) all cash and securities counted must be recorded on working papers subsequently filed on the current audit file. Reconciliations should be prepared where applicable (eg imprest petty cash float).

163. Follow up procedures should ensure that:

  (a) unbanked cheques/cash receipts have subsequently been paid in and agree to the bank reconciliation;
  (b) IOUs and cheques cashed for employees have been reimbursed; and
  (c) the balances as counted are reflected in the accounts (subject to any agreed amendments because of shortages etc).

Summary of cash and bank procedures

164. The following suggested substantive balance sheet tests summarise the principal audit procedures discussed above relevant to cash and bank balances.

  (a) Obtain standard bank confirmations from each bank with which the client conducted business during the audit period;

  (b) In respect of each bank account:
    (i) obtain a reconciliation of the year end balance and check its arithmetical accuracy;
    (ii) trace items outstanding from the bank reconciliation to the after date bank statements. Record details of any items not cleared at the time of the audit;
    (iii) verify by reference to pay-in slips that uncleared bankings are paid in prior to the year end;
    (iv) verify the bank balances with reply to standard bank letter;
    (v) scrutinise the cash book and bank statements before and after the balance sheet date for exceptional entries or transfers which have a material effect on the balance shown to be in hand.

  Note: as regards (ii) above ensure that all cheques are despatched immediately after signature and entry in cash book. Examine interval between dates of certain of the larger cheques in the cash book and payment by bank since this may indicate that cheques were despatched after year end (window dressing).

  (c) Identify whether any accounts are secured on the assets of the company.

  (d) Consider whether there is a legal right of set-off of overdrafts against positive bank balances.

  (e) Determine whether the bank accounts are subject to any restrictions.

  (f) In respect of cash in hand:
    (i) count cash balances held and agree to petty cash book etc:
      - count all balances simultaneously;
      - all counting to be done in the presence of the individuals responsible;
      - enquire into any IOUs or cashed cheques outstanding for unreasonable periods of time; or
    (ii) obtain certificates of cash in hand from responsible officials.

  (g) Confirm that bank and cash balances as reconciled above are correctly stated in the accounts.

TEST YOUR KNOWLEDGE
Numbers in brackets refer to paragraphs in this chapter

1. In what specific areas might the auditor seek confirmations from a specialist third party? (10)

2. How should the auditor evaluate the findings of a specialist? (18)

3. In what circumstances should the auditor attend a client's stocktaking? (34)

4. Where continuous stock-checking methods are being used what are the objectives of the auditor's tests? (39)

5. What are the principal procedures that should be carried out *before* the auditor attends a stocktaking? (42)

6. What matters should the auditor have regard to when reviewing a client's stocktaking procedures? (44)

7. What procedures should the auditor carry out to verify valuation of raw material and bought-in component stocks derived from a standard costing system? (56(b))

8. How will the auditor determine whether cost of finished goods exceeds net realisable value? (67, 68)

9. How does SSAP9 (revised) define a long-term contract? (72)

10. Summarise the audit procedures relevant to the audit of long-term contract work in progress. (75)

11. What audit procedures might the auditor carry out in respect of goodwill purchased during the period under review? (78(d)-(h))

12. What information should the auditor look out for when inspecting deeds to verify ownership of property? (81)

13. What audit procedures might the auditor perform in respect of depreciation applied to tangible fixed assets? (91 (4))

14. In what special circumstances may development expenditure be deferred? (97)

15. What audit work might the auditor perform in respect of investment income? (122)

16. In what circumstances might it be acceptable to carry out a debtors' circularisation prior to the year end to provide audit assurance as regards the balance sheet debtors figure? (131)

17. When might a 'positive' debtors' circularisation be undertaken? (134)

18. What classes of account require special attention when selecting a sample for a debtors' circularisation? (138)

19. What additional procedures should the auditor carry out when his circularisation is conducted prior to the year end? (143)

20. What procedures might the auditor carry out to determine whether the provision for bad and doubtful debts is reasonable? (147)

21. How might management seek to use the cash book at the year end to 'window dress'? (158)

22. What disciplines should apply during a cash count? (162)

Chapter 11

THE BALANCE SHEET AUDIT: LIABILITIES

Topics covered in this chapter:

- Creditors and accruals
- Loan capital
- Share capital, reserves and statutory books
- Taxation

Creditors and accruals

1. As with debtors above, creditors (liabilities) are likely to be a material figure in the balance sheet of most enterprises. The purchases cycle transactions audit work will have provided the auditor with some assurance as to the completeness of liabilities but he should be particularly aware, when conducting his balance sheet work, of the possibility of understatement of liabilities - this is a more likely cause of material error than overstatement. The primary objective of his balance sheet work will be to ascertain whether liabilities existing at the year-end have been completely and accurately recorded. As regards *trade* creditors, this primary objective can be subdivided into two detailed objectives:

    (a) Is there a satisfactory cut-off between goods received and invoices received, so that purchases and trade creditors are recognised in the correct year?

    (b) Do trade creditors represent bona fide amounts due by the company?

2. The third and final detailed objective will be to ascertain that accruals, representing benefits received in the current year but not recorded until the following year, and sundry creditors have been properly provided for.

3. Before we ascertain how the auditor designs and conducts his tests with these three objectives in mind, we need to establish the importance, as with trade debtors, of the list of balances.

Trade creditors listing and accruals listing

4. The list of balances will be the principal source from which the auditor will select his samples for testing. The listing should be extracted from the purchase ledger by the client. The auditor will carry out the following substantive tests to verify that the extraction has been properly performed:

    (a) check from the purchase ledger accounts to the list of balances and vice versa;
    (b) check the total of the list with the purchase ledger control account; and
    (c) cast the list of balances and the purchase ledger control account.

    The client should also prepare a detailed schedule of trade and sundry accrued expenses.

Purchases cut-off

5. The procedures applied by the auditor will be designed to ascertain whether:

    (a) goods received for which no invoice has been received are accrued;
    (b) goods received which have been invoiced but not yet posted are accrued; and
    (c) goods returned to suppliers prior to the year-end are excluded from stock and trade creditors.

6. At the year-end stocktake the auditor will have made a note of the last serial numbers of goods received notes. Suggested substantive procedures are as follows:

    (a) Check from goods received notes with serial numbers before the year end to ensure that invoices are either:
        (i)   posted to purchase ledger prior to the year end; or
        (ii) included on the schedule of accruals.
    (b) Review the schedule of accruals to ensure that goods received after the year end are *not* accrued.
    (c) Check from goods returned notes prior to year end to ensure that credit notes have been posted to the purchase ledger prior to the year end or accrued.
    (d) Review large invoices and credit notes included after the year end to ensure that they refer to the following year.
    (e) Reconcile daily batch invoice totals, around year end to purchase ledger control ensuring batches are posted in the correct year.
    (f) Review the control account around the year end for any unusual items.

The creditors circularisation

7. Verification of trade debtors by direct communication is virtually a standard procedure. Is it therefore also standard procedure to carry out a creditors circularisation? The answer is a qualified 'No'. The principal reason for this lies in the nature of the purchases cycle - third party evidence in the form of suppliers' invoices and even more significantly, suppliers' statements, are part of the standard documentation of the cycle. The auditor will hence concentrate on these documents when designing and conducting his tests to gain assurance in respect of objective (b) in paragraph 1 - 'Do trade creditors represent bona fide amounts due by the company'.

8. In the following circumstances the auditor may, however, determine that a circularisation *is* necessary:

    (a) where suppliers' statements are, for whatever reason, unavailable or incomplete;
    (b) where weaknesses in internal control or the nature of the client's business make possible a material misstatement of liabilities that would not otherwise be picked up;
    (c) where it is thought that the client is deliberately trying to understate creditors;
    (d) where the accounts appear to be irregular or if the nature or size of balances or transactions is abnormal.

    In these cases confirmation requests should be sent out and processed in a similar way to debtors' confirmation requests. 'Positive' requests will be the order of the day in these circumstances.

9. In normal circumstances the following substantive procedures, based on the accounting records and documentation maintained and retained by the company will be performed:

    (a) Select from the trade creditors listing and check to supporting documentation (invoices, goods received notes, purchase orders, etc) that the purchase was for the purpose of the business.
    (b) Reconcile a sample of purchase ledger balances with suppliers' statements.
    (c) Review balances for unusually low balances with major suppliers.
    (d) Compare ratio of trade creditors to purchases with previous year's figures.
    (e) Compare ratio of trade creditors to stock with previous year's figures.
    (f) Verify reasonableness of deductions from liability figures (eg discounts) by reference to subsequent events.
    (g) Ascertain reasons for significant debit balances.

Purchase of goods subject to reservation of title clauses

10. *Background*
    We have already mentioned briefly the existence of transactions where the seller may retain legal ownership of goods passed to a 'purchaser' in the context of the audit of debtors. The main burden is, however, on the auditor of the purchaser not the seller. It is now time to look at the audit implications of such 'reservation of title clauses' in more detail. Before we discuss the audit implications we must set the scene by identifying the principal legal decisions that prompted reaction, and subsequently guidance from the accountancy bodies.

11. *Romalpa.* On 16 January 1976 the Court of Appeal caused a considerable stir by refusing *Romalpa Aluminium Limited (Romalpa)* leave to appeal to the House of Lords over a dispute with *Aluminium Industry Vaasen BV ('AIV')* concerning the retention of title to goods by a supplier.

12. Very briefly, AIV had supplied aluminium foil to Romalpa but had stipulated in its terms of trade that their title to the property should remain until such time as Romalpa had remitted payment for the aluminium to them. The purpose of this condition was simply to protect AIV in the event of Romalpa defaulting.

13. Romalpa was perfectly entitled to sell the aluminium to a third party who would gain a good title to the goods, but Romalpa would be acting as an agent of AIV and as such would hold the sale proceeds for AIV. Similarly, they would have a claim on outstanding debts against any amount owing by third parties.

14. It is probable that contention would only arise in such circumstances where the intermediate purchaser becomes insolvent. This is exactly what happened to Romalpa in this case. This occurrence has further implications in that the monies paid by the third party into the intermediate purchaser's bank account are only traceable, under the principle established in *re Hallet*, where the account is in credit. Often, if the company is insolvent, the company will be overdrawn and the monies will be lost. In fact, because the monies were paid into a separate account, subsequent to the appointment of a receiver to Romalpa, the monies were recovered by AIV on the grounds of their fiduciary relationship with Romalpa.

15. The type of clause used by AIV had, until the Romalpa case, been rare in the UK. One of the immediate effects of the publicity given to the case was that reservation of title clauses became regarded as normal. The apparently wide reaching scope of the Romalpa case has, however, been limited by two more recent decisions which have shown that considerable care is needed in the construction of the clauses if they are to be effective. In the Romalpa case, AIV's claim against the goods still in Romalpa's possession was based on the fact that Romalpa was not the owner of the goods but acted as a bailee. Their claim against the sale proceeds received by Romalpa was, as already mentioned, made as by a principal against his agent.

16. In *Borden (UK) Limited v Scottish Timber Products Limited*, Borden (B) had supplied resin to Scottish Timber Products (S) on the basis of similar terms. S went into receivership and B attempted to recover from the stocks of the chipboard into which the resin had been incorporated and from the sale proceeds obtained from sales of the chipboard. The Court of Appeal held that S could not be a bailee as bailment implied the possibility of returning the goods in the same condition as in which they were delivered. It was also held that the clause was not effective in making S agents of B. B's only possible claim would have rested on them having a charge over the chipboard. To be effective, however, such a charge would have had to be registered under S95 Companies Act 1948 (now S395 Companies Act 1985). This was not done.

17. In *re Bond Worth*, Monsanto (M) supplied goods to Bond Worth (B) under the terms that

> *...equitable and beneficial ownership shall remain with us (M) until full payment has been received or until resale in which case our beneficial entitlement shall attach to the proceeds of resale....*

It was accepted that the legal ownership of the goods had passed to Bond Worth. The Court considered that M had attempted to set up a trust over the goods or the sale proceeds but that the trust was ineffective as the trustee (B) was left free to deal with the goods as he pleased in the ordinary course of the business. If the clause attempted to establish a floating charge, this was also ineffective for lack of registration (see above).

18. It is important to appreciate that these two more recent cases do not override Romalpa, but merely restrict the types of clause that are effective. It would now seem that a reservation of title clause may not be upheld unless:

(a) the legal ownership of the goods does not pass to the 'purchaser' as long as they remain in the original state;

(b) the clause states that the 'purchaser' holds the goods as bailee, and where he is permitted to dispose of them to his customers, he acts as agents for the supplier;

(c) where the goods are to be incorporated by the 'purchaser' into his products, it is made clear that the supplier has a charge over the products for the money owed to him and this charge will need to be registered under S395 Companies Act 1985;

(d) the supplier insists that the goods, any products made from them and any sale proceeds are kept separately and are readily identifiable.

The practical consequences of (c) and (d) are likely to reduce the popularity of reservation clauses.

19. In a joint statement, the members of the CCAB recommend that the commercial substance of a sale subject to reservation of title should take precedence over its strict legal form. In other words, although the title to the goods may not pass until the purchaser has paid for them, the two parties to the transaction should record it in their accounts as if it was a normal sale. It is felt that any other treatment would not give a true and fair view. There is one important exception to this rule. If there is any doubt as to whether the purchaser is a going concern, the transaction should be treated in accordance with the strict legal form. It should be obvious that, under these circumstances, to include goods sold subject to reservation of title in stocks would give a misleading impression of the company's true financial position.

20. It is recommended that companies entering into contracts of this type should disclose:

(a) the accounting treatment adopted;

(b) the fact that some of the liability to suppliers may, in effect, be secured and rank above creditors with a floating charge over the company's assets; and

(c) if possible, the amount owed to these suppliers in respect of these goods.

21. The Inland Revenue have written to the CCAB explaining that whereas they accept the proposals of the CCAB, they reserve the right to insist on the legal basis for both parties if one claims it.

22. The existence of this type of transaction will place an additional burden on the auditor of the purchaser. One point of special importance is the relevance of the going concern concept to the accounting treatment adopted. Generally, the auditor's approach should be as follows.

(a) Ascertain what steps the client takes to identify suppliers selling on terms which reserve title by enquiry of those responsible for purchasing and of the board;

(b) Ascertain what steps are taken to quantify the liability to such suppliers for balance sheet purposes, including liabilities not yet reflected in the creditors ledger;

(c) Where there are material liabilities to such suppliers:
(i) if the liabilities are quantified in the accounts, review and test the procedures by which the amounts disclosed have been computed;
(ii) if the directors consider that quantification is impracticable, but have either estimated the liabilities or indicated their existence, review and test the information upon which their disclosure is based;
(iii) consider the adequacy of the information disclosed in the accounts;

(iv) ensure that the basis on which the charge for taxation is computed takes account of the accounting treatment adopted and, where necessary, is adequately disclosed;

(d) Where liabilities to such suppliers are said not to exist or to be immaterial, review the terms of sale of major suppliers to confirm that this is so;

(e) Obtain formal written representation from the directors either that there are no material liabilities of this nature to be disclosed or that the information disclosed is, in their view, as accurate as it is reasonably possible to achieve.

23. It will be appreciated that the above procedures should, where applicable, be carried out as an integral part of the balance sheet audit of trade creditors, though the existence of suppliers selling on terms which reserve title (procedure (a)) should be clarified as early as possible in the audit to assist the balance sheet work.

Verification of sundry accruals: creditors and provisions

24. Sundry accruals is an area that lends itself to analytical review and reconciliation techniques, though care must be taken with statutory liabilities such as PAYE and VAT where there is, arguably, an expectation that the auditor verifies these liabilities regardless of materiality.

25. The following substantive procedures are suggested.

(a) From the client's sundry accruals listing check that accruals are fairly calculated and verify by reference to subsequent payments.

NB: for PAYE and VAT the following approach should be adopted:
(i) PAYE - Normally this should represent one month's deductions. Check amount paid to Revenue by inspecting receipted annual declaration of tax paid over, or returned cheque.
(ii) VAT - Check reasonableness to next VAT return. Verify paid cheque for last amount paid in year.

(b) Review the profit and loss account and prior years' figures and consider liabilities inherent in the trade to ensure that all likely accruals have been provided.

(c) Scrutinise payments made after year-end to ascertain whether any payments made should be accrued.

(d) Consider and document basis for round sum accruals and ensure it is consistent with prior years.

(e) Ascertain why any payments on account are being made and ensure that the full liability is provided.

(f) Review list of sundry accruals against previous year's figures and liabilities expected.

(g) For provisions (other than provisions for depreciation, tax and bad debts):
(i) prepare a schedule of any provisions indicating their purpose and basis, showing details of movement during the period;
(ii) decide whether any of the provisions are sufficiently material to be separately disclosed in the accounts.

Inter-company indebtedness

26. Where the company is a subsidiary or associate, it is likely that it may have a liability to its holding/investing company represented by current or loan account balances. In these circumstances it is suggested that confirmation of the balances owing is obtained and that cut-off procedures respect of inter-company transfers are tested. However, it is often the holding/investing company auditor who takes the initiative and requests the confirmations and hence the auditor of the subsidiary/associated company will be in the position of being required to confirm the balance(s). In any event the balances *must* be agreed - whosoever starts the ball rolling.

Loan capital

27. We are concerned here with long-term liabilities comprising debentures, loan stock and other loans repayable at a date more than 1 year after the year end.

28. The auditor's objective will be to determine whether long-term liabilities are properly classified and disclosed in the accounts and that the associated interest has been charged to the profit and loss account correctly and consistently.

29. The major complication for the auditor is that debenture and loan agreements frequently contain conditions with which the company must comply, including restrictions on the company's total borrowings and adherence to specific borrowing ratios. Furthermore, the auditor is sometimes *specifically* engaged to monitor and report to the debenture/loan stock trustees on the company's adherence to these conditions.

Substantive procedures applicable to all audits

30. The following suggested substantive procedures are relevant:

    (a) Obtain/prepare schedule of loans outstanding at the balance sheet date showing for each loan:

    Name of lender, date of loan, maturity date, interest date, interest rate, balance at the end of the period and security.
    - Compare opening balances to previous year's papers.
    - Test the clerical accuracy of the analysis.
    - Compare balances to the private ledger.
    - Check name of lender etc, to register of debenture holders or equivalent (if kept).
    - Trade additions and repayments to entries in the cash book.
    - Examine cancelled cheques and memoranda of satisfaction for loans repaid.
    - Verify that borrowing limits imposed either by Articles or by other agreements are not exceeded.
    - Examine signed Board minutes relating to new borrowings/repayments etc.

    (b) Obtain direct confirmation for lenders of the amounts outstanding and what security they hold.

    (c) Verify interest charged for the period and the adequacy of accrued interest.

(d) Review the permanent files to ensure that appropriate extracts from current loan agreements and other relevant information are included and that changes made during the year are appropriately noted.

(e) Review restrictive covenants and provisions relating to default:
   (i)   review any correspondence relating to the loan;
   (ii) review confirmation replies for non-compliance;
   (iii) if a default appears to exist, determine its affect, and schedule findings.

NB The above review should be conducted regardless of whether the auditor has a specific responsibility to report to the trustees under the terms of the loan agreement(s).

Reports to debenture and loan stock trustees

31. A company which issues debentures or loan stock will usually enter into an agreement with the trustees for the stockholders. This *trust deed* will usually impose certain restrictions on the company's activities (eg by placing a limit on its borrowings). It is also common for the deed to contain a provision for an annual report from the company's auditors as to the company's compliance or non-compliance with the trust deed. The form of the report may be specified by the trustees.

32. In 1986 the APC published an Audit Brief on the subject of reports to debenture and loan stock holders. Amongst other things the brief contains a number of specimen forms of report. It is useful to book at the specimen report addressed to trustees of unsecured loan stock because it gives some idea of the kind of work which the auditor will need to carry out in order to complete his report.

33. SPECIMEN REPORT: UNSECURED LOAN STOCK

31 December 19X1

"To ....Limited (as trustee of the Unsecured Loan Stock referred to below)

.........................Limited ("the Company") ....% .... Stock 19.. constituted by the Trust Deed dated ....19.. ('the Trust Deed')

Dear Sirs,

1. With reference to Clause .. of the Trust Deed we report that in our opinion:

"Adjusted capital and reserves"

2. The adjusted total of share capital and consolidated reserves at 31 December 19X1 as defined in and calculated in accordance with the provisions of the Trust Deed, that is to say based on the accounts for the year ended 31 December 19X0, adjusted as appropriate to 31 December 19X1, in accordance with the Trust Deed amounted to £..... .

"Overall borrowing limit"

3. The maximum aggregate amount permitted under Clause ... of the Trust Deed in respect of borrowings (as defined therein) at 31 December 19X1 calculated on the basis referred to in (2) above amounted to £...

"Inner borrowing limit"	4.	The maximum aggregate amount permitted under Clause ... of the Trust Deed in respect of secured borrowings of the Company and guarantor subsidiaries and borrowings of subsidiaries other than guarantor subsidiaries at 31 December 19X1, calculated on the basis referred to in (2) above amounted to £.... .
"Overall borrowings"	5.	The aggregate amount required to be taken into account as borrowings by the Company and its subsidiaries at 31 December 19X1 for the purpose of Clause ... of the Trust Deed amounted to £.... .
"Inner limit borrowings"	6.	The aggregate amount required to be taken into account as secured borrowings by the Company and guarantor subsidiaries and as borrowings of its subsidiaries other than guarantor subsidiaries as at 31 December 19X1 for the purpose of Clause ... of the Trust Deed amounted to £..... .
	7.	(NB: this final paragraph may be appropriate where the auditor has not carried out a full audit at the date at which he reports to the Trustees. In these circumstances the dates for the borrowings in paras (5) and (6) above may be other than that of the year-end).

Whilst we have obtained, wherever possible, independent confirmation of the borrowings of the Company and its subsidiaries at ......, we have not carried out an audit and have necessarily placed reliance on representations of management as to the completeness of the borrowings stated in (5) and (6) above.

Yours faithfully.

Share capital, reserves and statutory books

34. This section discusses three areas which, although only tenuously related, are often bracketed together for audit purposes. The audit objectives are to ascertain that:

    (a) share capital has been properly classified and disclosed in the financial statements and movements properly authorised;
    (b) movements on reserves have been properly authorised and, in the case of statutory reserves, only used for permitted purposes;
    (c) statutory records have been properly maintained and returns properly and expeditiously dealt with.

Share capital and reserves

35. *Share transfers*
The issued share capital as stated in the accounts must be agreed in total with the share register. Although the auditor does not usually carry out complete 'share transfer audits' an examination of transfers on a test basis should be made in those cases where a company handles its own registration work. Where the registration work is dealt with by independent registrars it is normally sufficient to examine the reports submitted by them to the company during the year and to obtain from them at the year end a certificate of the share capital in issue.

36. *Dividends*
Dividend payments should be checked on a sample basis to ascertain whether there are any outstanding dividends and unclaimed dividends unrecorded.

37. *Movements in share capital/reserves*
If shares have been issued at a premium it will be necessary to ensure that the share premium account has been properly credited. Special care will need to be taken if the company has purchased or redeemed any of its own shares (in the case of a private company such a purchase or redemption may be out of capital). Where such purchase or redemption is wholly or partly out of profits then a transfer must be made to capital redemption reserve equal to the nominal value of the shares purchased or redeemed less the proceeds of any fresh issue.

38. *Substantive procedures*
The following suggested substantive procedures are relevant:

(a) Agree the authorised share capital with the memorandum and articles of association. Agree any changes with properly authorised resolutions. File copy of certificate from the Registrar on the Permanent File.

(b) Verify any issue of share capital or other changes during the year with the minutes and ensure issue or change is within the terms of the memorandum and articles of association.

(c) Verify transfers of shares by reference to:
   (i) correspondence;
   (ii) completed and stamped transfer forms;
   (iii) cancelled share certificates; and
   (iv) minutes of directors' meeting.

(d) Check the balances on shareholders' accounts in the register of members and the total list with the amount of issued share capital in the nominal ledger.

(e) Agree dividends paid and proposed to authority in minute books and check calculation with total share capital issued. (NB: It will also be necessary to check that the dividends do not contravene the distribution provisions of the Companies Act 1985.)

(f) Check dividend payments with documentary evidence (eg returned dividend warrants).

(g) Check that advance corporation tax has been accounted for to the Inland Revenue and correctly treated in the accounts in accordance with SSAP8.

(h) Check movements on reserves to supporting authority. Scrutinise the minutes book for relevant resolutions. Ensure that movements are sanctioned by the Companies Act 1985 and the memorandum and articles of association. Confirm that the company can distinguish those reserves at the balance sheet date that are distributable from those that are non-distributable.

Statutory books

39. *What are the statutory books?*
This heading includes eight items (section references are to the Companies Act 1985):
- The register of directors and secretaries - S288
- Register of directors' interests in shares and debentures - S325

- Register of charges - S407
- The minute books of general and directors' meetings - S382
- The register of interests in shares - S211 (public companies only).
- The accounting records - S221
- Directors' service contracts - S318.
- The register of members - S352 (the auditor will review the register of members during his work to verify share capital).

40. In addition to the statutory books above, the auditor should also concern himself with the various regulatory returns to ensure that they have been filed promptly. With regard to accounting records, the auditor will need to be mindful of the requirements of the Act throughout his audit; nevertheless it is at the balance sheet stage that he must form an opinion as to whether proper accounting records have been kept. The auditor should also consider, at the same time, whether the nominal ledger and journal have been satisfactorily maintained.

Substantive procedures

41. Suggested substantive procedures are as follows.

   (a) *Register of directors and secretaries*
     (i) Up-date permanent file giving details of directors and secretary.
     (ii) Verify any changes with the minutes and ensure that the necessary details have been filed at Companies House.
     (iii) Verify that the number of directors complies with the regulations (if any) in the Articles.

   (b) *Register of directors' interests in shares and debentures*
     (i) Ensure that directors' interests are noted on the permanent file for cross referencing to directors' reports; and
     (ii) Ensure that directors' shareholdings are in accordance with any requirements of the Articles.

   (c) *Minute books*
     (i) Obtain photocopies or prepare extracts from the minute books of meetings concerning financial matters, cross-referencing them to appropriate working papers. Ensure that extracts of agreements referred to in the minutes are prepared for the permanent file.
     (ii) Check agreements with the company's seal book where one is kept.
     (iii) Note the date of the last minute reviewed, and
     (iv) Check that meetings have been properly convened and that quorums attended.

   (d) *Register of interests in shares (if applicable)*

   Scrutinise register and verify that prima facie it appears to be in order.

   (e) *Register of charges*
     (i) Up-date permanent file schedule from the register. Ensure that details of any assets which are charged as security for loans from third parties are disclosed in the accounts.
     (ii) If no entries appear in the register, obtain verbal confirmation that there are no charges to be recorded.
     (iii) Consider carrying out company search at Companies House to verify the accuracy of the register.

(f) *Accounting records*
   Consider whether the accounting records are adequate to:
   (i)   show and explain the company's transactions;
   (ii) disclose with reasonable accuracy, at any time, the financial position of the company;
   (iii) comply with the Act by recording money received and expended, assets and liabilities, year-end stock and stock-taking, sales and purchases; and
   (iv) enable the directors to ensure that the accounts give a true and fair view.

(g) *Nominal ledger and journal*
   (i)   Check opening balances in nominal ledger to previous year's audited accounts.
   (ii) Check additions of nominal ledger accounts.
   (iii) Review nominal ledger accounts and ensure significant transfers and unusual items are bona fide.
   (iv) Review the journal and ensure that significant entries are authorised and properly recorded; and
   (v)   Check extraction and addition of trial balance (if prepared by the client).

(h) *Returns*
   Check that the following returns have been filed properly:
   (i)   annual return and previous year's accounts;
   (ii) notices of change in directors or secretary;
   (iii) memoranda of charges or mortgages created during the period;
   (iv) VAT returns; and
   (v)   Forms CT61 (ACT).

(i) *Directors' service contracts*
   (i)   Inspect copies of directors' service contracts or memoranda; and
   (ii) ensure that these are kept at either:
        - the registered office;
        - the principal place of business; or
        - the place where the register of members is kept, if not the registered office;
   (iii) verify that long-term contracts (>5 years) have been approved in general meeting.

Taxation

42. The auditor's objectives will be to ascertain whether:

   (a) the profit and loss account fairly states the charge to taxation on the profits on ordinary activities for the year, including any adjustments required to the charge to taxation in prior years, and taxation attributable to extraordinary items, in accordance with SSAP8, SSAP15 and the Companies Act 1985; and
   (b) liabilities for taxation, current and deferred, are fairly stated and properly described in the balance sheet in accordance with SSAP8, SSAP15 and the Companies Act 1985.

43. On certain assignments the auditor may also have been engaged to take responsibility for the client's taxation affairs. However, the auditor will always have to form an opinion regarding the objectives above, whether or not he has prepared the supporting accounting summaries and computations. Many larger firms of accountants have specialist autonomous tax departments, and hence this is an audit area where the 'auditor' (ie the reporting partner and his audit team) may have to liaise with members of the tax department.

44. Tax information required for computations will be gathered as the audit progresses, in particular the identification and scheduling of disallowable items ('permanent differences') and movements on tangible fixed assets. Firms often use checklists to ensure that information for corporation tax purposes is complete.

Deferred taxation

45. The most difficult area for the auditor is frequently the deferred taxation provision, especially where the directors have determined that less than full provision is justified. Following the introduction of SSAP15 *Accounting for deferred tax* in 1978, companies were no longer required to provide for taxation timing differences (other than short-term differences) where they could demonstrate that such timing differences were unlikely to reverse in the foreseeable future. The ASC has published a revised version of SSAP15, effective for accounting periods beginning on or after 1 April 1985. The main changes contained in the revised standard are as follows.

    (a) Partial provision for deferred tax is still required, although there is a change in emphasis from 'provide unless it can be demonstrated that no liability will arise' to 'provide to the extent that it is probable that a liability will crystallise and do not provide to the extent that it is probable that a liability will not crystallise'.

    (b) Companies should assess the likelihood of any liability crystallising in the light of their own particular circumstances, rather than by reference to a minimum period of three years as laid down in the original SSAP15. The period of assessment relevant to any particular company may be relatively short (say three to five years) where the pattern of timing differences is expected to be regular, but may be longer where the pattern is expected to be irregular.

    (c) Deferred tax should be computed using the liability method. Thus the deferral method is no longer permitted.

    (d) Deferred tax should not be automatically provided on all short-term timing differences, as required by the original SSAP 15. Such differences should be considered with other timing differences in assessing whether or not a liability will crystallise.

    (e) Deferred tax net debit balances should not be carried forward except to the extent that recovery without replacement by equivalent debit balances is assured beyond reasonable doubt. The significance of this new requirement affects short-term debit balances such as ACT.

    (f) Where the potential amount of deferred tax on a revalued asset is not shown, because it does not constitute a timing difference due to the availability of capital losses or rollover relief, that fact should be stated.

46. Partial provision is a difficult area for the auditor, who must determine whether management's forecasts for the relevant period of assessment are reasonable and support the partial provision. The forecasts that the auditor may be concerned with include profit and cash flow, capital expenditure and disposals, and depreciation charges on allowable capital expenditure. It is useful to be reminded of the types of timing difference that might be encountered and in respect of which decisions as to the likelihood of crystallisation will have to be made.

(a) Timing differences arising from the use of the receipts and payments basis for tax purposes and the accruals basis in the accounts. Examples include:
- interest receivable in the accounting period, but taxed when received;
- dividends from foreign subsidiaries accrued in a period prior to that in which they arise for tax purposes;
- intra-group profits in stock deferred upon consolidation until realisation to third parties;
- interest or royalties payable accrued in the accounting period, but allowed when paid;
- pension costs accrued in the financial statements but allowed for tax purposes when paid or contributed at some later date;
- provisions for repairs and maintenance made in the financial statements but not allowed for tax purposes until the expenditure is incurred;
- bad debt provisions not allowed for tax purposes unless and until they become 'specific';
- provisions for revenue losses on closing down plants or for costs of reorganisation upon which tax relief is not obtained until the costs or losses are incurred; and
- revenue expenditure, deferred in the financial statements, such as development or advertising, if it is allowed for tax purposes as it is incurred.

(b) Accelerated capital allowances: These are timing differences which arise from the availability of capital allowances in tax computations which are in excess of the related depreciation charges in financial statements. The reverse may also occur whereby the depreciation charges in financial statements exceed the capital allowances available in tax computations.

(c) Revaluations of fixed assets:

(i) When a fixed asset is revalued above cost a timing difference potentially arises in that, in the absence of rollover relief, tax on a chargeable gain may be payable if and when the asset is disposed of at its revalued amount. Where it is probable that a liability will crystallise, provision for the tax payable on disposal is required to be made out of the revaluation surplus, based on the value at which the fixed asset is carried in the balance sheet. Whether or not a liability will crystallise can usually be determined, in the absence of rollover relief, at the time the enterprise decides to dispose of the asset.

(ii) *Revaluations not incorporated in the accounts.* Para 42 of the Standard requires that, where the value of an asset is not incorporated in the balance sheet but is given elsewhere such as in a note, the tax effects, if any, which would arise if the asset was realised at the noted value should also be shown. This also applies where the value is given in the directors' report instead of in the notes.

(iii) *Rollover relief.* Rollover relief has the effect of deferring the reversal of the timing difference arising on the revaluation of an asset beyond the date of sale, or of creating a timing difference on the sale of an asset that has not been revalued, or a combination of the two. Where rollover relief has been obtained on the sale of an asset, with the 'base cost' of the replacement asset for tax purposes thereby being reduced, and the potential deferred tax has not been disclosed, the standard requires disclosure of the fact that the revaluation does not constitute a timing difference and that tax has therefore not been quantified, as it will not otherwise be evident from the accounts.

47. The auditor must ensure, notwithstanding the subjective nature of forecasts, that the presumptions are reasonable having regard to the company's financial history and management's plans, as well as to external factors such as economic conditions and technical developments. The auditor should be alert to the fact that non-provision or overprovision of deferred tax provides yet another opportunity for 'window-dressing'.

Substantive procedures

48. The following procedures are suggested:

(a) Obtain or prepare analysis of movements in the nominal ledger tax accounts, current and deferred, for the period: and
   (i) test for mathematical accuracy;
   (ii) compare amounts paid during the current period to copies of assessments and cash book;
   (iii) compare refunds received to correspondence with the Inland Revenue.

(b) Verify, or prepare, the computation of the corporation tax charge:
   (i) verify calculations of non-allowable expenses, and other adjustments;
   (ii) verify fixed asset additions and disposals with fixed asset movements schedule and check calculation of capital allowances.

(c) Identify timing differences at year-end.

(d) Check provision for deferred tax is made at the corporation tax rate at the year end on all timing differences less losses and ACT, except to the extent that it is probable that a liability will not crystallise.

(e) Assess the justification for non-provision of part (or all) of the taxation deferred, by references to forecasts and projections for a sufficient period of years in the circumstances, in respect of cashflow, capital expenditure and disposals etc:
   (i) Consider reliability of forecasts made in previous years.
   (ii) Consider likelihood of management bias in forecasting.
   (iii) Test reasonableness of forecasts in the light of economic forecasts, industry trends, company trends.
   (iv) Perform sensitivity analysis on forecasts if there are doubts about reliability in order to establish materiality of possible misstatements.
   (v) Test check calculations and the resulting amount of tax provided and unprovided.

(f) (i) Check that deferred tax on asset revaluations above cost is provided where disposal is intended (and roll over relief is not available) out of the revaluation surplus.
   (ii) If asset revaluation not incorporated in the accounts, check that the note (or directors' report) indicates the tax effect (if any) which would arise if the asset were realised at the stated value.

(g) Confirm that the amount of any unprovided deferred tax in respect of the period is disclosed in the notes, analysed into its main components.

(h) Prepare a reconciliation of the tax charge in the profit and loss account (this is an overall check that accounts profits have been brought into tax, whether current or deferred).

(i) Check that profit and loss, balance sheet and notes classification and disclosure of taxation is fairly presented.

TEST YOUR KNOWLEDGE

Numbers in brackets refer to paragraphs in this chapter

1. In what circumstances might the auditor decide that a creditors circularisation is necessary? (8)

2. What were the circumstances of the *Romalpa* case? (11–14)

3. What procedures might the auditor adopt to establish whether his client purchases goods sold subject to reservation of title and to assess the impact on the accounts, if any? (22)

4. What statutory books are required by the Companies Act 1985? (39)

5. In what circumstances according to SSAP 15 should deferred tax be provided? (45)

Chapter 12

REVIEW OF FINANCIAL STATEMENTS

Topics covered in this chapter:

- The objectives of the review of financial statements
- The use of analytical review procedures
- Directors' emoluments and transactions with directors
- Financial information issued with audited financial statements

---

Introduction

1. Our detailed audit work to date has primarily been devoted to the evaluation and testing of the accounting and control systems and substantive work in relation to items or groups of items in the balance sheet. We must now concentrate on a review of the financial statements as a whole. Clearly one objective of this review must be to assess whether the financial statements conform with statutory and other regulatory requirements, including relevant SSAPs, but the review is also concerned more imaginatively with *interpretation* of the figures in the accounts to assess whether the accounts as a whole make sense. Are they consistent within themselves? Do they form part of a discernible and logical pattern over the last few years?

2. Our principal interpretative tool is the technique of analytical review - this technique is discussed in detail. To assist our statutory compliance review it is necessary to consider a rather complicated area; the auditor's responsibilities with regard to director's emoluments and transactions with directors. Finally, we identify the auditor's attitude to other financial information issued with the audited accounts including the directors' report (required of course by statute) but also employee accounts, chairman's statement etc.

The objectives of the review of the financial statements

3. Our starting point must be the Operational Standard. Paragraph 6 states:

   "The auditor should carry out such a review of the financial statements as is sufficient, in conjunction with the conclusions drawn from the other audit evidence obtained, to give him a reasonable basis for his opinion on the financial statements."

4. It is important to note the term 'in conjunction with': reviewing the accounts is further audit evidence, it is *not* an exercise in isolation. Thus the results of the review must be considered in the light of all the other audit evidence - compliance and substantive - obtained to date through stages 1-9 of the audit process identified in our diagrammatic approach.

5. To identify how we can achieve compliance with the Standard we should turn initially to the Guideline 'Review of financial statements'. First, the Guideline states that the objectives of the review are to determine whether:

    (a) the financial statements have been prepared using acceptable accounting policies which have been consistently applied and are appropriate to the enterprise's business;

    (b) the results of operations, state of affairs and all other information included in the financial statements are compatible with each other and with the auditor's knowledge of the enterprise;

    (c) there is adequate disclosure of all appropriate matters and the information contained in the financial statements is suitably classified and presented;

    (d) the financial statements comply with all statutory requirements and other regulations relevant to the constitution and activities of that enterprise; and ultimately whether:

    (e) the conclusions drawn from the other tests which he has carried out, together with those drawn from his overall review of the financial statements, enable him to form an opinion on the financial statements.

6. The following points should be borne in mind when determining the procedures necessary to achieve the above.

    (a) Throughout the review the auditor needs to take account of the materiality of the matters under review and the confidence which his other audit work has already given him in the accuracy and completeness of the information contained in the financial statements.

    (b) Skill and imagination are required to recognise the matters to be examined in carrying out an overall review and sound judgement is needed to interpret the information obtained. Accordingly, the review should not be delegated to someone lacking the necessary experience and skill. (The task will typically fall to the senior in charge in the first instance, but the manager and subsequently the reporting partner will need to be involved in the review process.)

    (c) An overall review of the financial statements based on the auditor's knowledge of the business of the enterprise is not of itself a sufficient basis for the expression of an audit opinion on those statements. However, it provides valuable support for the conclusions arrived at as a result of his other audit work. In addition apparent inconsistencies could indicate areas in which material errors, omissions or irregularities may have occurred which have not been disclosed by other auditing procedures.

Review procedures

7. The Guideline in broad terms considers that the review procedures should include the following:

" *Accounting policies*
The auditor should review the accounting policies adopted by the enterprise to determine whether such policies:

    (a) comply with statements of standard accounting practice or , in the absence thereof, are otherwise acceptable;

    (b) are consistent with those of the previous period;

    (c) are consistently applied throughout the enterprise;

(d) are disclosed in accordance with the requirements of statement of standard accounting practice No 2 *Disclosure of accounting policies*."

When considering whether the policies adopted by management are acceptable the auditor should have regard, inter alia, to the policies commonly adopted in particular industries and to policies for which there is substantial authoritative support.

"   *General review*
The auditor should consider whether the results of operations and the state of affairs of the enterprise as reported in the financial statements are consistent with his knowledge of the underlying circumstances of the business.

In addition to any analytical review procedures carried out during the course of the audit, the auditor should carry out an overall review of the information in the financial statements themselves and compare it with other available data. For such a review to be effective the auditor needs to have sufficient knowledge of the activities of the enterprise and of the business which it operates to be able to determine whether particular items are abnormal. This background information should be available in the auditor's working papers as a result of his planning and earlier audit procedures.

Presentation and disclosure
The auditor should consider the information in the financial statements in order to ensure that the conclusions which a reader might draw from it would be justified and consistent with the circumstances of the enterprise's business. In particular, he should bear in mind the need for the financial statements to reflect the *substance* of the underlying transactions and balances and not merely their *form*. He should consider also whether the presentation adopted in the financial statements may have been unduly influenced by management's desire to present facts in a favourable or unfavourable light.
(The existence of related parties or of related party transactions may affect the presentation and disclosure in the financial statements - this difficult area for the auditor is discussed later.)

The auditor should also consider whether the financial statements adequately reflect the information and explanations obtained and conclusions reached on particular aspects of the audit.

The auditor should consider whether his review has disclosed any new factors which affect the presentation or accounting policies adopted. For example, it may become apparent as a result of his review of the financial statements as a whole, that the enterprise has liquidity problems and the auditor should consider whether or not the financial statements should have been prepared on a going concern basis."

8.   The presentation and disclosure requirements for limited companies are now so onerous that many firms utilise a checklist - commonly referred to as an 'Accounting requirements checklist' - to ensure that the financial statements contain prima facie, all the disclosures required by the Companies Act 1985, SSAPs and, where applicable, The Stock Exchange. Mere completion of such a checklist, is of course, not an end in itself: further objective review will be necessary to determine whether the accounts present a true and fair view in the underlying circumstances. (It is beyond the scope of this text to provide such an accounting requirements checklist - reference should be made to an appropriate Financial Accounting source.)

9. When performing the general review identified above, it is the technique of analytical review that will provide the principal audit comfort - hence it is now time to identify how this technique can be applied to the review of financial statements.

The use of analytical review procedures

10. Analytical review is a substantive technique that can be used at the initial planning stage of the audit, during the course of the audit and at or near the completion of the audit when reviewing the financial statements. Our analytical review procedures in respect of the financial statements will serve as an overall test of the reasonableness of the figures contained therein and are intended to corroborate conclusions formed during the previous stages of the audit in respect of transactions and balances and hence *may* highlight areas requiring further investigation where unusual matters or inconsistencies with earlier audit evidence are disclosed.

The techniques

11. It is meaningless to attempt a standardised approach to analytical review - every industry is different and each company within that industry differs in certain respects. What can be stated for all audits is that the reviewer must have an in depth knowledge of the company, its history and the industry within which it operates.

12. To assist in analysing trends it is useful to make use of ratio analysis. The choice of ratios is a matter of judgement, based on knowledge of the client, the industry, and the general state of the economy. In any event, ratios mean very little when used in isolation. Ratios should be calculated for previous periods and for comparable companies. This may involve a certain amount of initial research, but subsequently it is just a matter of adding new statistics to the existing information each year. The permanent file should contain a section with summarised accounts and the chosen ratios for prior years.

13. Important ratios that could be examined include the following:

   (a) gross profit margins - in total and by product;
   (b) debtors ratio - ie average collection period;
   (c) stock turnover ratio - ie stock divided into cost of sales;
   (d) current ratio - ie current assets to current liabilities;
   (e) quick or acid test ratio - ie liquid assets to current liabilities;
   (f) gearing ratio - ie debt capital to equity capital;
   (g) return on capital employed.

14. In addition to looking at the more usual ratios the auditor should consider examining other ratios that may be relevant to the particular clients' business eg revenue per passenger mile for an airline operator client, fees per partner for a professional office.

15. One further important technique is to examine important related accounts in conjunction with each other. It is often the case that revenue and expense accounts are related to balance sheet accounts and comparisons should be made to ensure that the relationships are reasonable. Examples of such related accounts are:

    (a)   creditors and purchases;
    (b)   stocks and cost of sales;
    (c)   fixed assets and depreciation, repairs and maintenance expense;
    (d)   intangible assets and amortisation;
    (e)   loans and interest expense;
    (f)   investments and investment income;
    (g)   debtors and bad debt expense;
    (h)   debtors and sales.

16. Other areas that might be investigated in the analytical review include:

    (a)   sales - examine changes in products, customers and levels of returns, looking for any noticeable trends;
    (b)   assess the effect of price changes on the cost of sales;
    (c)   consider the effect of inflation, industrial disputes, changes in production methods, etc on the charge for wages;
    (d)   where appropriate obtain explanations for all major variances analysed using a standard costing system. Particular attention should be paid to those relating to the over or under absorption of overheads since these may, inter alia, affect stock valuations;
    (e)   compare trends in production and sales and assess the effect on any provisions for obsolete stocks;
    (f)   ensure that changes in the percentage labour or overhead content of production costs are also reflected in the stock valuation;
    (g)   other profit and loss expenditure; compare:
        (i)   rent with annual rent per rental agreement;
        (ii)   rates with previous year and known rates increases;
        (iii) interest payable on loans with outstanding balance and interest rate per loan agreement;
        (iv) hire or leasing charges with annual rate per agreements;
        (v)   other items related to activity level with general price increase and change in relevant level of activity (eg telephone expenditure will increase disproportionately if export or import business increases);
        (vi) other items not related to activity level with general price increases (or specific increases if known);
    (h)   review profit and loss account for items which may have been omitted (eg scrap sales, training levy, special contributions to pension fund, provisions for dilapidations etc);
    (i)   general; ensure expected variations arising from the following have occurred:
        (i)   review of minutes;
        (ii)   discussions with client officials;
        (iii) industry or local trends;
        (iv) known disturbances of the trading pattern (eg strikes, depot closures, failure of suppliers).

17. Certain of the comparisons and ratios measuring liquidity and longer-term capital structure will assist in evaluating whether the company is a going concern, in addition to contributing to the overall view of the accounts. We shall see in chapter 13, however, that there are factors other than declining ratios that may indicate going concern problems.

18. The working papers must contain the completed results of the analytical review. These might comprise:

    (a) the outline programme of the review work;
    (b) the summary of significant figures and relationships for the period;
    (c) a summary of comparisons made with budgets and with previous years;
    (d) details of all significant variations considered;
    (e) details of the results of investigations into such variations;
    (f) the audit conclusions reached;
    (g) information considered necessary for assisting in the planning of subsequent audits.

Directors' emoluments and transactions with directors

19. Provisions with regard to disclosure of directors' emoluments, are now contained in Parts V and VI Schedule 5 Companies Act 1985 whereas the complicated rules regarding transactions with directors are to be found in Part X Sections 330-344 (legality) and Parts I to III of Schedule 6 (disclosure).

20. The reason for the auditor's keen interest in these provisions is his express duty to include in his report (so far as he is reasonably able to do so) the required disclosure particulars of directors' emoluments and transactions with directors, if these requirements have not been complied with in the accounts (S237 (5)).

21. The above duty, in so far as it affects directors' emoluments, is well established and the auditor has, not surprisingly, developed techniques to provide him with audit comfort - though there are some areas that can cause difficulties. The auditor's responsibility regarding transactions with directors is much more recent, and much more onerous. We shall examine this legal and operational minefield in detail in paragraphs 36 to 61 below. First we can establish how the auditor performs his duties in respect of directors' emoluments.

Directors' emoluments - audit approach

22. *Background*
The auditor will have carried out an evaluation of salaries payroll procedures, including the system in operation for directors' salaries, earlier in the audit (stage 5 of our diagrammatic approach). He will subsequently have performed compliance tests where strong controls have been identified, and substantive tests on the underlying records. At the year end, assuming the results of his earlier testing were satisfactory, he can probably concentrate on limited substantive work designed to ensure that (i) the final figures in the accounting records are complete (it should be appreciated that certain figures such as directors' bonuses and commissions may not be computed until the last moment) and (ii) the disclosure requirements in respect of directors and higher paid employees have been complied with. The following disclosure areas may require special attention:

    (a) compensation for loss of office - generally speaking these payments are disclosable but doubt often arises over whether the approval of the company in general meeting is required;
    (b) where emoluments are paid other than by the company itself - disclosure is required regardless of who actually makes the payment but it may be difficult to obtain the necessary information;
    (c) benefits in kind are disclosable as well as fees and salaries and these are frequently difficult to quantify.

23. *General procedures*
The auditor should carry out the following general procedures.

(a) Ascertain whether monies payable or benefits in kind provided have been properly approved in accordance with the company's memorandum and articles of association and that they are not prohibited by the Act;

(b) Confirm that all monies payable and benefits receivable in relation to the current accounting period have been properly accounted for, unless the right to any of these has been waived. There can be problems here in relation to non-recurring payments and benefits in kind, as, if the auditor has no previous knowledge of the existence of such items, they are often difficult to detect. Consideration should always be given as to whether some of the more common types of benefit exist (eg company car, cheap loans, share options granted by the company etc);

(c) Review directors' service contracts;

(d) Review the company's procedures to ensure that all directors are made aware of and properly discharge their statutory responsibility (s 231 (4)) to advise the board of all disclosable emoluments. On the following page is an example of a form to be submitted annually by each director to the company secretary containing the emoluments information. The auditor should obtain copies of these letters. The auditor will often, in addition, obtain a confirmation statement of aggregate emoluments from the company secretary. As we shall see a little later, it is good practice for the company secretary to request each director to include, in addition, information in respect of transactions as well as emoluments;

(e) Review the procedures for ensuring that any payments made to former directors of the company are identified and properly disclosed;

(f) Consider the need for any amounts included in directors' remuneration to be further disclosed in accordance with the provisions of the Companies Act 1985 (eg property rented by directors from a company at below market rental).

To: The company secretary

Director's name:..

Dear Sir,

In accordance with Section 231 (4) of the Companies Act 1985 I hereby give notice of the following matters to be disclosed by me under Part V Sch 5 in respect of the company's financial period ended.................

EMOLUMENTS		*From the company* £	*From subsidiary companies* £	*From any other person* £
1.	*Emoluments for the year*			
	Remuneration as director	....	....	....
	Remuneration as an executive (salary, bonus etc)	....	....	....
	Expenses allowance insofar as chargeable to UK Income tax	....	....	....
	Pension contributions paid by the company	....	....	....
	Estimated money value of benefits received other than in cash	....	....	....
		£_____	£_____	£_____

2. *Expense allowance of previous years*
Not then reported as chargeable
to UK Income tax but which have been
in whole or in part so charged during
the year   £_____ £_____ £_____

3. *Pensions received* other than under
a scheme wholly maintained by
contributions   £_____ £_____ £_____

4. *Compensation for loss of office*   £_____ £_____ £_____

5. *Emoluments waived for the year*   £_____ £_____ £_____

I hereby confirm that the above particulars are in accordance with the provisions of Part V Schedule 5 of the Companies Act 1985 and that the information disclosed relates to all the emoluments, pensions and compensation for loss of office receivable, or waived, by me in respect of my services to the company and its subsidiaries whether these emoluments are payable by the company, by its subsidiaries or by any other person or company.

Yours faithfully,

Director.

24. In the following paragraphs we consider the three areas identified in paragraph 22 that may raise potential disclosure problems.

25. *Compensation for loss of office*
In the normal course of events, statute requires that any payments made to a director in compensation for loss of office (or in connection with his retirement) should have received the prior approval of the company in general meeting. The following difficulties in interpretation may, however, arise.

(a) The prior approval of the members is not required in respect of payments which are made 'bona fide' by way of damages for breach of contract or by way of pension in respect of past services. The auditor must ascertain the terms and length of the unexpired portion of the director's service contract and consider the reasonableness of the payments made against this background. If, following such consideration, the amount paid appears excessive, then it may be evidence that the payment made was not 'bona fide';

(b) Where a payment made is described as 'ex gratia' it could be considered to be unrelated to the office and therefore not requiring the prior approval of the members, but the auditor should consider carefully all the circumstances surrounding the payment and not automatically assume that approval was not required;

(c) Where a payment is made to a director after he has resigned, it has been argued that the prior approval of the members is not required, as the Act does not require the prior approval of payments made to past directors.

26. The interpretations referred to in paragraph 25 (b) and (c) above are not definitive and it would normally, therefore, be advisable for the company to seek legal advice on such interpretations in the light of the prevailing circumstances. Where the auditor is not entirely satisfied with the advice received by the company he should consider taking independent legal advice on the matter.

27. *Payments made by persons other than the company*
As noted earlier, directors' emoluments must be disclosed even if they have not been paid by the company itself. This would most commonly arise in the following situations:

    (a) where payment is made either by a holding company or fellow subsidiary;
    (b) where payment is made by a management company which is not part of the group or a company owned by the director, a charge being made to the company (where financial statements are being reported on) for the services of the director. In addition to being remuneration, any such arrangement may also require disclosure under the provisions of the Companies Act 1985 in relation to transactions in which directors have a material interest.

28. In either of the above cases it is possible that a blanket charge is made to the company by the other company involved, such charge covering not merely the directors' emoluments but also other costs (eg general administration costs). In such a situation the amount requiring disclosure may not be separately identifiable (in the case of payments made by another group company there may be no recharge at all) and the auditor would therefore be justified in accepting an apportionment, especially where no recharge is made and the director is a director of several group companies. The auditor should also bear in mind that the information is only disclosable 'so far as ..... the company has the right to obtain it from the persons concerned'. Where the necessary information cannot be obtained, then the facts should be disclosed by way of note.

29. The auditor may be faced with a further complication if a company claims that emoluments paid by its parent company were purely in respect of the director's services to the parent company. If this is the case, then such emoluments are only disclosable in the accounts of the parent company if the director is also a director of the parent company (unless the parent company is a foreign company). The auditor must consider the acceptability of such a claim in the light of the circumstances prevailing.

30. *Valuation of benefits in kind*
In accordance with statute (Sch V Para 22(3) Companies Act 1985) the amount to be disclosed for a benefit in kind is its *estimated money value*. Unfortunately the Act gives no guidance as to how this phrase should be interpreted. It is often the case that taxable amounts are used but it is difficult to reconcile these with 'money values' for certain types of benefit. If one is concerned with the information needs of members then perhaps a more suitable interpretation would be to consider a value based upon the personal benefit derived by the director.

31. Where the value used is based upon estimates the auditor must ensure that such estimates are made at an appropriate level (eg by the board of directors). On occasions it may be almost impossible to place a meaningful value on the benefit and this is particularly true with regard to share options. The consensus of opinion seems to be that a benefit arises when the option is granted rather than at the time it is exercised. However, this view makes valuation difficult especially where there is no ready market for the shares.

32. In such cases it might be advisable for the directors to provide an explanatory note at the foot of the directors' emoluments notes. The wording of such a note might be as follows:

'Included in the above figures is £892, being the estimated money value of an option granted during the year to Mr A N Other. Under this option, which must be exercised before 30 June 19XX, Mr A N Other may subscribe for 800 25p ordinary shares of the company at a price of £1.25 per share.'

33. *Conclusion*
The auditor must be aware of the detailed statutory disclosure requirements relating to directors' remuneration. It is not considered appropriate to reproduce all the details here but if you are in any doubt as to what these requirements are, you should refer to an appropriate financial accounting text.

34. You are reminded that if the company fails to make the required disclosures then the auditor has a statutory responsibility to include the necessary details in his audit report, insofar as he is reasonably able to do so.

35. As all companies must have at least one director then the audit problems associated with director's remuneration can arise in *any* audit.

Transactions with directors: legality and disclosure regulations

36. Before we identify the audit procedures necessary to establish that financial statements contain all the information relating to transactions with directors, it is important that we clarify the existing rules affecting:
    - legality; and
    - disclosure of such transactions.

37. *Legality*
Under S190 Companies Act 1948 a company was prohibited from:

    (a) making a loan to a director, or to a director of its holding company; and
    (b) guaranteeing or providing security in connection with a loan made to such a director by another party.

38. S190 Companies Act 1948 was repealed and replaced by S49 Companies Act 1980. The provisions of S49 are now re-enacted in S330 Companies Act 1985. This section contains the prohibitions in paragraph 37 above but also the following restrictions.

    (a) No company may:
        (i) arrange to have assigned to it, or to assume, the rights or liabilities under a transaction that would have been prohibited if it had initially been entered into by the company. This clause is designed to prevent the basic rule being circumvented by involving third parties. For example, previously, it would have been legal for a third party to make a loan to a director and for the company to then purchase the third party's rights in respect of the principal and interest;

(ii)   take part in any sort of arrangement whereby a third party receives some benefit from the company, its holding company, subsidiary of fellow subsidiary and, in return, enters into a transaction with a director which would have been prohibited if it had been entered into by the company. For example, the clause covers arrangements when one company makes loans to the directors of another company in return for loans made to its own directors. It also covers cases where a director arranges for his company to deposit money with a building society in return for receiving a personal mortgage on favourable terms;

(b)   No *relevant company* may enter into, guarantee or provide security in connection with:
   (i)   a loan agreement with a person 'connected' with a director or a director of its holding company;
   (ii)   a *quasi loan* with such a director or connected person;
   (iii)   a *credit transaction* with such a director or connected person.

39.   S330 introduces some important terms which are defined in s331.

(a)   The term *relevant company* means any public company and any private company which is a member of a group containing one or more public companies;

(b)   Persons *connected* with a director include:
   -   the spouse and infant children of the director;
   -   companies with which the director is associated. A director is associated with a company if, he together with any persons connected with him, held more than 20% of the equity capital or voting rights of the company;
   -   the trustee of a trust of which the director or a person connected with him is a beneficiary;
   -   any partners of the director or of a person connected with him.

(c)   A company makes a *'quasi loan'* to a person when it pays or agrees to pay money for or on behalf of that person on the understanding that the money will be reimbursed by that person. A typical example is where a director uses a company credit card to buy goods for his personal use on the understanding that he will reimburse the company at a later time;

(d)   A *'credit transaction'* in the context of this legislation includes any transaction involving the acquisition of land, goods or services for which payment is deferred. It includes leasing transactions.

All these terms are significant as they represent an extension of pre 1980 Act prohibitions.

40.   There are, however, certain exceptions to the general prohibitions above. The most important are:

(a)   *De minimis* exemption - small loans.
   A company is not prohibited from making loans to any of its directors or to any director of its holding company, provided the aggregate of the *'relevant amounts'* does not exceed £2,500.

(b)   Subject to the approval procedures detailed below, a company is not prohibited from doing anything to provide any of its directors with funds to meet expenditure incurred or to be incurred by him for the purposes of the company or to enable him properly to perform his duties as officer of the company or to enable any of its directors to avoid incurring such expenditure.

The approval procedures stipulate that either:

(i)   prior approval of the company in general meeting must be obtained; or

(ii)   retroactive approval must be sought at or before the next annual general meeting after the loan is made. Failing this, the loan must be repaid within six months of the conclusion of that meeting.

The purpose and amount must be disclosed at the general meeting during which approval of the loan is sought.

In the case of a *relevant* company this exception is restricted in that such a company may not enter into any transaction if the aggregate of the *'relevant amounts'* exceeds £10,000.

(c)   A company is not prohibited from making a loan or quasi-loan to its holding company or from entering into a guarantee or providing any security in connection with such a loan or quasi-loan. Similarly, a company is not prohibited from entering into a credit transaction as creditor for its holding company or entering into a guarantee or providing any security in connection with such a credit transaction.

(d)   Intra-group transactions. Where a director of a relevant company or of its holding company is *'associated'* (see definition of connected person in para 28 above) with a subsidiary of either of those companies, the relevant company is not prohibited by reason of that association alone from making a loan or quasi-loan to the subsidiary; nor is it prohibited from entering into a guarantee or providing any security in connection with such a loan or quasi-loan.

(e)   All credit transactions made in the ordinary course of the company's business and others where the *'relevant amount'* does not exceed £5,000.

(f)   Transactions entered into by money lending companies in the ordinary course of their business and on terms that are no more favourable than those that would be available to an unconnected person of similar standing. In the case of a relevant company the *'relevant amount'* must not exceed £50,000 (but see (h) below);

(g)   For transactions entered into by recognised banks the provisions are the same as in (f) but without any financial limit (but see (h) below);

(h)   Loans made to directors of money lending companies or recognised banks for the purchase or improvement of their sole or main residence provided that they are granted on terms that are no more favourable than those given to other employees and the 'relevant amount' does not exceed £50,000.

NB. The relevant amount is the value of all existing transactions between, on the one hand the party in relation to whom a new transaction is being contemplated and any persons connected with him and, on the other hand, the company and any of its subsidiaries or fellow subsidiaries, plus the value of the transaction being contemplated.

41.   In general a loan or other transaction which is entered into in contravention of the Act is voidable at the instance of the company. The director(s) responsible and other persons aware of the illegality of the transaction may be criminally liable. The director (or connected person) is also liable to account to the company for any gain he has made.

42. *Contracts of employment*
    Prior to the 1980 Act, there were no restrictions on service contracts between directors and the company. This has meant that, in the past, companies have sometimes been forced to pay substantial compensation for loss of office to directors who were removed by the shareholders under S184 Companies Act 1948.

43. Under S319 of the Companies Act 1985 the general rule is now that a company may not incorporate into any agreement a term under which a director's employment with the company or (if he is a director of a holding company) his employment within the group is to continue or may be continued otherwise that at the company's option for a period that exceeds five years unless the company has the absolute right to terminate the employment by notice or the term has been approved by the company in general meeting.

44. It is interesting to note that the Act goes further than the Stock Exchange Listing Agreement which requires that no service contract shall be longer than ten years unless approved by the company in general meeting.

45. *Substantial property transactions*
    The 1985 Act contains restrictions in respect of substantial property transactions between companies and their directors. The basic rule under S320 is that any acquisition or disposal by the company of a non-cash asset from or to a director, a director of its holding company or a connected person is prohibited. The major exceptions are:

    (a) arrangements approved by the company in general meeting;
    (b) arrangements when the value of the assets is less than £1,000 or, if greater, is less than the lower of £50,000 and 10% of the company's net assets (as reported in the last accounts);
    (c) if the asset is to be acquired by a holding company from any of its wholly owned subsidiaries or from a holding company by any of its wholly owned subsidiaries, or by one wholly owned subsidiary to another wholly owned subsidiary of the same holding company;
    (d) the arrangement is entered into by a company which is being wound up unless the winding-up is a members' voluntary winding-up.

46. *Disclosure requirements*
    The 1980 Act extended the disclosure requirements of earlier ones considerably. The existence of detailed rules for disclosure is of course, the main safeguard against directors abusing their position in the company. The 1985 Act requires that not only should prohibited transactions be disclosed, but also many transactions that would have been prohibited but for the specific exceptions given in the Act. To give the provisions some force, they are not only covered by general rules which make non-compliance with disclosure requirements a criminal offence, but also as we are aware, the auditors must give in their report any of the required information not given in the financial statements.

47. The disclosure requirements relate to:

    (a) *any* loans, quasi loans or other arrangements specified in S330 (see para 37 and 38 above) that the company or one of its subsidiaries has entered into or agreed to enter into;

(b) any other transaction or arrangement with the company or one of its subsidiaries in which a director of the company, its holding company or a person connected with such director had, either directly or indirectly a *material* interest. The term material is not defined by the Act. It is left to the opinion of the majority of the other directors or, failing their agreement, to the court. (It should be appreciated that directors are required to disclose to the board details of any transaction or arrangement in which they, or persons connected with them, are interested - S317.)

48. The main information required to be disclosed is (Sch 6 para 9):

(a) the principal terms of the transaction or arrangement;
(b) a statement that it took place or existed during the year;
(c) the name of the director involved and where relevant, the name of the connected person;
(d) as regards loans:
    (i)   the amount of the liability (including interest) at both the beginning and the end of the financial year and the maximum amount during the year;
    (ii) the amount of any unpaid interest;
    (iii) the amount of any provision the company has made against the debt;
(e) similar requirements exist for guarantees, loans, quasi loans etc;
(f) the *'value'* of any other transactions. This would mean, for example, the disclosure of the arm's length value of any goods, land or services;
(g) for officers, other than directors, the Act requires the disclosure of the aggregate amount outstanding at the end of the year and the number of officers involved for each of the following types of transaction (Sch 6 Para 16):
    (i)   loans and related guarantees; and
    (ii) quasi loans and related guarantees; etc;
    (iii) credit transactions and related guarantees; etc.

49. There are disclosure exemptions. These are the principal ones:

(a) transactions etc between two companies where the interest of a director of one solely arises because he is also a director of the other;
(b) service contracts - these must however be available for inspection by members under S318;
(c) credit transactions (and related agreements) when the aggregate amount outstanding on all such transactions for the director involved does not exceed £5,000;
(d) any transaction or arrangement covered by para 47 (b) where the aggregate value of all such transactions is less than £1,000 or if it exceeds £1,000, is less than the lower of £5,000 or 1% of the company's net assets;
(e) any transaction etc which was not entered into during the financial year and which did not subsist at any time during that year.

50. *Summary*
The rules regarding legality and disclosure are clearly complex - it is therefore important not to lose track of the main thrust of the legislation. In summary:

(a) Legality:
Subject to the specified exceptions -
    -   For *all* companies: loans and guarantees in respect of loans are illegal
    -   For relevant (ie public) companies: (i) quasi loans and credit transactions for directors are illegal; and (ii) loans, quasi loans and credit transactions for their connected persons are illegal.

(b) Disclosure:
Subject to the specified exceptions -
- For *all* companies: *all* classes of transaction in (a) above (regardless of legality) require disclosure; plus
- Any other transaction in which a director or connected person has a *material* interest.

Transactions with directors: audit approach

51. We must now investigate how the auditor can ensure, so far as he is reasonably able to do so, that all statutory disclosure requirements have been complied with. The approach below reflects the guidance provided in a 1984 APC Audit Brief entitled 'Directors' loans, other transactions and remuneration'.

52. The first potential problem for the auditor is the difficulty faced in order to satisfy himself that he has been able to identify properly all disclosable transactions. These difficulties may result from:

(a) the low value of certain transactions, making them difficult to detect when using normal audit procedures;
(b) the requirements of the Act for disclosure of transactions between the company and the connected persons of a director, given that it may not always be an easy task for the auditor to identify such connected persons;
(c) the fact that there may be little or no documentary evidence of transactions requiring disclosure, given that the Act covers not just formal agreements and arrangements, but also informal ones.

In the light of the above, the auditor's approach must be largely dependent on the vigilance of the auditor and on management representations.

53. The second major problem facing the auditor is the complexity of the legislation itself, which may in turn give rise to difficulties of interpretation, eg the Act does not actually include a definition of a loan and so the auditor must be aware that not every form of indebtedness amounts to a loan.

54. As a first step, the auditor should make enquiry as to the company's procedure for ensuring that all disclosable transactions are properly identified and recorded. Such procedures might reasonably be expected to include the following:

(a) advising all directors and officers that they have a responsibility to disclose transactions in which they have an interest, either directly or through connected persons. Such disclosure should take place at a meeting of the directors of the company;
(b) the recording of all transactions notified in the minutes of directors' meetings;
(c) maintaining some form of register in which details of all transactions requiring disclosure are recorded;
(d) the establishment of some method of:
  (i) identifying proposed transactions which will require the approval of the members in general meeting;
  (ii) ensuring that the company does not enter into any illegal transaction;

(e) monitoring the system by checking on a regular basis (as a minimum, once a year) that each director is in agreement with the company's record of his disclosable transactions and is satisfied that such records are both complete and accurate;

(f) at the end of each financial year, obtaining from each director a formal statement indicating the disclosures necessary for the purposes of the statutory accounts. This statement might conveniently be combined with the director's emoluments letter identified in paragraph 23(d)).

55. The establishment of procedures such as the above would normally be the responsibility of the company secretary. Certainly, this is likely to be the case with larger companies, but, particularly with smaller organisations, the auditor may well find that either there are no formalised procedures or that such as there are appear to be inadequate. In such cases, the auditor should consider the provision of details of the statutory requirements from each of the directors, with a request that they provide written confirmation of their interests in disclosable transactions.

56. Where, in the auditor's opinion, the establishment of formal procedures would be a practicable proposition, the auditor should, as necessary, be prepared to advise the client on the institution of such procedures or the revision of such procedures as are established where they appear to be inadequate.

57. Following on from the above, further audit procedures to be adopted should include:

(a) an inspection of Board minutes and other records of transactions with directors and connected persons to consider their adequacy and whether or not they appear to have been kept up to date;

(b) an examination of any agreements and contracts involving directors and connected persons, including tracing the details of such transactions to any source documentation available;

(c) consideration of whether transactions disclosed are on commercial terms, as, although in many cases it would not affect the legality of the transaction, the very fact that it is on commercial terms will perhaps aid the wording of any note to the accounts detailing such transactions and will provide greater 'comfort' to the user of the accounts;

(d) consideration of the recoverability of amounts due from directors or connected persons;

(e) consideration as to the legality of the disclosable transactions recorded by the company. Where the auditor is of the opinion that a transaction is illegal, he should immediately advise the directors of such opinion and also give careful consideration as to whether any reference to the matter will be required in the audit report;

(f) advising the client to seek legal advice in those cases where there are doubts as to the legality and/or disclosable nature of a transaction. Should the client decline to do so, or if the auditor is still not satisfied with the advice received by the client then he should consider taking independent legal advice on the matter;

(g) considering the possibility that the company's details of disclosable transactions may be incomplete as regards those directors (and connected persons) who have not been in office throughout the year;

(h) reviewing post balance sheet events in order to consider whether they might have any impact on the matters requiring disclosure.

58. As a final step the auditor should consider obtaining written representations from each director giving confirmation of disclosable transactions which relate to themselves and their connected persons. An appropriate form of letter might be as follows:

"Dear Sirs,

Transactions involving directors and connected persons
(Companies Act 1985 S232, Sch 6 Part I)

I hereby confirm that I have examined the financial statements of Standard plc as at 31 December 19XX and that these financial statements contain all the information required by section 232 and Sch 6 Part I of the Companies Act 1985 in respect of myself and all persons connected with me.

Yours faithfully,"

An alternative form of letter might make reference to an attached list of transactions (where financial statements incorporating the information are not available). In these circumstances the auditor would need to check that the information on the list was correctly transferred to the financial statements.

59. In the case of those companies where more formal procedures have been established it might be appropriate to obtain copies of the statement mentioned in paragraph 54 (f) above, addressed to the company secretary from each director confirming the information required to be disclosed (if any). In addition it might be advisable to obtain a statement from the company secretary on behalf of the board covering directors' transactions *in aggregate*. An example of such a statement, extended to cover aggregate directors' emoluments (see paragraph 23(d)), is reproduced below:

"Dear Sirs,

I hereby confirm that the attached summaries of particulars of directors' emoluments and of loans and other transactions involving persons who were directors or officers at any time during the year ended 31 December 19XX properly state all the information required by the Companies Act 1985.

Yours faithfully,

(Company Secretary)

	Paid by		
Particulars of directors' emoluments	*Company*	*Subsidiary*	*Any other person*
1.	£	£	£
Fees for services as director	1,000	–	–
Emoluments for services in connection with the management of the company or any subsidiary	65,264	15,896	33,990
Pension contributions	7,766	1,872	4,029
Estimated benefits in kind (company cars and cheap loans)	1,200	400	600
	75,230	18,168	38,619
Ex gratia payment to former director	–	30,000	–
	75,230	48,168	38,619

The amounts shown in the right-hand column were paid by the holding company.

2. Details of emoluments excluding pension contributions:
   (a) The emoluments of the chairman were £25,654
   (b) The emoluments of the highest paid director were £34,590
   (c) The number of other directors whose emoluments fell
   in each range of £5,000 were:

Up to £5,000	2
£15,001 to £20,000	2
£20,001 to £25,000	1

Particulars of loans and other transactions involving directors and officers

3. *Loans*
   (a) The following interest-free loans were made to directors, prior to their joining the Board, in accordance with the company's policy of providing housing finance to employees who have been transferred:

Name	Principal amount of loan	1/1/XX	Outstanding principal and interest Maximum during year	31/12/XX
	£	£	£	£
T Evans	10,000	–	10,000	10,000
R Brown	15,000	15,000	15,000	–

   (b) At 31 December 19XX a total of £40,000 was outstanding from five officers of the company in respect of housing finance.

4. *Credit transactions*
   A house is let by the company to an officer. At 31 December 19XX the amount outstanding in respect of this transaction was £550.

5. *Transactions in which directors have (or had) a material interest*
   During the year, S Limited, a subsidiary of the company, received a loan of £120,000 from A Limited, a company controlled by P Smith. This loan bears interest at a rate of 3% above bank base rate and is repayable in full in 19XX.

60. If a company does not comply with the disclosures of the Act, it is the responsibility of the auditors to include the details in their report as far as they are reasonably able to do so. Set out below is an example of such a report.

'AUDITORS' REPORT TO THE MEMBERS OF........

We have audited the financial statements on pages ... to ... in accordance with Auditing Standards.

The following details of a loan required by S232 of the Companies Act 1985 to be disclosed in the financial statements, have not been so disclosed. During the year, the company made a loan of £8,000 to Master A X, a minor son of Mr B X, a director of the company. The maximum amount of the liability (including interest) during the year amounted to £8,300. The amount of the liability at the end of the year was £7,300 of which £3,000 was interest due but not paid at that date.

Except for the absence of the above disclosure, in our opinion the financial statements give a true and fair view of the state of the company's affairs at 31 December 19XX and of its profit and source and application of funds for the year then ended and have been properly prepared in accordance with the Companies Act 1985.

NB. This is an example of an audit report qualified on the grounds of disagreement - failure to comply with legislation. The significance of the presentation and precise wording of the above report will become clearer when chapter 14 has been studied.

61. In summarising the auditors' responsibilities in respect of directors' transactions one can do little better than to quote from paragraph 44 of the APC Audit Brief:

"This is an extremely difficult area of the law for the auditor since the audit approach is heavily reliant on internal evidence in general and on representations by management in particular. It is important therefore that the suggested audit procedures described above are considered at an early stage in the audit so that the auditor is satisfied that adequate audit evidence will be available. In some cases, especially in smaller businesses, the auditor will find that there is little or no written evidence and that directors will need advice as to the nature of their responsibilities under the legislation."

Related party transactions

62. Central to a number of DTI investigations (Pinnock Finance, London Capital Group) have been companies trading with organisations or individuals other than at arms length. Such transactions were made possible by a degree of control or influence exercised by directors (usually chief executives) over both parties to the transactions, and in some cases resulted in financial loss to shareholders, creditors or both.

63. Auditors have been criticised for failing to deal adequately with such transactions. In the United States, similar pressures led in 1975 to the issue of an Auditing Statement on the subject (SAS 6). The Canadian profession has more recently followed suit (Handbook statement 3840, 1979). As yet no Guideline has been issued in the UK (though one is planned) but an International Auditing Guideline No 17 entitled 'Related parties' was published in October 1984, and moreover, disclosure of related party transactions in accounts is required by International Accounting Standard 25 and proposed to be required by ED 46.

64. Some types of related party transactions are covered by existing statutory or Stock Exchange requirements; eg. the complex provisions of the Companies Act 1985 covering transactions by directors and connected persons discussed above and 'Class IV' circulars which listed companies are required to send to shareholders wherever an acquisition or disposal of assets is made from or to a director, substantial shareholder or associate. But the concept of related parties is wider than implied in existing UK statutory and regulatory pronouncements.

65. The international auditing guideline provides us with a broader interpretation. It contains the following definitions:

"Related party - parties are considered to be related if one party has the ability to influence the other party to make financial and operating decisions it might not make in the absence of such influence. Such influence may be exercised through:

  (a) control;
  (b) ownership, directly or indirectly, of a substantial interest in the voting power of the enterprise; or
  (c) participation in the policy-making process of the enterprise, often by representation on the board of directors, but also arising from material inter-company transactions, interchange of key managerial personnel, or dependence on technical information.

When the same party has such influence with two or more other parties through ownership of voting power, all such parties are considered to be related.

Related party transaction - a transfer of benefits or obligations between related parties, whether or not consideration is given.

Control - ownership, directly or indirectly through subsidiaries, of more than one half of the voting power of a company."

66. Transactions between related parties are a normal feature of commerce and business. The auditor needs to be aware of them because:

  (a) The existence of related parties or related party transactions may affect the financial information. For example, the tax laws in various countries require special consideration when related parties exist which may affect the entity's tax liability and expense.

  (b) The source of audit evidence affects the auditor's assessment of its reliability. A greater degree of reliance is normally placed on audit evidence that is obtained from or created by unrelated third parties. (Related party influence can be used to defeat audit procedures, as in the American example of the Giant Stores Corporation, where the company persuaded its suppliers to give false confirmations of balances to its auditors.)

  (c) The potential for fraud is greater when two or more parties to a transaction are related.

67. The auditor's responsibilities effectively fall under three headings:

  - identifying related parties: it is important that this is done at the planning stage of the audit;
  - identifying transactions involving related parties which are, or may be, suspect;
  - deciding whether appropriate disclosure has been made in the financial statements and what, if any, comment should be made in the audit report.

Identification of related parties

68. The following procedures should assist the auditor in identification of related parties:

  (a) inquiry of management as to the names of all related parties;

  (b) inquiry as to the affiliation of directors and officers with other entities (review of the register of directors and secretaries will provide crucial information);

  (c) review of register of members and register of debenture-holders, if applicable, to identify parties with major interests;

  (d) review of personal ledgers, sales and purchases, to establish major trading partners.

69. *Identification and examination of transactions with related parties*
    The names of related parties identified by the procedures above should be provided to the audit personnel involved in the audit of the entity and its components so that they will be alerted to recognise transactions with such parties if they are encountered within the scope of the audit.

70. In studying and evaluating the accounting system and related internal controls on which he intends to rely, the auditor should include the procedures and controls over the authorisation and recording of related party transactions. For example, he should review the procedures over the control of information provided individually by directors or key management personnel outlining related party transactions of which they are aware including those applicable to themselves and their immediate families.

71. During the ordinary course of the audit, the auditor's procedures may identify transactions with related parties. Examples of such procedures include:

    (a) Reviewing minutes of meetings of shareholders, board of directors, and executive or sub-committees of the board of directors.

    (b) Reviewing accounting records for large or unusual transactions or balances, paying particular attention to transactions recognised at or near the end of the reporting period.

    (c) Reviewing confirmations of loans receivable and payable for indication of guarantees and determining the nature and relationship, if any, of guarantees to the reporting entity.

    (d) Reviewing investment transactions, for example, purchase of an equity interest in a joint venture or another company.

72. The auditor should also consider whether related party transactions have occurred that are not recorded, such as the receipt or provision of management services at no charge.

73. While performing his procedures, the auditor should be alert for transactions which appear unusual in the circumstances, as they may indicate the existence of previously unidentified related parties and examples include:

    (a) Transactions which have abnormal terms of trade, such as unusual prices, interest rates, guarantees, and repayment terms.
    (b) Transactions which appear to lack a logical reason for their occurrence.
    (c) Transactions in which substance differs from form.
    (d) Transactions processed in other than the normal way for processing similar transactions.
    (e) High volume or significant transactions with certain customers or suppliers as compared to others.

74. In examining the identified related party transactions, the auditor should apply the procedures he considers necessary to obtain reasonable assurance as to the purpose, nature and extent of these transactions. However, evidence of a related party transaction may be limited, such as a simple instruction from a parent company to a subsidiary to record a royalty expense. In these types of circumstances, the auditor should consider performing additional procedures, such as:

    (a) Confirming the terms and amount of the transaction with the other party to the transaction, or with the other party's auditor.

(b) Inspecting evidence in possession of the other party to the transaction.

(c) Confirming or discussing information with persons associated with the transactions, such as banks, lawyers, guarantors and agents.

It is desirable that a management representation be obtained, preferably in writing, as to related party transactions.

75. *Audit consequences where related party transactions are discovered*
Assuming that the auditor has discovered some transactions which do not appear to be on a normal commercial basis, he has then to decide what action, if any, to take. To start with, he should make sure that he fully understands the substance of the transaction himself: for instance extended credit granted by his client to a customer may have further implications if the customer is controlled by a director of the client. He should then ask himself whether any differences between the description of the transactions given or implied in the accounts and its real substance are sufficiently material to mislead the shareholders. If he decides that they are he may wish to insist on fuller disclosure in the accounts, or he may consider that, with or without such disclosure, a mention in the audit report is needed, either in the form of an emphasis of matter or a qualification.

76. The following list of items gives an indication of the types of related party transactions which may require disclosure:
  - purchases or sales of goods (finished or unfinished)
  - purchases or sales of other assets (property and other assets)
  - rendering or receiving of services
  - agency arrangements
  - leasing arrangements
  - transfer of research and development
  - licence agreements
  - finance (including loans and equity contributions in cash or in kind)
  - guarantees and collaterals

Financial information issued with audited financial statements

77. S237(6) Companies Act 1985 states:

"It is the auditors' duty to consider whether the information given in the directors' report for the financial year for which the accounts are prepared is consistent with those accounts; and if they are of opinion that it is not, they shall state that fact in their report."

78. The Act does not provide any interpretative assistance as to what is meant by an 'inconsistency' or indeed what matters may give rise to an inconsistency in this context. What is in no doubt, however, is that this requirement - introduced by the Companies Act 1981 - is *not* equivalent to forming an opinion on the directors' report itself.

79. This new statutory provision has prompted the APC to develop guidance for the auditor. This is in the form of a detailed operational guideline entitled 'Financial information issued with audited financial statements' issued in September 1985, from which the comments below are derived.

80. It should also be noted, however, that this guideline clarifies the auditor's responsibilities in relation to other financial information which may be published with audited financial statements (eg five year summary, employee report) and that it will be relevant to the audit of enterprises other than those incorporated under the Companies Act 1985 (or earlier Acts).

The directors' report: statutory responsibilities

81. As already noted, the Companies Act 1985 does not require the auditor to form an opinion on the directors' report itself and, for this reason, the page references given in the first paragraph of an audit report on the annual financial statements of an enterprise should not extend to those pages containing the directors' report.

82. The auditor should therefore, under normal circumstances, confine his work to satisfying himself that the directors' report does not contain any matters which are inconsistent with the financial statements.

83. The guideline suggests that matters which may give rise to inconsistencies would include the following:

    (a) an inconsistency between actual figures or narrative appearing in, respectively, the audited financial statements and the directors' report;
    (b) an inconsistency between the bases of preparation of related items appearing in the financial statements and the directors' report, where the figures themselves are not directly comparable and the different bases are not disclosed;
    (c) an inconsistency between figures contained in the audited financial statements and a narrative interpretation of the effect of those figures in the directors' report.

84. Where the auditor considers that some inconsistency exists, he should consider carefully its implications and hold discussions with the client's management in order to try and achieve its elimination.

85. If management are not prepared to put through the adjustments considered necessary by the auditor, then the further action to be taken by the auditor will depend on where he believes that the adjustment is required.

86. If, in the auditor's opinion, the adjustment is required in the directors' report, he should, in a separate paragraph in his report on the financial statements, refer to the inconsistency.

87. If, in the auditor's opinion, the adjustment is required in the *audited financial statements* then he should consider qualifying his report on the financial statements, in accordance with the Auditing Standard 'The audit report' (see chapter 14). The auditor will also have to make reference in his report to the inconsistency between the financial statements and the directors' report as it will still exist. Since the identification of such inconsistencies will normally occur only when the audit has been largely completed, it would, however, be exceptional if it was the financial statements which required amendment.

Non-statutory responsibilities

88. The auditor has no statutory responsibilities in respect of items in the directors' report which in his opinion are misleading but not inconsistent with the financial statements, (for example there may be a statement given in the directors' report for which there is no corresponding financial information in the financial statements but which is nevertheless misleading), or in respect of other financial information contained elsewhere in the annual report (eg chairman's statement).

89. However, where information of this kind is published as part of, or in conjunction with, the annual report, the auditor should review that information. The auditor does this as part of his overall professional responsibility to ensure that the credibility of the financial statements is not undermined, and in so doing meets the expectations of those to whom the information is directed.

90. Where the auditor considers that there is a material inconsistency between the financial statements and other financial information or that an item is misleading in some other respect, he should consider its implications and hold discussions with directors, or other senior members of management, and may also make his views known in writing to all the directors in order to achieve its elimination. Where communication with directors and their representatives does not result in elimination of the problem, he should consider whether an amendment is required to the financial statements, the directors' report or the other financial information.

91. If, in the auditor's opinion, it is the financial statements which require amendment he should follow the guidance given in paragraph 87 above.

92. Assuming it is not the financial statements which require amendment, there is no statutory requirement for the auditor to comment in his report. However, there may be occasions when a matter is potentially so misleading to a reader of the financial statements that it would be inappropriate for the auditor to remain silent. In these circumstances the auditor should seek legal and other professional advice on what action may be appropriate.

93. If the auditor decides that he should refer to the matter in his report, he should be aware that Counsel has advised that the qualified privilege (ie the defence to an action for defamation) which an audit report normally enjoys may not extend to comments on:

(a) an item in the directors' report which, while not inconsistent with the financial statements, is misleading in some other respect; or

(b) financial information contained elsewhere in an annual report which is inconsistent with the financial statements or otherwise misleading.

94. The auditor may make use of his right under section 387 of the Companies Act 1985 to be heard at any general meeting of the members on any business of the meeting which concerns him as auditor. This includes the right to draw attention to those matters described in paragraph 93.

95. The auditor should urge the company not to publish its annual report until after he has completed his review of the other financial information and he should make arrangements to see, prior to publication, any documents in which the financial statements are to be included. The auditor should deal with these procedures in the audit engagement letter. Where, notwithstanding this, the auditor is not given an opportunity to complete his review before the date of issue, he should complete it before the general meeting at which the financial statements are laid before the members. In the event that there is something with which he disagrees, the auditor should take legal and other professional advice and consider taking the course of action set out in paragraph 94.

96. Only very rarely will the auditor encounter problems of inconsistencies or misleading information - either in the directors' report or in the other financial information - where the directors are unwilling to amend as necessary. This particular audit task should normally be achieved relatively painlessly.

Summary

97. This chapter comprises topics of variable examination impact. The following areas are fundamental:

   - The auditing guideline 'Review of financial statements'
   - Use of analytical review procedures. Examination questions on this topic frequently require the interpretation of financial data and hence ratio analysis techniques are of particular significance.
   - Financial information issued with the audited financial statements. The auditor's responsibility to review the directors' report for consistency with the financial statements is still relatively novel. It is important to have a thorough knowledge of the *disclosure* requirements of the directors' report in order to cope with detailed questions on this topic.

98. The regulations in respect of transactions with directors are highly complex as we have seen. Although the examination impact to date of this topic has been minor, as time passes it must be regarded as 'fair game' for the examination.

TEST YOUR KNOWLEDGE

Numbers in brackets refer to paragraphs in this chapter

1. What is the ultimate audit objective of reviewing the financial statements? (3)

2. What factors should the auditor have regard to when determining his review procedures? (6)

3. When reviewing accounting policies what matters should concern the auditor? (7)

4. Identify six key ratios that could be incorporated into an analytical review programme. (13)

5. What general procedures might the auditor perform to satisfy himself that the accounts contain the correct disclosures in respect of directors' emoluments? (23)

6. What amount does the Act require to be disclosed for a benefit in kind? (30)

7. What is a 'relevant company'? (39)

8. What 'persons' may be connected with a director? (39)

9. In what circumstances may a company make loans to any of its directors? (40)

10. What information is required to be disclosed in respect of a loan to a director or connected person? (48)

11. What procedures might be incorporated by a company to ensure that all disclosable directors' transactions are identified and recorded? (54)

12. In what circumstances might parties be considered to be 'related'? (65)

13. What three headings do the auditors' responsibilities effectively fall under in connection with related parties? (67)

14. In what respect may transactions appear unusual such that they may indicate the existence of related parties? (73)

15. What matters might give rise to an inconsistency between information in the directors' report and the financial statements? (83)

16. What action might the auditor take if he identifies items that are *misleading* in the directors' report? (90, 94)

Chapter 13

THE AUDIT CONCLUSION

Topics covered in this chapter:

- Post balance sheet events
- Going concern evaluation
- Representations by management
- The audit completion review
- Quality control considerations

Introduction

1. Most of the audit evidence contributing to the auditor's judgement of sufficiency has been obtained from tests of transactions and balances, analytical review, reliance on internal controls (where applicable) and review of financial statements, but there are, nevertheless, some small but significant pieces still to be fitted into the audit evidence jigsaw. It is an important general principle that the auditor's responsibility extends to the date on which he signs his audit report and indeed, as we shall see a little later, he may retain some responsibility after that date. Certain audit procedures, therefore, are timed to take place as close as possible to the date of signing the audit report. The two principal procedures are:

   - review of post balance sheet events; and
   - the obtaining of audit evidence in the form of written representations from the directors confirming oral representations made to the auditor during the course of the audit.

2. The significance of the above procedures has been formally recognised by the APC who have issued guidance in the form of two operational guidelines entitled 'Events after the balance sheet date' and 'Representations by management' respectively. These guidelines are considered in detail.

3. There are, furthermore, important control and review considerations in this 'breathing space' period at the latter end of the post balance sheet period before the audit report is signed. It cannot be emphasised too strongly that it is the reporting partner who is responsible for the audit opinion - hence now is the time for a final review to be performed so that he can be satisfied that all members of the audit team have performed their duties to the required standard and to confirm that the results support the audit conclusions reached.

4. Paragraph 15 of the auditing guideline 'Planning, controlling and recording' states:

   "The final stages of an audit require special attention. At this time, when pressures are greatest, control of the audit work is particularly required to ensure that mistakes and omissions do not occur. The use of an audit completion checklist, with sections to be filled in by the reporting partner and his staff, will help to provide such control."

5. An approach to controlling the final stages of the audit, including the use of audit completion checklists, is developed in this chapter. It is also convenient to consider in this chapter the development and application of further review techniques designed to monitor a firm's quality control procedures in response to the operational guideline 'Quality control' - these techniques are discussed in the closing section of the chapter.

The final management letter

6. It will be recalled from the audit overview developed in chapter 6 that it will often be considered appropriate to send a second management letter to the client at the completion of the audit following up the initial letter submitted at the conclusion of the interim audit - in these circumstances this will be another task that falls into the final phase of the audit. The technique of the management letter has been dealt with in detail in chapter 8 so suffice it to say that a second letter would normally include the following:

   - any additional matters under the same headings as the initial letter;
   - inefficiencies or delays in the agreed timetable for preparation of the accounts or of workings schedules which delayed the completion of the audit and may have resulted in increased costs;
   - any significant differences between the accounts and any management accounts or budgets which not only caused audit problems but also detract from the value of management information;
   - any results of the auditor's analytical procedures of which management may not be aware and may be of benefit to them.

The audit of post balance sheet events

7. The Guideline 'Events after the balance sheet date' has clarified the responsibilities of the auditor regarding examining and reporting upon post balance sheet events, including the significance of the date of the audit report. The following is a summary of the principal matters, written in the context of the audit of a limited company, affecting the dating of the audit report:

   (a) The auditor should always *date* his audit report - the date used should, generally, be that on which he *signs* his report on the financial statements. If, for administrative reasons, final copies of the financial statements are not available at the date at which the auditor declares himself willing to sign his report, he may use that date, provided the delay in the preparation of final copies is only of short duration.

   (b) The auditor's responsibility is to report on the financial statements as presented by the directors - these statements do not exist in law until approved by the directors and, indeed, SSAP17 requires disclosure of the date of approval in the financial statements. It follows that the auditor cannot date his report *earlier* than the date of approval by the directors. Before signing he should obtain evidence that the financial statements have been approved by the directors; this might typically be a board minute.

(c) At the date on which the financial statements are approved by the directors, they do not have to be in the final typed form, but the auditor should satisfy himself that the approved financial statements are materially complete. Hence they should not leave unresolved any matters requiring exercise of judgement or discretion.

(d) The auditor should plan his work so that, wherever practicable, his report is dated as close as possible to the date of approval of the financial statements. In practice, the auditor's report date and directors' approval date will be the same, assuming the auditor has completed all his post balance sheet work to his satisfaction.

Action up to the date of the audit report

8. As the auditor's responsibility extends to the date on which he signs his report it follows that he must obtain reasonable assurance up to that date in respect of all significant events. The procedures necessary to achieve this assurance are described later in this chapter. The auditor should ensure that any such significant events are, where appropriate, accounted for or disclosed in the financial statements - if not, a qualification of his report may be necessary.

Action after the date of the audit report

9. This is a tricky area, for the auditor's responsibilities are not clear cut as they are in the period prior to the date of his report. The following is a summary of his responsibilities and practical problems that could arise:

(a) After the date of the audit report the auditor does not have a duty to *search* for evidence of post balance sheet events. However, if he becomes aware of information before the general meeting at which the financial statements are laid before the members (normally, of course, the AGM) of information, from sources either within or outside the company, which might have led him to give a different audit opinion had he possessed the information at the date of his report he should act as follows:

   (i) Discuss the matter with the directors and then consider whether the financial statements should be amended by the directors (the auditor does not have powers to amend accounts).

   (ii) If the directors are unwilling to take action which the auditor considers necessary to inform the members of the changed situation, the auditor should consider exercising his statutory rights to make a statement at the general meeting. He should also consider taking legal advice on his position. The auditor does *not* have a statutory right to communicate directly in writing with the members except where he wishes to resign or where it is proposed to remove him.

   (iii) If the directors wish to amend after the auditor has signed his report but *before* they have been sent to the members, the auditor will need to consider whether the proposed amendments affect his report. His report should not be dated before the date on which the amended financial statements are approved by the directors. The auditor should perform the procedures described in paragraphs 27-45 below before making his report on the amended financial statements.

   (iv) Where, *after* the financial statements have been sent to the members, the directors wish to prepare and approve an amended set of financial statements to lay before the members, further post balance sheet audit work as in (iii) above will be necessary to cover events up to the revised date of his audit report. In this *latter* report he should refer to the original financial statements and his report thereon.

(b) If *after* the general meeting the auditor becomes aware of information which suggests that the financial statements which were laid before that meeting are wrong, he should inform the directors. He should ascertain how the directors intend to deal with the situation. In particular he should ascertain whether they intend to communicate with the members. If the auditor considers that the directors are not dealing correctly with the situation he may, exceptionally, wish to take legal advice.

10. It is useful to summarise the broad audit responsibilities in diagrammatic form:

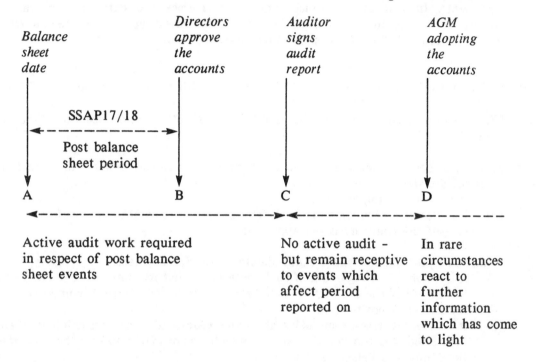

The period between B and C should be kept as short as possible. Ideally, assuming the auditor has performed the underlying post balance sheet work satisfactorily, these events will occur on the same day. C can never *precede* B, as the financial statements do not legally exist until approved by the directors.

Accounting requirements of SSAP17 and SSAP18

11. Before describing the steps taken by the auditor to obtain reasonable assurance in respect of post balance sheet events it is prudent to revise the accounting requirements of the relevant accounting standards SSAP17 *Accounting for post balance sheet events* and SSAP18 *Accounting for contingencies.*

12. *Accounting for post balance sheet events*
SSAP17 *Accounting for post balance sheet events* was issued in August 1980 and has been effective for accounting periods starting on or after 1 September 1980. The standard defines post balance sheet events in the following terms:

"*Post balance sheet events* are those events, both favourable and unfavourable, which occur between the balance sheet date and the date on which the financial statements are approved by the board of directors.

Adjusting events are post balance sheet events which provide additional evidence of conditions existing at the balance sheet date. They include events which because of statutory conventional requirements are reflected in financial statements.

Non-adjusting events are post balance sheet events which concern conditions which did not exist at the balance sheet date.

The date on which the financial statements are approved by the board of directors is the date the board of directors formally approves a set of documents as the financial statements. In respect of unincorporated enterprises the date of approval is the corresponding date. In respect of group accounts, the date of approval is the date when the group accounts are formally approved by the board of directors of the holding company.

13. Standard practice in respect of the disclosure of post balance sheet events is as follows:

"Financial statements should be prepared on the basis of conditions existing at the balance sheet date.

A material post balance sheet event requires changes in the amounts to be included in financial statements where:
(a)   it is an adjusting event; or
(b)   it indicates that application of the going concern concept to the whole or a material part of the company is not appropriate.

A material post balance sheet event should be disclosed where:
(a)   it is a non-adjusting event of such materiality that its non-disclosure would affect the ability of the users of financial statements to reach a proper understanding of the financial position; or
(b)   it is the reversal or maturity after the year end of a transaction entered into before the year end, the substance of which was primarily to alter the appearance of the company's balance sheet.

14. In respect of each post balance sheet event which is required to be disclosed under the sub-paragraph immediately above, the following information should be stated by way of note in the financial statements:

(a)   the nature of the event; and
(b)   an estimate of the financial effect, or a statement that it is not practicable to make such an estimate.

15. Finally the date on which the financial statements were approved by the board should be disclosed.

16. There is an important overriding consideration that should be applied to non-adjusting events. In order to accord with the prudence concept, an adverse event which would normally be classified as non-adjusting may need to be reclassified as adjusting - in such circumstances, full disclosure of the adjustment would be required.

17. By way of illustration, if a company suffered serious damage to property and/or trading stocks in the post balance sheet period this would normally be classified as a non-adjusting event requiring disclosure in the notes to the financial statements. If, however, the resulting loss was under-insured, or uninsured, prudence may indicate that the event should be reclassified as adjusting, hence requiring amendment to the financial statements and disclosure as an exceptional or extraordinary item.

18. It is important to stress the two categories of material post balance event requiring changes in the amounts to be included in the financial statements:

    (a) the adjusting event described above; and
    (b) the event indicating that application of the going concern concept to the whole or a material part of the company is not appropriate.

19. The auditor's post balance sheet review must clearly concern itself with both categories of event and, as we shall see, many of the procedures that the auditor adopts are specifically designed to appraise whether the company is a going concern.

20. *Accounting for contingencies*
    SSAP 18 *Accounting for contingencies* was issued in 1980 and has been effective for accounting periods starting on or after 1 September 1980. The standard defines contingencies in the following terms:

    "*Contingency* is a condition which exists at the balance sheet date, where the outcome will be confirmed only on the occurrence or non-occurrence of one or more uncertain future events. A contingent gain or loss is a gain or loss dependent on a contingency."

21. Standard practice in relation to contingencies is as follows:

    "In addition to amounts accrued under the fundamental concept of prudence in SSAP2 *Disclosure of accounting policies,* a material contingent loss should be accrued in financial statements where it is probable that a future event will confirm a loss which can be estimated with reasonable accuracy at the date on which the financial statements are approved by the board of directors.

    A material contingent loss not accrued above should be disclosed except where the possibility of loss is remote.

    Contingent gains should not be accrued in financial statements. A material contingent gain should be disclosed in financial statements only if it is probable that the gain will be realised."

22. In respect of each contingency required to be disclosed the following information should be stated by way of note in the financial statements:

    (a) the nature of the contingency;
    (b) the uncertainties which are expected to affect the ultimate outcome; and
    (c) a prudent estimate of the financial effect, made at the date on which the financial statements are approved by the board of directors; or a statement that it is not practicable to make such an estimate.

23. Where there is disclosure of an estimate of the financial effect of a contingency, the amount disclosed should be the potential financial effect. In the case of a contingent loss, this should be reduced by:

    (a) any amounts accrued; and
    (b) the amounts of any components where the possibility of loss is remote.

    The net amount only need be disclosed.

24. This accounting standard is by no means easy to interpret and apply as it is in the nature of a contingency that the outcome is uncertain. It is helpful, therefore, first to identify some examples of contingencies and then interpret the tests of 'probability' and 'remoteness' required by the standard. Examples of contingencies are as follows.

    (a) Contingent gains:
        - an insurance recovery expected in respect of a loss previously provided for
        - legal claims initiated by the client, where damages are expected to be awarded;
        - compensation payable by a foreign government for assets nationalised and written off.

    (b) Contingent liabilities:
        - legal claims against the client in respect of faulty goods or other alleged breaches of contract;
        - product warranties or guarantees;
        - bills discounted with recourse;
        - pension liabilities, if unfunded and not provided;
        - guarantees on behalf of subsidiary companies.

25. The standard does not require disclosure of 'remote' contingencies, whether assets or liabilities. Remoteness is best interpreted in terms of *probability* rather than of *time scale*. The table below sets out the different degrees of probability (although no attempt is made to place a figure upon them) and the resulting treatment in the financial statements, based on the standard.

	Contingent asset	*Contingent liability*
Remote	No disclosure	No disclosure
Possible/probable	No disclosure	Disclosure
Highly probable	Disclosure	Provision
Virtually certain	Accrual	Provision

26. It is argued that there is a greater probability of 'crystallisation' needed for disclosure of a contingent asset than for disclosure of a contingent liability. The degree of probability is for management to assess. The opinion of independent advisers, for example, solicitors in the case of a pending legal claim against the client, may be of assistance to management.

Procedures for the audit of events after the balance sheet date

27. The Guideline 'Events after the balance sheet date' identifies that certain events falling within the ambit of SSAP17 are examined by the auditor as part of his normal verification work on the balance sheet. Examples include the checking of cash received from certain debtors after the balance sheet date or the amounts realised from the sale of stock after the year-end to assess net realisable value. There are, however, *additional* procedures described as a 'review of events after the balance sheet date' - also commonly referred to as a 'subsequent event review' - that the auditor should carry out.

28. The Guideline states that the review should consist of discussions with management relating to such events, and may also include consideration of:

   (a) procedures taken by management to ensure that all events after the balance sheet date have been identified, considered and properly evaluated as to their effect on the financial statements;
   (b) any management accounts and relevant accounting records;
   (c) profit forecasts and cash flow projections for the new period;
   (d) known 'risk' areas and contingencies, whether inherent in the nature of the business or revealed by previous audit experience;
   (e) minutes of shareholders', directors' and management meetings and correspondence and memoranda relating to items included in the minutes;
   (f) relevant information which has come to attention, from sources outside the enterprise including public knowledge of competitors, suppliers and customers.

29. This review should be updated to a date as near as practicable to that of the audit report by making enquiries of management and considering the need to carry out further tests.

30. The review above is necessarily broad-brush in approach to cater for all circumstances, but it should be appreciated that it contains procedures to investigate the three critical post balance sheet areas:

   (a) adjusting events;
   (b) evaluation of the company as a going concern; and
   (c) contingencies.

31. To develop a more practical approach it is useful to look at procedures relevant to going concern evaluation and the audit of contingencies in greater detail.

Going concern evaluation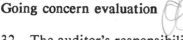

32. The auditor's responsibility to form an opinion as to whether a company is a going concern at the date of his report is beyond dispute, but it is only recently that formal guidance has been issued by the APC identifying procedures that the auditor should carry out to discharge his duties. The guidance is in the form of an Auditing Guideline entitled 'The auditor's considerations in respect of going concern' published in August 1985.

33. It is an important theme of the Guideline that it is very rare for an enterprise to cease to carry on business without any prior indications and hence any procedures that provide early identification that the enterprise may be unable to continue in business will be of assistance to management as well as the auditor. Nevertheless, going concern considerations cannot be confined to the early stages of the audit and hence the procedures need to be continued to the date of the audit report. Of particular practical assistance in the Guideline are the paragraphs identifying possible symptoms of going concern problems. These paragraphs are reproduced here as a listing to make them more palatable:

   (a) Symptoms indicating an inability to meet debts as they fall due:
       Adverse financial figures or ratios:
       - recurring operating losses
       - financing to a considerable extent out of overdue suppliers and other creditors (for example, VAT, PAYE, National Insurance)
       - heavy dependence on short-term finance for long-term needs
       - working capital deficiencies
       - low liquidity rates
       - over-gearing, in the form of high or increasing debt to equity ratios
       - under-capitalisation, particularly if there is a deficiency of share capital and reserves.
       Borrowings in excess of limits imposed by debenture trust deeds
       Default on loans or similar agreements
       Dividends in arrear
       Restrictions placed on usual trade terms
       Excessive or obsolete stock
       Long overdue debtors
       Non-compliance with statutory capital requirements
       Deterioration of relationship with bankers
       Necessity of seeking new sources or methods of obtaining finance
       The continuing use of old fixed assets because there are no funds available to replace them
       The size and content of the order book
       Potential losses on long-term contracts.
   (b) Other factors not necessarily suggesting inability to meet debts:
       Internal matters:
       - loss of key management or staff
       - significantly increasing stock levels
       - work stoppages or other labour difficulties
       - substantial dependence on the success of a particular project or particular asset
       - excessive reliance on the success of a new product
       - uneconomic long-term commitments
       External matters:
       - legal proceedings or similar matters that may jeopardise a company's ability to continue in business
       - loss of a key franchise or patent
       - loss of a principal supplier or customer
       - the undue influence of a market dominant competitor
       - political risks
       - technical developments which render a key product obsolete
       - frequent financial failures of enterprises in the same industry.

34. The indications above vary in importance and some may only have significance as audit evidence when viewed in conjunction with others. Many audit firms incorporate symptoms such as those itemised above in formal checklists - often referred to as 'Going concern review checklists' - to provide documentary evidence of their review. The significance of the indications above may diminish because they are matched by audit evidence indicating that there are mitigating factors. Indications that the enterprise, for instance, is unable to meet its debts may be mitigated by factors relating to alternative means for maintaining adequate cash flows - for example, the ability to dispose of assets or postpone replacement of assets without adversely affecting operations, to obtain new sources of finance or to renew or extend loans and to restructure debts.

35. The auditor should carry out procedures as early as possible in the audit in order to determine whether any of the indications described above are present and to give management more time to consider its response if symptoms are discovered.

36. In the post balance sheet period the auditor will tend to concentrate on the review of forecasts and budgets as indicated in paragraph 28(c) above, but such information may well be lacking in necessary detail in the case of small enterprises. Where the auditor considers that an enterprise is facing difficulties based on his ongoing review he may well have to insist that forecast and budgetary information will need to be developed, *regardless of the size of the enterprise;* although small companies need not be expected to provide the same amount and quality of evidence as large companies.

37. When forming his opinion at the conclusion of the post balance sheet period the auditor should have regard to the term 'foreseeable future' identified in SSAP2 in the context of going concern. While the foreseeable future must be judged in relation to specific circumstances, the auditor should normally consider information which relates to a minimum of *6 months* following the date of the audit report or *1 year* after the balance sheet date, whichever is the *later*. It will also be necessary to take account of events which will or are likely to occur later, for example, where the enterprise is due to repay significant indebtedness. Where there is doubt about the enterprise's ability to continue in business then the auditor may have to consider qualifying his audit report - the auditor should *not* refrain from qualifying his report report on the grounds that it may lead to the appointment of a receiver or liquidator.

Contingencies: obtaining audit evidence

38. The importance of the auditor considering the existence and treatment of contingencies as part of his subsequent event review has been stressed in paragraph 28. He will have to pay particular regard to the different treatment required by SSAP18 on grounds of prudence for contingent gains on the one hand and contingent losses on the other. He will also need to use his judgement in determining 'remoteness' and 'probability' in individual cases. The audit of contingencies is the subject of an early guidance statement (U16) published by the ICAEW in 1970. Although this statement predates the accounting standard, SSAP18, its recommendations are still broadly relevant to contingencies such as legal claims.

39. The following audit procedures are suggested for the verification of the *existence* of such contingencies as pending lawsuits or other actions against the company, though they will not necessarily provide the auditor with adequate information of the likely amounts for which the company may ultimately be responsible:

    (a) reviewing the client's system of recording claims and the procedure for bringing these to the attention of the management or board;

    (b) discussing the arrangements for instructing solicitors with the official responsible for legal matters;

    (c) examining the minutes of the Board of Directors and or executive or other relevant committee for references to, or indications of, possible claims;

    (d) examining bills rendered by solicitors and correspondence with them, in which connection the solicitors should be requested to furnish bills or estimates of charges to date, or to confirm that they have no unbilled charges;

    (e) obtaining a list of matters referred to solicitors from the appropriate director or official with estimates of the possible ultimate liabilities;

    (f) obtaining a written assurance from the appropriate director or official that he is not aware of any matters referred to solicitors other than those disclosed.

40. In appropriate circumstances, the auditor may decide to obtain written representations in respect of legal actions from the company's legal advisers. Requests for such confirmation should be kept within the solicitor-client relationship and should thus be issued by the client with a request that a copy of the reply be sent direct to the auditors. As with a debtors circularisation it should be appreciated that the auditor does not have a right to communicate with third parties directly.

41. In order to ascertain whether the information provided by the directors is complete an auditor may, especially in certain overseas countries, decide to arrange for solicitors to be requested to advise whether they have matters in hand which are not listed in the letter of request, and to provide information as to the likely amounts involved. When considering such a non-specific inquiry, the auditor should note that the Council of the Law Society has advised solicitors that it is unable to recommend them to comply with requests for information which are more widely drawn than the specimen form of wording set out below:

> "In connection with the preparation and audit of our accounts for the year ended.... the directors have made estimates of the amounts of the ultimate liabilities (including costs) which might be incurred and are regarded as material in relation to the following matters on which you have been consulted. We should be obliged if you would confirm that in your opinion these estimates are reasonable.
>
> *Matter*   *Estimated liability, including costs."*
> ....

42. Despite the above views of the Council of the Law Society regarding non-specific enquiries, there may be circumstances in which it is necessary as an audit procedure for an enquiry of a general nature to be addressed to the solicitors in order to confirm that the information provided by the directors is complete in all material particulars.

43. If the outcome of his enquiries appears satisfactory, the auditor would not normally regard the absence of a corroboration of the completeness of a list of legal matters as a reason in itself for qualifying his report. If the enquiries lead to the discovery of significant matters not previously identified, the auditor will wish to extend his enquiries and to request his client to address further enquiries to, and arrange a meeting with, the solicitors, at which the

auditor will wish to be present. If, having regard to all the circumstances, the auditor is unable to satisfy himself that he has received all the information he requires for the purpose of his audit, he must qualify his report.

44. It is not uncommon for the auditor, notwithstanding the procedures considered above, to conclude that he has not been able to obtain adequate evidence to support estimates and use his experience to reach an opinion as to their reasonableness in the case of major litigation. In these circumstances he may consider it necessary to qualify his report.

Evidence of review of post balance sheet events

45. The audit working papers must contain a record of the work carried out to identify events after the balance sheet date. In practice, many firms use a checklist, often referred to as a 'subsequent events review programme', to ensure that the identification of adjusting events and contingencies and their treatment is adequately documented, together with the 'going concern review checklist' identified in paragraph 34. Where discussions have taken place with management regarding matters arising from the subsequent events review, a record should be retained by the auditor. The auditor may wish to obtain formal representations from management concerning events after the balance sheet date or the fact that there have not been any - if such representations are obtained, they should be dated as close as possible to the date of the audit report. This is just one example of a management representation, a concept further developed in the following section.

Representations by management

46. Representations by management are a source of audit evidence. The Auditing Guideline 'Representations by management' provides the auditor with useful guidance as to the nature and scope of such representations, and the following comments are derived from the Guideline.

47. Oral representations are made throughout an audit in response to specific enquiries. Whilst representations by management constitute audit evidence, the auditor should not rely solely on the unsupported oral representations of management as being sufficient reliable evidence when they relate to matters which are material to the financial statements. In most cases, oral representations can be corroborated by checking with sources independent of the enterprise or by checking with other evidence obtained by the auditor, and therefore do not need to be confirmed in writing.

48. However, in certain cases, such as:
    - where knowledge of the facts is confined to management; or
    - where the matter is principally one of judgement and opinion,

the auditor may not be able to obtain independent corroborative evidence and could not reasonably expect it to be available. In such cases, the auditor should ensure that there is no other evidence which conflicts with the representations made by management and he should obtain written confirmation of the representations.

49. Where written representations are obtained, the auditor will still need to decide whether in the circumstances these representations, together with such other audit evidence as he has obtained, are sufficient to enable him to form an opinion on the financial statements.

Procedures

50. Where oral representations by management are uncorroborated by sufficient other audit evidence and where they relate to matters which are material to the financial statements, they should be summarised in the audit working papers. The auditor should ensure that these representations are either:
    - formally minuted as being approved by the board of directors; or
    - included in a signed letter, addressed to the auditor, and known as a 'letter of representation'.

    It is the latter alternative - the letter of representation - that is favoured in practice.

51. Because the representations are those of management, standard letters may not be appropriate. In any event, management should be encouraged to participate in drafting any letter of representation or, after review and discussion, to make appropriate amendments to the auditor's draft, provided that the value of the audit evidence obtained is not thereby diminished.

52. A letter of representation should be signed by persons whose level of authority is appropriate to the significance of the representations made - normally by one or more of the executive directors on behalf of the whole board. The signatories of the letter should be fully conversant with the matters contained in it. The auditor should request that the consideration of the letter, and its approval by the board for signature, be minuted. He may request that he be allowed to attend the meeting at which the board is due to approve the letter - such attendance may also be desirable where the representations are to be formally minuted rather than included in a letter.

53. Procedures regarding written representations should be agreed at an early stage in order to reduce the possibility of the auditor being faced with a refusal by management to co-operate in providing such representations. In the case of a new engagement it is good practice to draw the directors' attention to the fact that the auditor will seek representations as part of his normal audit procedures in a paragraph in the letter of engagement.

54. In the past one of the reasons why management refused to co-operate was that they considered the representation letter to be an attempt by the auditor to shift responsibility for the audit opinion - an attitude with some justification, as the auditor frequently sought representations in respect of virtually all the material figures in the balance sheet involving *any* degree of judgement and opinion. Now that representations are to be confined to material matters that are *principally* areas of judgement and opinion - and matters where knowledge of the facts is confined to management - there should be relatively few representations to be sought and this approach should hence lessen the reluctance of management to co-operate.

55. However, management may at the outset indicate that they are not willing to sign letters of representation or to pass minutes requested by the auditor. If they do so indicate, the auditor should inform management that he will himself prepare a statement in writing setting out his understanding of the principal representations that have been made to him during the course of the audit, and he should send this statement to management with a request for confirmation that his understanding of the representations is correct.

56. If management disagrees with the auditor's statement of representations, discussions should be held to clarify the matters in doubt and, if necessary, a revised statement prepared and agreed. Should management fail to reply, the auditor should follow the matter up to try to ensure that his understanding of the position, as set out in his statement, is correct.

57. In rare circumstances the auditor may be unable to obtain the written representations which he requires. This may be, for instance, because of a refusal by management to co-operate, or because management properly declines to give the representations required on the grounds of its own uncertainty regarding the particular matter. In either case, if the auditor is unable to satisfy himself, he may have to conclude that he has not received all the information and explanations that he requires, and consequently may need to consider qualifying his audit report.

Dating of formal record of representations

58. The formal record of representations by management should be approved on a date as *close as possible* to the date of the audit report and after all other work, including the review of events after the balance sheet date, has been completed. It should never be approved *after the* audit report since it is part of the evidence on which the auditor's opinion, expressed in his report, is based.

59. If there is a substantial delay between the approval of the formal record of representations by management and the date of the audit report, the auditor should consider whether to obtain further representations in respect of the intervening period and also whether any additional post balance sheet audit procedures need to be carried out.

Contents and wording of the letter of representation

60. Set out on the next page is an example letter of representation relating to matters which are material to financial statements *prepared by an auditor for the company*, and to circumstances where the auditor cannot obtain independent corroborative evidence and could not reasonably expect it to be available. You should note its relative brevity - there are only five representations, one of which - relating to transactions with directors - is a good example of a situation 'where knowledge of the facts is confined to management'. The others are principally matters of judgement and opinion.

Dear Sirs,

We appreciate that there are matters which are material to the financial statements where you cannot obtain independent corroborative evidence and could not reasonably expect it to be available, and hence require written representations from us.

We confirm to the best of our knowledge and belief, and having made appropriate enquiries of other directors and officials of the company, the following representations given to you in connection with your audit of the company's financial statements for the year ended..............:

General

We acknowledge as directors our responsibility for the financial statements (which you have prepared for the company). All the accounting records have been made available to you for the purpose of your audit and all the transactions undertaken by the company have been properly reflected and recorded in the accounting records. All other records and related information, including minutes of all management and shareholders' meetings, have been made available to you.

Legal claim

The legal claim by Mr.......... has been settled out of court by the company paying him £.......... No further amounts are expected to be paid and no similar claims by employees or former employees have been received or are expected to be received.

Deferred tax

Deferred tax has been provided to the extent that liabilities will crystallise and at the rates at which they are expected to crystallise.

In connection with deferred tax not provided, the following assumptions reflect the intentions and expectations of the company:

(a) Capital investment of £....... is planned over the next ...... years.

(b) There are no plans to sell revalued properties.

(c) We are not aware of any indications that the situation is likely to change so as to necessitate the inclusion of a provision for tax payable in the financial statements in respect of the unprovided element.

Transactions with directors

The company has had at no time during the year any arrangement, transaction or agreement to provide credit facilities (including loans, quasi-loans or credit transactions) for directors nor to guarantee or provide security for such matters, except as disclosed in note ... to the financial statements.

Post balance sheet events

Other than the fire damage and related insurance claims described in note ... to the financial statements, there have been no events since the balance sheet date which necessitate revision of the figures included in the financial statements or inclusion of a note thereto. Should further material events occur, which may necessitate revision of the figures included in the financial statements or inclusion of a note thereto, we will advise you accordingly.

Yours faithfully,

(Signed on behalf of the Board of Directors)
_____ Financial Director

61. The paragraphs included in the example letter relate to a specific set of circumstances. Set out below are some examples of additional paragraphs which, depending on the circumstances, may be appropriate for inclusion in a letter of representation or board minutes. It is most unlikely that the auditor will need to obtain all these representations as a matter of routine.

(a) There have been no breaches of the income tax regulations regarding payments to subcontractors in the construction industry which may directly or indirectly affect the view given by the financial statements.

(b) Having regard to the terms and conditions of sale imposed by major suppliers of goods, trade creditors include no amounts resulting from the purchase of goods on terms which include reservation of title by suppliers, other than £...... due to ABC plc.

(c) With the exception of the penalties described in note 17, we are not aware of any circumstances which could produce losses on long-term contracts.

(d) DEF Limited, an associated company, is about to launch a new product which has received excellent test results. As a result, the amount of £....... outstanding since 6 January 19.. is expected to be fully recoverable.

(e) The company has guaranteed the bank overdraft of its subsidiary A Limited but has not entered into guarantees, warranties or other financial commitments relating to its other subsidiary or associated companies.

(f) The transaction shown in the profit and loss account as extraordinary is outside the course of the company's normal business and is not expected to recur frequently or regularly.

(g) Since the balance sheet date, the company has negotiated a continuation of its bank overdraft facilities with a limit of £...... There have been no other events which are likely to affect the adequacy of working capital to meet foreseeable requirements in the year following the adoption of the financial statements.

The audit completion review

62. The procedures considered to date in this chapter are concerned with obtaining further vital audit evidence in the post balance sheet period up to the date of the audit report. This section sets out the review responsibilities of the senior members of the audit team to provide a check that the audit has been performed to an acceptable standard and to form the foundation of the following year's audit. It is accepted good practice that work performed by each member of the audit team is reviewed by more senior persons. During the final stages of the audit it is vital that the review process involves not just the senior in charge and manager but also the partner who is responsible for the audit opinion. This review process may, indeed, be supplemented by consultation with other senior colleagues and further reviews of a quality control nature performed by senior staff independent of the audit team.

63. The final review in summary should enable the auditor to:

(a) ensure that the figures in the draft accounts make sense in the light of the audit evidence;

(b) assess the impact of any unadjusted errors and decide whether to press for adjustments;

(c) check that all appropriate disclosure and other requirements have been complied with in the financial statements;

(d) check that there is sufficient relevant reliable audit evidence to support the audit opinion;

(e) consider what recommendations can be made to client in the management letter(s);

(f) prepare the way for the following year's audit by summarising any points which will be relevant to that audit and by ensuring that the permanent file is up-to-date.

64. In addition, where there is a separate interim audit, the review of the interim work provides a link between that visit and the final audit. In order better to appreciate the nature of the review process the following paragraphs define typical manager and partner responsibilities - they should be seen merely as a guide as it is difficult, and undesirable, to lay down hard and fast rules.

Manager review

65. The manager is responsible for:

   (a) review of detailed working papers prepared by the senior and assistants. This will include an examination of the permanent file, the detailed audit programme, supporting working papers and conclusions drawn;
   (b) consideration of analytical review evidence;
   (c) review of the financial statements, supplementing the review performed by the senior in charge evidenced by completion of an accounting requirements checklist;
   (d) consideration and editing of the 'points for partner' schedule: this schedule is normally prepared by the senior in charge and typically contains the following elements to aid the partner in his review:
      - a brief explanation of the results and financial position as shown by the draft accounts and of any changes from prior years, budget and expectations;
      - an explanation of any audit problems including areas where major judgements have been exercised;
      - a brief explanation of any outstanding work which it has proved impossible to complete;
      - a summary of the costs of the audit to date (plus an estimate to complete) together with an explanation of any variances from budget; and
      - a schedule of unadjusted errors, showing cycle by cycle the effect on the profit and loss account and the balance sheet.
   (e) review and editing of management letter, letter of representation, audit time summary and fee note;
   (f) review of corporation tax computations and supporting schedules.

Reporting partner review

66. He is responsible for:

   (a) examination and review of the audit files in sufficient detail to be satisfied that the audit staff, including the manager, have performed their work satisfactorily;
   (b) review of 'points for partner' schedule with manager and formulation of decisions;
   (c) approval of the management letter for submission to the client (this may be a second letter, following up one sent after completion of the interim audit, or a letter covering the whole audit);
   (d) approval of the financial statements having reviewed analytical review evidence and the subsequent events programme;
   (e) ensuring that all material points are cleared - at his discretion he might decide to consult with his colleagues to obtain a second opinion in respect of any contentious matters;
   (f) review and approval of representation letter and fee note;
   (g) approval of the final typed financial statements.

67. It will be appreciated from the above summary that the partner is primarily a reviewer and decision maker. Having satisfactorily completed his final review he will be in a position to form his audit opinion - qualified or unqualified - and subsequently sign and date the audit report (after formal approval of the financial statements by the directors).

68. In a practical world it should be appreciated that the final review stage is not only a check on the quality and effectiveness of the audit, it is also the opportunity to assess the service given to the client and determine improvements that can be made in future years.

69. The responsibilities identified above provide the framework for an effective final review function but as a further aid to an efficient and comprehensive review the auditor will often use - not for the first time in the audit process - a checklist. This checklist commonly referred to as an 'audit completion checklist' is conventionally set up in sections to emphasise the separate manager and partner review responsibilities.

De-briefing meeting

70. It is becoming common practice to introduce a further review stage in the audit process, referred to as the debriefing meeting. This meeting is timed to take place as soon as practicable after completion of the audit. Its purpose is to review the conduct of the audit as a whole with the objective of improving performance of individuals and conduct of future audits and more specifically to develop the initial plan for the following year's audit. The debriefing meeting for the audit just completed could hence alternatively be considered as the first stage of the following year's audit. It is usually considered expedient to hold the meeting no more than a few weeks after the audit report has been signed and dated so that the audit is still relatively fresh in the minds of the audit team. The meeting is normally chaired by the reporting partner and in attendance will be the assignment manager, senior in charge and other support staff at the discretion of the partner.

Quality control considerations

71. The review procedures discussed in the previous section are concerned with ensuring that work on an individual audit is properly controlled in the context of the operational guideline 'Planning, controlling and recording' such that the reporting partner can form the audit opinion. Para 17 of the guideline states that the auditor 'should also consider how the overall quality of the work carried out within the firm can best be monitored and maintained'. This is quality control in a broader sense and, indeed, is applicable not only to auditing but to the entire range of professional services provided by a firm. The APC published an operational guideline entitled 'Quality control' in January 1985 to assist firms in complying with para 17 above. This guideline defines quality control as 'the means by which a firm obtains reasonable assurance that its expression of audit opinions always reflects observance of approved auditing standards, any statutory or contractual requirements and any professional standards set by the firm itself. Quality control should also promote observance of the personal standards relevant to the work of an auditor, which are described in the ethical statements published by the Accountancy Bodies'.

Scope of quality control procedures

72. The guideline stresses that the objectives of quality control procedures are the same for all firms and proceeds to define six specific objectives which it considers to be universally applicable. The procedures that a firm may adopt to meet the objectives will depend on its size, the nature of its practice, the number of its offices and its organisation. The *objectives* are as follows:

   (a) *Communication*
      Each firm should establish procedures appropriate to its circumstances and communicate them to all partners and relevant staff, and to other professionals employed by the firm in the course of its audit practice.

(b) *Acceptance of appointment and reappointment as auditor*
Each firm should ensure that, in making a decision to accept appointment or reappointment as auditor, consideration is given to the firm's own independence and its ability to provide an adequate service to the client.

(c) *Professional ethics*
There should be procedures within the firm to ensure that all partners and professional staff adhere to the principles of independence, objectivity, integrity and confidentiality, set out in the ethical statements issued by the Accountancy Bodies.

(d) *Skills and competence*
The firm's partners and staff have attained the skills and competence required to fulfil their responsibilities.

(e) *Consultation*
There should be procedures for consultation.

(f) *Monitoring the firm's procedures*
The firm should monitor the effectiveness of its application of the quality control procedures outlined above.

73. The guideline provides a brief description of the procedures that firms may adopt to meet the above objectives - placing particular emphasis on the procedures appropriate to smaller firms. Worthy of detailed consideration are the procedures necessary to meet the objectives (d), (e) and (f) above.

Skills and competence

74. This involves procedures relating to:
    (a) recruitment;
    (b) technical training and updating;
    (c) on-the-job training.

Staff should be informed of the firm's procedures for example by means of manuals and standardised documentation or programmes. The firm's procedures should be regularly updated.

75. (a) *Recruitment*
Effective recruitment of personnel with suitable qualifications including any necessary expertise in specialised areas and industries involves both planning for staffing needs and determining criteria for recruitment based on such needs. Such criteria should be designed to ensure that cost considerations do not deter the firm from recruitment of audit staff with the experience and ability to exercise the appropriate judgement.

(b) *Technical training and updating*
All partners and staff should be required to keep themselves technically up-to-date on matters that are relevant to their work. The firm should assist them to meet this requirement. Such assistance should include:
- circulating digests or full texts, where appropriate, of professional publications and relevant legislation;
- maintaining a technical library;
- issuing technical circulars and memoranda on professional developments as they affect the firm;
- encouraging attendance at professional courses;
- maintaining appropriate training arrangements.

The methods of implementing the above procedures may vary according to the size of the firm. For example, a smaller firm can ensure that it has copies of essential reference books relevant to its practice where a fuller technical library would be impracticable. Also manuals do not need to be produced internally by the smaller firms but can be acquired from various professional bodies and commercial sources; and co-operative arrangements with other firms can help meet training needs.

(c) *On-the-job training*

The guideline 'Planning, controlling and recording' relates staff assignment to the needs of the particular audit visit but, in the context of quality control generally, a further factor in staff assignment should be the opportunity for on-the-job training and professional development. This should provide staff with exposure to different types of audit and with the opportunity to work with more experienced members of the team who should be made responsible for the supervision and review of the work of junior staff. It is important that the performance of staff on audits is evaluated and that the results of these assessments are communicated to the staff concerned, giving the opportunity for staff to respond to comments made and for any action to be agreed.

Consultation

76. Procedures for consultation would include:

(a) a structured approach to audit file review (so that the review procedures recommended in the auditing guideline 'Planning, controlling and recording' are effective for *every* audit);
(b) reference of technical problems to designated specialists within the firm; and
(c) resolution of matters of judgement.

77. For smaller firms, and particularly for sole practitioners, consultation at the appropriate professional level within the firm may not be possible. Consultation with another practitioner or with any relevant professional advisory service, may be a suitable alternative, provided that confidentiality of the client's affairs is maintained.

Monitoring the firm's procedures

78. The monitoring process should provide reasonable assurance that measures to maintain the professional standards of the firm are being properly and effectively carried out. This process should include periodic review of a sample of the firm's audit files by independent reviewers from within the firm. The firm should:

(a) have procedures for selection of particular audits for review, and for the frequency, timing, nature and extent of reviews;
(b) set the levels of competence for the partners and staff who are to participate in review activities;
(c) establish procedures to resolve disagreements which may arise between the reviewers and audit staff.

79. The purpose of this independent review is to provide an assessment of the overall standards of the firm, and so it is quite separate from the purpose of the earlier review procedures concerned with control over the individual audit. Where, in the smaller firm, independent review within the firm is not possible, attendance at professional courses and communication with other practitioners can provide the opportunity of comparison with the standards of others, thereby identifying potential problem areas. Whatever action is taken by the firm to monitor the effectiveness of quality control procedures, the firm should ensure that recommendations that arise are implemented.

80. It is instructive to expand a little on the requirements of (a), (b) and (c) in paragraph 78 by identifying how firms in practice set up their monitoring procedures. A distinction is commonly drawn between so called 'hot' and 'cold' reviews. The characteristic of a hot review is that it is carried out before the audit report is signed and dated, hence providing an opportunity to take remedial action resulting from the review findings before the completion of the audit. The cold - or post - audit review - takes place after the audit report has been signed. In both classes of review, the partners or staff who carry out the review *must* be independent of the audit team involved in the assignment under scrutiny. In other words, hot and cold reviews are characterised by their *timing* not by who performs them.

81. In terms of scope and objectives three types of review are commonly performed:
    - the detailed review
    - the brief review
    - the special purpose review

    Each of the above in terms of *timing* may be performed 'hot' or 'cold'.

The detailed review

82. The objectives of a detailed review may be summarised as follows:

    (a) to check the extent of compliance with the firm's standards and policies with regard to:
       (i)   auditing procedures;
       (ii) accounting and reporting principles;
       (iii) working paper preparation and presentation;
    (b) to determine whether the scope and results of the audit work (ie audit evidence) is adequate to support the audit opinion;
    (c) to review the performance of the audit staff and to assist them in improving their future performance;
    (d) to identify areas of weakness in the firm's procedures, or application thereof, and to establish new procedures and implement them;
    (e) to ensure that unnecessary work is eliminated and efficiency thus improved.

83. The key objective above that distinguishes the detailed review from the brief review considered below is the determination of the adequacy of audit evidence to support the audit opinion. The review must hence be detailed enough for the reviewer to be able to form his own opinion as to the sufficiency, relevance and reliability of the audit evidence.

84. It is essential that the reviewer has access to all the audit files, including the permanent file, and it is recommended in practice that the reviewer commences his review with the permanent/interim files (if applicable) and then the final audit file and financial statements – he hence reviews each phase of the audit in the same order, as far as possible, as the work was carried out.

85. Clearly, this particular cold review technique is time-consuming as it is an in-depth investigation, but it is probably a more valuable quality control tool than the brief review technique considered below.

The brief review

86. It is clear that the commitment in time and effort demanded of a reviewing partner to carry out a detailed review is formidable. It is expedient, therefore, to supplement detailed reviews with a programme of brief reviews, which provide a realistic opportunity to review all, or at worst, the majority of audits in a practice on a regular basis.

87. The brief review is of necessity superficial and its limited objective is to ascertain from a relatively brief scrutiny of the audit files whether, prima facie, the firm's procedures and standards have been applied. It is not possible to draw valid conclusions regarding the sufficiency of audit evidence when applying this technique (except in a negative sense where it is apparent that there is a conspicuous lack of evidence).

88. The most effective way to carry out the review is to commence with the financial statements subject to the review and work 'backwards' through the current and permanent files (NB this directional approach is the opposite of that for detailed reviews above.)

The special purpose review

89. The special purpose review is a review of specific aspects of an audit designed to achieve a particular limited objective. Such reviews tend to be performed on an ad hoc basis and often concentrate on 'high risk' or contentious areas of an audit. The objectives of such reviews clearly vary widely and it is not possible to suggest a standardised approach but it is perhaps useful to give examples of the type of problem areas that might be the subject of a special purpose review:

   (a) review to check compliance with a newly implemented firm procedure;

   (b) review of a number of specially selected audits to check consistency of audit approach and application of a particular statement of standard accounting practice;

   (c) review of a particular audit area which is consistently causing problems – as evidenced, perhaps, by brief and detailed reviews. This type of review may often be more effectively performed by a reviewer with the appropriate specialist knowledge, but he must, as always, be independent of the audit subject to the review.

Frequency of reviews and communication of results

90. The guideline does not give any indication as to how frequently reviews should be performed; it merely suggests that there must be a policy regarding selection. Many firms set up a selection policy that requires all audits of listed companies, major public and private companies and 'high risk' clients to be reviewed each year usually applying the rigorous detailed review technique. Certainly the selection process should ensure that at least one audit of each partner is reviewed each year.

91. A vital aspect of a post audit review is the communication of the findings. These must be fully discussed with the partner whose work has been subject to the review, but it must be made abundantly clear that the review is intended as a constructive process not a witch hunt.

92. It is important after the end of a series of reviews, to draw the results together in summary form, and it is then generally considered prudent to destroy the results of individual reviews as they are potentially self-incriminating.

93. The firm, perhaps via a technical committee, should then consider the areas of weakness highlighted in the summary and consider what appropriate action might be taken and finally devise an action programme

Postscript - peer reviews

94. The concept of a peer review, whereby the accounting and auditing procedures and practice management of a firm of accountants is examined by another firm, was introduced in the USA in 1971 by the American Institute of Certified Public Accountants as a voluntary education programme. Mandatory peer reviews have subsequently been imposed on many US firms by the Securities and Exchange Commission (SEC) since 1973.

95. Peer reviews are hence an American concept - there is *no mention* of this technique in the guideline 'Quality control' discussed above. There is of course every possibility that the technique could become better established in the UK in the future by a self regulatory process or statutory enforcement. It could involve either:

    (a) the profession as a whole establishing panels of experts to review and report on the practices and procedures of a firm of auditors; or simply,

    (b) another independent firm of auditors carrying out the review.

96. The main object of such an exercise is to improve the quality and performance of audit work generally, but undoubtedly an important part of the 'brief' of the reviewer would be to consider whether the firm under review was sufficiently independent of its clients.

Summary of the chapter

97. This chapter deals with a number of topics that are already well established as examiners' favourites:

    (a) the letter of representation;
    (b) the audit of post balance sheet events;
    (c) factors indicating going concern problems and the auditor's responsibility to evaluate going concern.

98. As each of these topics is the subject of an operational guideline, the examiner can reasonably expect students to be able to apply the intentionally broad procedures developed by these guidelines to more specific case study type questions. The concept of quality control is - compared with the topics above - relatively novel, and for that reason alone is likely to be highly examinable in the foreseeable future.

TEST YOUR KNOWLEDGE
Numbers in brackets refer to paragraphs in this chapter

1. When should the auditor date his report? (7)

2. What action need an auditor take after he has signed and dated his audit report? (9)

3. Distinguish between 'adjusting' and 'non-adjusting' events. (12)

4. What procedures, in summary form, should be incorporated in a subsequent event review programme? (28)

5. What does the auditor understand by the term 'foreseeable future'? (37)

6. What procedures should the auditor carry out to verify the existence of contingencies? (39)

7. In what circumstances may the auditor seek to obtain written representations from the directors of a company? (48)

8. What steps should the auditor take if management indicates that they are unwilling to sign a letter of representation or to pass minutes requested by the auditor? (55)

9. When should the letter of representation be dated? (58)

10. What is a 'de-briefing meeting'? (70)

11. What are the six universal quality control objectives applicable to any firm? (72)

12. What is the difference between a 'hot review' and a 'cold review'? (80)

SECTION 4: ILLUSTRATIVE QUESTIONS

1. (a) Discuss the role of an internal audit department in a large organisation.
   (b) Compare the role of an internal auditor with that of an external auditor.
   (c) Discuss the extent to which there can be effective liaison between internal and external auditors, and the precautions which should be taken by an external auditor before placing reliance on the work of an internal auditor.
   (d) State to whom, in your opinion, the internal auditor should report in a public company.

2. The management of Brandon Limited have asked you as auditor to review their system of control over the purchase, receipt, storage and issue of raw materials. They are aware of the fact that improvements need to be made and would like you to write a letter to them with your suggestions for improvement. You have prepared the following comments with regard to the current procedures used by Brandon Limited:

   (a) Raw materials consist mainly of expensive electronic components and are kept in a locked storeroom. Storeroom personnel include a supervisor and four clerks. All are well trained, competent and the firm has taken out fidelity guarantee policies. Raw materials are only removed from the storeroom upon written or oral authorisation from one of the production foremen.

   (b) There are no perpetual inventory records and therefore the storeroom clerks do not keep records of goods received or issued. In order to compensate for the lack of perpetual records, a physical count is made every month by the storeroom clerks who are well supervised, and proper procedures are followed in counting the stock.

   (c) After the physical count the storeroom supervisor matches quantities counted against a predetermined reorder level. If the count for any item is below this level the supervisor enters the part number on a materials requisition list which he sends to the accounts department for the attention of the purchase ledger clerk. The latter prepares a purchase order for a predetermined reorder quantity for each part required and mails this order to the supplier from whom the part was last purchased.

   (d) When the materials which were ordered arrive at Brandon Limited they are received by the storeroom clerks who count them and agree the total with the suppliers' delivery note. All suppliers' delivery notes are initialled, dated and filed in the storeroom to act as receiving reports.

   Required:

   You are to write a letter to the management of Brandon Limited highlighting the weaknesses of the present system and to give your recommendations as to the improvements which you consider they should adopt. Pay particular attention to the layout of your letter.

3. Evidence supporting the financial statements consists of the underlying accounting data and all other corroborating information available to the auditor. In the course of his examination of the financial statements the external auditor will perform detailed tests taking samples of transactions from various large-volume populations. The auditor may also audit various types of transactions by tracing a single transaction of each type through all stages of the accounting system.

Required:

(a) What are the various audit objectives associated with selecting a sample of transactions from a large-volume population?

(b) What evidence would the auditor expect to gain from auditing various types of transactions by tracing a single transaction of each type through all stages of the accounting system?

4. You are required to present the arguments for and against the use of statistical sampling in auditing and reach a conclusion on the subject.

5. An extremely important aspect of an auditor's examination of the financial statements is his observation of the physical stocktaking.

Required:

(a) What are the main objectives of the auditor's observation of the physical stocktaking? (You are not required to describe the techniques adopted to achieve these objectives.)

(b) During the course of your attendance at the year-end physical stocktaking of Howard Shoe Company Limited you observe after the count has been in process for some time that two teams of stocktakers are not following instructions. Stock is located at five different areas and there are two separate count teams for each area with two staff in each team. It was intended that stock in the five locations should be counted independently by the two separate teams who should return their completed stock sheets to the stock controller. You notice that in one location only the two teams are working together, counting the stock simultaneously and agreeing their figures before completing the stock sheets and returning to the controller.

What action should you, as auditor, take in respect of this breach of instructions?

(c) In observing the stock of liquid shoe polish you note that a particular lot is five years old and an inspection of some bottles in an open box reveals that the liquid in most of the bottles has solidified.

What action should you, as auditor, take in respect of this stock?

6. Bright Sparks Limited distributes domestic electrical equipment from one warehouse. Customers are mainly installers of such equipment, but there is a 'cash and carry' counter in the warehouse for retail customers. The warehousemen are responsible for raising invoices and credit notes relating to credit sales as well as handling cash sales.

You have carried out your interim audit in respect of the year ending 31 December 19X0 which included a circularisation of 80 debtors as at 30 September 19X0 selected from a total credit customer list of 1,000. Replies were received from all debtors circularised. The interim audit work disclosed the following:

(1) Of the 80 customers accounts circularised, 8 disagreed but could be reconciled by bringing into account payments stated by the customers concerned to have been made before 30 September 19X0 but which in each case were recorded in Bright Sparks Limited's books between 14 and 18 days after the dates stated by the customers as the date of payment.

(2) Your tests suggested that some 25% of credit customers were allowed settlement discounts of 2½ % although payments were consistently received after the latest date eligible for discount.

(3) A large number of credit notes were raised representing approximately 12% of the total number of invoices raised. A review of the copy credit notes indicated that they usually arose from arithmetical and pricing errors on invoices raised.

You are required to set out the conclusions you would draw as a result of the interim audit and the work you would plan to carry out at the final audit on debtors at 31 December 19X0 based upon those conclusions.

7. You are due to commence the final audit of Patchit Limited, a machine tool manufacturer, for the year ended 31 December 19X2, and have been presented with a draft set of financial statements for the year which have been prepared by management. Your interim audit was conducted earlier in the year and you came to the conclusion at that stage that systems were satisfactory. The main objective of your audit is to enable you to express an opinion on whether the financial statements give a true and fair view and you wish to examine the draft financial statements to assist you in your audit planning, by identifying significant audit areas and potential audit problems at the start of the assignment. You are aware of the fact that the company is at present contemplating an issue of £2,000,000 15% debenture stock (redeemable in the year 2000) in order to assist the remodelling of its present production facilities. The majority of the directors are in favour of making the issue but a few are reluctant to do so in view of the fact that the machine tools industry is subject to wide ranging fluctuations in sales and profits.

Abbreviated financial statements for Patchit Limited together with typical ratios for firms in the machine tool industry are as follows:

PROFIT AND LOSS ACCOUNTS FOR THE YEARS ENDED 31 DECEMBER 19X2 AND 19X1

	19X2		19X1	
	£'000	£'000	£'000	£'000
Sales		23,500		20,500
Cost of goods sold		16,000		14,000
Gross profit		7,500		6,500
Selling expenses	2,700		1,900	
Administration expenses	2,300		2,600	
		5,000		4,500
Net operating profit		2,500		2,000
Interest paid		500		300
Net profit before taxation		2,000		1,700
Taxation		1,200		1,020
Net profit after taxation		800		680
Dividends paid		525		280
Profit for the year retained		275		400
Retained profit: beginning of year		6,090		5,690
End of year		6,365		6,090

BALANCE SHEETS AS AT 31 DECEMBER

	19X2		19X1	
	£'000	£'000	£'000	£'000
Net assets employed				
Fixed assets (net)		6,315		5,600
Other assets		800		750
		7,115		6,350
Current assets				
Stock	5,100		3,200 *	
Debtors	2,900		1,900 **	
Prepayments	100		100	
Cash and bank	600		590	
	8,700		5,790	
Creditors: amounts falling due within one year	3,600		2,400	
		5,100		3,390
Total assets less current liabilities		12,215		9,740
Creditors: amounts falling due after more than one year				
8% debenture stock (1990–1993)		5,500		3,300
		6,715		6,440
Capital and reserves				
Called up share capital:				
Ordinary 50p shares authorised, issued and fully paid		350		350
Retained profits		6,365		6,090
		6,715		6,440

* (Stock valuation at 31.12.X0 was £2,500,000)

** (Debtors' balance at 31.12.X0 totalled £1,700,000)

Typical industrial average for 19X2 and 19X1 are:

Gross profit on sales	34%
Net profit before tax on sales	11%
Net profit before tax on net assets employed	19.5%
Working capital ratio	2.5:1
Acid test ratio	1.2:1
Average age of debtors	30 days
Average age of stock	73 days
Interest cover	8 times

Required:

(a) Review the above financial statements and industry averages and list the main features therein which require most attention during your forthcoming final audit. Give your reasons.

(b) With regard to those areas which may cause you some concern outline the main matters which you would need to investigate (a detailed audit programme is not required).

8. Just Crust Limited bakes bread products and supplies various supermarkets. The company operates from one central bakery and uses a fleet of vans to deliver to its customers. Minimal stocks are held at any time. The company employs a small number of accounts staff but maintains detailed production and delivery records and prepares monthly accounts.

   You are preparing the audit plan and considering placing greater reliance upon analytical review procedures than previously.

   You are required to explain to what extent analytical review can be used as part of your audit and to detail the analytical review procedures you might use for your audit of Just Crust Limited.

9. You are the auditor of Sheraton Limited, the year end of which is 30 November. You are currently planning the 19X1 audit and want to incorporate procedures which will ensure that, in finalising its financial statements, the company has complied with SSAP17, on post balance sheet events.

   You are required to:
   (a) detail the procedures that you would incorporate into the audit plan; and
   (b) describe the types of events, as defined in the Standard, and their accounting treatment.

10. You are the auditor of Manufacturers Limited, an engineering company producing components for the motor car industry. Following your discussion with the finance director, it appears that the company may have a liquidity problem.

    You are required to describe the factors which, by themselves, or taken together, could indicate that the going concern concept may be brought into question.

1. (a) Internal auditing is a relatively new branch of the profession and, as it evolves, the role of the internal audit department is constantly changing. Initially the internal audit department devoted a substantial proportion of its time to accounting and financial matters but today there may be a considerable amount of time devoted to other areas, eg. operational auditing. Internal audit has been defined by the Institute of Internal Auditors as "an independent appraisal activity within an organisation for the review of operations as a service to management. It is a managerial control which functions by measuring and evaluating the effectiveness of other controls". This definition only defines the boundaries of audit and does not define what the internal audit department actually does. The job of the internal audit department is defined by the organisation of which it is a part. The internal audit department's work can embrace the following:

    (i)   review of accounting systems and related internal controls;
    (ii)   examination of financial and operating information for management, including detailed testing of transactions and balances;
    (iii) review of the economy, efficiency and effectiveness of operations and of the functioning of non-financial controls;
    (iv)   review of the implementation of corporate policies, plans and procedures;
    (v)   special investigations.

    (b) The internal auditor and the external auditor operate to quite a large extent in the same field on financial matters and they both have an interest in ascertaining that the accounting system is adequate to provide information necessary for the preparation of true and fair financial statements. They also have a common interest in an effective system of internal control, designed to prevent errors and fraud. Despite the common interests already stated there are fundamental differences. The scope of an internal auditor's work is determined by management to whom he is responsible. On the other hand the scope of the external auditor's work is decided by himself in order to fulfil his statutory responsibility to report to the shareholders. No restriction can be placed on the external auditor's work. The approach of the external auditor is geared towards establishing the truth and fairness of the statutory accounts whereas the internal auditor's approach is geared towards meeting the objectives laid down for him by management. There is also a difference in the degree of independence in that the external auditor is independent of the management whereas the internal one is an employee. However, the latter *can* be independent in that he reports to the board of directors or to an audit committee.

    (c) Before deciding upon the extent to which he can place reliance on the work of an internal auditor, an external auditor should review the qualifications and experience of the latter. He should preferably be a member of one of the professional bodies of which the Institute of Internal Auditors is one. He should have either trained with a professional firm or have received special training through a company's own training programme. The external auditor should also assess the objectivity of the internal auditor by ascertaining the management level to which he reports, and he should review recommendations in such reports and see what action has been taken thereon. The external auditor must evaluate the internal auditor's fieldwork by examining working papers to see the scope of work performed, programme of work, adequacy of working papers, conclusions, reports etc. He should also perform a minimum of tests to substantiate the reports. Once the external auditor has followed the above steps he can properly judge the reliance which he can place on the internal auditor, and will restrict his own work to the minimum compatible with his being able to give an audit opinion. If he is not satisfied with any aspect of the internal audit function he should make representations to senior management to remedy the situation.

Ways in which there can be liaison for the mutual benefit of the external and internal auditor are:

(i) At an early stage in the financial period discussions can be held between the two parties to decide upon a joint approach which will enable both to restrict their tests to a minimum compatible with their individual responsibilities and to ensure that all important audit areas are covered.

(ii) This joint approach means that both teams can sensibly share important procedures such as attendance at stock counts, particularly in companies with widely spread branches.

(iii) Work performed and information produced by the internal auditor can be used by the external auditor and will prevent duplication of effort and extra time e.g. debtors circularisation, asset verification.

(iv) The internal auditor's intimate knowledge of the company may be of assistance to the external auditor and the latter may be able to rely to a large extent on the internal auditor to monitor the continuous operation of the system of internal control. On the other hand the external auditor's wide experience may be of assistance to the internal auditor. The external auditor could also assist in company training programmes which should improve communication between both sets of auditors.

(v) It is essential that an internal auditor be as independent as possible and to achieve this he should report directly to the top level of management. If the company has set up an audit committee then ideally this is the body to whom the internal auditor should report. Where there is no such committee then reports should go to the board, chairman or managing director. It is not advisable that the internal auditor reports to the head of the finance or accounting functions, except on purely routine and procedural matters.

2. PRIVATE AND CONFIDENTIAL   30 Montpelier Road
   The Directors   Acton
   Brandon Limited   London W3A 1BX
   15 Commercial Road
   London EC1 2CV   30 June 19X1

   Dear Sirs,

                            Internal Control Review

   Following your request for us to carry out a review of the firm's system of control over the purchase, receipt, storage and issue of raw materials we have now concluded our review. We have set out below the weaknesses which we found in the present system together with our suggestions for improvement.

   Weakness
   1. Raw materials may be removed from the storeroom upon oral authorisation from one of the production foremen.

   Recommended Improvement
   1. These materials should only be removed upon written authorisation from an authorised production foreman. The authorisation forms must be prenumbered, list quantities and job number and be signed and dated. Controls should be maintained over the blank authorisation forms, and regular checks made on missing numbers from those issued. Alternately, the possibility of including the authorisation forms in the paperwork issued by the Production Control Department when the jobs are issued to the shop floor should be considered.

Weakness

2. The practice of monthly stock counts does not compensate for the lack of a perpetual inventory system. Quantities on hand at the end of a month may not be sufficient to last until next month's count and if this is taken into account in reorder levels the company may be investing too much in stock.

Recommended Improvement

2. A perpetual inventory system should be established under the control of someone other than the storekeepers and should record quantities and values for each item. The physical counts can be taken as at present and agreed to the perpetual records. Differences should be investigated and if the records are in error they should be investigated. Controls are required over obsolete and slow-moving stocks.

Weakness

3. The purchase ledger clerk handles the buying function in addition to keeping the detailed suppliers' accounts. This is not a satisfactory separation of duties.

Recommended Improvement

3. There should be a separate buying department which should not be concerned with keeping suppliers' accounts. The buying department should be responsible for all orders which should be made on pre-numbered forms. A copy of such orders should be sent to the receiving department and to the accounting department.

Weakness

4. Raw materials are always purchased from the same supplier.

Recommended Improvement

4. The buying department should consider obtaining quotes on all purchases over a specified amount.

Weakness

5. Raw materials are always purchased at a predetermined reorder level and in pre-determined quantities. Since production levels may often vary during the year quantities ordered may be too great or too small for current production demands.

Recommended Improvement

5. Requests for purchases should come from the production department and be based on production schedules and quantities on hand per the perpetual records.

Weakness

6. There is no receiving department or receiving report. There should be a proper separation of duties with personnel other than the storeroom clerks responsible for receiving goods.

Recommended Improvement

6. A receiving department should be established and personnel in the department should count or weigh all goods received and prepare a prenumbered receiving report. These reports should be signed and dated and one copy should be sent to the buying department, one to the accounting department and one with the goods to the storeroom.

Weakness

7. There is no inspection department. Since expensive electronic components are usually required to meet certain specifications they should be tested for these requirements when received.

Recommended Improvement

7. An inspection department should be established to inspect goods when received. Prenumbered inspection reports should be prepared and accounted for and a copy of such reports should be sent to the accounting department.

If you have any queries or comments concerning our recommendations we shall be pleased to discuss these with you at your earliest convenience.

Yours faithfully,

Arthur Daley & Co,
Certified Accountants.

3. (a) In a large-volume population, eg cash receipts transactions, it would normally be impractical and undesirable to test all transactions in detail but where the set of transactions has a material effect on the financial statements at the end of the period it is necessary for the auditor to examine a sample of such transactions. The auditor must make an objective examination of such a sample and a subjective review alone is not sufficient.

One objective of auditing the sample is to determine whether the system of internal control is actually operating as it is purported to do and whether such a system is adequate to ensure the accuracy and reliability of the records. Where an auditor is testing for compliance he may prefer to use statistical sampling techniques which would allow him to evaluate the error rate at an acceptable confidence level.

In addition to the use of sampling for the purpose of compliance tests the auditor may also take a sample of transactions from large-volume populations in order to verify directly an item in the financial statements. An example of this is where he may select a sample of debtors for circularisation at the end of the accounting period. The objective of the circularisation is to substantiate the existence and valuation of an item in the financial statements. A secondary objective of the circularisation is to confirm the reliability of the accounting records and thus of the internal control system with regard to sales and debtors' accounts, and therefore in this case the sample is in effect being selected as a dual purpose test. In substantive testing as in compliance testing statistical sampling may be used.

(b) The first stage in carrying out an effective audit is to understand and record the client's accounting system and system of internal control. This recording could take the form of ICQs, flow charts or notes, which are prepared after a review of the system as it exists on paper and in the perceptions of client personnel. After completing this recording stage but *before* a thorough evaluation of the system the auditor should confirm his understanding of the system as he has recorded it by carrying out what is known as a 'walk-through test'. This involves selecting one or two transactions of each type and tracing them through the client's accounting system. The objective of such a step is to ensure that the system has been correctly understood and accurately recorded. This procedure is particularly appropriate where the client has prepared the record of the system which the auditor is to use.

4. An inevitable characteristic of audit testing is that a sample only of transactions or items can be examined. The auditor examines a sample of items and thereby seeks to obtain assurance that the whole group is acceptable.

Provided that conditions are appropriate for its use, a statistical approach to sampling is likely to have many advantages over the alternative of judgement sampling.

Conditions favouring the use of statistical sampling are:
- existence of large and homogeneous groups of items;
- low expected error rate and clear definition of error;
- reasonable ease of identifying and obtaining access to items selected.

If these conditions are present, statistical sampling is likely to have the following advantages:
- at the conclusion of a test the auditor is able to state a definite level of confidence he may have that the whole population conforms to the sample result, within a stated precision limit;
- sample size is objectively determined, having regard to the degree of risk the auditor is prepared to accept for each application;
- it may be possible to use smaller sample sizes, thus saving time and money;
- the process of fixing required precision and confidence levels compels the auditor to consider and clarify his audit objectives;
- the results of tests can be expressed in precise mathematical terms;
- bias is eliminated.

Statistical sampling is not without disadvantages
- the technique may be applied blindly without prior consideration of the suitability of the statistical sampling for the audit task to be performed. This disadvantage may be overcome by establishing soundly-based procedures for use in the firm, incorporating guidelines on sampling in the firm's audit manual, instituting training programmes for audit staff and proper supervision.
- unsuspected patterns or bias in sample selection may invalidate the conclusions. The probability of these factors arising must be carefully judged by the auditor before he decides to adopt statistical sampling;
- it frequently needs back-up by further tests within the population reviewed - large items, non-routine items, sensitive items like directors' transactions;
- at the conclusion of a statistical sampling-based test the auditor may fail to appreciate the further action necessary based on the results obtained. This potential disadvantage may be overcome by adequate training and supervision, and by requiring careful evaluation of all statistical sampling tests;
- statistical sampling may be applied carelessly, without due confirmation that the sample selected is acceptably random;
- the selection exercise can be time consuming;
- the degree of tolerance of acceptable error must be predetermined.

The disadvantages listed above can all be overcome if the technique is applied sensibly and competently.

Provided that the conditions favouring its use are present, statistical sampling is a useful technique for several auditing tasks:
- compliance testing
- substantive testing
- debtor and creditor circularisation
- fraud investigation using discovery sampling.

Statistical techniques should be used when they are convenient and of positive use to the auditor in achieving a level of reliability in his results. If they are used selectively - ie. in cases where their advantages are conspicuous and their disadvantages can be reduced to a minimum - they can make a significant contribution towards greater quality control on an audit. But it is hard to resist the argument that properly devised and controlled 'judgement methods' can achieve the same high standards with fewer administrative or technical problems.

5. (a) It is the responsibility of the management of an enterprise to ensure that the amount at which stocks are shown in the financial statements represents stocks physically in existence and includes all stocks owned by the enterprise. Management satisfies this responsibility by carrying out appropriate procedures which will normally involve ensuring that all stocks are subject to a count at least once in every financial year.

Where stocks are material in the enterprise's financial statements, and the auditor is placing reliance upon management's stocktake in order to provide evidence of existence, then the auditor should attend the stocktaking. This is because attendance is normally the best way of providing evidence of the proper functioning of management's stocktaking procedures, and hence of the existence of stocks and their condition. Where the auditor attends any physical count of stocks in order to obtain audit evidence, this does not reduce the responsibility of the directors to ensure that the amount shown for stocks in the financial statements represents stocks physically in existence.

(b) One of the main objectives of attending the count is to ensure that the company is following instructions prepared before the count. These instructions should have already been reviewed for their adequacy by the auditor who should, if necessary, discuss these with company officials. If the instructions are adequate but they are not carried out properly then clearly the auditor must take action, since the departures decrease the reliability of the count. In this case the auditor must immediately point out to the stock count controller that there has been a breakdown in procedures in one location which must be corrected at once. In addition the auditor will have to make extra counts of the material counted by the teams involved to satisfy himself that they were not making an unusual number of count errors. If such errors arose a complete recount could be necessary. In order to ensure that such a breakdown does not occur in future the matter should be noted by the auditor in his working papers as a matter for discussion with management.

(c) Stock is required to be valued in the financial statements at the lower of cost or net realisable value. In the case of the bottles where the liquid has solidified there is no realisable value in such stock and thus such items should be recorded on the stock sheets but their value should be shown as nil. The auditors should make a note in his working papers of the stock involved and check at the time of the count with the client's stock sheets to ensure that the condition of the stock has been noted on the stock sheets. After the count he can then check that a nil value has been placed on such items. The auditor could require that another box be opened and if a further inspection of some bottles confirms the position as shown by the first box he can make a reasonable assumption that most of the stock is unsaleable and should be valued accordingly. It would also be prudent to value the few bottles which are in order at a nil value because of their age. There is considerable doubt when stock is of such age that it will in fact be sold and, even if it is, the likelihood is that the disposal will be at a nominal value.

6. (a) *Conclusions to be drawn as a result of the interim audit*
        The following weaknesses exist in the company's systems:
        (i)   In any system of internal control, one person should not be able to process a whole
             transaction, ie:
             - authorisation
             - execution
             - recording

             The most serious deficiency in the company's system is that warehousemen can:
             - sell goods
             - receive cash from cash sales
             - raise sales invoices for credit sales
             - raise credit notes.

             Moreover, there appears to be no procedure for checking any of their work. Since the
             accounting records are written up on the evidence of these invoices and credit notes,
             any errors made by the warehousemen will be carried into the records. It may also be
             the case that the issue of credit notes is not authorised by a senior member of
             staff.

             Possible consequences:
             - Errors in invoices may not be detected except by customers;
             - Risk of unauthorised or fraudulent invoices or credit notes being raised without
               detection;
             - Risk of goods leaving the premises without being invoiced, whether through error or
               fraud. This is particularly dangerous in a business such as this, with a variety
               of high-value items;
             - Time wasted by needless disagreements with customers about amounts owing.

        (ii) There appears to be a weakness in the recording of cash received by the company. The
             dates recorded in the books are presumably the dates when the entries were written
             up. If so, there is clearly an excessive delay in recording cash received, and
             possibly also in banking it. There may also be no record of cash received made when
             incoming mail is opened.

             Possible consequences
             - Errors and defalcations can arise where a cash received system is weak;
             - The longer the gap between receipt and recording, the more likely it is that
               discrepancies can occur;
             - Specific possibilities:
               - falsification of records leading to misappropriation of cash (teeming and lading)
               - mislaying of cheques if not banked promptly;
               - errors in the records, especially concerning dates;

        (iii) Stricter control is needed over the granting of cash discounts (assuming that it is
             the actual receipt of cash which is later than the due date, not merely the late
             recording of same).

             Possible consequence:
             - Discounts given to a standard list of customers who may be friends of staff or
               regular customers, not necessarily prompt payers.

SECTION 4: SUGGESTED SOLUTIONS

(b) *Audit work on debtors at the final audit*

(i) *Second circularisation*
- Consider circularising all debtors, or at least a larger sample than before of debtors not circularised at 30 September.
- Circularise, and investigate disagreeing replies. Discover if reasons are similar to those given at 30 September circularisation.

(ii) *Other checks*
- Check the sales invoices which make up the balances with backing documentation, eg. orders and despatch notes (if the latter exist).
- Check calculations and pricing of such invoices.
- Ascertain extent of cash received from debtors after the year-end; reconcile the individual invoices to ensure that no discrepancies exist.
- Carry out further tests on settlement discounts and ascertain whether the position has improved or deteriorated since the time of the interim audit.
- Carry out cut-off tests at 31 December to ensure that all goods leaving the premises by that date (and only those) have been included in sales.
- If a control account is maintained from sales day book and cash book totals, reconcile the balance at 31 December with the total of the balances on the debtors' ledger. (NB: a sales day book may well not be kept by this company.)
- Examine ageing analysis and verify adequacy of provision for doubtful debts. Check that irrecoverable amounts have been written off and that write-offs are properly authorised.
- Check that all returns of goods after the year-end relating to 19X0 sales have been correctly recorded.
- Check all credit notes issued since the year-end and discover whether they are authorised. Ensure that all credit has been properly given.

7. (a) *Stock* - Represents a significant proportion of current assets (59%) and the average age of stock has increased from 74 days in 19X1 to 95 days in 19X2 compared to an industry average of 73 days.

Average age of stock = $\dfrac{\text{Average stock x 365}}{\text{Cost of Sales}}$

Debtors - Represents a significant proportion of current assets (33.3%) and the average age of debtors has increased from 32 days in 19X1 to 37 days in 19X2 compared to an industry average of 30 days.

Average age of debtors = $\dfrac{\text{Average debtors x 365}}{\text{Sales}}$

Fixed Assets - Of the net assets employed in the business 52% is invested in fixed assets. (Is the valuation of fixed assets reasonable in view of the need for a debenture issue to enable part of the plant to be remodelled?)

Net profit before tax on net assets employed - The percentage return has declined from 17.5% in 19X1 to 16.4% in 19X2 and compares unfavourably with an industry average of 19.5%. It appears that there is a particular problem on profit margins.

Net profit and gross profit before tax on sales - The net profit before tax on sales has marginally increased from 8.3% for 19X1 to 8.5% in 19X2 but compares poorly with an industry average of 11%. The gross profit on sales barely changed, being 31.7% in 19X1 and 31% in 19X2 but the industry average is 34%.

Expenses - There has been a saving on administration expenses but selling expenses are now 11½ % on sales as compared to 9¼ % in 19X1.

Other matters - An analysis of current liabilities is required so that this item can be further investigated. The interest cover was 5 times in 19X2 as against 6.7 times in 19X1 whereas the industry average is 8 times.

(b) The areas which cause particular concern are stock, gross profit on sales, sales expenses, debtors and the proposed debenture issue.

Stock - The average age of stock has shown a marked increase with a result that there are increased holding costs with the greater amount of stock, loss of capital tied up in stock, dangers of obsolescence, pilferage etc. As a consequence the auditor will need to pay particular attention to the provision made against obsolete, slow moving and damaged stock; he must ensure that stock is adequately insured and he should carefully examine the system of stock recording and reporting to management of stock movements and levels. He will also require a detailed breakdown between raw materials, work in progress, completed machines, consumables etc. In addition to the normal checks on these figures, questions need to be asked as to the proportion of spares held as a service to customers and company policy as to retention of spares for obsolete machines including their valuation.

Gross profit on sales - The reason why Patchit is earning less than the industry average could be due to a number of different factors, e.g. lower sales prices, more costly materials, poor materials, higher production costs, poor workmanship, stock control or valuation problems. The auditors should be aware that any of these areas could lead to gross profit reductions and his audit work should encompass these areas.

Sales expenses - The auditor will require an analysis of this between fixed salaries, commission, travelling expenses, entertainment etc. before he can investigate further. He will be particularly concerned that management are aware of the increases which have been authorised by them and that they are able to provide satisfactory explanations. During his routine audit tests he will examine the documentation relating to certain of the payments made.

Debtors - The average age of debtors has slightly increased but this is an area which should be tightly controlled as the firm is losing money due to the fact that debtors are taking longer to pay. There is also a greater danger of bad debts being incurred. The auditor must therefore pay particular attention to the adequacy of the provision for doubtful debts and the systems of credit control. He should of course carry out a debtors circularisation.

Proposed debenture issue - Although this is a matter for the directors to decide, the auditor's advice may be sought or he may feel that he ought to advise the directors in any case. It has already been pointed out that the interest cover is not as good as the industry average and if the further issue is made the cover could in fact be worse. This is particularly the case with an industry which it is stated is unpredictable. Is it wise to have such heavy borrowings in such an industry? There is a possibility that if business deteriorates there could be a strain on liquidity as interest payments must be met. A possible alternative could be a bonus issue by capitalisation of part of the reserves followed by a rights issue to raise the additional cash.

8. (a) *Use of analytical review*
    The Guideline on Audit Evidence issued by the Auditing Practices Committee suggests analytical review as one of the ways of obtaining audit evidence, ie. information used by an auditor in arriving at the conclusions on which his audit opinion is based.

    It is not a substitute for other audit work but an extension of substantive testing which seeks to provide assurance about the completeness, accuracy and validity of the information contained in a client's accounting records and financial statements.

    Analytical review procedures are used especially at the planning stage and the overall review of financial statements, but are not confined to those stages. Audit tests may show that the client's systems and controls are operating correctly and that transactions are properly recorded, but an extra element is required to assure the auditor that the results he has obtained make sense in the context of the business *as a whole*.

    (b) *Analytical review procedures*
    Analytical review procedures should include the following:
    (i)   making comparisons using significant accounting ratios, in particular those relating to:
          - profitability
          - liquidity
          - capital gearing
    (ii) comparing items with budgets or forecasts, and with previous periods. Specific comparisons should include:
          - breakdown of sales into products;
          - costs of productive labour compared with sales;
          - costs of variable overheads compared with sales;
          - returned and unsold goods compared with production;
          - fixed assets, depreciation, and vehicle running costs;
    (iii) determining monthly trends, using management accounts;
    (iv) analysing variations, obtaining explanations and carrying out further audit work where explanations are not wholly satisfactory (eg. further vouching of expenses in the profit and loss account);
    (v)   carrying out analytical review procedures to ensure the reasonableness of the accounts figures, eg:
          - investigate monthly figures for new business, comparing them with previous year and budget;
          - obtain adequate explanations for variations;
          - review hire charges for each type of contract, in comparison with any stated price changes and with national level of inflation;
          - compare general scale of charges with major competitors;
          - ensure level of income accords with any definite expansion/contraction in the business during the period;
          - obtain explanations for any material changes in 'sales mixture' - ie. relative proportion of each type of contract.

9. (a) *Detailed procedures for incorporation in audit plan*
    (i) Ensure that all staff are fully briefly on the requirements of the accounting standard SSAP17 and the related standard SSAP18 (contingencies);
    (ii) Ensure that the following procedures are included in the audit programme:
        - discuss with management the steps taken to identify and act upon post balance sheet events in preparing the financial statements.
        - examine all financial records for the period between the balance sheet date and the date of the audit report, with special reference to:
        - cash book for payments indicating liabilities at the balance sheet date
        - debtors' records for subsequent payment, issue of credit notes
        - files of correspondence with debtors
        - accounts payable records and unpaid invoice files for unrecorded liabilities
        - sales at special prices, indicating need for stock write-downs
        - journal entries
        - examine interim management accounts
        - consideration of areas requiring special attention as high risk areas
        - minutes of directors' meetings
        - ensure that all large or unusual items, or significant variations, are allocated to the correct period and properly recorded.
    (iii) Confirm that the letter of representation covers post balance sheet events.
    (iv) Confirm that the going concern review includes a consideration of the impact of post balance sheet events.
    (v) Confirm that the effect of post balance sheet events on contingencies is considered.
    (vi) Consider the materiality of post balance sheet events identified by auditors of subsidiary and associated companies.
    (vii) Ensure that the possible effect of events between the date of the audit report and the date of the annual general meeting are considered, where such events come to the notice of the auditors.
    (viii) Discuss the situation with the internal auditors (if any).
    (ix) Discuss any matters that may arise as a result of the tests with the management to assess what further action is necessary.

    (b) *Types of event, and accounting treatment*
    Post balance sheet events may be either
    (i) adjusting events
    (ii) non-adjusting events

Adjusting events are post balance sheet events which provide additional evidence of conditions existing at the balance sheet date. Financial statements should reflect all material adjusting events.

Non-adjusting events are post balance sheet events which concern conditions which do not exist at the balance sheet date. Material non-adjusting events should be disclosed by note to the financial statements, unless they cast doubt on the going concern status of the company, in which case the financial statements should be amended. Any note should explain the nature of the event, an estimate of its pre-tax effect and the taxation implications.

SECTION 4: SUGGESTED SOLUTIONS

10. A company rarely ceases to carry on business without any prior indications, either of inability to meet debts as they fall due or of other problems that raise questions about the continuation of business. The indications may vary in importance depending upon specific circumstances. They may be interdependent and some may only have significance as audit evidence when viewed in conjunction with others. Further, their significance may diminish because they are mitigated by other audit evidence. The following lists indicate factors that may indicate that Manufacturers Ltd is experiencing liquidity problems:

   (a) Indications that the company may be unable to meet its debts as they fall due include:
   - recurring operating losses
   - financing to a considerable extent out of overdue suppliers and other creditors (for example, VAT, PAYE, National Insurance)
   - heavy dependence on short-term finance for long-term needs
   - working capital deficiencies
   - low liquidity ratios
   - over-gearing in the form of high or increasing debt to equity ratios, and under-capitalisation, particularly if there is a deficiency of share capital and reserves
   - borrowings in excess of limits imposed by debenture trust deeds
   - default on loan or similar agreements
   - dividends in arrears
   - restrictions placed on usual trade terms
   - excessive or obsolete stock
   - long overdue debtors
   - non-compliance with statutory capital requirements
   - deterioration of relationship with banks
   - necessity of seeking new sources or methods of obtaining finance
   - the continuing use of old fixed assets because there are no funds to replace them
   - the size and content of the order book
   - potential losses on long-term contracts

   (b) Indications of problems that raise questions about the continuation of the business and which might lead to an inability to meet its debts include:

   Internal matters
   - loss of key management or staff
   - significantly increasing stock levels
   - work stoppages or other labour difficulties
   - substantial dependence on the success of a particular project or on a particular asset
   - excessive reliance on the success of a new product
   - uneconomic long-term commitments

   External matters
   - legal proceedings or similar matters that may jeopardise a company's ability to continue in business
   - loss of a key franchise or patent
   - loss of a principal supplier or customer
   - the undue influence of a market dominant competitor
   - political risks
   - technical developments which render a key product obsolete
   - frequent financial failures of enterprises in the same industry

(c) *Mitigating factors*

Indications that the company may be unable to meet its debts might be mitigated by factors relating to alternative means for maintaining adequate cash flows. Such factors include, for example, the ability to dispose of assets or to postpone the replacement of assets without adversely affecting operations, to lease assets rather than purchase them outright, to obtain new sources of finance, to renew or extend loans, to restructure debts and to raise additional share capital.

Similarly, indications of problems that raise questions about the continuation of business might be mitigated by factors relating to the company's capacity to adopt alternative courses of action, for example the availability of suitable persons to fill key positions, the likelihood of finding alternative sales markets when a principal customer is lost, the ability to replace assets which have been destroyed and the possibility of continuing the business by making limited reductions in the level of operations or by making use of alternative resources.

SECTION 5

THE AUDIT REPORT

Chapter 14

THE AUDIT REPORT

Topics covered in this chapter:

- The report to members: statutory requirements
- The Auditing Standard 'The audit report' (revised March 1989)
- The revised version of the Standard

The report to members: statutory requirements

1. The audit report is the tangible means by which the auditor expresses his opinion on the truth and fairness of a company's financial statements for the benefit principally of the shareholders, but also other users. Statute has consistently recognised its importance by requiring that certain mandatory statements appear in the report. The 1948 Act required the auditor to confirm in his report that:

   - he had received all the information and explanations he required
   - proper books of account had been kept
   - the accounts were in agreement with the books and returns

   in addition to stating whether the balance sheet and profit and loss account gave a true and fair view and had been prepared in accordance with the Act.

2. The 1967 Act introduced the technique of 'exception reporting' to the audit report, whereby in an unqualified audit report, the auditors must state certain things specifically and their silence will imply satisfaction with various other matters. Hence the auditor was still required to establish that the matters indicated above had been complied with, but only had to mention them in his report - ie 'qualify' - to the extent that any of the requirements had *not* been met. A typical form of *unqualified* report, therefore, which was employed to comply with the 1967 Act is reproduced here:

   "AUDITORS' REPORT TO THE MEMBERS OF SWINGING SIXTIES LIMITED

   In our opinion, the accounts set out on pages ... to ... together give a true and fair view of the state of affairs of the company at 31 December 1969 and of its profit for the year ended on that date and comply with the Companies Acts 1948 and 1967."

14: THE AUDIT REPORT

Requirements of the 1985 Act

3. The statutory approach since the 1967 Act through to the 1985 Act has been to retain the exception reporting approach. There are, however, further matters introduced subsequent to the 1967 Act that the auditor has a specific duty to include in his report if the accounts fail to do so. The following is the *complete* list of matters with which the auditor implies satisfaction in his unqualified report as now consolidated into the Companies Act 1985:

    (a) proper accounting records have been kept and proper returns adequate for the audit received from branches not visited (S237 (1)(a) and (2));
    (b) the accounts are in agreement with the accounting records and returns (S237 (1)(b) and (2));
    (c) all information and explanations have been received from the company's officers as the auditor thinks necessary and he has had access at all times to the company's books, accounts and vouchers (S237 (3) and (4));
    (d) details of directors' emoluments, pensions and compensation for loss of office and particulars of higher paid employees in accordance with Parts V and VI of Schedule 5 have been correctly disclosed in the financial statements (S237(5));
    (e) particulars of loans and other transactions in favour of directors and officers in accordance with Parts I to III of Schedule 6 have been correctly disclosed in the financial statements (S237 (5)); and
    (f) the information given in the directors' report is consistent with the accounts (S237 (6)).

4. The Act also requires the following *explicit* statements:

    (a) whether in the auditor's opinion the balance sheet and profit and loss account and (if it is a holding company submitting group accounts) the group accounts have been properly prepared in accordance with the Act (S236 (2)(a));
    (b) without prejudice to the above, whether in the auditor's opinion a true and fair view is given:
        (i)   in the balance sheet, of the state of the company's affairs at the end of the financial year;
        (ii) in the profit and loss account of the company's profit or loss for the financial year; and
        (iii) in the case of group accounts of the state of affairs and profit or loss of the company and its subsidiaries dealt with by those accounts, so far as concerns members of the company (S236 (2)(b)).

5. The legislation does *not* require any comments as to the nature and scope of the audit conducted but as we shall see in the following section, this *is* a requirement of the Auditing Standard! Finally, we should remind ourselves *when* an audit report is required:

    "A company's auditors shall make a report to its members on the accounts examined by them, and on every balance sheet and profit and loss account, and on all group accounts, copies of which are to be laid before the company in general meeting during the auditor's tenure of office" (S236 (1)).

The auditing standard 'The audit report'

6. The full text of part 1 of the Standard 'The audit report' runs as follows:

> "1. This Auditing Standard applies to all audit reports issued as a result of audits within the meaning of the Explanatory Foreword to Auditing Standards and Guidelines. Although this standard is not primarily intended to apply to other forms of report provided by auditors, many of the principles of this standard will normally be applicable to such reports.
>
> 2. The audit report should state clearly:
>
>   (a) the addressee;
>   (b) the financial statements audited;
>   (c) the auditing standards followed;
>   (d) the audit opinion;
>   (e) any other information or opinions prescribed by statutory or other requirements;
>   (f) the identity of the auditor; and
>   (g) the date of the report.
>
> 3. If the auditor is unable to express an audit opinion without reservation he should qualify his report by referring to all those matters which he considers to be material and about which he has reservations.

Effective date

> 4. This Auditing Standard is effective for audit reports dated on or after 1 September 1989."

7. Paragraph 2(e) is particularly important, emphasising that the standard does not override any relevant statutory requirements - hence the Companies Act 1985 statements, explicit and implied, will apply to the limited company audit report as will the express references of paragraph 2 of the standard.

8. This standard represents a modest shift towards a more positive style of reporting to the extent that it requires a statement that the audit has been carried out in accordance with auditing standards - but it goes no further. Crucially, there is no requirement to describe what steps have been taken to ensure compliance, eg the levels of detailed testing, sampling basis, extent of reliance on internal controls etc.

9. As indicated in paragraph 1 of the statement, the standard applies to all reports in which the auditor has carried out an audit as defined by the Explanatory Foreword. The APC's explanatory notes to the standard make the following points, which should be noted carefully.

  (a) The auditor should specify the auditing standards that he has followed. Normally these will have been the APC's Auditing Standards.
  (b) When expressing an opinion that financial statements give a true and fair view the auditor should be satisfied, inter alia that:
     (i) all relevant SSAPs have been complied with, except where non-compliance is justified; and

(ii)   any significant accounting policies which are not the subject of SSAPs are appropriate to the circumstances of the business;

(c)   The auditor should comply with any reporting requirements imposed by legislation and any other reporting requirements relevant to the financial statements (eg stock exchange requirements for a listed company).

10.   Set out below are two examples demonstrating the manner in which unqualified reports might be worded which meet the requirements of the Standard *and* the Companies Act 1985. The examples, the first for a non-group company, the second for a company submitting group accounts, are based on the examples contained in the Appendix to the Auditing Standard.

Example 1

AUDITORS' REPORT TO THE MEMBERS OF ABC LIMITED

We have audited the financial statements on pages 7 to 21 in accordance with Auditing Standards.

In our opinion the financial statements give a true and fair view of the state of the company's affairs at 31 December 19... and of its profit and source and application of funds for the year then ended and have been properly prepared in accordance with the Companies Act 1985.

Arthur Daley & Co, Certified Accountants
London, 2 February 19...

Example 2

AUDITORS' REPORT TO THE MEMBERS OF XYZ LIMITED

We have audited the financial statements on pages 8 to 32 in accordance with Auditing Standards.

In our opinion the financial statements give a true and fair view of the state of affairs of the company and the group at 31 December 19... and of the profit and source and application of funds of the group for the year then ended and have been properly prepared in accordance with the Companies Act 1985.

Arthur Daley & Co, Certified Accountants
London, 2 February 19...

The fact that the audit report examples are contained in an Appendix and do not comprise a part of the Standard itself indicates that there needs to be flexibility to cope with changes in legislation and other circumstances - it also allows for a limited degree of drafting freedom. All reports should be *signed and dated*.

11. The form of the report can conveniently be considered under two principal headings, 'scope' and 'opinion'.

    (a) *Scope*
       (i) The audit report must clearly identify the persons to whom it is addressed, namely the shareholders in the case of a limited company audit, so that all interested users are reminded that the audit is designed primarily to satisfy and protect the shareholders' interests before those of anyone else. The auditor should however, take into account the interests of other persons likely to rely on his opinion; it must be remembered that recent cases such as 'Jeb Fasteners' have established that the auditor may owe a duty of care to third parties in certain circumstances.

       (ii) The audit report must clearly identify the financial statements to which it relates. This is best done by referring to page numbers on which those statements are set out. The financial statements will normally comprise the balance sheet, profit and loss account, source and application of funds and notes - *not* the directors' report. The auditor has to satisfy himself that the directors' report is consistent with the financial statements - it is not a part of those financial statements.

       (iii) It is a basic principle of any report that it should explain the scope and nature of the examination on which it is based. Auditing Standards prescribe the basic principles and practices which auditors are expected to follow. Compliance with them gives the auditor a basis from which to express an opinion and it is informative for the reader to know that the examination has been performed in accordance with these Standards, but as we have already mentioned, there is currently no requirement to amplify how the Standards have been applied.

    (b) *Opinion*
    The report must contain an expression of opinion in 'truth and fairness' terms. The OED defines 'opinion' as 'judgement or belief based on grounds short of proof'. Hence, it is *not* equivalent to a hard and fast guarantee or a certificate of indemnity covering the financial statements audited. It is rather a personal statement based on conclusions drawn after an independent, expert, examination of the available evidence. Many of the judgements made during the course of an audit are open to debate particularly those resulting from an appraisal of a company's accounting policies. The audit report is, therefore, not a certificate - it is a judgemental statement not a factual statement.

Emphasis of matter

12. Also dealt with in the explanatory notes is the idea of an 'emphasis of matter' paragraph. It has always been a generally accepted principle that the auditor issuing an unqualified opinion should not make reference to specific aspects of the financial statements in the body of his report, as such reference may be be misconstrued as being a qualification. However, the APC take the view that, in rare circumstances, the reader will obtain a better understanding of the financial statements if his attention is drawn to important matters. Suggested examples are an unusual event, accounting policy or condition, awareness of which is fundamental to an understanding of the financial statements.

13. In order to avoid giving the impression that a qualification is intended, references which are simply intended as emphasis of matter should be contained in a *separate subsequent paragraph* and introduced with a phrase such as 'Without qualifying our opinion above, we draw attention to ....' and should *not* be referred to in the opinion paragraph. An emphasis of matter paragraph should be positioned *after* the opinion paragraph as in this way, one could reduce the risk of being seen to include the emphasis of matter within the scope of the audit opinion.

14. The APC stress that emphasis of matter should *not* be used to rectify a lack of appropriate disclosure in the financial statements, nor should it be regarded as a substitute for a qualification.

15. The auditor should exercise great care in the use of this reporting technique because, as indicated in paragraph 12 above, it is only 'in rare circumstances' that 'the auditor may wish to draw the reader's attention to important matters in the financial statements to ensure that these are not overlooked.'

16. When considering the use of an emphasis of matter paragraph, the auditor must bear in mind that his responsibility is to report on whether the financial statements produced by management give a true and fair view. It is, of course, management's responsibility to prepare and present the financial statements and to ensure that the information which they disclose is adequate. If, therefore, in the auditor's opinion, the information disclosed is insufficient to give a true and fair view then he should qualify his opinion. The auditor's only purpose, in using an emphasis of matter paragraph, can be either to give greater prominence to important matters which are already contained within the financial statements, or to highlight the fact that certain information has not been provided the lack of which, however, does not impair the true and fair view. An example of the former circumstance is contained in the Audit Report Examples illustrated below - example 3.

17. SSAP10 requires, with certain exceptions, that financial statements should include a statement of source and application of funds. Omission of such a statment from accounts to which SSAP10 applies presents a particular problem to the auditor in that the omission of a funds statement does not in itself justify a qualified report on the profit and loss account and balance sheet. It is considered that the requirements of the Standard will be met if the auditor reports the omission of the funds statement by adding a separate emphasis of matter paragraph to his report.

Qualifications in audit reports

18. Prior to the publication of the Auditing Standards in 1980 there was much public criticism of qualified audit reports. The principal problem was that the report often failed to convey the meaning that the auditor intended; this was partly due to inconsistent terminology which did not promote clarity. Also the distinction between a qualification and an emphasis of matter was by no means clear. The objectives of an Auditing Standard on qualifications might therefore be defined as:

    (a) to outlaw certain ambiguous ways of qualifying that were previously encountered;
    (b) to attempt to categorise the circumstances giving rise to a qualification and then prescribe suggested wording and format associated with each category (this would promote consistent use of language);
    (c) to reinforce the concept that a qualification is only appropriate where the matters concerned are material to the users of the financial statements, and as an extension of this concept to distinguish the material from the even more significant 'fundamental' problem that seriously undermines the true and fair view; and
    (d) generally, to promote better drafting by using non-technical language and clearer presentation.

The qualification 'matrix'

19. The Auditing Standard 'The audit report' gives the circumstances in which each sort of qualification would be appropriate.

   Where the auditor is unable to report affirmatively on the matters contained in the paragraphs above, he should qualify his report by referring to all material matters about which he has reservations. A full explanation of the reasons for the qualification should be given, together with, whenever possible, a quantification of its effect on the financial statements. Where appropriate, reference should be made to non-compliance with relevant legislation and other requirements.

20. It has long been accepted that it is not sufficient that a qualified audit report should merely 'prompt further inquiry'. The standard re-affirms this view and stresses the fact that *a qualified audit report should leave the reader in no doubt as to its meaning and its implications for an understanding of the financial statements.* In order to promote a more consistent understanding of qualified audit reports, the APC recommend that the forms of qualification described in the Standard should be used unless, in the auditor's opinion, to do so would fail to convey clearly the intended meaning.

21. The APC take the view that the nature of the circumstances giving rise to a qualification of the auditor's opinion will generally fall into one of two categories:

   (a) where there is uncertainty which prevents the auditor from forming an opinion on a matter (uncertainty); or

   (b) where the auditor is able to form an opinion on a matter but this conflicts with the view given by the financial statements (disagreement).

22. Either case, uncertainty or disagreement, may give rise to alternative forms of qualification. This is because the uncertainty or disagreement can be:

   (a) of fundamental importance to the overall true and fair view; or
   (b) material but not fundamental.

23. The Standard requires that the following forms of qualification should be used in the different circumstances outlined below:

QUALIFICATION MATRIX

Nature of circumstances	Material but not fundamental	Fundamental
Uncertainty	Subject to	Disclaimer of opinion
Disagreement	Except for	Adverse opinion

24. The meaning of the above forms can be summarised as follows:

    (a) a disclaimer of opinion is one where the auditor states that he is unable to form an opinion as to whether the accounts give a true and fair view;

    (b) an adverse opinion is one where the auditor states that in his opinion the accounts do not give a true and fair view;

    (c) a 'subject to...' opinion is one where the auditor disclaims an opinion on a particular aspect of the accounts which is not considered fundamental;

    (d) an 'except for ...' opinion is one where the auditor expresses an adverse opinion on a particular aspect of the accounts which is not considered fundamental.

Circumstances giving rise to uncertainties

25. In the explanatory notes to the standard, the APC suggest that circumstances giving rise to uncertainties include the following:

    (a) *Limitations in the scope of the audit.* Scope limitations will arise where the auditor is unable for any reason to obtain all the information and explanations which he considers necessary for the purpose of his audit. Limitations in the scope of the audit would result from the absence of proper accounting records or an inability to carry out audit procedures considered necessary as, for example, where the auditor is unable to obtain satisfactory evidence of the existence or ownership of material assets, or of the amounts at which they have been stated on the basis adopted.

    (b) *Inherent uncertainties.* Inherent uncertainties result from circumstances in which it is not possible to reach an objective conclusion as to the outcome of a situation due to the circumstances themselves rather than to any limitation of the scope of the audit procedures. This type of uncertainty may relate to major litigation, the outcome of long-term contracts or doubts about the ability of the enterprise to continue as a going concern. Inherent uncertainties will not normally include instances where the auditor is able to obtain adequate evidence to support estimates and use his experience to reach an opinion as to their reasonableness; for example as regards collectability of debts or realisability of stock.

26. The wording in expressing the audit opinion describes the effect of uncertainties on that opinion and does not distinguish those arising from a limitation of scope from those which are inherent. The cause of the uncertainty will be described elsewhere in the audit report.

Circumstances giving rise to disagreements

27. The explanatory notes suggest that circumstances giving rise to disagreement include the following:

    (a) inappropriate accounting policies; (for a limited company this could mean failure to comply with the accounting requirements of the Companies Act 1985, and/or SSAPs or additional Stock Exchange disclosures);

    (b) disagreement as to the facts or amounts included in the financial statements;

    (c) disagreement as to the manner or extent of disclosure of facts or amounts in the financial statements;

    (d) failure to comply with relevant legislation or other requirements.

28. In relation to statutory requirements, the auditor will also need to consider whether the circumstances which give rise to his qualification impinge on his statutory duties to report. For example, shortcomings in the purchase records which give rise to a qualified opinion on the financial statements will generally mean that proper accounting records, as required by S221 CA 1985, have not been maintained. Similarly, limitations in scope may mean that the auditor has not obtained all the information and explanations he considers necessary. In the case of directors' emoluments and transactions with directors the normal judgements in relation to materiality are overruled. If the company has failed to disclose such information satisfactorily, the auditor must step in and do so in his report; in other words such items are, by definition, 'material' and the auditor will hence qualify his report on the grounds of failure to comply with legislation.

29. The audit report should include a brief recital of the reasons for a qualification and should quantify the effects on the financial statements if this is relevant and practicable. Whilst it is acceptable practice to make reference to relevant notes in the financial statements, such reference should not be used as a substitute for a description of the basic circumstances in the audit report itself.

30. The auditor should refer in his report to all material matters about which he has reservations. Thus, a qualification on one matter should not be regarded as a reason for omitting other unrelated qualifications which otherwise would have been reported - 'multiple' qualifications are, in other words, a possibility.

31. The manner in which the reasons for qualifying are disclosed is for the auditor to decide in the particular circumstances of each case, but the overall objective should be clarity. The APC suggest that the inclusion of a separate 'explanatory' paragraph before the paragraph in which the auditor gives his opinion is likely to be the clearest method of outlining the facts giving rise to the qualification.

Materiality

32. In deciding whether to qualify his audit opinion, the auditor should have regard to the materiality of the matter in the context of the financial statements on which he is proposing to report. In general terms a matter should be judged to be material if knowledge of the matter would be likely to *influence the user* of the financial statements. Materiality may be considered in the context of the financial statements as a whole, the balance sheet, the profit and loss account, or individual items within the financial statements. In addition, depending upon the nature of the matter, materiality may be considered in relative or absolute terms.

33. If the auditor concludes that judged against the criteria he believes to be most appropriate in the circumstances, the matter does not materially affect the view given by the financial statements, he should not qualify his opinion.

34. Where the auditor has decided that a matter is sufficiently material to warrant a qualification in his audit report, a further decision is required as to whether or not the matter is fundamental, so as to require either an adverse opinion or a disclaimer of opinion on the financial statements as a whole. An *uncertainty* becomes *fundamental* when its impact on the accounts is so great as to render the financial statements as a whole *meaningless*. A

disagreement becomes *fundamental* when its impact on the financial statements is so great as to render them totally *misleading*. The combined effect of all uncertainties and disagreements must be considered.

35. The adverse opinion and the disclaimer of opinion are the extreme forms of the two main categories of qualification of opinion arising from disagreement and uncertainty. In most situations the 'except for' or 'subject to' form of opinion will be the appropriate form to use; the adverse opinion and the disclaimer should be regarded as measures of last resort.

Audit report examples

36. In this section a number of audit report examples are reproduced from the Appendix to the Standard. Note that the first of the examples from the guideline has already been reproduced in paragraph 10 above.

37. It is *not* necessary to learn these examples by heart - they are, in any event, only of illustrative status - rather, they should be reviewed and appreciated in the light of the requirements of the Standard and explanatory notes discussed in the earlier sections. It should be noted that all the reports are incomplete to the extent that they have not been signed and dated by the auditor.

Example 3
UNQUALIFIED AUDIT REPORT

Emphasis of matter

AUDITORS' REPORT TO THE MEMBERS OF XYZ LIMITED
We have audited the financial statements on pages ... to ... in accordance with Auditing Standards.

In our opinion the financial statements give a true and fair view of the state of the company's affairs at 31 December 19... and of its profit and source and application of funds for the year then ended and have been properly prepared in accordance with the Companies Act 1985.

Without qualifying our opinion above, we draw attention to note ..... which refers to the substantial uncertainties relating to litigation and taxation, the provisions for which will continue to be reviewed by the directors as events unfold.

Example 4
UNQUALIFIED AUDIT REPORT

Other information or opinion prescribed by statutory or other requirements
AUDITORS' REPORT TO THE MEMBERS OF XYZ LIMITED

We have audited the financial statements on pages .... to .... in accordance with Auditing Standards.

In our opinion the financial statements give a true and fair view of the state of the company's affairs at 31 December 19.. and of its result and source and application of funds for the year then ended and have been properly prepared in accordance with the Companies Act 1985.

In our opinion, the information given in paragraph ... of the directors' report is not consistent with these financial statements. That paragraph states without amplification that the company's trading resulted in a profit before tax of £X. The profit and loss account, however, states that the company incurred a loss before tax for the year of £Y and, as an extraordinary item, a profit from the sale of land of £Z.

Example 5

QUALIFIED AUDIT REPORT

Uncertainty - subject to (scope limitation)
AUDITORS' REPORT TO THE MEMBERS OF XYZ LIMITED

We have audited the financial statements on pages .... to .... in accordance with Auditing Standards except that the scope of our work was limited by the matter referred to below.

£XX of the company's recorded turnover comprises cash sales. There was no system of control over such sales on which we could rely for the purpose of our audit and there were no satisfactory audit procedures that we could adopt to confirm independently that all cash sales were properly recorded. In this respect alone we were unable to satisfy ourselves as to the completeness and accuracy of the accounting records.

Subject to any adjustments that we might have found to be necessary had we been able to satisfy ourselves as to the matter referred to above, in our opinion the financial statements give a true and fair view of the state of the company's affairs at 31 December 19.. and of its profit and source and application of funds for the year then ended and have been properly prepared in accordance with the Companies Act 1985.

Notes:
1. In this example the uncertainty arising from the scope limitation is not regarded as fundamental. If the impact of the uncertainty had been regarded as so great that the financial statements as a whole could be misleading, a disclaimer of opinion would be required.

2. Where the auditors of a company incorporated in Great Britain fail to obtain all the information and explanations which, to the best of their knowledge and belief, are necessary for the purposes of their audit, section 237 of the Companies Act 1985 requires them to state that fact in their audit report. Therefore where there has been a limitation of the scope of the audit, the auditors of the company should consider whether such a statement should be made, for example by amending the last sentence of the second paragraph of the report as follows:

'In this respect alone we have not obtained all the information and explanations that we considered necessary for the purpose of our audit and we were unable to satisfy ourselves as to the completeness and accuracy of the accounting records.'

Example 6

QUALIFIED AUDIT REPORT

Uncertainty - subject to
AUDITORS' REPORT TO THE MEMBERS OF XYZ LIMITED

We have audited the financial statements on pages .... to .... in accordance with Auditing Standards.

As more fully explained in note .... to the financial statements a claim has been lodged by a customer against the company in respect of one of its major contracts. The claim calls for rectification and for substantial compensation for alleged damage to the customer's business. The directors have made a provision of £XX for the estimated cost of rectification but no provision for compensation as that part of the claim is being strongly resisted. At this time it is not possible to determine with reasonable certainty the ultimate cost of rectification and compensation, if any, which may become payable.

Subject to the adjustments, if any, that might have been necessary if the outcome of the uncertainties referred to above had been known, in our opinion the financial statements give a true and fair view of the state of the company's affairs at 31 December 19.. and of its profit and source and application of funds for the year then ended and have been properly prepared in accordance with the Companies Act 1985.

Example 7

QUALIFIED AUDIT REPORT

Uncertainty - subject to
AUDITORS' REPORT TO THE MEMBERS OF XYZ LIMITED

We have audited the financial statements on pages .... to .... in accordance with Auditing Standards.

The financial statements have been prepared on a going concern basis. This basis may not be appropriate because the company incurred a loss after taxation of £XX during the year ended 31 December 19.. and at that date its current liabilities exceeded its current assets by £XX. Further, the company is currently negotiating for long-term facilities to replace the loan of £XX which is repayable on ..... These factors, which are explained in note .... indicate that the company may be unable to continue trading.

Should the company be unable to continue trading, adjustments would have to be made to reduce the value of assets to their recoverable amount, to provide for any further liabilities which might arise and to reclassify fixed assets and long-term liabilities as current assets and liabilities.

Subject to the company being able to continue trading, in our opinion the financial statements give a true and fair view of the state of the company's affairs at 31 December 19.. and of its loss and source and application of funds for the year then ended and have been properly prepared in accordance with the Companies Act 1985.

Example 8

QUALIFIED AUDIT REPORT

Disagreement - except for
AUDITORS' REPORT TO THE MEMBERS OF XYZ LIMITED

We have audited the financial statements on pages .... to .... in accordance with Auditing Standards.

No provision has been made against an amount of £X owing by a company which is in liquidation. In our opinion XYZ Limited, as an unsecured creditor, will not receive full payment and a provision of £Y should have been made.

Except for the absence of the above provision, in our opinion, the financial statements give a true and fair view of the state of the company's affairs at 31 December 19.. and of its profit and source and application of funds for the year then ended and have been properly prepared in accordance with the Companies Act 1985.

Example 9

QUALIFIED AUDIT REPORT

Disagreement - except for
AUDITORS' REPORT TO THE MEMBERS OF XYZ LIMITED

We have audited the financial statements on pages .... to .... in accordance with Auditing Standards.

As explained in note .... no provision has been made for the depreciation of freehold buildings. This is not in accordance with the requirements of Statement of Standard Accounting Practice No 12 and of Sch 4 to the Companies Act 1985. In our opinion a provision of £XX (19.. £XX) should have been made; the effect of the company's accounting policy has been to overstate the company's profits before and after tax by this amount.

Except for the absence of the above provision, in our opinion the financial statements give a true and fair view of the state of the company's affairs at 31 December 19.. and of its profit and source and application of funds for the year then ended and have been properly prepared in accordance with the Companies Act 1985.

Note: It might also be appropriate to indicate the cumulative effect on retained profits and other balance sheet items where the amounts are material in the context of the balance sheet.

Example 10

QUALIFIED AUDIT REPORT

Uncertainty - disclaimer of opinion
AUDITORS' REPORT TO THE MEMBERS OF XYZ LIMITED

We have audited the financial statements on pages .... to .... in accordance with Auditing Standards.

As indicated in note .... the estimates of losses to completion of long-term construction contracts depend on a number of assumptions including those relating to substantially increased productivity which has yet to be achieved. In view of this uncertainty we are unable to confirm that the provision for losses of £XX is adequate.

Because of the potential impact of this uncertainty, we are unable to form an opinion as to whether the financial statements give a true and fair view of the state of the company's affairs at 31 December 19XX and of its profit and source and application of funds for the year then ended. In all other respects, in our opinion the financial statements have been properly prepared in accordance with the Companies Act 1985.

Notes:
1. In this example it is assumed that the potential impact of the uncertainties relating to estimates of losses on long-term construction contracts is fundamental in relation to the company's balance sheet, profit and loss account and funds statement.

2. In this case the area of uncertainties is well defined so that the auditor is able to reach an opinion as to whether the financial statements are in all other respects properly prepared in accordance with company legislation. Such a conclusion would not normally be possible where more pervasive uncertainties are involved.

Example 11

QUALIFIED AUDIT REPORT

Disagreement - adverse opinion
AUDITORS' REPORT TO THE MEMBERS OF XYZ LIMITED

We have audited the financial statements on pages .... to .... in accordance with Auditing Standards.

As more fully explained in note .... no provision has been made for losses expected to arise on certain long-term contracts currently in progress because the directors consider that such losses should be off-set against expected but unearned future profits on other long-term contracts. In our opinion provision should be made for foreseeable losses on individual contracts as required by Statement of Standard Accounting Practice No 9. If losses had been so recognised the effect would have been to reduce the profit before and after tax for the year and the contract work in progress at 31 December 19.. by £XX.

In view of the impact of the failure to provide for the losses referred to above, in our opinion the financial statements do not give a true and fair view of the state of the company's affairs at 31 December 19.. and of its profit and source and application of funds for the year then ended. In all other respects, in our opinion the financial statements have been properly prepared in accordance with the Companies Act 1985.

Note: In this example it is assumed that the impact of the disagreement is fundamental in relation to the company's balance sheet, profit and loss account and funds statement.

Example 12

QUALIFIED AUDIT REPORT

Qualification on profit and loss account only
AUDITORS' REPORT TO THE MEMBERS OF XYZ LIMITED

We have audited the financial statements on pages .... to .... in accordance with Auditing Standards except that the scope of our work was limited by the matter referred to below.

We were not appointed auditors of the company until .... and in consequence did not report on the financial statements for the year ended .... There were no satisfactory audit procedures that we could adopt to confirm the amount of stock and work in progress included in the preceding period's financial statements at a value of £XX. Any adjustments to this figure would affect the profit for the year ended 31 December 19..

In our opinion the financial statements give a true and fair view of the state of the company's affairs at 31 December 19.. Subject to any adjustments that we might have found to be necessary had we been able to satisfy ourselves as to the matter referred to above, in our opinion the financial statements give a true and fair view of the company's profit and source and application of funds for the year then ended and have been properly prepared in accordance with the Companies Act 1985.

Example 13

QUALIFIED AUDIT REPORT

Multiple qualification
AUDITORS' REPORT TO THE MEMBERS OF XYZ LIMITED

We have audited the financial statements on pages .... to .... in accordance with Auditing Standards except that the scope of our work was limited by the matter referred to at (1) below.

1. £XX of the company's recorded turnover comprises cash sales. There was no system of control over such sales on which we could rely for the purpose of our audit and there were no satisfactory audit procedures that we could adopt to confirm independently that all cash sales were properly recorded. In this respect alone we were unable to satisfy ourselves as to the completeness and accuracy of the accounting records.

2. No provision has been made against an amount of £X owing by a company which is in liquidation. In our opinion XYZ Limited, as an unsecured creditor, will not receive full payment and a provision of £Y should have been made.

Subject to any adjustments that we might have found to be necessary had we been able to satisfy ourselves as to the matter referred to at (1) above, and except for the absence of the provision referred to at (2) above, in our opinion the financial statements give a true and fair view of the state of the company's affairs at 31 December 19.. and of its profit and source and application of funds for the year then ended and have been properly prepared in accordance with the Companies Act 1985.

Notes:
1. The example of a multiple qualification is based on examples 5 and 8.
2. For ease of reference the explanatory paragraphs have been numbered.

The revised version of the Standard

38. The original standard was restricted to reports giving a 'true and fair' audit opinion. An audit opinion need not be a 'true and fair view' and the revised Standard recognises this point. This is designed to cope with the increasing number of local authority audits, for example, where the audit opinion refers to whether the financial statements 'present fairly' the position of the authority.

39. The revised standard does not require the auditor to refer to the particular accounting convention used. In the majority of cases the financial statements will be prepared on a historical cost basis. If this is not so, the accounting convention used should be clearly explained in the accounting policies note in the financial statements themselves.

40. The requirement that the auditor's report should be dated was introduced in the revised Standard. The guidance on this matter is consistent with the Auditing Guideline 'Events after the balance sheet date'. Therefore, the date on which the auditor signs his report should be that on which he signs his report on the financial statements, which have been approved by management. If this is not possible the delay between these two dates should be as brief as possible.

41. The APC make it clear that while the existing Standards are written in the context of the audit of limited companies, the revised Standard is intended to apply to other types of audit too. Therefore, the auditor should specify the Standards he has followed in conducting his audit. Normally he will have complied with Auditing Standards and his report should refer to this fact. If the auditor is required by statute to follow other comparable standards he should refer to these in the audit report.

42. In the original Standard it was implied that the auditor need not refer to departures from accounting standards in the audit report, if he concurred with the accounting treatment adopted and with the disclosure of the fact in the financial statements. In the revised Standard, such a departure should normally be referred to in the audit report.

43. However, probably the major changes included in the revised Standard concern the use of 'emphasis of matter' statements and on the acceptance of management representations for small companies. The latter are discussed in the next chapter.

Summary of the chapter

44. The subject of audit reporting is an important examination topic. It is vital to understand the discipline underlying the construction of audit reports - qualified and unqualified. Do not attempt to learn the report examples parrot fashion - appreciate the requirements and objectives of the Standard and then peruse the report examples ensuring that, for each qualification example, you can appreciate the circumstances and hence the wording and construction.

45. Many of the examination questions invoking the principles of the *qualified standard* are of a 'case study' type. The examiner will only rarely provide background information such that an adverse opinion or disclaimer is warranted - remember that these are 'measures of last resort'.

It is more likely that you will be required to consider circumstances resulting in a 'material but not fundamental' decision, and hence the 'except for' or 'subject to' opinion will be appropriate.

TEST YOUR KNOWLEDGE

Numbers in brackets refer to paragraphs in this chapter

1. What are the matters with which the auditor of a limited company implies satisfaction in an unqualified report? (3)

2. What are the express references in an audit report required by 'The audit report' Standard? (6)

3. Draft in full an unqualified report for a non-group company. (10)

4. In what circumstances might an 'emphasis of matter' be justified? (16)

5. What are the two principal categories of circumstance giving rise to a qualification? (21)

6. What does an 'adverse opinion' imply? (24 (b))

7. What is the distinction between an uncertainty arising due to a limitation in the scope of the audit and an inherent uncertainty? (25)

8. What circumstances might give rise to a disagreement? (27)

9. When does an uncertainty become fundamental? (34)

10. In what manner should the auditor draw attention to the fact that the directors' report is inconsistent with the financial statements? (37 Example 4)

---

1. The Auditing Standard issued by the Accountancy Bodies contains the following example of an unqualified audit report for a company without subsidiaries:

    "AUDITORS' REPORT TO THE MEMBERS OF......

    We have audited the financial statements on pages ... to ... in accordance with Auditing Standards.

    In our opinion the financial statements give a true and fair view of the state of the company's affairs at 31 December 19... and of its profit and source and application of funds for the year then ended and have been properly prepared in accordance with the Companies Act 1985."

    Any reader of an audit report presented in the format shown above is entitled to assume that the financial statements are prepared on the basis of the 'going concern' concept and that there are no significant departures from any statements of standard accounting practice. You are the partner in a firm of certified accountants, in charge of the audit of Hebite Limited. The audit senior has completed the audit for the year to 31 March 19X0 and has presented you with the financial statements for the year together with the working papers. You are now conducting your final review prior to signing the audit report. The senior has stated in his final notes to you that Hebite Limited has not presented a statement of source and application of funds because the directors felt that such a statement is meaningless having regard to the nature of Hebite's business.

    Required:

    (a) Assuming you agree with the directors, draft a suitably worded audit report, clearly stating the principles involved in drafting the report.
    (Make any assumptions you consider necessary.)

    (b) List any seven questions which you feel that your senior should have asked himself in order to determine whether the 'going concern' concept was appropriate.

    (c) Assume that the senior, having made appropriate 'going concern' enquiries, has ascertained that certain borrowings totalling £2 million are due for repayment on 31 July 19X0, but the company is currently negotiating for an extension of the repayment period, the outcome of which will determine the continuance or otherwise of the enterprise. State what modifications you would make in these circumstances to the audit report given in your answer to part (a) of the question. State clearly the principles involved in preparing your answer (you can again make any assumptions you consider necessary).

2. You are the auditor of Builders Merchants Limited, a company which distributes materials to the construction industry from eight depots in the south of England, and you are currently finalising the audit for the year ended 31 March 19X1. Your audit tests have proved satisfactory with the exception of the following two matters.

    (a) The physical stocktaking sheets for one of the depots were lost before they were made available to you, and you have not been able to confirm the stock quantities and values for this depot by alternative methods. The directors have valued this part of the stock at £75,000 and this figure is included in the overall stock valuation of £640,000.

(b) Included in trade debtors, which total £580,000, is a debt amounting to £45,000 from a customer which went into liquidation on 15 June 19X1. You have ascertained from the Liquidator that your client is unlikely to receive a distribution. The profit and loss account for the year shows a pre-tax profit of £110,000 but the directors are not prepared to provide for this debt.

You are required to prepare an audit report to the members of Builders Merchants Limited in respect of the year under review.

1. (a) AUDITORS' REPORT TO THE MEMBERS OF HEBITE LIMITED

We have audited the financial statements on pages 20 to 30 in accordance with Auditing Standards.

In our opinion the financial statements give a true and fair view of the state of the company's affairs at 31 March 19X0 and of its profit for the year then ended and have been properly prepared in accordance with the Companies Act 1985.

Without qualifying our opinion above, we draw attention to the fact that the financial statements do not specify the manner in which the operations of the company have been financed or in which its financial resources have been used during the year as required by Statement of Standard Accounting Practice No 10.

Principle involved: The omission of a funds statement does not justify, on this ground alone, a qualified report on the profit and loss account and balance sheet. The final paragraph above is hence an 'emphasis of matter' not a qualification.

(b) The following seven questions are amongst those which the senior should have considered:
(i)   What is the debt to equity ratio and how does it compare to previous periods?
(ii) What is the rate of stock and debtors turnover, and how does it compare to previous periods and to industry averages?
(iii) What is the working capital ratio and how does it compare to previous periods?
(iv) Has the firm had to finance long-term projects, such as plant expansion or product development by using short-term or medium-term borrowings?
(v)   Has the firm had to dispose of income-generating fixed assets in order to improve the cash position?
(vi) Has the firm reached or almost reached the limits of its borrowing powers and will it require further finance in the near future?
(vii) Are there any post balance sheet events which could cause problems, e.g. a serious fire, failure of a substantial debtor etc?

(c) The following qualified report will be necessary in the circumstances outlined:

AUDITORS' REPORT TO THE MEMBERS OF HEBITE LIMITED

We have audited the financial statements on pages 20 to 30 in accordance with Auditing Standards.

The financial statements have been prepared on a going concern basis. This basis may not be appropriate as the company is currently negotiating for an extension of the repayment period in respect of borrowings of £2 million due for repayment on 31 July 19X0. This factor, which is explained in note 18, indicates that the company may be unable to continue trading.

Should the company be unable to continue trading, adjustments would have to be made to reduce the value of assets to their recoverable amount, to provide for any further liabilities which might arise, and to reclassify fixed assets and long-term liabilities as current assets and liabilities.

Subject to the company being able to continue trading, in our opinion the financial statements give a true and fair view of the state of the company's affairs at 31 March 19X0 and of its profit for the year then ended and have been properly prepared in accordance with the Companies Act 1985.

We draw attention to the fact that the financial statements do not specify the manner in which the operations of the company have been financed or in which its financial resources have been used during the year as required by Statement of Standard Accounting Practice No 10.

Principle involved: A going concern qualification is an example of an inherent uncertainty giving rise, in this instance, to a 'subject to' opinion as the matter is judged to be material but not fundamental. Where the uncertainty about the appropriateness of the going concern assumption is so fundamental as to prevent the auditor from forming an opinion on the financial statements, he will need to disclaim an opinion.

2. AUDITORS' REPORT TO THE MEMBERS OF BUILDERS MERCHANTS LIMITED

We have audited the financial statements on pages 4 to 18 in accordance with Auditing Standards except that the scope of our work was limited by the matter referred to below.

The physical stocktaking sheets of one of the company's depots were lost before they were made available to us and there were no practicable alternative auditing procedures that we could apply to confirm quantities. Accordingly, we have been unable to satisfy ourselves as to the existence and value of the stock quantities in question. These have been valued by the Directors at £75,000 and included as part of the total stock of £640,000 in the balance sheet. In our opinion, in the case of the stocks referred to above, proper accounting records have not been kept as required by Section 221, Companies Act 1985.

No provision has been made against an amount of £45,000 owing by a company which has been placed in liquidation since the year-end. The liquidator has indicated that unsecured creditors are unlikely to receive any payment and in our opinion full provision for this debt should be made in the accounts under review. If this loss had been recognised, the effect would have been to reduce the profit for the year before tax, and the figure of debtors at 31 March 19X1, by £45,000.

In view of the significant effect of the failure to provide for the debt owing by the liquidated company, in our opinion the financial statements do not give a true and fair view of the state of the company's affairs at 31 March 19X1 and of its profit and source and application of funds for the year then ended. In all other respects, in our opinion the financial statements have been properly prepared in accordance with the Companies Act 1985.

Principle involved: Although both the qualification matters identified in the question merit mention in the audit report, the doubtful debt of £45,000, which is an adjusting event, is of fundamental significance in the context of the pre-tax profit of £110,000 and results in an opinion that the financial statements do not give a true and fair view (disagreement – fundamental).

SECTION 6

SPECIALISED TOPICS

Chapter 15

THE PROBLEMS OF AUDITING
SMALL BUSINESSES

Topics covered in this chapter:

- Control in a small business environment
- Application of auditing standards to small businesses
- The need for a full statutory audit
- Unaudited financial statements
- Modified accounts
- Dormant companies
- Publication of accounts other than by filing

Introduction

1. All limited companies are required by statute to have their accounts audited, with the exception of dormant companies whose shareholders have the power to dispense with an audit. Moreover, the Companies Act 1985 does not differentiate in any way between the scope of an audit for large and small companies; nor does it make any difference whether they are public or private - the auditor's rights and duties the same.

2. The revived debate on whether or not small companies ought to continue to have an audit must not cloud the fact that the auditor is required at the present time not only to comply with the Companies Act 1985, but also to apply auditing standards. In this chapter we identify the control procedures and methods that distinguish small companies, in particular the importance of proprietor involvement. We consider how the auditor must modify the operational approach of the systems audit to obtain audit assurance in respect of small companies, and the reporting consequences.

3. In March 1985 the Department of Trade and Industry issued a report entitled 'Burdens on business'. It gave a useful insight into how businesses see the administrative and legislative burdens imposed on them by government. Most noticeable was the fact that company law - embracing the statutory audit - was ranked a lowly thirteenth as a burden, way behind such 'favourites' as VAT, PAYE and employment protection. It is perhaps surprising that the DTI has subsequently issued a consultative document entitled 'Accounting and audit requirements for small firms', especially since the ground that it covers is already well-trodden as a result of the consultation undertaken in 1979 prior to introducing the EEC Fourth Directive into UK law and which culminated in the publication of an Audit Brief entitled 'Small companies: the need for an audit?' The case for and against retaining the statutory audit of small companies is discussed in detail.

4.   Finally in this chapter we consider the responsibilities of the practising accountant when he is engaged to prepare accounts for clients but not to audit them, and the concept of modified accounts.

Control in a small business environment

5.   We are concerned in this chapter with the application of modified audit procedures to so called 'small enterprises'. It would therefore make life relatively straightforward if we could, at the outset, define small enterprises in absolute terms - perhaps by reference to those companies defined as small for the purpose of modified accounts eligibility. Sadly perhaps, but wisely, the Auditing Standards and Guidelines do not attempt to be so precise. The key, as we have signalled in chapter 5, is internal control or, to be more precise, the relative lack of formal controls. The explanatory note to a withdrawn APC standard stated:

> "However, the operating procedures and methods of recording and processing transactions used by small enterprises often differ significantly from those of large enterprises. Indeed, many of the controls which would be relevant to the large enterprise are not practical, appropriate or necessary in the small enterprise. The most effective form of internal control for small enterprises is generally the close involvement of the directors or proprietors. This involvement will, however, enable them to override controls and purposely to exclude transactions from the records. This possibility can give rise to difficulties for the auditor not because there is a lack of controls but because of insufficient evidence as to their operation and the completeness of the records."

6.   The type of business we are dealing with here will have a small staff and, as a result, segregation of duties will often appear inadequate. Similarly, because of the scale of the operation, organisation and management controls are likely to be rudimentary at best or non existent. The onus is therefore on the proprietor, by virtue of his day-to-day involvement, to compensate for the lack of the above controls. Such involvement should hence embrace other control types - physical, authorisation, arithmetical and accounting, and supervision.

7.   Hence it is important to stress that there *is* internal control in a well run small company. Such companies must not be an accounting and control shambles - it should be recalled, in any event, that *all* companies have to comply with the Companies Act accounting records requirements and maintain a satisfactory *accounting system*.

8.   We referred above to 'the proprietor'; this term normally implies both ownership *and* management. The auditor will have to be particularly careful where the manager of the small enterprise does not have an equity stake and consequently does not, perhaps, have the same commitment to the running of the business. In these circumstances the auditor may have to consider the adequacy of controls exercised by the shareholders over the manager.

Minimum business controls

9.   Having established that proprietor involvement is the key to internal control in the small enterprise, the next stage is to be rather more precise and identify the types of control relevant to each principal accounting area. These proprietor dominated controls are commonly referred to as 'minimum business controls'. It is important to appreciate that such controls

will not, and cannot, be evaluated and relied on by the auditor in a systems audit sense, but they provide some overall comfort to the auditor when determining whether to seek to rely on management assurances as to the completeness of the accounting records.

10. The following checklist provides illustrative examples of such minimum standards of internal control:

Mail
(a)　Is all mail received and opened by the proprietor?
(b)　If the proprietor does not himself open the mail, is it opened by a person not connected with the accounts (eg the proprietor's secretary) and read by him before it is distributed to the staff?

Receipts
(a)　Are all cheques and postal orders received by post counted by the proprietor before they are passed to the cashier?
(b)　Are all cheques and postal orders crossed to the company's branch of its bankers 'Not negotiable - account payee only'.
(c)　Are cash sales and credit sale receipts over the counter controlled by locked cash register tapes which only the proprietor can open?
(d)　Does the proprietor reconcile the cash register totals with the cash sales receipts daily?
(e)　Is the person performing the duties of cashier barred any responsibility concerning the sales, purchase or nominal ledgers?

Banking
(a)　Is all cash received banked intact at intervals of not more than three days?
(b)　Does the proprietor reconcile all monies received with the copy paying-in slips at regular intervals?

Payments
(a)　Are all payments except sundry expenses made by cheques?
(b)　Does the proprietor sign all cheques?
(c)　Are cheques signed by the proprietor only after he has satisfied himself that:
　　(i)　he has approved and cancelled all vouchers supporting the payment;
　　(ii)　all cheques are crossed:
　　　　- not negotiable?
　　　　- account payee only?
　　(iii)　all cheque numbers are accounted for?
(d)　Are petty cash expenses controlled by the imprest system?
(e)　Does the proprietor review all expenses and initial the petty cash book before reimbursing the cashier?

Bank statements
(a)　Are bank statements and paid cheques sent direct to the proprietor and opened only by him?
(b)　Does the proprietor scrutinise all paid cheques to ensure that he has signed them all before he passes them to the cashier?
(c)　Does the proprietor:
　　(i)　prepare a bank reconciliation each month? or
　　(ii)　review in detail a reconciliation produced by the cashier?

Orders
(a)   Are all purchase orders issued:
    (i)   serially numbered by the printer;
    (ii)   pre-printed duplicate order forms?
(b)   Does the proprietor approve all orders?

Receipt of goods
Are delivery notes:
(a)   checked with goods;
(b)   compared with the copy order;
(c)   compared with the invoice?

Wages
(a)   Is a separate cheque drawn for the exact amount to pay wages and PAYE/National Insurance?
(b)   Does the proprietor either prepare or examine the wages records before signing the cheque?
(c)   Does the proprietor initial the wages records after his examination?
(d)   Does the proprietor oversee the distribution of the wages packets or does he distribute them himself?

Debtors
(a)   If credit is granted to customers does the proprietor:
    (i)   authorise every extension of credit to a customer; or
    (ii)   approve credit limits for each customer?
(b)   Does the proprietor authorise all:
    (i)   write offs of bad debts?
    (ii)   sales returns and allowances?
    (iii) discounts other than routine cash discounts?
(c)   Does the proprietor receive a monthly list of debtors, showing the age of the debts?
(d)   Are all authorisations by the proprietor evidenced by his initials?

Goods outwards
(a)   Are pre-numbered despatch notes prepared for *all* goods leaving the premises?
(b)   Are all despatch notes:
    (i)   accounted for?
    (ii)   cross referenced with invoices and credit notes?
(c)   Is the proprietor satisfied that all goods leaving the premises have been accounted for?

Stock
Does the proprietor scrutinise the stocks regularly to:
(a)   keep abreast of what is in stock?
(b)   discover obsolete items?
(c)   discover damaged articles?
(d)   ensure that stock levels are kept under control?

11.   Although the above types of control are desirable and feasible, they are nevertheless relatively informal. Consequently evidence of their *performance* tends to be lacking and they may indeed be overridden as there is no check on the proprietor himself.

Application of auditing standards to small businesses

12. The key question is clearly 'Can the auditing standards be applied to small companies?' having regard to the control problems identified above. The answer is 'yes'! The following paragraphs identify the particular points of operational significance that affect the auditor's approach to such businesses:

   (a) *Planning, controlling and recording*
   Planning may not necessarily be a weighty task in the case of a small client, but some planning is clearly necessary. Control over work delegated to staff is just as important in the case of a small client as it is in a large one, and the need to record the audit work done and evidence obtained is equally apparent.

   (b) *Accounting systems*
   The need to ascertain and assess a client's accounting system arises even in respect of small clients. If there is no organised system of gathering together the basic accounting data (details of purchases, sales, cash received and paid etc) no amount of auditing will provide assurance that the accounts show a true and fair view. The guideline does not suggest that such a system of data collection need be anything other than simple, but it must be comprehensive and must also comply with the accounting records requirements of S221 Companies Act 1985.

   (c) *Audit evidence*
      (i) The collection of sufficient audit evidence is, of course, what auditing is all about. The APC has stated in the context of small enterprises:

      "The auditor needs to obtain the same degree of assurance in order to give an unqualified opinion on the financial statements of both small and large enterprises.

      In many situations it may be possible to reach a conclusion that will support an unqualified opinion on the financial statements by combining the evidence obtained from extensive substantive testing of transactions with a careful review of costs and margins. However, in some businesses such as those where most transactions are for cash and there is no regular pattern of costs and margins, the available evidence may be inadequate to support an opinion on the financial statements."

      (ii) In other words, the auditor will be carrying out an exclusively substantive audit comprising:
      - extensive tests of transactions (applying the techniques described in chapter 6);
      - extensive verification of assets and liabilities (applying the techniques described in chapter 7); and
      - analytical review (including review of financial statements - see (e) below).

      In terms of timing, it is not unusual for the transactions and balance sheet work to be combined and carried out in one single phase commencing, typically, shortly before the year end. In these circumstances the management letter will be sent at the conclusion of the audit work after the client's year end.

      (iii) The auditor's objective should always be to obtain sufficient evidence to support, if possible, an unqualified opinion. Nevertheless it is often the case with a small company that, at the conclusion of his field work, the auditor will have obtained insufficient evidence as to the completeness of the entries in the accounting records.

      "There will be other situations where the evidence available to the auditor is insufficient to give him the confidence necessary for him to express an unqualified opinion but this uncertainty is not so great as to justify a total disclaimer of

opinion. In such situations the most helpful form of report may be one which indicates the need to accept the assurances of management as to the completeness or accuracy of the accounting records. Such a report should contain a 'subject to....' opinion. It would only be appropriate to use this form of report if the auditor has taken steps to obtain all the evidence which can reasonably be obtained and is satisfied that:
(1) the system of accounting and control is reasonable having regard to the size and type of the enterprise's operations; and is sufficient to enable management to give the auditor the assurances which he requires;
(2) there is no evidence to suggest that the assurances may be inaccurate."

(iv) The requirement for the auditor to satisfy himself in respect of (1) and (2) above is important. The system of accounting and control must be reasonable. The use of a minimum business controls checklist, incorporating the types of question identified in paragraph 10, may provide the auditor with comfort as regards requirement (1). When assessing the possibility that management assurances might be inaccurate, the auditor must consider whether his examination of the records, the audit evidence available to him and his knowledge of all the circumstances affecting the company are consistent with and support the assurances. He must also form an opinion as to the honesty and reliability of management, based on previous experience, and having due regard to the prevailing circumstances. The important principle here is that reliance on management assurances is not a routine matter, it must be justified.

(d) *Internal controls*
The format of the Auditing Standards makes it quite clear that there is no need for the auditor to seek to rely on a system of internal control. We have seen that, although the needs for internal control may be fulfilled in part by the proprietor himself, for that reason the auditor may find little, if any, evidence that such control has been properly exercised. It is only where there is evidence of the operation of internal control that the auditor can rely on it.

(e) *Review of financial statements*
The need to review financial statements is well established in respect of clients of all sizes. The use of techniques such as analytical review is universal. The accounts of small companies have, of course, to comply with the requirements of the Companies Act 1985 and SSAPs as much as do those of large companies. These financial statements must be reviewed by the auditor to ensure that compliance is achieved.

Reporting consequences

13. At the conclusion of his field work the auditor may be in a position to form an unqualified opinion of the accounts of his small company client. In these happy circumstances, the style of report will be as illustrated in chapter 14 (example 1). But it is more likely that he will conclude that a qualification of his report is necessary on the grounds that he needs to accept the assurances of management as to the completeness of the accounting records. In these circumstances - provided he is satisfied that the assurances are reliable - he may wish to give his report a 'subject to' qualification, as follows:

AUDITOR'S REPORT TO THE MEMBERS OF.....................

We have audited the financial statements on pages ... to .... in accordance with Auditing Standards having regard to the matters referred to in the following paragraph.

In common with many businesses of similar size and organisation the company's system of control is dependent upon the close involvement of the directors (who are major shareholders). Where independent confirmation of the completeness of the accounting records was therefore not available we have accepted assurances from the directors that all the company's transactions have been reflected in the records.

Subject to the foregoing, in our opinion the financial statements give a true and fair view of the state of the company's affairs at 31 December 19X0 and of its profit and source and application of funds for the year then ended and have been properly prepared in accordance with the Companies Act 1985.

14. The auditor's judgement in these circumstances is that the problem (ie uncertainty) is material but not fundamental. The auditor should consider referring to the specific area or areas of the financial statements in which he has had to rely on assurances (eg credit sales).

15. Where the lack of evidence of the operation of internal controls coupled with the inability to adopt alternative procedures to compensate is regarded as so fundamental as to prevent an effective audit being carried out, a *disclaimer* of opinion will be necessary. The auditor might encounter such a situation in small companies where sales are substantially for cash (it will be appreciated that third party confirmation of debtors will be irrelevant for such companies).

16. It must be emphasised that the auditor should only qualify his audit report on the accounts of a small business in situations where he is unable to gather sufficient audit evidence on which to base his opinion. The audit report above must not be regarded as a 'standard' form of audit report for small companies. In the past this sort of audit report has been called a 'small company qualification' as if it had been issued as a suitable form of audit report for all small companies, rather than as an example of one type of qualified report. This misconception could result in a qualified report being given when it was not required, or in insufficient audit work being done if the auditor decided from the outset that his audit report was going to be qualified in this way.

17. The current options for the small company auditor can therefore be summarised as follows.

   (a) *Give an unqualified audit report*
   This is appropriate where the auditor has obtained satisfactory audit evidence, corroborating management representations by, for example, analytical review and other substantive tests. The auditor should normally in such cases make no reference to any management representations he may have obtained, since any such reference could be misinterpreted as a form of qualified opinion.

   (b) *Give a qualified audit report (either 'subject to' or disclaimer)*
   (i) This is appropriate where the auditor has not been able to obtain satisfactory audit evidence to corroborate management representations. He should specify in his qualified audit report the areas and amounts in the financial statements affected by the uncertainty. It will normally in such cases be possible for the auditor to specify the areas and amounts in this way.

   (ii) In exceptional cases, there may be a general uncertainty pervasive to the whole financial statements, making it impracticable for the auditor to attempt to specify the areas and amounts affected. When the uncertainty is so far-reaching that its effects cannot be specified at all, the potential impact could be to cause the financial statements as a whole to be misleading, and a disclaimer of opinion should be considered.

If the uncertainty is not so far-reaching, a 'subject to' qualification should be used, where the opinion is subject to a reservation expressed in general rather than in specific terms.

18. The duties and responsibilities of the auditors in respect of the individual small company client are the same as in larger audits and the satisfactory accomplishment of the work requires the skilful adaptation and application of the principles of auditing to the individual case. Because the relationship with the directors is frequently less formal, and because other professional services including accountancy work are often provided, it is particularly important that the arrangement and scope of the work should be clearly defined and confirmed in the engagement letter. It should be noted that paragraph 1.4 of the specimen engagement letter in chapter 7 draws management's attention to the possibility that the auditor may seek to rely on management assurances where appropriate.

The need for a full statutory audit

19. We have seen that it is possible to apply the operational standard to the audit of small companies, though the resulting audit report may well be qualified. The question we ask in this section is 'Is it worth it?' In other words, is the statutory audit of small companies of sufficient value to anyone to justify the administrative and financial burden imposed on the company?

20. As indicated in the introduction, this debate has recently been revived by the government. The DTI consultative document 'Accounting and audit requirements for small firms' seeks to elicit views of interested parties with regard to both the abolition of the audit requirement and relaxation of accounting rules for small companies.

21. In examining the arguments for and against exempting small companies from the statutory audit requirement, it suggests that the protection afforded by an audit is not essential where all shareholders are directors, who should normally be in a position to get a view of the company's affairs without being required to commission an independent audit. Nevertheless, it is acknowledged that the interests of other investors such as banks and trade creditors require protection and such persons could require their own independent audits in the absence of any statutory requirement. The options for change identified by the paper are as follows.

   (a) Abolish the audit requirement for small companies, all of whose members are directors.

   (b) Abolish the audit requirement for all small companies below a certain size, though not for all small companies as presently defined.

   (c) Abolish the audit requirement for all small companies and allow members to decide the company's policy on auditing of accounts in the light of its particular circumstances.

22. The consultative document then proceeds to discuss the form and content of accounts. It explains that when the Fourth Directive was implemented, there was a choice either to allow small companies to do no more than prepare and file a modified balance sheet with supporting notes, or

to maintain the requirement that full accounts be circulated to shareholders but to allow the publication of modified accounts. In view of the lack of any consensus at the time, the latter alternative was adopted as a compromise solution, which protected shareholders' interests and still afforded the company a measure of privacy from the outside world. In exploring the possibility of any further relaxation from the current requirements, the following options are put forward.

(a) Allow small owner-managed companies to produce modified accounts only.
(b) Allow all small companies to produce modified accounts only, subject to shareholder approval.
(c) Allow a sub-category, which is not defined in the consultative document, of small companies to produce modified accounts only, again subject to shareholder approval.

23. Finally, the consultative document asks for comments on whether the present size criteria for small and medium sized companies should be raised in order to take account of inflation. This follows the recent adoption by the EEC of a short directive increasing the original financial threshholds contained in the Fourth Directive (see the section on modified accounts later).

24. It would appear from press reports that the ACCA remains broadly in favour of retaining the audit of small companies though the ICAEW consider that companies, under stringent conditions, might be allowed to vote not to have one. To examine in greater detail the pros and cons it is useful to refer to the Audit Brief 'Small companies: the need for audit' issued as a consultative document back in 1979 prior to the implementation of the Fourth Directive in the Companies Act 1981.

'Small companies: the need for an audit' – APC 'Audit Brief'

25. *Pros and cons*
The case for retaining the present system rests on the value of the statutory audit to those who have an interest in audited accounts, ie the users. The Audit Brief defines these interested parties as:
- shareholders
- banks and other institutional creditors
- trade creditors
- taxing authorities
- employees
- management
(this is an almost identical list to our familiar list of users derived from the Corporate Report).

26. The Brief proceeds to put forward arguments for and against change from the viewpoint of each of the above parties as follows:

(a) *Shareholders:*
For change   where all the shareholders are also executive directors or closely related to them, the benefit gained from an audit may not be worth its cost.

Against change   (i)   shareholders not involved in management need the reassurance given by audited accounts. Furthermore, the existence of the audit deters the directors from treating the company's assets as their own to the detriment of minority shareholders;

(ii)   audited financial statements are invaluable in arriving at a fair valuation of the shares in an unquoted company either for taxation or other purposes.

(b) *Banks etc:*
Against change   banks rely on accounts for the purposes of making loans and reviewing the value of security.

For change   (i)   there is doubt whether banks rely on the audited accounts of companies to a greater extent than those of unincorporated associations of a similar size which have not been audited;

(ii)   a review of the way in which the bank accounts of the company have been conducted and of forecasts and management accounts are at least as important to the banks as the appraisal of the audited accounts;

(iii)   there is no reason why a bank should not make an audit a precondition of granting a loan.

(c) *Trade creditors:*
Against change   creditors and potential creditors should have the opportunity to assess the strength of their customers by examining audited financial statements either themselves or through a credit company;

For change   in practice, only limited reliance is placed on the accounts available from the Registrar of Companies as they are usually filed so late as to be of little significance in granting short term credit.

(d) *Tax authorities*
Against change   the Inland Revenue and Customs and Excise rely on accounts for computing corporation tax and checking VAT returns;

For change   there is little evidence to suggest that the tax authorities rely on audited accounts to a significantly greater extent than those, which, whilst being unaudited have been prepared by an independent accountant.

(e) *Employees*
Against change   employees are entitled to be able to assess audited accounts when entering wage negotiations and considering the future viability of their employer;

For change   there is little evidence to suggest that, in the case of small companies, such assessments are made.

(f) *Management*
Against change   the audit provides management with a useful independent check on the accuracy of the accounting systems and the auditor is frequently able to recommend improvements in those systems;

> For change   if the law was changed, the management of a company could, if they so desired, still elect to have an independent audit. It is likely, however, that a review accompanied by a management consultancy report would represent a greater benefit for a similar cost.

27. As a further argument for change, the Brief identifies the problems of auditing small companies and the likelihood that a significant number of qualified reports will result. It argues that a widespread increase in such reports will damage the standing of the audited financial statements of such companies. In the years that have elapsed since the Brief was issued it is certainly true that qualification of the accounts of small companies is commonplace; whether such qualifications have seriously affected the credibility of the financial statements reported on, is, however, arguable.

28. *Review as an alternative to full-dress audit*
    If the case for changing the law relating to the audit of small companies were accepted, the Brief argues that two main alternatives are available:

    (a) a statutory requirement for a *review* by an independent suitably qualified accountant; or
    (b) no legal requirement for any external examination of financial statements.

    It would of course be open to a company to opt for a full audit. Indeed it is quite possible that an audit would be required unless, say, 90% of the members voted for the change. (This restriction would, of course, be additional to those relating to the size of the company.) It must be remembered that, for all companies, the directors will remain responsible for producing accounts that give a true and fair view (unless that requirement were also to be abolished for small companies).

29. It has been argued that a review would be of no practical value as it would still be an expense to the company whilst not providing the assurance to be gained from an audit. Furthermore, it could be misleading to the users of the financial statements who may, seeing that the name of a firm of accountants is associated with the statements, believe that they have been audited. A lot of the criticism against the review option has, however, arisen because its supporters have often failed to define its nature and scope. The Brief attempts to clarify the main principles and objectives of a review and in so doing draws on the experience of countries where this form of external examination of financial statements is already used.

30. The review is defined as:
    "A procedure whereby an accountant, relying upon the assumption that his client has made a full and fair disclosure of all the relevant information, satisfies himself (after completing work in accordance with an approved review standard) that on the basis of the information and explanations so provided the financial statements give a true and fair view (or that there is no evidence to encourage the opinion that the financial statements do not show a true and fair view)."

31. The main parts to the review would be:

    (a) establishing that the client has employed reasonable procedures to ensure the accuracy of his financial statements, including:
        (i) having books and records which are reasonably adequate for the purpose of recording transactions and providing the necessary information;

(ii)   employing satisfactory procedures for such matters as ascertaining stock;

(iii)   taking reasonable precautions to verify the accuracy of the statements by such means as reconciling bank statements, reviewing suppliers' statements received after the balance sheet date, etc.

(b)   reviewing the accounting policies adopted by the client for consistency and appropriateness and reviewing with him the significant judgemental areas in the statements such as the recoverability of debts, stock obsolescence, depreciation etc;

(c)   carrying out analytical review procedures on the statements with a view to identifying anomalies or unexpected items or relationships and obtaining satisfactory explanations for them;

(d)   reviewing the financial statements as a whole for fairness of presentation, compliance with statutory disclosure requirements and compliance with accounting standards.

It will be seen that this work is not dissimilar to that which a competent accountant would perform if he was asked to prepare financial statements without carrying out an audit. What the reviewer would *not* be required to do is collect independent evidence or carry out an examination of internal control.

32.   In formulating a report appropriate to a review there are three basic options:

(a)   a disclaimer of opinion stating that a review rather than an audit has been carried out;

(b)   (a) above, together with a statement along the lines 'the financial statements are in accordance with the underlying records and with the explanations and information given to us';

(c)   a form of negative assurance such as 'we are not aware of any circumstances which suggest that the financial statements do not show a true and fair view'.

The first two options have the advantage that the accountant makes it clear that he has not carried out an audit. It is suggested, however, that the third form would be the most useful provided the scope of the work carried out by the review is clearly defined. This might be done, for example, in an appropriate review standard produced by the APC. The third form is also similar to that used successfully in the US where reviews of small company financial statements have been conducted for many years.

33.   The following specimen form of *accountants'* report illustrates the 'negative comfort' approach of option (c) above:

ACCOUNTANTS' REPORT TO THE MEMBERS OF XYZ LIMITED

We have reviewed the accompanying financial statements set out on pages ... to ... in accordance with approved Review Standards and have obtained the information and explanations which we required for this purpose.

Our review which consisted primarily of enquiries, comparisons and discussions was substantially less in scope than an audit, and in particular did not include the independent verification of information supplied to us. It is, therefore, inappropriate for us to express an audit opinion on the financial statements.

> Having carried out our review, we report that the financial statements are in accordance with the underlying records. We are not aware of any material respects in which the financial statements do not show a true and fair view of the state of the company's affairs at 31 December 19X0 and of its profit for the year ended on that date or fail to comply with the Companies Act 1985.

34. The argument for a review promoted by this Audit Brief was lost. Furthermore, review does not merit mention in the DTI's 'Accounting and audit requirements for small firms' consultative document. However, should there ultimately be any relaxation in the audit requirements for small companies it could well be that the concept of review might yet be revived as an alternative.

Unaudited financial statements

35. Many accountants in professional practice frequently prepare financial statements for clients but do not audit them. This may, for example, occur when the client is a sole trader or a partnership. Although the accountant has not signed an audit report, there is always a chance that the client will imply to a third party that they have been approved by his accountant. It is therefore important for the accountant, where his name is in any way associated with financial information which has not been audited, to make quite clear the precise capacity in which he has acted, and the extent of the work he has performed. This means that before agreeing to prepare or review, but not audit, financial information it is advisable for the accountant to obtain written instructions setting out precisely as possible his duties (mention of 'review' indicates that, although this term does not yet have any statutory or regulatory status with regard to limited companies, it is a concept the accountant is familiar with in the context of non-statutory engagements).

36. In all cases where an accountant's name is associated with any unaudited financial statements, he should attach to them a report outlining the work he has done and the status of the financial information reported on. The word 'audit' should be avoided except to say that no audit has been carried out.

37. Even when an accountant has not carried out an audit, he cannot entirely avoid responsibility for materially misleading statements where a minimum review would have revealed the true facts.

Any financial statements should conform with generally accepted accounting principles. Where unusual accounting principles have been followed these should be spelled out in the accountant's report.

Engagement letter

38. In any non-audit engagement the responsibility of the accountant and the extent of the work he carries out are governed by the instructions of the client. The client must be asked to put his instructions in writing, and in order to ensure that this is achieved the accountant employs the technique of drafting a confirmatory engagement letter for the client to endorse.

39. Although the detail of each letter must, of course, be drafted in terms appropriate to the particular engagement, there are, with regard to any non-audit assignment, three points which must always be stressed. These are:

(a) that an audit is not carried out and that this is a fact to which the accountant's report will refer;

(b) that the accounts will contain a declaration by the client that he has made available all relevant records and information for their preparation; and

(c) that the work carried out should not be relied upon to disclose defalcations and irregularities.

40. The details of accountancy work should be sufficiently informative to make clear the scope of the work to be carried out. If the scope or nature of the assignment changes at any time, the accountant must write a further letter to confirm the changed circumstances.

Assistance in reducing work

41. The engagement letter will indicate precisely the accountancy (and taxation) responsibilities and in most circumstances the accountant will rely on the client to prepare for him necessary summary information to help him provide his service on the most cost effective basis. It is generally politic to indicate to the client as early as possible after appointment the particular areas in which he can take some action to reduce the workload.

Planning, controlling and recording

42. The accountant must ensure that his accountancy work is performed to the same high standard as his audit work, hence such assignments require a degree of planning and controlling and working paper preparation must be of consistent quality.

43. Generally, the chronological sequence of events applicable to an accountancy engagement will be on the following lines:
    - hold initial meeting with client
    - prepare budget/design or update accounts preparation programme
    - brief staff
    - receive books etc from client (or attend at client's premises)
    - write up books and/or draft accounts (scope will be as agreed in the engagement letter)
    - discuss draft accounts with client
    - close off ledgers and return books to client
    - send final accounts to client for approval and signature
    - prepare and submit fee account
    - submit approved accounts to appropriate parties
      - Inland Revenue (with tax returns)
      - Bank
    - close files.

Nature of work to be performed

44. It is often difficult to decide how much work should be carried out in the absence of a full audit, but inevitably some of the work will have an audit flavour, invoking analytical review techniques and limited substantive testing of balances rather than transactions. The following minimum procedures might constitute such a review for an unincorporated concern:

(a) reasonableness check (analytical review):
   (i)   check key figures and ratios:
       - gross profit; and
       - debtors to sales;
   (ii) obtain explanations for marked differences between the figures in the accounts under review and those for previous years;
   (iii) review the accounting records for large or unusual items;
   (iv) review the accounts for conformity with generally accepted accounting principles including SSAPs;

(b) balance sheet verification:
   (i)   cash: obtain bank certificate and check reconciliations;
   (ii) debtors: examine:
       - control account reconciliations;
       - larger accounts for subsequent receipts;
       - adequacy of bad debt provision;
   (iii) creditors: examine:
       - control account reconciliations;
       - larger creditors against supplier statements;
       - larger accounts for subsequent payments;
       - reconciliation of VAT, PAYE and NIC;
   (iv) stock: enquire into and examine material aspects of period end cut-off. Scrutinise opening and closing stock sheets and test check arithmetic. If stock has been estimated, this fact should be indicated on the face of the balance sheet;
   (v)   fixed assets: examine
       - reconciliation of opening and closing balances;
       - major additions and disposals;
       - computations and consistency of depreciation.

Client's approval

45. After discussion with the proprietor or partners at the conclusion of the work and before signing the accountant's report, the accountant should obtain the client's approval of the financial statements, preferably in writing. A practical way of obtaining this is to attach to the financial statements a certificate of approval for the client to sign. Such a certificate might read:

ACCOUNTS APPROVAL CERTIFICATE

Approval of accounts to................19.....

I/we approve these accounts and confirm that I/we have made available all relevant records and information for their preparation and give my/our authority for these to be submitted to the Inland Revenue.

Accountant's report

46. Having carried out a minimum review, it is then possible to issue a report, which on unaudited financial statements should always be described as an 'accountants' report', and which might read as follows:

ACCOUNTANTS' REPORT TO..............

In accordance with your instructions we have prepared without audit the accounts set out on pages ... to ... from your books and records and from information and explanations supplied to us. (We have carried out procedures to the limited extent agreed between us in writing on ....19....)

Arthur Daley & Co
Date:.......

Modified accounts

47. The 1981 Act introduced the concept of 'modified' accounts, a dispensation permitting certain companies defined as 'small' or 'medium-sized' to file an abbreviated set of accounts with the Registrar of Companies, referred to as the modified accounts, in substitution for the full accounts approved by the shareholders.

48. A company is treated as a 'small' company, or as a 'medium-sized' company if it does not exceed more than one of the criteria in the relevant section of the table detailed below (S 248 CA85):

Category	Criteria	
Small	'Turnover' not more than	£2,000,000
	'Balance sheet total' not more than	£975,000
	'Average' number of employees not more than	50
Medium-sized	'Turnover' not more than	£8,000,000
	'Balance sheet total' not more than	£3,900,000
	'Average' number of employees not more than	250

49. It should be carefully noted that all companies must continue to prepare full accounts for presentation to their shareholders and that the exemptions only apply to the details which have to be filed with the Registrar of Companies.

50. When considering whether or not the above criteria apply to a company, the following definitions are used.

   (a) *Turnover:* here conforms to its generally accepted definition. If the accounting period of a company is not a period of twelve calendar months, then the maximum figure of turnover set out in the table will have to be proportionately adjusted;
   (b) *Balance sheet total:* should be taken as the sum of all the assets, without any deduction for liabilities;
   (c) *Average number of employees:* must be determined on a weekly basis. That is to say, the number of full-time plus part-time employees (who are each treated as one for this purpose) in each week of the year must be totalled. The sum of the weekly totals is then divided by the number of weeks in the accounting period to arrive at the average.

51. Other than those companies which are specifically excluded from doing so by the Act, all classes of companies may take advantage of the provisions relating to modified accounts. Those companies which are specifically excluded from taking advantage of the provisions are:

(a) *public* companies (however small);

(b) banking, insurance or shipping companies (as defined by the Act);

(c) companies which are members of an ineligible group (basically an ineligible group is one which contains any company falling within category (a) or (b) above).

52. Generally speaking, a company may be regarded as small or medium-sized in the financial year to which the accounts relate if it meets the required conditions in respect of both the current year and the previous year. If a company fails to meet the required conditions in a future year its status will not be lost in that year. However, if the failure were to run into a second consecutive year, then the status would be lost. Once a company has lost its status, it will have to meet the required conditions for two consecutive years before the status can be regained. These conditions are hence the ones that apply to established companies. There were special transitional provisions for established companies when the Act was implemented - these are fortunately now behind us.

53. A newly incorporated company may be regarded as being small or medium-sized in its first year of trading if it meets the required conditions for that year. This is an exception to the general rule that a company must meet the criteria in two consecutive years in order that it may be regarded as small or medium-sized.

The small company modifications

54. Where a company is classified as a small company, it may elect to file modified accounts with the Registrar of Companies comprising only an abbreviated version of its normal balance sheet and certain specified notes. A small company need *not* file a profit and loss account, a directors' report, or any information relating to the emoluments of directors, or higher paid employees, nor indeed a source and application of funds (this latter exemption arises not by virtue of the Act, but because modified accounts are not intended to give a true and fair view and hence the *disclosure* requirements of SSAPs do not apply, including SSAP10).

55. The abbreviated balance sheet need only show the total amount for each category of asset and liability, as designated by a letter or Roman numeral in the two permissible balance sheet formats in Schedule 4 of the 1985 Act. It should be noted, however, that the aggregate amount of debtors and creditors must be split between the amounts receivable or payable within one year and the amounts receivable or payable in more than one year. (The split must be disclosed either on the face of the balance sheet or in the notes.)

56. Under these exceptions for small companies, only the following disclosure requirements of Schedule 4 apply in respect of the notes to the financial statements:

(a) accounting policies;

(b) share capital;

(c) particulars of allotments;

(d) particulars of creditors payable in over five years, and particulars of security given;

(e) the basis used in translating foreign currency amounts into sterling.

The medium-sized company modifications

57. Where a company is classified as a medium-sized company, then it may file modified accounts which will comprise a full balance sheet, notes and directors' report, but only an abbreviated version of its profit and loss account. The modifications in respect of the profit and loss account mean that the following items can be combined and shown as one item under the heading of 'gross profit or loss':

    (a) *in the formats where expenses are classified by function:*
        Turnover, cost of sales, gross profit or loss and other operating income;
    (b) *in the formats where expenses are classified by type:*
        Turnover, change in stocks of finished goods and in work-in-progress, own work capitalised, other operating income, raw materials and consumables, and other external charges.

58. In addition to the above, the notes to the financial statements may omit the analysis of turnover and profit or loss before taxation called for in Schedule 4 paragraph 55 of the Act. There are no further exemptions with respect to the notes.

59. It will be appreciated, therefore, that the medium-sized company modifications are considerably less dramatic than those for the small company. Nevertheless as such modified accounts are also not intended to give a true and fair view, no source and application of funds will be necessary for the same reason as identified above for small company modified accounts. There is, however, nothing to prevent companies from including information required to be disclosed by SSAPs - including SSAP10 - if they wish to do so.

60. *Eligibility of groups and holding companies*
    For the purpose of determining whether a holding company should be classified as a small or medium-sized company, a group of companies must be viewed as though it were a single entity. If, in aggregate, the group companies fall within the relevant criteria, then, as appropriate, the holding company may be classified as small or medium-sized.

61. Where the holding company itself would be classified as a small company, but the group would be viewed as medium-sized, then the holding company must also be considered as medium-sized for the purposes of its individual accounts. By the same token, if the group does not meet the criteria for a medium-sized company, then the holding company is not entitled to any exemptions in respect of its individual accounts, even though the holding company itself *did* fall within the relevant criteria.

62. If a holding company is entitled to submit modified individual accounts and the directors rely on the exemptions in delivering any such accounts to the Registrar of Companies, they may also deliver modified group accounts in respect of the same period, as opposed to full group accounts prepared under the 1985 Act.

The auditors' responsibilities

63. Where modified accounts are filed, the balance sheet must include, immediately above the directors' signatures, a statement by the directors that they are entitled to file modified accounts. An example of such a statement, which would comply with the Act, would be as follows:

"We have relied on the exemptions for individual accounts, in accordance with Sections 247 to 249 Companies Act 1985, on the grounds that XYZ Limited is entitled to the benefit of those exemptions as a (small/medium-sized) company."

64. Before modified accounts are filed it will be necessary for the company's auditors to consider whether, in their opinion, the conditions required for exemption have been satisfied. Where the auditors are not satisfied in this respect, they must report this fact to the directors, and in this situation, the company could not properly proceed with the production of modified accounts.

65. Where the auditors are satisfied that the requirements of the Act have been met then they must prepare a 'special report' to this effect. This report needs to express the auditors' opinion that the directors are entitled to deliver modified accounts as claimed in the directors' statement and that the accounts have been 'properly prepared' in accordance with Schedule 8 of the Act. The 'special report' must include the full text of the auditors' report under section 236 of the Act. An example of such a report, which should be addressed to the directors of the company, is set out below:

AUDITORS' REPORT TO THE DIRECTORS UNDER PARAGRAPH 10
SCHEDULE 8 OF THE COMPANIES ACT 1985

In our opinion the directors are entitled under sections 247-249 of the Companies Act 1985 to deliver modified accounts in respect of the year ended 31 December 19XX, and the modified accounts on pages .... to .... have been properly prepared in accordance with Schedule 8 of that Act.

We reported, as auditors of XYZ Limited, to the members on (date) on the company's financial statements prepared under section 227 of the Companies Act 1985 for the year ended 31 December 19XX, and our audit opinion was as follows:

"We have audited the financial statements on pages ... to ... in accordance with Auditing Standards.

In our opinion the financial statements give a true and fair view of the state of the company's affairs at 31 December 19XX and of its profit and source and application of funds for the year then ended and have been properly prepared in accordance with the Companies Act 1985."

Arthur Daley & Co, Certified Accountants
(date)

The report above will be delivered to the registrar with the modified accounts.

66. It is felt that the work performed by the auditor on a company's main financial statements coupled with a review of the modified accounts is under normal circumstances, sufficient for the purposes of making the required reports.

67. The auditors' review of the modified accounts is aimed at ensuring that they include, as appropriate, at least the minimum information referred to above and that the amounts therein agree with the corresponding amounts in the company's full financial statements. It should be remembered that an audit as such is not required, and that, as previously stated, the modified accounts are not intended to give a true and fair view.

68. In a situation where there is to be a change of auditors, it would be preferable that the retiring auditor reports on the modified accounts. If this does not happen, the new auditor will have to adopt the procedures he would normally perform in preparation for his first audit of the full financial statements. Such procedures should be in accord with the APC's Auditing Guideline 'Amounts derived from the preceding financial statements', and might include correspondence with the previous auditor concerning his audit work in respect of the year just ended, and an inspection of the company's accounting records for the year.

69. The auditor must consider whether he can report under the Act where the audit report on the main financial statements has been qualified in the current or previous period in relation to one of the criteria for exemption. He must be satisfied that the maximum effect of the qualification does not take the turnover and/or total assets over the exemption limits.

70. Where the auditors' qualification on the main financial statements does not affect the turnover or 'items' included in the balance sheet total, then it would not normally affect the auditors' opinion in his Schedule 8 report. The auditor will not need to expand his report on the modified accounts to clarify his qualified opinion on the main financial statements.

71. There is no provision in the Act for filing of a qualified special report under Schedule 8 Para 10 (1) with the Registrar of Companies. It would appear, therefore, that the directors would be in breach of the Act, if modified accounts were delivered to the Registrar with other than an unqualified Schedule 8 report from the auditor.

Dormant companies

72. Under the Companies Act 1985 S252 a company which:

   (a) is not required to prepare group accounts;
   (b) is entitled to the benefit of the accounting exemptions applicable to 'small' companies, or would have been so entitled but for the fact that it was a member of an ineligible group; and
   (c) has been dormant since the end of the previous financial period,

   may agree, by *special resolution*, not to appoint an auditor.

73. Any such resolution should be passed at a general meeting of the company at which a set of the company's financial statements prepared under Section 241 are laid, or before a company's first such general meeting if it has been dormant since incorporation.

74. A company will be regarded as dormant during any period where no 'significant accounting transaction' occurs. Such a transaction is defined as one which is required under Section 221 to be entered into the company's accounting records, except for one arising from the taking of shares in the company by a subscriber to the memorandum.

75. Where the directors file the accounts of a dormant company which has resolved not to appoint an auditor, they should not attach a statement as required by Schedule 8 of the Act concerning modified accounts. Instead, there should be added to the balance sheet a statement that the company was dormant throughout the financial period. No special auditors' report will be required.

76. Where a company which has taken advantage of the above provisions ceases to be dormant, or, for some other reason, becomes ineligible, it immediately ceases to be exempt from the obligation to appoint an auditor. An auditor must be appointed by the directors (or if they do not do so, the shareholders may do so) to hold office until the conclusion of the next general meeting at which accounts are laid.

77. Once a company has passed a special resolution excluding it from the obligation to appoint auditors the previously incumbent auditors (if any) clearly have no further statutory duties as auditors.

78. The provisions in respect of dormant companies are particularly designed to help public groups with dormant subsidiaries, but group auditors should be alive to situations in which a dormant company may cease to qualify where, for example, there is a change in group structure so that the dormant subsidiary becomes a holding company required to prepare group accounts.

79. It should be noted, in passing, that the dormant company as defined above is currently the only class of company that can dispense with an audit. It remains to be seen, in due course, whether the latest government initiatives proposing the abolition of the audit of 'small' companies will find favour and reach the statute book.

Publication of accounts other than by filing

80. Modified accounts are, we have established, a 'slimmed down' version of the shareholders' accounts. Modified accounts must not be confused with another concept introduced originally by the Companies Act 1981 - 'abridged accounts'.

81. Abridged accounts are taken to be any statement purporting to be a balance sheet or profit and loss account dealing with any *financial year*, which is published separately from the company's 'full' financial statements, and will include such reports as preliminary announcements. Full financial statements in this context *includes* modified accounts. In other words, full financial statements are the accounts to be laid before the company in general meeting and delivered to the registrar of companies.

82. Where a company publishes 'abridged accounts' in a newspaper or elsewhere, the Act requires the company to publish with them, a statement indicating (S255(3) CA 1985):

   (a) that the accounts are not full;
   (b) whether full individual or group accounts have been filed with the Registrar of Companies;
   (c) whether the auditors have reported on the company's full accounts for the period under S236; and
   (d) whether the auditor's report was unqualified.

A company is *prohibited* by the Act from reproducing the text of the auditor's report on the full financial statements alongside the abridged accounts.

83. Where the auditor's report on the full financial statements has been qualified the company might wish to insert an 'explanation' for it in part (d) of the statement which has to be published with the abridged accounts. Any such 'explanation' may or may not be wholly factual. Whilst the Act places no responsibility upon the auditor in relation to such statement, he should be aware of the possibility of the company seeking to provide an explanation for any qualification given by the auditor. If possible the auditor should try to obtain a preview of the statement, before it is published, with a view to advising the directors, as necessary, on its wording.

84. Conversely, where a company publishes 'full' financial statements, it *must* also publish the auditor's report. Where a company which is obliged to prepare group accounts publishes full individual financial statements, then its group and individual accounts must be published together, along with the auditor's report; and where a company publishes full group accounts without full individual ones, it must also publish the relevant auditor's report (S254 CA 1985).

Summary

85. This chapter is concerned with the practical and the topical. Appreciate the operational *and* reporting problems confronting the auditor of small companies. Be prepared for general and specific questions on the operational approach. Remember that the design of substantive tests of transactions and balances is considered in detail in earlier chapters; this chapter merely stresses the need for the auditor, when gathering audit evidence, to adopt a broadly substantive approach.

86. The resurrection of proposals for the abolition of the audit of small companies clearly presents a golden opportunity for the examiner to test a student's awareness of current developments. As with all contentious issues, be prepared to argue for and against the proposition, whatever your convictions.

87. Be sure that you master both the accounting *and* audit implications of modified accounts and the related area of dormant companies.

TEST YOUR KNOWLEDGE
Numbers in brackets refer to paragraphs in this chapter

1. What control types are likely to be lacking or inadequate in a small company? (6)

2. What minimum business controls would be appropriate to mail opening and receipts in a small company? (10).

3. Can an auditor justify an unqualified opinion on the accounts of a small company? (12(c)(i))

4. If the auditor determines that he needs to accept the assurances of management as to the completeness of the accounting records, in respect of what matters must the auditor satisfy himself? (12(c)(iii))

5. Draft in full a qualified audit report reflecting the circumstances in 4 above. (13)

6. What additional paragraph might be inserted into the engagement letter for a small company? (18)

7. What three special points should be stressed in a non-audit assignment engagement letter? (39)

8. Draft an accountant's report applicable to unaudited financial statements. (46)

9. When may a company be treated as:
   (a) 'small'
   (b) 'medium sized'? (48)

10. What is the meaning of 'balance sheet total'? (50)

11. What classes of company are specifically excluded from filing modified accounts? (51)

12. What notes to the accounts are required in 'small company' accounts? (56)

13. Can a holding company file modified accounts? (60)

14. What is a dormant company? (74)

15. How and when may a dormant company dispense with its auditors? (72)

Chapter 16

THE AUDIT OF COMPUTERISED ACCOUNTING SYSTEMS

Topics covered in this chapter:

- The nature and importance of controls in a computer environment
- The auditor's operational approach
- The auditor's use of CAATs
- Control problems in small computer systems

Introduction

1. The advent of mini and micro computers has had a spectacular effect on the business environment – the use of computers for accounting purposes in particular has dramatically increased. This expansion will certainly continue and the auditor must hence be able to cope with the special problems that arise when auditing in a computer environment and keep abreast of technical innovation. This chapter investigates the main areas of concern to the auditor.

2. First we look in a rather general way at the nature of controls in a computer environment and the auditor's operational approach. Broad guidance is provided for the auditor in the form of the operational guideline 'Auditing in a computer environment' issued by the APC in June 1984. The introduction to this guideline sets the scene:

    > "Auditing standards prescribe the basic principles and practices to be followed in the conduct of an audit. The auditor's operational standard and the guidelines on planning, controlling and recording, accounting systems, audit evidence, internal controls and review of financial statements apply irrespective of the system of recording and processing transactions. However, computer systems do record and process transactions in a manner which is significantly different from manual systems, giving rise to such possibilities as a lack of visible evidence and systematic errors. As a result, when auditing in a computer environment, the auditor will need to take into account additional considerations relating to the techniques available to him, the timing of his work, the form in which the accounting records are maintained, the internal controls which exist, the availability of the data and the length of time it is retained in readily usable form, as further described below.

Computers have a wide range of capabilities and changes continue to be made as a result of new technology. With the introduction of smaller computers, there is greater likelihood of weak internal controls. This will normally lead to greater emphasis being placed on substantive testing of transactions and balances, and on other procedures such as analytical review, rather than on compliance testing. Furthermore, where smaller volumes of transactions are processed, substantive testing may in the circumstances be the more efficient method of obtaining audit evidence."

3. The comments in the initial sections of this chapter are, in the main, derived from the guideline. In later sections we move beyond the scope of the guideline to examine, in greater detail, control and audit problems posed by minis and micros.

The nature and importance of controls in a computer environment

4. Internal controls over computer based accounting systems may conveniently be considered under the following two main headings.

   (a) *Application controls*. These relate to the transactions and standing data appertaining to each computer-based accounting system and are therefore specific to each such application. The objectives of application controls, which may be manual or programmed, are to ensure the completeness and accuracy of the accounting records and the validity of the entries made therein resulting from both manual and programmed processing.

   (b) *General controls*. Controls, other than application controls, which relate to the environment within which computer based accounting systems are developed, maintained and operated, and which are therefore applicable to all the applications. The objectives of general controls are to ensure the proper development and implementation of applications and the integrity of program and data files and of computer operations. Like application controls, general controls may be either manual or programmed.

5. Application controls and general controls are inter-related. Strong general controls contribute to the assurance which may be obtained by an auditor in relation to application controls. On the other hand, unsatisfactory general controls may undermine strong application controls or exacerbate unsatisfactory application controls.

6. The draft version of the guideline 'Auditing in a computer environment' contained useful appendices identifying typical, and desirable, application and general controls. The authorised guideline did not retain these appendices; nevertheless, a relatively detailed knowledge of controls *is* required, so consequently the appendices are reproduced below in order to put some meat on the bare bones of the definitions in paragraph 4.

Examples of application controls

7. To achieve the overall objectives of application controls identified in paragraph 4 (a) above, the specific requirements are:
   (a) controls over the completeness, accuracy and authorisation of input;
   (b) controls over the completeness and accuracy of processing;
   (c) controls over the maintenance of master files and the standing data contained therein.

8. *Controls over input*
   Control techniques for ensuring the completeness of input in a timely fashion include:
   (a) manual or programmed agreement of control totals;
   (b) one for one checking of processed output to source documents;
   (c) manual or programmed sequence checking;
   (d) programmed matching of input to a control file, containing details of expected input;
   (e) procedures over resubmission of rejected controls.

9. Controls over the accuracy of input are concerned with the data fields on input transactions. Control should be exercised not only over value fields, such as invoice amounts, but also important reference fields, such as account number or date of payment. Some of the completeness control techniques, such as a batch total, will also control accuracy but others, such as sequence checks, will not. Additional techniques to ensure accuracy include:

   (a) programmed check digit verification (a check digit included in a reference number is arithmetically checked to ensure that it bears the required relationship to the rest of the number);
   (b) programmed reasonableness checks, including checking the logical relationship between two or more files;
   (c) programmed existence checks against valid codes;
   (d) manual scrutiny of output.

10. Controls over authorisation involve checking that all transactions are authorised and that the individual who authorised each transaction was so empowered. This will generally involve a clerical review of input transactions, although a programmed check to detect transactions that exceed authorisation limits may be possible. The clerical review should be done either after a control total has been established or after processing, to ensure that unauthorised transactions cannot be introduced after the review.

11. *Controls over processing*
    Controls are required to ensure that:
    (a) all input data is processed;
    (b) the correct master files and standing data files are used;
    (c) the processing of each transaction is accurate;
    (d) the updating of data, and any new data generated during processing, is accurate and authorised;
    (e) output reports are complete and accurate.

12. The control techniques used to ensure the completeness and accuracy of input may also be used to ensure the completeness and accuracy of processing provided the techniques are applied to the results of processing, such as a batch reconciliation produced after the update and not the one produced after the initial edit. Another technique for ensuring the completeness and accuracy of processing is summary processing.

13. *Controls over master files and the standing data contained therein*
    Techniques for ensuring the completeness, accuracy and authorisation of amendments to master files and standing data files and for ensuring the completeness and accuracy of the processing of these amendments are similar to the techniques for transaction input. However, in view of the

greater importance of master files and standing data, there is often sufficient justification for using the more costly control techniques such as one for one checking. It may also be appropriate to users to check all master files and standing data, perhaps on a cyclical basis.

Controls are also required to ensure the continuing correctness of master files and the standing data contained therein. Frequently control techniques such as *record counts or hash totals* for the file, are established and checked by the user each time the file is used.

Examples of general controls

14. To achieve the overall objectives of general controls identified in paragraph 4 (b) above, controls are required:
    (a) over application development;
    (b) to prevent or detect unauthorised changes to programs;
    (c) to ensure that all program changes are adequately tested and documented;
    (d) to prevent or detect errors during program execution;
    (e) to prevent unauthorised amendments to data files;
    (f) to ensure that systems software is properly installed and maintained;
    (g) to ensure that proper documentation is kept; and
    (h) to ensure continuity of operations.

15. *Controls over application development*
    The auditor might consider the adequacy of such matters as: system design standards, programming standards, documentation controls and standards, texting procedures, approval of development stages by users and computer management, internal audit involvement, segregation of duties for system design, programming and operations, training and supervision.

16. *Controls to prevent or detect unauthorised changes to programs*
    This covers both accidental and fraudulent corruption of program logic during program maintenance or program execution. In addition to such matters as the segregation of duties and the training and supervision of staff for program maintenance, the auditor would consider such matters as: authorisation of jobs prior to processing, the record of program changes and its review to detect unauthorised changes, password protection of programs, emergency modification procedures, integrity of back up copies of programs, physical protection of production programs and programs stored off-line, and comparison of production programs to controlled copies. For program execution, the auditor would consider: the operations manual procedures to prevent access to programs during execution, controls over use of utility programs, restricted access to the computer and remote terminals, review of job accounting reports and investigation of unusual delays, and rotation of duties.

17. *Controls to ensure that all program changes are adequately tested and documented*
    As program changes may range from a small alteration of an output report to a major redesign, most installations will have more than one set of standards for testing and documenting changes. The auditor would consider the adequacy of such matters as: testing procedures, documentation controls and standards, approval of changes by users and computer management, internal audit involvement, and segregation of duties, training and supervision of the staff involved.

18. *Controls to prevent or detect errors during program execution*
The auditor might consider the adequacy of operations controls included in the systems software, use of job control procedure libraries, an operations manual detailing set up and execution procedures, job scheduling, emergency back up procedures and training and supervision. These procedures should provide protection against errors such as incorrect data files, wrong versions of production programs, running programs in the wrong sequence, incorrect response to a program request and job control errors.

19. *Controls to prevent unauthorised amendment to data files*
Controls to prevent unauthorised amendments to data files are dependent upon the application controls over the file, the manner in which the file is maintained and the file management software used. The auditor might consider the adequacy of such general control procedures as: authorisation of jobs prior to processing, procedures to detect unauthorised amendments, password protection and procedures for recording and investigating unauthorised access attempts, emergency modification procedures, integrity of back up files, physical protection of data files, restricted use of utility programs and the segregation of duties.

20. *Controls to ensure that systems software is properly installed and maintained*
Systems software includes the operating system, teleprocessing monitors, data base management systems, spooling systems and other software used to increase the efficiency of processing and to control processing. The auditor should consider not only the controls exercised by the software but also the controls over the software, such as: frequency of amendments, amendment procedures, access controls and the segregation of duties.

21. *Controls to ensure that proper documentation is kept*
Proper documentation aids efficient and accurate operations by users and computer personnel, setting up and amendments to applications, and recovery from disaster. The auditor would consider such matters as: quality of documentation, quality of standards used, enforcement of standards, internal audit involvement and updating procedures.

22. *Controls to ensure continuity of operation*
As part of his overall assessment of the enterprise the auditor might consider the back up procedures, testing of back up facilities and procedures, protection of equipment against fire and other hazards, emergency and disaster recovery procedures, maintenance agreements and insurance.

Auditor's operational approach – an overview

23. Audits are performed in a computer environment wherever computer-based accounting systems, large or small, are operated by an enterprise, or by a third party on behalf of the enterprise, for the purpose of processing information supporting the amounts included in the financial statements.

24. The nature of computer-based accounting systems is such that the auditor is afforded opportunities to use either the enterprise's or another computer to assist him in the performance of his audit work. Techniques performed with computers in this way are known as Computer Assisted Audit Techniques (CAATs) of which the following are the major categories:

(a) *Use of audit software* - computer programs used for audit purposes to examine the contents of the enterprise's computer files;

(b) *Use of test data*- data used by the auditor for computer processing to test the operation of the enterprise's computer programs.

Audit software and test data are considered in detail later in the chapter.

25. Where there is a computer-based accounting system, many of the auditor's procedures may still be carried out manually. For instance, the ascertainment of the accounting system and the assessment of its adequacy will normally be performed manually, and in appropriate circumstances the auditor may also decide to select manual audit techniques.

Knowledge and skills

26. When auditing in a computer environment, the auditor should obtain a basic understanding of the fundamentals of data processing and a level of technical computer knowledge and skills which, depending on the circumstances, may need to be extensive. This is because the auditor's knowledge and skills need to be appropriate to the environment in which he is auditing, and because ethical statements indicate that he should not undertake or continue professional work which he is not himself competent to perform unless he obtains such advice and assistance as will enable him competently to carry out his task. The impact of the computer environment on the conduct of the audit is now considered by looking at each paragraph of the operational standard in turn.

Planning, controlling and recording

27. Paragraph 2 of 'The auditor's operational standard' states that 'the auditor should adequately plan, control and record his work'. The principles relating to planning, controlling and recording are the same in a computer environment as in other circumstances, but there are additional considerations that need to be taken into account.

28. *Planning*
    In order to plan and carry out an audit in a computer environment, the auditor will need an appropriate level of technical knowledge and skill. As part of his additional planning considerations, he should decide at an early stage what effect the system itself and the way it is operated, will have on the timing of and the manner in which he will need to perform and record his work. In this respect he may have had the opportunity to consider these matters during the development and implementation of the system.

29. The auditor should also consider the use of CAATs, as this may have a significant effect on the nature, extent and timing of his audit tests. As indicated in paragraph 30 below, in certain circumstances the auditor will need to use CAATs in order to obtain the evidence he requires, whereas in other circumstances he may use CAATs to improve the efficiency or effectiveness of his audit. For example, the availability of audit software may mean that substantive tests can be performed more economically or quickly than substantive tests performed manually, which may persuade him to place less reliance on internal controls and to reduce his compliance testing accordingly.

30. In choosing the appropriate combination of CAATs and manual procedures, the auditor will need inter alia to take the following into account.

    (a) Computer programs often perform functions of which no visible evidence is available. In these circumstances it will frequently not be practicable for the auditor to perform tests manually.

    (b) In many audit situations the auditor will have the choice of performing a test either manually or with the assistance of a CAAT. In making this choice, he will be influenced by the respective efficiency of the alternatives, taking into account:
        (i)   the extent of compliance or substantive testing achieved by both alternatives;
        (ii) the pattern of cost associated with the CAAT;
        (iii) the ability to incorporate within the use of the CAAT a number of different audit tests.

    (c) In some cases, the auditor will need to report within a comparatively short time-scale. In such cases it may be more efficient to use CAATs because they are quicker to apply, even though manual methods are practicable and may cost less.

    (d) There is a need before using a CAAT to ensure that the required computer facilities, computer files and programs are available. Furthermore, given that enterprises do not retain copies of computer files and programs for an indefinite period, the auditor should plan the use of any CAAT in good time so that these copies are retained for his use.

    (e) The operation of some CAATs requires frequent attendance or access by the auditor. The auditor may be able to reduce the level of his tests by taking account of CAATs performed by the internal auditors, but the extent to which he can do this in any given situation will depend, amongst other things, on his assessment of the effectiveness and relevance of the internal audit function.

    (f) Where the enterprise's accounting records include computer data, the auditor will need to have access to that data. Further, where the auditor wishes to perform a CAAT, it is often necessary for the enterprise to make computer facilities available to the auditor to enable him to discharge his responsibilities.

31. *Controlling*
    Whether or not the audit is being carried out in a computer environment, audit procedures should always be controlled to ensure that the work has been performed in a competent manner. Where CAATs are used, however, particular attention should be paid to:

    (a) the need to co-ordinate the work of staff with specialist computer skills with the work of others engaged on the audit;
    (b) the approval and review of the technical work by someone with the necessary computer expertise.

32. It is acceptable for an auditor to use a CAAT on copies of computer records or programs, provided he has taken steps to gain reasonable assurance that the copies are identical to the originals.

33. *Recording*

    The standard of the audit working papers relating to computer-based accounting systems, and the retention procedures in respect of them, should be the same as those adopted in relation to other aspects of the audit. Where the technical papers differ materially from the other working papers, for instance where they consist of computer output of magnetic media, it may be convenient to keep these separate from the other working papers.

34. Where a CAAT is used, it is appropriate that the working papers indicate the work performed by the CAAT, the results of the CAAT, the auditor's conclusions, the manner in which any technical problems were resolved and may include any recommendations about the modification of the CAAT for future audits.

Accounting systems

35. Paragraph 3 of 'The Auditor's Operational Standard' states that 'the auditor should ascertain the enterprise's system of recording and processing transactions and assess its adequacy as a basis for the preparation of financial statements'. The principles relating to this are the same in a computer environment, but it should be borne in mind that many computer-based accounting systems are specified in far greater detail than non-computer-based accounting systems. In assessing the adequacy of the accounting system as a basis for the preparation of financial statements, the auditor is likely to receive a more detailed record of the enterprise's system than would otherwise be the case.

Audit evidence

36. Paragraph 4 of 'The Auditor's Operational Standard' states that 'the auditor should obtain relevant and reliable audit evidence sufficient to enable him to draw reasonable conclusions therefrom'. The principles relating to the obtaining of audit evidence do not change because the audit is being carried out in a computer environment.

37. However, the availability of computer facilities results in opportunities for auditors to use computers. CAATs may be used at various stages of an audit to obtain audit evidence. For instance where the auditor chooses to place reliance on internal controls, he may use a CAAT to assist in the performance of compliance tests. Furthermore, he may also use CAATs to perform substantive tests, including analytical review procedures.

Internal controls

38. Paragraph 5 of 'The Auditor's Operational Standard' states that 'if the auditor wishes to place reliance on any internal controls, he should ascertain and evaluate those controls, and perform compliance tests on their operation'. The principles relating to internal controls are the same in a computer environment as in any other environment, but there are additional considerations which are discussed in the following paragraphs.

39. As with controls in other circumstances, the evaluation of application controls and general controls will be assisted by the use of documentation designed to help identify the controls on which the auditor may wish to place reliance. Such documentation can take a variety of forms but might consist of questions asking whether there are controls in a system which meet specified overall control objectives (ICQs), or which prevent or detect the occurrence of specified errors

or omissions (ICEQs). For application controls, an integrated set of internal control questions may be used covering controls over both the manual part and the programmed part of the application, and the impact of relevant general controls.

40. Where preliminary evaluation of the application controls and general controls discloses the absence of, or uncompensated weaknesses in, controls, and therefore the auditor cannot rely on the controls, he should move directly to substantive tests which may be assisted by the use of CAATs.

41. However, where preliminary evaluation reveals application controls or general controls which may meet the auditor's objectives, he should design and carry out compliance tests if he wishes to rely on those controls. In determining whether he wishes to place reliance on application controls or general controls, the auditor will be influenced by the cost effectiveness and ease of testing and by the following matters.

   (a) Where application controls are entirely manual the auditor may decide to perform compliance tests in respect of the application controls only, rather than to place any reliance on general controls. However, before he can place reliance on application controls which involve computer programs, the auditor needs to obtain reasonable assurance that the programs have operated properly, by evaluating and testing the effect of relevant general controls or by other tests on specific parts of the programs.

   (b) Sometimes a programmed accounting procedure may not be subject to effective application controls. In such circumstances, in order to put himself in a position to limit the extent of his substantive testing, the auditor may choose to perform his compliance tests by testing the relevant general controls either manually or by using CAATs, to gain assurance of the continued and proper operation of the programmed accounting procedure. Where as a result of his compliance tests the auditor decides he cannot place reliance on the controls, he should move directly to substantive tests.

   (c) As indicated in paragraph 2, there is in a computer environment, the possibility of systematic errors. This may take place because of program faults or hardware malfunction in computer operations. However, many such potential recurrent errors should be prevented or detected by general controls over the development and implementation of applications, the integrity of the program and data files, and of computer operations. As a result, the controls which the auditor may evaluate and test may include general controls.

   (d) On the other hand, the extent to which the auditor can rely on general controls may be limited because many of these controls might not be evidenced, or because they could have been performed inconsistently. In such circumstances, which are particularly common where small computers are involved, if he wishes to limit his substantive tests, the auditor may obtain assurance from compliance tests on manual application controls or by tests on specific parts of the programs.

42. In performing compliance tests on application or general controls, the auditor should obtain evidence which is relevant to the control being tested. Procedures the auditor may consider include observing the control in operation, examining documentary evidence of its operation, or performing it again himself. In the case of programmed application controls, the auditor may test specific parts of the programs, or re-perform them, by taking advantage of CAATs. He may also obtain evidence by testing relevant general controls.

Review of financial statements

43. Paragraph 6 of 'The Auditor's Operational Standard' states that 'the auditor should carry out such a review of the financial statements as is sufficient, in conjunction with the conclusions drawn from the other audit evidence obtained, to give him a reasonable basis for his opinion on the financial statements'. CAATs (particularly audit software) may be of assistance to auditors in carrying out certain aspects of this work.

The auditor's use of CAATs

44. Traditionally, the ways in which an auditor could approach the audit of computer based systems fell into the following two categories:
    (a) 'round the computer' approach;
    (b) 'through the computer' approach.

    A few years ago it was widely considered that an accountant could discharge his duties as auditor of a company with computer based systems without having any detailed knowledge of such systems. The auditor would commonly audit 'round the computer' by ignoring the procedures which take place within the computer programs and concentrating solely on the input and corresponding output. Audit procedures would include checking authorisation, coding and control totals of input and checking the output with source documents and clerical control totals.

45. This view is now frowned upon and it is recognised that one of the principal problems facing the auditor is that of acquiring an understanding of the workings of the EDP department and of the computer itself. It is now customary for auditors to audit 'through the computer'. This involves an examination of the detailed processing routines of the computer to determine whether the controls in the system are adequate to ensure complete and correct processing of all data. With the advent of 'embedded audit facilities' (see paragraphs 57-62) we are increasingly seeing the introduction of auditing from 'within the computer'.

46. One of the major reasons why the 'round the computer' audit approach is no longer considered adequate is that as the complexity of computer systems has increased there has been a corresponding loss of audit trail. An audit trail is the means by which an individual transaction can be traced sequentially through the system from source to completion, and its loss will mean that normal audit techniques will break down.

Audit trail

47. The original concept of an audit trail was to print out data at all stages of processing so that an auditor could follow transactions stage-by-stage through a system to ensure that they had been processed correctly. Computer auditing methods have now cut out much of this laborious, time-consuming stage-by-stage working, and make use of:

    (a) a more limited audit trail;
    (b) efficient control totals;
    (c) use of enquiry facilities;
    (d) audit packages;
    (e) file dumps.

48. An audit trail should ideally be provided so that every transaction on a file contains a unique reference back to the original source of the input (eg a sales system transaction record should hold a reference to the customer order, delivery note and invoice). Where master file records are updated several times, or from several sources, the provision of a satisfactory audit trail is more difficult, but some attempt should nevertheless be made to provide one.

49. Typical audit problems that arise as audit trails move further away from the hard copy trail include:
    (a) testing computer generated totals when no detailed analysis is available;
    (b) testing the completeness of output in the absence of control totals.

    In these situations it will often be necessary to employ computer assisted audit techniques.

Types of CAAT

50. As indicated in paragraph 24 there are two principal categories of CAAT - test data and audit software. As test data has a primarily compliance objective we shall look at this technique first. Audit software is particularly appropriate to substantive testing of balances and hence will often be of greater impact during the final stages of the audit.

Test data

51. *Description*
    Audit test data consists of data submitted by the auditor for processing by the enterprise's computer based accounting system. It may be processed during a normal production run ('live' test data) or during a special run at a point in time outside the normal cycle ('dead' test data).

52. *Audit objectives*
    The primary use of test data is in compliance testing of application controls. For example, an application control to ensure the completeness of input may consist of programmed agreement of batch totals. The auditor may choose to compliance test his control by submitting test data with correct and incorrect batch totals. Rather more advanced CAATs with compliance objectives referred to as 'embedded audit facilities' are considered in paragraphs 57-62.

53. *Planning*
    The level of expertise necessary for use of audit test data and other compliance CAATs varies greatly depending on the complexity of the testing procedures. The user of test data will need at least a basic understanding of data processing and a good understanding of the accounting system and the operating environment which will process the test data. Extensive technical expertise in the areas of systems analysis, programming languages and operating systems may not be needed in a straightforward application of audit test data but may well be necessary when using an embedded audit facility.

54. In planning the use of test data the auditor should consider whether he intends to submit data during a normal production run or during a special processing run. If live test data is submitted the auditor will need to ensure that any resulting corruption of the data files is corrected. Where dead test data is submitted the auditor will need to gain reasonable assurance

that the programs processing this test data are those in use during normal processing. Where the auditor is using test data for compliance testing purposes he must also obtain reasonable assurance that the programs processing his test data were used throughout the audit period, whether by testing relevant general controls or by repeating the test at other times during the period.

55. The use of test data requires the same operational disciplines as those expected during the running of normal production data. However, as some uses of test data involve the submission of data over several processing cycles the auditor will need to control the sequence of submission with great care. In more complex circumstances it may be appropriate for the auditor to perform trials containing small amounts of test data before submitting his main audit test data. Other important points to note are:

(a) Provided that there is adequate evidence to demonstrate that the test data was run against the correct versions of the programs it is not necessary for the auditor to be present during processing. In considering the adequacy of this evidence the auditor will consider the effectiveness of the general controls at the installation.

(b) The auditor will need to predict the results of the test data separately from the test data output. He should predict the results anticipated from each transaction and not merely check off the results on the output.

56. *Recording*
As the use of test data does not always provide any visible evidence of the audit work performed, both direct and indirect evidence should also be recorded. Working papers will normally include details of the controls to be tested and an explanation of how they are to be tested, details of the transactions and master files used, details of the predicted results, the actual results and evidence of the predicted and actual results having been compared.

Embedded audit facilities

57. The use of test data provides compliance comfort to the auditor in respect of the *whole* period only if he obtains reasonable assurance that the programs processing his test data were used throughout the period under review (see paragraph 54). To allow a *continuous* review of the data recorded and the manner in which it is treated by the system, it may be possible to use CAATs referred to as 'Embedded audit facilities'. An embedded facility consists of program code or additional data provided by the auditor and incorporated into the computer element of the enterprise's accounting system. Two frequently encountered examples are:
- Integrated test facility (ITF); and
- Systems control and review file (SCARF).

58. ITF is the more complex of the two techniques. It involves the creation of a fictitious entity (eg department, customer etc) within the framework of the regular application. Transactions are then posted to the fictitious entity along with the regular transactions, and the results produced by the normal processing cycle are compared with those predetermined. It is important to ensure that the fictitious entities do not become part of the financial reporting of the organisation and several methods can be adopted to prevent this. The simplest and most secure method is to make reversing journal entries at appropriate cut-off dates. ITF enables management and auditors to keep a constant check on the internal processing functions applied to all types of valid and invalid transactions.

59. SCARF is a relatively simple technique to build into an application. It is best described by illustrating an example - in this case, a general (nominal) ledger application.

60. Each general ledger account has two fields. These are a Yes/No field indicating whether or not SCARF applies to this account; and a monetary value which is a threshold amount set by the auditor.

61. If SCARF does not apply to the account then all transactions posted to the account which have a value in excess of the threshold amount are also written to a SCARF file. The contents of that file can be read by the user, but usually can only be altered or deleted by the organisation's external auditors. The same restriction applies to the Yes/No and threshold fields associated with each account. When a new account is opened, it is automatically assigned as a SCARF account (Yes) and with a threshold of £zero. Only the external auditor can change these fields.

62. Sometimes the organisation is permitted to change the threshold, by reducing but not increasing it. To protect the auditor's exclusive access, the programs to alter threshold and clear SCARF files can be initiated by applying a formula, held only by the auditor, to a set of random numbers generated by the machine, the answer being similar to a password. SCARF thus enables the organisation and its auditor to monitor material transactions or sensitive accounts with ease and provides an assurance that all such transactions are under scrutiny.

Audit software

63. *Description*
Audit software comprises computer programs used by the auditor to examine an enterprise's computer files. It may consist of package programs or utility programs which are usually run independently of the enterprise's computer-based accounting system. It includes interrogation facilities available at the enterprise. The features of the main types of audit software are as under:

(a) *Package programs:* consist of prepared generalised programs for which the auditor will specify his detailed requirements by means of parameters, and sometimes by supplementary program code.

(b) *Purpose written programs:* involve the auditor satisfying his detailed requirements by means of program code specifically written for the purpose.

(c) *Utility programs:* consist of programs available for performing simple functions, such as sorting and printing data files.

64. *Audit objectives*
Although audit software may be used during many compliance and substantive procedures, its use is particularly appropriate during substantive testing of transactions and especially balances. By using audit software, the auditor may scrutinise large volumes of data and concentrate skilled manual resources on the investigation of results, rather than on the extraction of information.

65. During substantive testing the auditor may, for example, use audit software to reperform calculations, by adding individual transactions, to verify aged account balances, to select individual transactions for subsequent manual substantive tests, or to obtain information relevant to his analytical review.

66. When performing compliance tests of application controls, the auditor may use audit software to assist in various ways. For example, when testing the controls that ensure that completeness of input, audit software may be used to simulate programmed controls such as those used to identify any missing items from a sequence.

67. *Planning*
The level of expertise necessary for the use of audit software and its related techniques varies considerably. As a minimum, where the auditor is using generalized audit software to achieve straightforward audit objectives with simple detailed specifications, he will require a basic understanding of data processing and the enterprise's computer application together with a detailed knowledge of the audit software and the computer files to be used. Depending on the complexity of the application, the auditor may need to have a sound appreciation of systems analysis, operating systems, and where program code is used, experience of the programming language to be utilised.

68. During his planning of the use of audit software, the auditor will need to ensure that the required versions of the computer files are created and retained for his use. Similarly, he will need to ensure that appropriate computer facilities are available at a convenient time.

69. *Controlling*
In common with other computer programs, audit software requires design, compilation and testing. Although audit software normally checks the format of parameters, it cannot check to ensure that the logic and the values specified meet the auditor's detailed specifications. The auditor should, therefore, check his parameters and logic. Where program code is used, this detailed check may consume a considerable amount of time. Important points to note are:

(a) It will normally be desirable for the auditor to request computer staff from the installation where the audit software is to be run to review the operating system instruction to ensure that the software will run in that installation.

(b) It is usually appropriate for the auditor to test his software on small test files before running on the main data files to avoid excessive consumption of computer time.

(c) Once the audit software has been run, the auditor should check the identity and version of the data files used, whether supplied by the client or additional data supplied by himself. This will normally involve checking with external evidence, such as control totals maintained by the user.

(d) Given that there is evidence to provide reasonable assurance that the audit software functioned as planned, it is not necessary for the auditor to be present during its use, although there are frequently practical advantages from doing so. In considering the adequacy of this evidence, the auditor will consider the results of his compliance tests of general controls at the installation.

70. *Recording*
As the use of audit software does not usually provide any visible evidence of the audit work performed, additional evidence should be recorded. This will normally include detailed specifications (including file layouts), parameters listing, source listings, results of testing, and other evidence to provide reasonable assurance that the software functioned as planned.

Controls in on-line and real-time systems

71. *Nature of on-line and real-time systems*
Whilst traditional batch processing is still a common method of using a computer to process accounting data there is a rapid increase in the use of an on-line system, including those in real-time. On-line systems provide the facilities for data to be passed to and from the central computer via remote terminals. Real-time systems are a further development of on-line systems and permit immediate updating of computer held files. The data input and file update phases are therefore merged and the system accepts individual transactions rather than batches of data.

72. Real-time systems, which are often referred to as one-write systems, are the computerised equivalent of bookkeeping systems like Kalamazoo or Twinlock. In those systems, several accounting records are prepared simultaneously by the use of carbon paper between specially aligned sheets of paper, the bottom sheet being, say, a sales day book, followed by the customer's account, then the customer's statement.

73. Most minis and micros can operate in real time. We shall consider the problems associated with such systems later. The following paragraphs are concerned primarily with larger, multi-terminal, on-line systems.

74. *Control problems and strengths*
On-line systems vary considerably, but as implied in paragraph 71, a broad distinction can be drawn between those with remote input devices which collect data for subsequent processing in batches and those operating in real time. There are, however, certain control problems and advantages associated with most on-line systems. The main points to remember are:

(a) *segregation of duties:* when remote terminals are located at the point at which data is originated, it may be found that the same person is responsible for producing and processing the same information. To compensate for the reduction in internal check, supervisory controls should be strengthened;

(b) *data file security:* the ability of a person using a remote terminal to gain access to the computer at will results in the need for special controls to ensure that files are neither read nor written to (nor destroyed), either accidentally or deliberately, without proper authority. The controls may be partly physical. For example:
(i)   access to terminals is restricted to authorised personnel;
(ii) the terminals and the rooms in which they are kept are locked when not in use;
and partly operated by the operating system, including:
(i)   the use of
  - passwords (or lockwords)
  - special badges or keys
sometimes linked to a user's personal identification code which must be used before the terminal operator can gain access to the computer/particular files. In some systems it is found that one password or other identification is required before it

is possible to read a file, a second before it is possible to write new data and yet a third if both operations are permitted. Obviously, the code given to a particular individual will depend on his job function and status within the organisation;

(ii)   the restriction, by the operating system, of certain terminals to certain files. For example, the terminal in the wages department may only be given access to the wages files;

(iii)   the logging of all attempted violations of the above controls possibly accompanied by the automatic shut down of the terminal used. Obviously all violations should be speedily and thoroughly investigated.

(c)   *program security:* the points discussed above apply equally to the use of programs;

(d)   *file reconstruction:* dumping, the method of allowing for the reconstructing of direct access files in batch processing systems, is of limited use in on-line systems as the contents of the file are being continually changed. Although the complete file will be dumped periodically, it is also necessary to maintain a file giving details of all transactions processed since the last dump;

(e)   one of the greatest advantages of on-line systems is the ability to make editing more effective. This is partly because the immediate access to a master file and pipeline files allows more sophisticated checks to be performed (eg. more extensive use of computer matching where the information input may be checked for accuracy against that held on file) and partly because the terminal operator will be able to correct certain types of error immediately. It should be noted, however, that it is essential that strict control is kept over rejections particularly in systems using a database. It may otherwise be found that subsequent processing is performed in ignorance of the fact that master files, which should have been updated, have not been.

75.   In a batch processing system, the establishment of batch totals provides a strong control over the completeness and accuracy of processing. In an on-line system, this facility will, to a greater or lesser extent, be absent. Occasionally it is found that input documents are batched retrospectively, the totals obtained then being reconciled to those generated by the computer. The fact that this technique is not popular is because it is time consuming (and therefore expensive) and because, in many systems, it may prove difficult, if not impossible, to identify the cause of any discrepancies after the processing for a selected period has been completed. In most on-line systems it is, therefore, essential that there are strong controls, particularly supervisory controls, over data capture and input. These may be backed up, for example, by programming the computer to check whether all serial numbered documents up to a given number have been processed. After input, the computer can accumulate totals for different classes of transactions which can then be used to control subsequent processing.

76.   *Database management systems (DBMS)*
DBMS are normally designed for use in real-time environments and enable elements of data to be accessed by different programs. This avoids the duplication of data which inevitably occurs in a traditional system. As data is normally only stored once, and may be accessible to all users that require it, the principal control problems raised concern the authorisation of data amendments and restriction of access to data. Any data amendments must take into account the requirements of all the users. It is good practice to set up an administration function specifically to run and control the day to day operation of the database, thereby enhancing segregation of duties (this function will be independent of the systems development personnel and programmers and data processing manager).

77. The following controls, some of which are common to all real-time systems, might be incorporated into DBMS:

  (a) Controls to prevent or detect unauthorised changes to programs
      (i)   No access to live program files by any personnel except for the operations personnel at the central computer.
      (ii) Password protection of programs.
      (iii) Restricted access to the central computer and terminal.
      (iv) Maintenance of a console log and scrutiny by the data processing manager and by an independent party such as the internal auditors.
      (v)   Periodic comparison of live production programs to control copies and supporting documentation.

  (b) Controls to prevent or detect errors during operation
      (i)   Restriction of access to terminals by use of passwords and restrictions of programs themselves to certain fields.
      (ii) Satisfactory application controls over input, processing and master files and their contents, including retrospective batching (see paragraph 75).
      (iii) Use of operations manuals and training of all users.
      (iv) Maintenance of logs showing unauthorised attempts to access and regular scrutiny by the data processing manager and internal auditors.
      (v)   Physical protection of data files.
      (vi) Training in emergency procedures.

  (c) Controls to ensure integrity of the database system
      (i)   Restriction of access to the data dictionary (this contains standard descriptions, including definitions, characteristics and inter-relationship of data - this codification and cross referencing is important as the various user departments may apply inconsistent terminology);
      (ii) Segregation of duties between the data processing manager, the data base administration function (including its manager) and systems development personnel;
      (iii) Liaison between the data base administration function and systems development personnel to ensure integrity of systems specifications;
      (iv) Preparation and update as necessary of user manuals in conjunction with the data dictionary in (i) above.

78. The audit of DBMS creates particular problems as the two principal CAATs - test data and audit software - tend to work unsatisfactorily on the programs and files contained within such systems. The auditor may, however, be able to use embedded audit facilities such as described in paragraphs 57-62. Close liaison with the internal auditors may also provide audit comfort depending on the nature and continuity of their DBMS review functions. The auditor *must* realistically be involved at the evaluation, design and development stages so that he is able to determine his audit requirements and identify control problems *before* implementation.

Bureaux and software houses

79. *Services provided*
Computer service bureaux are third party service organisations who provide EDP facilities to their clients. Most bureaux are members of COSBA (Computer Services and Bureaux Association) which provides a code of practice for its members.

80. The main types of bureaux are:

   (a) independent companies formed to provide specialist computing services;

   (b) computer manufacturers with bureaux;

   (c) computer users (eg universities) with spare capacity who hire out computer time when it is not required for their own purposes. This type of bureau is now much less common than it was some years ago.

81. The following list contains some of the main areas in which bureaux will offer services:

   (a) *data preparation:* this means transcribing data from source documents into a machine readable form eg. on punched cards or magnetic tape;

   (b) *hiring computer time:* the bureau will process the clients' data on its computer. The client may be responsible for providing the programs, but many bureaux offer software packages (eg. for payroll);

   (c) *do-it-yourself:* here the bureau will provide the computer but the client will provide operators, programs etc. This type of service is often provided by computer users with spare capacity;

   (d) *time sharing:* the customer has access to the bureau's computer by means of communication links (normally the Post Office's Datel System). Since all clients' files will usually be held permanently on-line, file security is of paramount importance;

   (e) *complete service:* the bureau provides a comprehensive service covering systems analysis and design, programming and implementation. Often the system will be in the form of a standard package used by many customers;

   (f) *consultancy:* many bureaux will offer assistance or advice on any type of data processing problem;

   (g) *software:* customers can obtain programs or sets of programs, either specially written for them or part of a regular application package.

82. However, few bureaux will provide services in all these areas. The costs of the services will vary with the type and with the volume of work. For standard applications there will normally be a fixed scale of fees whereas fees for individual work will be negotiated at the time the contract is made.

83. *Why use a bureau?*
   The following are the most common reasons for using a bureau:

   (a) *new user:* a company that is considering acquiring a computer may find it extremely beneficial to use a bureau because:
   (i)   it can evaluate the type of computer it is interested in;
   (ii) it can test and develop its programs prior to the delivery of its own computer;
   (iii) its staff will become familiar with the requirements of a computer system.
   In some cases a new system may be initially implemented using a bureau. This will involve file conversion and pilot or parallel running;

   (b) *cost:* many companies cannot justify the installation of an in-house computer on cost-benefit grounds. With the enormous increase in the number of VRCs and mini computers available this basis is becoming less common;

(c) *peak loads:* some computer users find it convenient to employ a bureau to cope with peak loads arising for example from seasonal variations in sales; bureaux may be used for data preparation work for file conversion, prior to the implementation of a new computer system;

(d) *stand by:* a bureau's computer may be used in the event of breakdown of an in-house machine;

(e) *specialised skills:* management feel that the job of data processing should be left to the experts;

(f) *consultancy:* bureaux can provide advice and assistance in connection with feasibility studies, system design, equipment evaluation, staff training etc.;

(g) *for one-off use.*

84. *Advantages and disadvantages to the user*
The reasons for using a bureau effectively constitute a list of their advantages. It should be emphasised, however, that very few users can afford to pay for the services of systems analysts and programmers of the quality that will be found working for the large bureaux. A company using a bureau will probably not need them Other advantages include:

(a) use of a bureau should enable a customer to obtain the use of up-to-date computer technology in the bureau;
(b) unloading responsibility on to the bureau (eg. payroll);
(c) use of a bureau does not require a high capital outlay.

85. The principal disadvantages of using a bureau are:

(a) loss of control over time taken to process data and in particular the inability to reschedule work should input delays occur;
(b) problems may be encountered in the transfer of data to and from the bureau;
(c) the bureau may close down leaving the customer without any DP facilities;
(d) many potential users will not employ a bureau's services because they feel that they will lose control over an important area of their business and furthermore that it is bad security to allow confidential information to be under the control of an outsider. Their fears are normally ungrounded; the bureau will certainly not try to run the business and its security may well be considerably better than that of its customers;
(e) its employees will be uninterested in and often unaware of the type of data they are processing;
(f) standards of service and the provision of adequate documentation control and any audit trail are also important considerations.

86. *Planning and control exercised by the user*
When a system using a bureau is set up it is essential that a full feasibility study and system design should be carried out. In practice the bureau may provide assistance in performing these tasks.

87. A *small* DP department should be set up to liaise with the bureau and to ensure that adequate systems controls are maintained. The controls kept by the client should cover:

(a) physical movement of data to and from the bureau;
(b) accuracy and completeness of processing;
(c) resubmission of rejected data;
(d) correct distribution of output;
(e) system testing involving all clerical procedures at the user company;
(f) control over the maintenance of data on master files;
(g) adequate back-up facilities both for processing and for file reconstruction;
(h) security of data.

88. *The audit approach where controls are in the hands of third parties*
To set the scene we can briefly return to the guideline 'Auditing in a computer environment'. Under the heading 'Third party service organisations' it states:

"Where enterprises use a third party service organisation such as a computer service bureau or a software house for the purpose of maintaining part or all of their accounting records and procedures, the auditor still has a responsibility to follow 'The auditor's operational standard'. However, the auditor may encounter practical obstacles, as the enterprise may be placing some reliance on the proper operation of internal control exercised by the third party. Consequently, where the auditor finds it impracticable to obtain all the information and explanations that he requires from the enterprise itself (because the enterprise may not be maintaining sufficient controls to minimise that reliance) he should perform other procedures. These may include taking the steps he considers necessary to enable him to rely on the work performed by other auditors or carrying out procedures at the premises of the third party."

89. The above statement implies that, wherever possible, the auditor would opt to obtain assurance by testing his client's controls, provided they are adequate, rather than by seeking to rely on controls operated by the bureau. This may be feasible, and cost effective, where, for instance, batch processing is involved. Visible data is generally abundant and loss of audit trail is normally not encountered. Reliance will be sought from the user controls at the input and output stages which should provide evidence of the proper functioning of programmed procedures performed by the bureau. However, the auditor will also be concerned with the operation of general controls at the bureau, in particular (f) (g) and (h) identified in paragraph 87:
- security over the client's data (sensitive information such as names of customers and employees should be coded if necessary);
- adequate facilities for reconstruction; and
- control over master file data (all master file amendments should be printed out and checked to ensure that they have all been authorised by the user).

90. Where the auditor wishes to evaluate and test the controls at the bureau (whether general and/or application), and *permission is obtained*, there appear to be two courses of action available:

(a) a separate examination of controls by the auditors of each of the bureau's clients;
(b) an examination of controls by a third party reviewer (probably another firm of auditors - perhaps even the bureau's own auditors) and issue of a report which can be made available to auditors of each of the bureau's clients.

91. The first option may meet with some opposition from the bureau since it may understandably be alarmed at the prospect of each of its clients' auditors performing separate examinations of its controls.

92. The second option also has some problems.

    (a) A particular auditor may be unwilling to place reliance on an examination of controls commissioned by the computer bureau.
    (b) The interaction between the general controls exercised by the bureau and the application controls exercised by the client may be unclear.
    (c) It is often the case that different users place varying degrees of reliance on certain controls and auditors need to gain different levels of knowledge about these controls.

93. The auditor may conclude that he can rely on an examination by a third party review if he is satisfied that all the procedures which he himself would have wished to perform have indeed been carried out and with the same level of expertise as he would have applied. This is likely to involve consultations with the third party reviewer, where the evidence provided by him is, in the auditor's opinion, insufficient for his particular purposes. Remember that the bureau is the client of the third party reviewer and as such must give permission before a consultation can take place.

94. Finally, it is important in all cases for the auditor to consider the circumstances of the use of the computer bureau's services and the extent to which the control procedures within the computer bureau and at the client are comprehensive. Where the auditor is unable to rely on an examination by a third party reviewer and is not granted permission to perform his own examination of the controls at the bureau, he may have to resort to extensive substantive testing (unless he can obtain sufficient assurance from the user controls). There is no reason why the auditor should not employ CAATs such as test data and audit software to assist him where his client uses a bureau. In the case of audit software, permission of the client *and* bureau would normally be necessary.

Control problems in small computer systems (minis and micros)

95. The design of modern mini-computers is well-adapted to these systems; the one-write concept has been developed to the point where an order clerk can enter details of an order using a VDU terminal and the system will immediately proceed to update the inventory, sales ledger, customer account, and general ledger and print the picking list, delivery notes, and invoice in respect of that transaction.

96. A big advantage of these systems, apart from the degree of automation, is that the organisation's accounting records are always up to date. However, if the system is not fully and properly controlled, serious problems can arise for management and auditor alike.

97. In this section we look at the control and audit problems peculiar to minis and micros. It is, incidentally, rather difficult to specify which machines fall into the category of mini as distinct from micro. One categorisation is to define the 'mini' as capable of supporting multiple keyboards and VDUs whereas the 'micro' is desksize, comprising a processor with single keyboard and VDU, a printer and, probably, magnetic (floppy) disc storage. From the audit viewpoint the distinction is not significant – all the machines have the common features of relatively compact size and ability to operate in a normal office environment (as distinct from the protected environment necessary with mainframes). For consistency's sake, the term 'mini' is used throughout this section.

Summary of the control problems

98. The majority of the potential problems arise due to the departure from the formal structure of the traditional data processing department, where a controlled environment was provided over the acquisition, maintenance and distribution of computer information. In the world of the mini-computer this controlled structure does not exist and the environment is more informal.

99. These problem areas surrounding mini computers can be grouped under three headings:

    (a) lack of planning over the acquisition and use of minis:
    (b) lack of documentary evidence; and
    (c) lack of security and confidentiality.

100. All these areas could produce problems for the auditor, giving him difficulties when attempting to assess the documentation, the adequacy of design processes and testing, the completeness, accuracy and authority of data and, of course, audit trails. Each of the three problem areas is now considered in more detail.

Lack of planning over the acquisition and use of mini–computers

101. *Authorisation*
When an organisation sets out to acquire a computer system, a series of steps should be undertaken before making the decision to purchase.

102. A feasibility study should be carried out, examining the requirements, the costs and the benefits, to ensure that the expense is justified. Suppliers should be invited to tender, and responses from the suppliers should be evaluated and compared. Contracts should be negotiated with the final choice of supplier and only then should the equipment be installed. All interested parties within the organisation should be identified and involved throughout the whole procedure, *irrespective of the size of the system* which is being purchased.

103. *Suitability*
There is a risk when purchase of a mini is under consideration that the client will not have the expertise to evaluate the relative merits of systems. This could give rise to compatability and/or capacity problems thereby restricting future developments, unless in the last resort, the entire system is replaced. Many first time users tend to purchase standard software packages which creates an even greater risk as regards suitability, for such systems may not fit precisely the company's trading methods. Moreover, the first time user is unlikely to have the expertise required to tailor such packages.

104. *Support facilities*
The support facilities offered by the supplier and/or software house should be ascertained to ensure that:

    (a) in the event of machine breakdown, prompt service and, if necessary, backup facilities are available;
    (b) any bugs in the programme can be sorted out;
    (c) minor modifications to the program can be carried out;

    (d) adequate systems documentation and operator manuals have been provided – such documentation falls into three generally accepted categories:

        (i)   *program documentation:* This states in detail how each program within each part of the system operates, what files are being opened and accessed, and what functions are being performed;

        (ii) *operator instructions:* These are designed to be 'desk-top' instructions enabling the micro user to access and use the system as required;

        (iii) *user manual:* This is the 'layman's guide' to the operation of the whole system and would usually include the operator instructions; and

    (e) operators have received adequate instruction.

105. *Standards*

In a formal data processing environment there will normally be standards to which all procedures regarding hardware and software should conform. All programs, whether written by the user or brought in from outside, should meet specified criteria and satisfy minimum standards, covering aspects such as controls and accounting principles. With minis, where the time taken from ordering, through installation to operation, may be a matter of weeks only, there is great danger that standards are not set.

106. Strict disciplines must be imposed to ensure that recognised systems development controls *are* applied and sufficient administration procedures are implemented.

Lack of documentary evidence

107. *Use of VDUs*

We have identified that many mini-computers operate in real time via VDUs, which allows users to have direct access to the computer thus enabling them to input data, update files and make one-off enquiries on data held on files. The necessity for edit programs and hard copy is avoided. Although this may be conceived as an 'advantage' from the viewpoint of computer operators/users, management and the auditor will recognise the inherent control problems. Control can be enhanced by ensuring that edit programs *are* in-built at the design stage and by incorporating into the system a user-usage file which logs details of the user's identification, the application involved, the records accessed or updated etc. Such a file can be reviewed periodically by a responsible official and the auditor.

Lack of audit trail

108. Frequently in mini computer systems there is no trail to follow since all the processing is done inside the computer and no intermediate printouts are produced. The quality of audit evidence can be questionable if there is a lack of primary records (eg telephone sales orders entered straight into the computer via the VDU to take our example in paragraph 95). It may be prudent to implement manual controls to ensure that transactions can only be processed when supported by an appropriate initiating document. Similarly, manual batching can be imposed.

Lack of security and confidentiality

109. *Lack of segregation of duties*
Poor segregation of duties all too easily occurs since frequently the same person prepares the data, feeds it into the computer, supervises the processing and acts as end user. This lack of division of duties leads to enhanced opportunities for fraud - the user having access to assets and the recording and disposal of assets. The auditor may well have to perform extensive substantive verification work to compensate for this serious lack of control.

110. *Lack of control over users*
Because mini-computers do not require a protected environment the terminals are readily available to any user. In order to safeguard the records, controls to prevent unauthorised users from using the computer are necessary (eg use of locks, passwords etc).

111. *Lack of control over alterations to programs*
We have emphasised in paragraph 103 that a lack of expertise, particularly in the case of first time users, may lead to imprudent purchase in terms of capacity and compatability. Conversely, there are dangers arising because of the relative ease with which expertise may be acquired once a machine is installed and operational. Mini-computers employ high level languages and a working knowledge can be grasped within a short time. In the wrong hands there is a danger that programs might be altered without detection or that programs are written at the time data is being processed without adequate testing.

112. Stringent supervisory arrangements are required to prevent unauthorised personnel from having access to the programs together with programmed controls preventing unauthorised running. A degree of security will be guaranteed to the extent that the programs are permanently etched onto silicon chips and are hence an integral part of the hardware ('ROMs'). Such programs can only be altered by specialist electronics engineers.

The future

113. The continuing development of more and more advanced mini/micro systems, particularly in terms of capacity, means that the control problems currently confronting the auditor are likely, at best, merely to continue, and at worst to increase. The auditor must carefully evaluate such systems, but the almost inevitable conclusion is going to be that an extensive amount of substantive testing is necessary. The main hope for the future is that CAATs, which have been developed principally to operate on large mainframe applications, can be scaled down to be effective on minis and micros.

Summary of the chapter

114. The examination emphasis placed on auditing in a computer environment clearly reflects the practical impact of computerisation over the last decade and the fact the auditor is almost bound to encounter computer-based systems in his professional work.

115. Questions can, however, vary in their style and intensity. Some are concerned merely with control techniques, others are concerned with the controls *and/or* audit techniques designed to test the controls and systems, in particular the auditor's use of CAATs.

116. Quite justifiably, the examiner tends to concentrate on the smaller types of computer system - minis and micros - rather than sophisticated mainframe applications. It is therefore recommended that, once an overall perspective has been acquired, the control problems inherent in mini/micro systems are studied in depth.

TEST YOUR KNOWLEDGE
Numbers in brackets refer to paragraphs in this chapter

1. What is the definition of general controls? (4 (b))

2. What application controls might ensure *completeness* of input? (8)

3. In which eight areas should general controls operate? (14)

4. What are the two principal categories of CAAT? (24)

5. What factors will determine whether the auditor performs a test manually or by using a CAAT? (30)

6. In what circumstances may the reliance that the auditor wishes to place on general controls be limited? (41(d))

7. What is meant by 'audit trail'? (47)

8. What planning points arise when the auditor wishes to use test data? (54)

9. What is the advantage of an embedded audit facility? (57)

10. What is an 'integrated test facility'? (58)

11. What special control points should be considered when the auditor uses audit software? (69)

12. What control problems and strengths can be identified in on-line computer systems? (74)

13. Suggest three categories of controls which might be incorporated into database management systems. (77)

14. List four disadvantages of using the services of a computer bureau. (85)

15. What support facilities should be offered by a mini-computer supplier? (104)

16. What security and confidentiality problems are likely to be encountered in a small computer environment? (109 - 111)

---

1. In many small businesses incorporated as limited companies, the system of internal control is dependent upon the close involvement of the directors who may or may not be major shareholders. Often, when reporting upon such businesses, the auditor has to qualify his report.

    You are required to describe the circumstances in which an auditor can report, without qualification, on a small company.

2. There is no point in trying to audit the unauditable. Small companies should therefore be exempt from the requirements of an audit.

    Discuss.

3. Computer security is of vital importance not only to the accountant in industry but also to the accountant in practice who may be advising his client as to suitable security controls or who may be auditing a computer system. Security is the means by which losses are controlled and therefore involves the identification of risks and the institution of measures to either prevent such risks entirely or to reduce their impact.

    Required:
    (a) Identify the main areas of risk which may arise in relation to a computer system.
    (b) Describe the different forms of control which should be instituted to safeguard against computer security risks.

4. You are the auditor of Super Group plc which operates a chain of garages through its 15 subsidiaries. In the past each subsidiary has been responsible for its own accounting procedures and has had its own accounts department. Standards of accounting throughout the group are good. During 19X0 the holding company set up a centralised group computer department using a mainframe computer with responsibility for processing accounting information for all companies within the group. The new computer department will commence operations on 1 January 19X1 with a total staff of 20 including the departmental manager, systems development staff, control staff and operational staff.

    The finance director has asked you to review and report to him on the proposed controls within the computer department.

    You are required to set out the controls you would expect to find in these circumstances.

1. Whether a limited company be large or small, the directors have a statutory duty to prepare accounts which show a true and fair view of the profit or loss for the period and of the state of affairs at the period-end, and to present these accounts to the members in general meeting. The auditor of the company has a statutory duty to form an opinion - where possible - on the truth and fairness of the accounts and to give this opinion to the members in his audit report attached to the company's balance sheet.

    However, the auditor needs to obtain the same degree of assurance in order to give an unqualified opinion on the financial statements of both small and large companies. But the operating procedures and methods of recording and processing transactions used by small companies often differ significantly from those of larger companies. Indeed, many of the controls which would be relevant to the large enterprise are not practical, appropriate or necessary in the small company. The most effective form of internal control for small companies is generally the close involvement of the directors or proprietors. This involvement will, however, enable them to override controls and purposely to exclude transactions from the records. This possibility can give rise to difficulties for the auditor not because there is a lack of controls but because of insufficient evidence as to their operation and the completeness of the records.

    In many situations it will be possible to reach a conclusion that will support an unqualified opinion on the financial statements by combining the evidence obtained from extensive substantive testing of transactions and balances with a careful review of costs and margins applying analytical review techniques. These tests and reviews may lead the auditor to believe that the accounting records are complete and reliable, and that the figures in the balance sheet can be substantiated. The auditor would, as in the case of any company audit, obtain from the directors a Letter of Representation, the purpose of which is to obtain positive confirmation of assurances given to the auditor and to ensure that there is no misunderstanding of the information and opinions given and as to the identity and authority of those by whom they are given. The particular wording of the Letter of Representation will need to be considered carefully in the light of the circumstances prevailing in the small business.

    However, in some businesses such as those where most transactions are for cash and there is no regular pattern of costs and margins, the available evidence may be inadequate to support an opinion on the financial statements.

    There will be other situations where the evidence available to the auditor is insufficient to give him the confidence necessary for him to express an unqualified opinion but this uncertainty is not so great as to justify a total disclaimer of opinion. In such situations the most helpful form of report may be one which indicates the need to accept the assurances of management as to the completeness or accuracy of the accounting records. Such a report should contain a 'subject to...' opinion. It would only be appropriate to use this form of report if the auditor has taken steps to obtain all the evidence which can reasonably be obtained and is satisfied that:

    (a) the system of accounting and control is reasonable having regard to the size and type of the company's operations, and is sufficient to enable management to give the auditor the assurances which he requires;

    (b) there is no evidence to suggest that the assurances may be inaccurate.

2. The long-standing debate concerning the relevance or otherwise of independent audits for small companies has recently been refired by the publication of the Department of Trade and Industry's consultative document 'Accounting and audit requirements for small firms'. The debate, however, centres not so much on the "auditability" of such enterprises but more upon whether the benefit of the compulsory audit justifies the attendant cost. The statement in the question on the other hand argues that small companies should be exempt because they are incapable of being audited.

    It is the involvement of owners as managers which distinguishes this sector from other companies. Such involvement results in substantial domination of the accounting and financial management functions by one person. Furthermore, there are limitations in the effectiveness from the audit point of view of the system of internal control rendered inevitable by the small number of employees. The implications of these shortcomings in internal control are that its value may be so reduced that the auditor will not be able to place reliance thereon as a justification for reducing levels of subsequent substantive tests and verification work on assets and liabilities. Moreover, it may become necessary despite an extension of detailed substantive audit procedures to rely to a more significant extent upon the representations of management where alternative confirmation of transactions is not available or supported either by outside evidence or by opinions of, or records maintained by, other personnel of the company. In these circumstances the auditor must consider whether his examination of the company's records, the evidence available to him and his knowledge of all the circumstances affecting the company are consistent with and support the representations of management and provide sufficient evidence on which to assess the reliability of the records. While it is a matter for the cautious exercise of the auditor's judgement it does not necessarily follow that representations of management for which direct confirmatory evidence is not available may not be relied upon by the auditor. He must consider whether the surrounding evidence as a whole is consistent with and sufficient to support these representations to his satisfaction.

    If in all the circumstances the auditor forms an opinion that the records are adequate and have been properly maintained, he may place reliance on them as a basis for the preparation of financial statements showing a true and fair view. If on the other hand the auditor cannot form such an opinion it is necessary for the audit report to state such reservations clearly.

    It follows from the above therefore that small companies are auditable, and on these grounds alone should not be exempted from the requirement for an audit. Whether it is constructive for small company clients and users, for their accounts to be frequently qualified consequent to reliance on management assurances is another question. Perhaps the profession needs a way to report positively. This would require an amendment to the present requirement that Auditing Standards apply to all audit engagements.

3. (a) The main areas of risk to which a computer system is exposed, and some of the factors which may lead to the exposure are:
    (i)   Accidental destruction or loss of data by operator or software error. The auditor should pay particular attention during his audit to recovery procedures. In addition the possibility of accidental destruction of programs or hardware - particularly the dropping of a disk pack - by an operator, and the consequences thereof, should not be overlooked.
    (ii) The acceptance of inaccurate input data due to inadequate edit or other checks is another frequent cause of loss of data.
    (iii) A complete systems failure can lead to loss of data and may be caused by a failure in the power supply or possibly a failure of the air conditioning or other environmental controls.
    (iv) Theft of data from a batch processing system by an operator copying or removing data files, particularly where these are on easily transportable media such as magnetic tapes.

(v) Theft of data from an on line or real time system by a person obtaining unauthorised access to the system via a remote terminal and either using passwords illegally or alternatively using a 'piggyback system' (in which a valid transmission is intercepted and the final 'logging off' operation stopped in transmission to permit the illegal operator to continue in operation masquerading as the authorised user).

(vi) Theft of software either by operators copying or removing the program file, and in the latter case possibly demanding a ransom from the rightful owner, or alternatively by programming staff copying and attempting to sell the source documentation, with or without the object program.

(vii) Deliberate destruction of the hardware has been known to occur, and where adequate protection has not been provided, such acts have also led to the simultaneous destruction of software and data. Similar results may occur as a result of fire or explosion either in the computer room or adjoining premises.

(b) The different forms of control which should be instituted may be sub-divided into three main headings.

Physical security
(i) Strict control of access to the computer area, using such devices as magnetic keys, alarm systems, etc.

(ii) Effective precautions against fire or other natural disruption including alarm systems, automatic extinguishing systems and regular inspections.

(iii) Established and well-practised emergency procedures in the event of fire etc. and alternative power supply.

(iv) Location of the computer so that it is difficult for unauthorised personnel to have access with the minimum of entrances and exits.

(v) Possibility of remote storage of security copies of data.

(vi) Location of the computer room so that it is, if possible, situated away from known hazards such as:
- Flooding
- Radiation from X-Ray equipment, radio systems etc,
- Fire/Explosion risks in adjoining premises.

Software security
(i) Effective control over the preservation of information contained on files by ensuring that before a file is to be overwritten a check is made on the file label.

(ii) Prevention of unauthorised access by the use of devices such as passwords.

Systems security
(i) Strict control and verification of all input data, with control totals prepared outside the computer department and with all tabulations balanced thereto.

(ii) All input should pass through an 'edit' program as the first stage in being entered on to the computer files. This program clearly indicates all items accepted and rejected, the latter to be investigated by the user department.

(iii) Adequate controls should be in force to ensure that amendments to programs are properly authorised, checked out and validated before use.

(iv) There should be adequate recovery, restart and standby procedures in the event of power failure, machine breakdowns etc, which can be facilitated by a 'log' of all work performed and by frequent dumping of files.

(v) Controls should be instituted to ensure that computer output is properly distributed, especially confidential print-outs, payments etc.

(vi) Proper control over storage and issue of magnetic media with manual records being kept of physical maintenance performed. Such records frequently also record current status of the media and the details of the file(s) currently stored upon it.

4. The controls which an auditor would expect to find in the company's computer department are as follows:

Division of responsibilities
(a) Division of responsibilities:
    (i) between the computer department and user departments; and
    (ii) within the computer department, between:
        – systems development staff
        – control staff
        – operational staff;
(b) An organisation chart should be prepared and the principal tasks in the department allocated to specified individuals or groups.
(c) Only the control and data preparation sections should have access to the documents containing the original data to be processed by the computer.
(d) Computer department staff should not have access to any of the company's clerically maintained financial records.
(e) Only computer operators should have access to the computer during production runs.
(f) Only computer operators and the file librarian should have access to files and current programs.
(g) Only the user department staff and control section should be allowed to amend input data.
(h) The staff of the control section and the librarian should not have any other duties within the computer department.
(i) Computer department staff should not initiate transactions and changes to master files.
(j) Access to the computer room should be restricted to authorised persons at authorised times.

Control over operational staff
(a) The use of manuals laying down general standards of operating discipline.
(b) Scheduling of work.
(c) The provision of detailed operating instructions for each program.
(d) The frequent and independent review of computer usage by reference to time and fault logs prepared by operators, and where there is a console typewriter by reference to operating logs produced thereon.
(e) The requirement of a minimum of two operators per shift.
(f) Rotation of operators' duties.
(g) Programming that all operator intervention appears on the console print-outs where available. Console print-outs should be on pre-numbered paper or alternatively have the intervention numbered consecutively by the computer.

File control
(a) File storage procedures should be the responsibility of a librarian, whose duties should include:
    (i) controlling the issue and return of files according to scheduled time-tables;
    (ii) maintaining external file labels;
    (iii) ensuring that tapes containing information which is no longer of value (generally known as scratch tapes) cannot be confused with data tapes;
    (iv) allocating identification numbers to storage devices and maintaining usage records;
    (v) ensuring that access to files is restricted to authorised personnel.
(b) File identification procedures. For example, each file should be allocated a unique identity number. This would be physically recorded on the storage device and checked before use of that device.
(c) File reconstruction procedures. Several generations of master files and relevant files containing transactions data should be retained.

(d) Fire precautions and standby arrangements, including:
   (i)   lockable, fireproof conditions for the computer and associated hardware;
   (ii) lockable, fireproof storage for all files;
   (iii) retention of duplicate files in another location;
   (iv) adequate standby arrangements such that the essential accounting functions can be performed in the event of a long breakdown of the company's own computer.

Systems development controls
(a) *Standard procedures and documentation*
   This should include documentation of both the systems and the programs.

(b) *Systems and program testing*
   It is particularly important that all new systems are tested by pilot running or in parallel with the existing system.

(c) *File conversion*
   All master files which are set up must be checked in detail before operational processing begins.

(d) *Acceptance and authorisation procedures*
   Each major stage of development should be reviewed by the head of the computer department and by the user departments concerned.

(e) *Systems and program amendments*
   These should be subject to the same controls as the initial development.

Note: It has been assumed in this answer that general controls are envisaged by the question rather than detailed application controls. However, controls which should be in operation for every application could be relevant here, including:
- controls which ensure that all data is processed;
- physical controls over data received for processing;
- controls over the distribution of processed output.

TABLE OF CASES

SUBJECT INDEX

414